HUNTING JUSTICE

This book presents a long-term study of the activist campaign that contested the Botswana government's much-publicized removal of the San and Bakgalagadi people from the Central Kalahari Game Reserve. Sapignoli's multiple points of observation and analysis range from rural Botswana to the nation's High Court, and a variety of United Nations agencies in their Headquarters, focusing on rights claimants and officials from NGOs, states, and the United Nations as they acted on the grievances of those who had been displaced. In offering a comprehensive discussion of the San people and their claims-making through formal institutions, this book maintains a consistent focus on the increased recourse to law and the everyday experience of those who are asserting their rights in response to the encroachments of the state and the opportunities inherent in new indigenous advocacy networks.

MARIA SAPIGNOLI is a research fellow in the Department of Law and Anthropology at the Max Planck Institute for Social Anthropology. Since 2006 she has carried out ethnographic work in Botswana, most recently in Namibia, and in several international organizations, including the United Nations Permanent Forum on Indigenous Issues. She is the author of numerous articles and book chapters. She is the co-editor of *Palaces of Hope: The Anthropology of Global Organizations* (Cambridge 2017).

CAMBRIDGE STUDIES IN LAW AND SOCIETY

Cambridge Studies in Law and Society aims to publish the best scholarly work on legal discourse and practice in its social and institutional contexts, combining theoretical insights and empirical research.

The fields that it covers are: studies of law in action; the sociology of law; the anthropology of law; cultural studies of law, including the role of legal discourses in social formations; law and economics; law and politics; and studies of governance. The books consider all forms of legal discourse across societies, rather than being limited to lawyers' discourses alone.

The series editors come from a range of disciplines: academic law; socio-legal studies; sociology; and anthropology. All have been actively involved in teaching and writing about law in context.

A list of books in the series can be found at the back of this book.

HUNTING JUSTICE

Displacement, Law, and Activism in the Kalahari

Maria Sapignoli

Max Planck Institute for Social Anthropology

CAMBRIDGE
UNIVERSITY PRESS

CAMBRIDGE
UNIVERSITY PRESS

University Printing House, Cambridge CB2 8BS, United Kingdom

One Liberty Plaza, 20th Floor, New York, NY 10006, USA

477 Williamstown Road, Port Melbourne, VIC 3207, Australia

314–321, 3rd Floor, Plot 3, Splendor Forum, Jasola District Centre, New Delhi – 110025, India

79 Anson Road, #06-04/06, Singapore 079906

Cambridge University Press is part of the University of Cambridge.

It furthers the University's mission by disseminating knowledge in the pursuit of education, learning, and research at the highest international levels of excellence.

www.cambridge.org
Information on this title: www.cambridge.org/9781107191570
DOI: 10.1017/9781108123570

First published 2018

Printed in the United Kingdom by Clays, St Ives plc

A catalogue record for this publication is available from the British Library.

Library of Congress Cataloging-in-Publication Data

Names: Sapignoli, Maria.
Title: Hunting justice : displacement, law, and activism in the Kalahari / Maria Sapignoli, Max Planck Institute for Social Anthropology
Description: Cambridge, United Kingdom ; New York, NY, USA : Cambridge University Press, 2018. | Series: Cambridge studies in law and society | Includes bibliographical references and index.
Identifiers: LCCN 2017042285 | ISBN 9781107191570 (hardback)
Subjects: LCSH: Indigenous peoples—Land tenure—Botswana—Central Kalahari Game Reserve. | National parks and reserves—Law and legislation—Botswana—Central Kalahari Game Reserve. | San (African people)—Legal status, laws, etc.—Botswana. | Kgalagadi (African people)—Legal status, laws, etc.—Botswana.
Classification: LCC KQK254.17 .S27 2018 | DDC 323.1196/106883—dc23 LC record available at https://lccn.loc.gov/2017042285

ISBN 978-1-107-19157-0 Hardback

To Giorgio Sapignoli

CONTENTS

ACKNOWLEDGMENTS

A book that tries to look at a well-known case in a new way is bound to acquire debts along the way from those whose work came before and whose insights provided inspiration.

I am particularly grateful to Robert Hitchcock for the discussions and the materials he shared with me, especially from his fantastic private library relating to the Central Kalahari, his collaboration while in the field, and his mentoring through the years. I am deeply grateful for the long-standing support of Colin Samson, friend and advisor, and for the many compelling discussions over the years, not just during my PhD but beyond. My gratitude also goes to Ronald Niezen for his stimulating comments and suggestions, an important source of inspiration for my work.

I also wish to thank John Berger, Sally Engle Merry, Richard Wilson and three anonymous reviewers who encouraged me in this project from the beginning, with important insights on my proposal. Richard Wilson also offered insight at the other end of the process, with some timely suggestions for the Introduction just as I was moving toward completion of the manuscript. Brian Donahoe made an invaluable contribution to the editing process. There are many others to whom I owe thanks for inspiring me and collaborating at various points and in various ways: Arthur Albertson, Stefano Allovio, Gerhard Anders, Wayne Babchuk, Alan Barnard, Gordon Bennett, Megan Biesele, Maude Brown, Christoph Brumann, Julian Burger, Jean and John Comaroff, Antonella Cordone, Stephen Corry, David Cownie, Delme Cupido, Ute Dieckmann, Anita Diphetogo, Baba Festus, Marie-Claire Foblets, Carlos Gigoux, Mark Goodale, Catie Gressier, Mathias Guenther, Ørnulf Gulbrandsen, John Holm, Kazunobu Ikeya, Johnjohn Kempf, Stuart Kirsch, Andrea Klein, Kuela Kiema, Jenny Lawy, Richard Lee, Kali Mercier, Keikabile Mogodu, Matsipane Mosetlhanyane, Job Morris, Juan Núñez, Willem Odendaal, Sidsel Saugestad, Habe Tibi Setshego, Katrin Sidel, Broddi Sigurdarson, Sonia Smallacombe, Jacqueline Solway, Elsa Stamatopolou, Rob Stones, Renee Sylvain, Akira Takada,

Mike Taylor, Bert Turner, Joram /Useb, Coby and Hessel Visser, Pnina Werbner, Richard Werbner, Xukuri Xukuri, Manuela Zips-Mairitisch, the late Alec Campbell, the late Janet Hermans, and the late George Silberbauer. Maps and figures were drafted by Marieka Brouwer-Burg and Andrea Santoni. The list is as complete as I can make it, but there may be others I have neglected to mention, and to them I also extend my thanks. Having received the benefit of many suggestions and sources of inspiration, it is important for me to acknowledge that I am solely responsible for the content of this book.

Financial support for this project was provided by the Department of Law and Anthropology, Max Planck Institute for Social Anthropology, to which I want to express my deepest appreciation. Funding was also provided by the Department of Sociology, University of Essex, and First Peoples Worldwide. The government of Botswana and the University of Botswana's Schapera Research Program gave me official permission to conduct the work in Botswana.

I am grateful for the institutional support I received from the Botswana National Archives, Ditshwanelo, First People of the Kalahari, First Peoples Worldwide, the Botswana Khwedom Council, the Kuru Family of Organizations, the International Fund for Agricultural Development (IFAD), the Legal Assistance Centre of Namibia, the Open Society Initiative for Southern Africa, the San Youth Network, the Secretariat of the PFII, Survival International, the University of Botswana, and of course all my colleagues in the Max Planck Institute for Social Anthropology.

This book would not have been possible without the collaboration, assistance, insights, and information provided by the people of the Central Kalahari Game Reserve, Ghanzi District, Kweneng District, and the capital of Botswana, Gaborone. My work has in particular been enriched by many hours of conversation with Jumanda Gakelebone and Roy Sesana. I cannot thank them enough for all their help and openness to sharing with me their daily lives.

Finally, I wish to express my deepest gratitude for the long-standing support and love of my parents and my brothers.

ABBREVIATIONS

ACHPR	African Commission on Human and Peoples' Rights
ARV	Anti-Retroviral Drugs
AU	African Union
BBC	British Broadcasting Corporation
BCC	Botswana Council of Churches
BCP	Botswana Congress Party
BDF	Botswana Defence Force
BDO	Bushmen Development Officer
BDP	Botswana Democratic Party
BDP	Bushmen Development Programme
BMD	Botswana Movement for Democracy
BNA	Botswana National Archives
BNF	Botswana National Front
BOCONGO	Botswana Council of Non-Governmental Organisations
BPP	Botswana People's Party
CBNRM	Community-Based Natural Resource Management
CAT	Committee against Torture
CBO	Community Based Organization
CCHA	Community Controlled Hunting Area
CERD	Committee on the Elimination of Racial Discrimination
CKGR	Central Kalahari Game Reserve
CSC	Communal Service Centre
CSIR	Council for Scientific and Industrial Research
CUZ	Community Use Zone
DANIDA	Danish International Development Agency

DRIP	Declaration on the Rights of Indigenous Peoples
DOCIP	Indigenous Peoples' Centre for Documentation, Research and Information
DWNP	Department of Wildlife and National Parks
ECOSOC	Economic and Social Council
EMRIP	Expert Mechanism on the Rights of Indigenous Peoples
FAO	Food and Agriculture Organization
FMD	foot-and-mouth disease
FNDI	First Nations Development Institute
FPIC	Free, Prior and Informed Consent
FPK	First People of the Kalahari
FPW	First Peoples Worldwide
GDP	Gross Domestic Product
HIV	Human Immunodeficiency Virus
HRC	Human Rights Council
KDT	Kuru Development Trust
KFO	Kuru Family of Organizations
KFP	Kalahari Peoples Fund
IFAD	International Fund for Agricultural Development
ILO	International Labor Organization
INGOs	International Non-Governmental Organizations
IPACC	Indigenous Peoples of Africa Co-ordinating Committee
IPO	Indigenous Peoples Organization
IWGIA	International Work Group for Indigenous Affairs
MLGLH	Ministry of Local Government, Lands, and Housing
MLRR	Ministry of Lands, Resettlement, and Rehabilitation
MP	Member of Parliament
MWET	Ministry of Wildlife, Environment, and Tourism
NGO	Non-Governmental Organization
NORAD	Norwegian Agency for Development Co-operation
NSP	National Settlement Policy

OHCHR	Office of the High Commissioner for Human Rights
OIPA	Organization of Indigenous Peoples in Africa
OSISA	Open Society Initiative for Southern Africa
PFII	Permanent Forum on Indigenous Issues
RAC	Remote Area Communities
RAD	Remote Area Dwellers
RADO	Remote Area Development Officer
RADP	Remote Area Development Programme
RAS	Remote Area Settlements
RETENG	Multicultural Coalition of Botswana
SASI	South African San Institute
SGL	Special Game License
SI	Survival International
SIAPAC	Social Impact Assessment and Policy Analysis Corporation
SPFII	Secretariat of the Permanent Forum on Indigenous Issues
SSG	Special Support Group (Botswana Police)
SYN	San Youth Network
TGLP	Tribal Grazing Land Policy
UDC	Umbrella for Democratic Change
UN	United Nations
UNDRIP	United Nations Declaration on the Rights of Indigenous Peoples
UNPFII	United Nations Permanent Forum on Indigenous Issues
UNUPR	United Nations Universal Periodic Review
UNWGIP	United Nations Working Group on Indigenous Populations
UPR	Universal Periodic Review
WB	World Bank
WGIP	Working Group on Indigenous Populations
WGIPA	Working Group on Indigenous Populations/Communities in Africa
WIMSA	Working Group of Indigenous Minorities in Southern Africa

WIPO	World Intellectual Property Organization
WMA	Wildlife Management Area
WTO	World Trade Organization
WWF	World Wildlife Fund

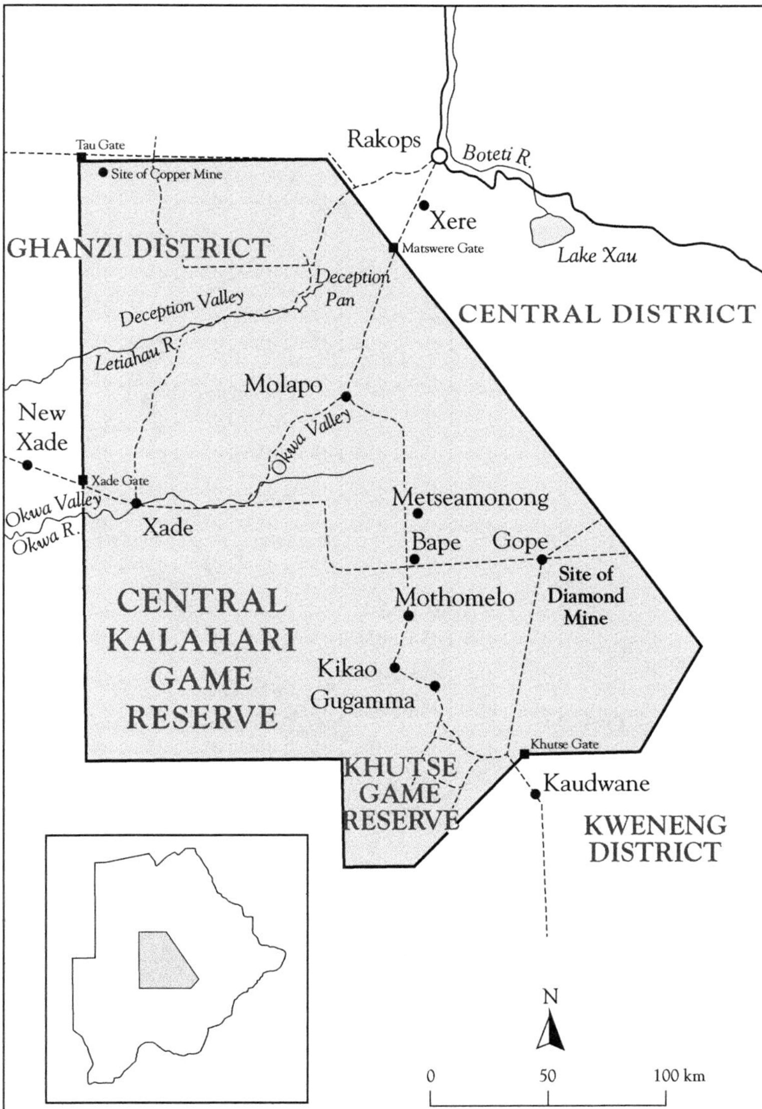

Figure 1 The Central Kalahari Game Reserve and surrounding areas

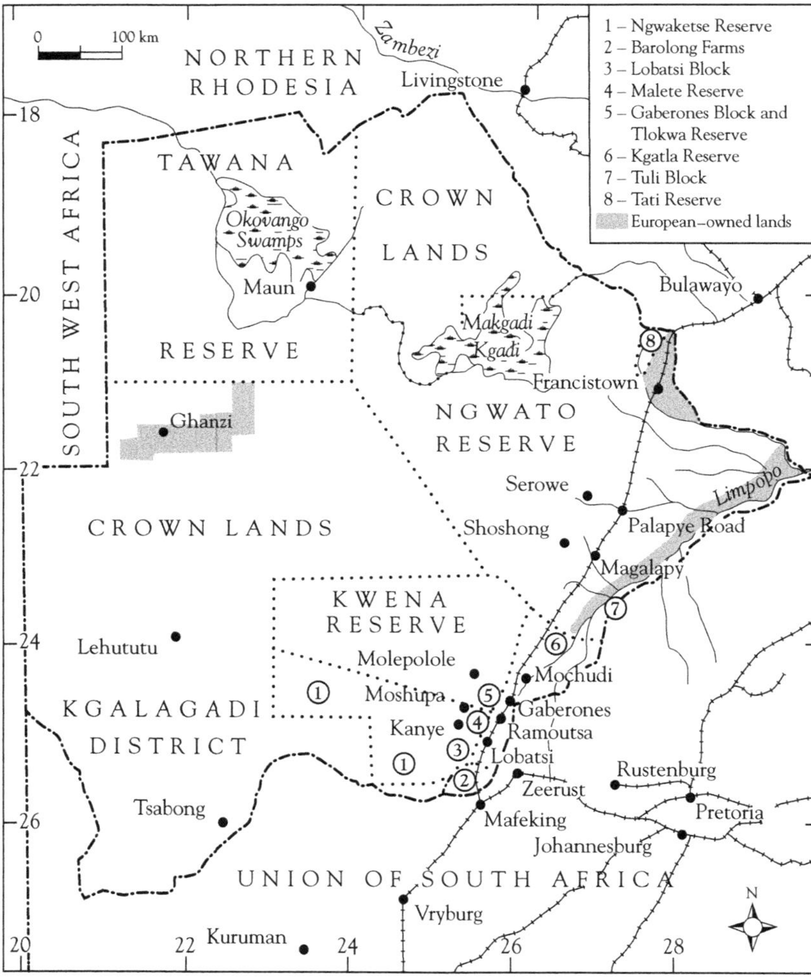

Figure 2 The Bechuanaland Protectorate

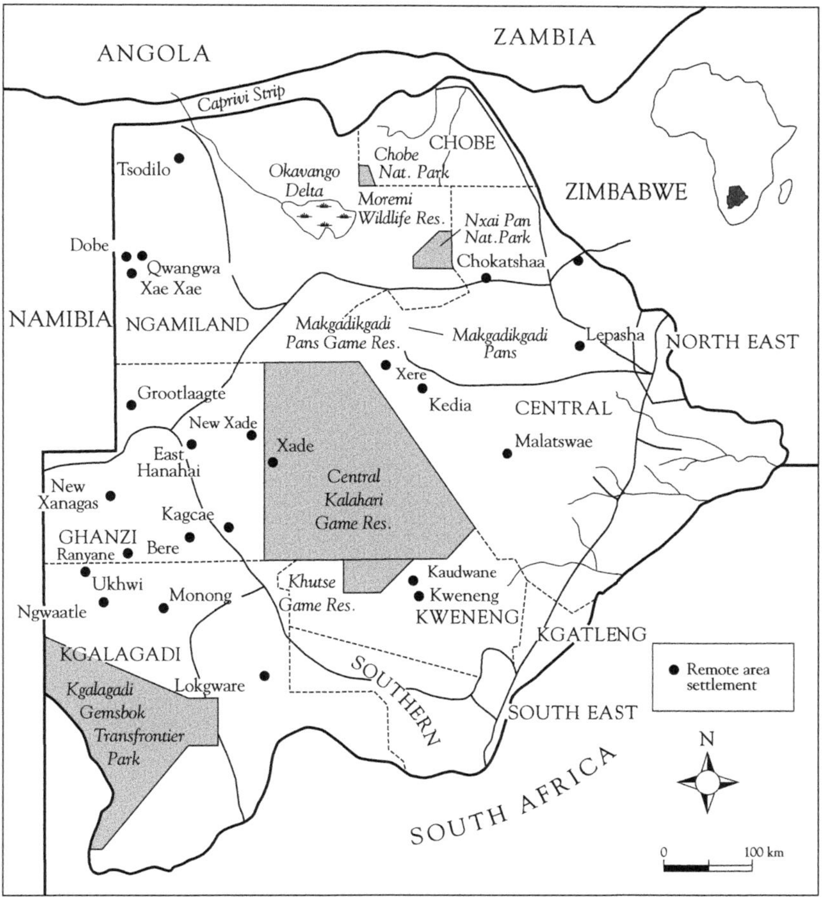

Figure 3 Remote Area Settlements, Botswana

1

INTRODUCTION

THE HUNT FOR JUSTICE

Activism using the tools of law and formal organizations has become essential for many who, through their justice claims, refer to themselves as indigenous peoples. Their varied uses of state courts, global organizations, NGOs, and media are a growing phenomenon, marking an epochal shift toward increasing activist engagement with formal organizations and legal processes. Rights claimants are forming broad alliances, often using the latest communication technologies, to advocate for new international legal standards and forms of accountability (Becker 2013). The multiple strategies of justice campaigns have been applied toward issues that include forced displacement, criminalization of ways of life, genocide, and land dispossession, becoming necessary parts of the ways that many indigenous peoples define and defend their rights and secure their livelihoods. The conditions for participating in these processes are beyond the reach of many, producing inequalities, exclusions, and the risk of keeping structural imbalances of power in place. At the same time, these campaigns express hope for restitution, recognition, and a just future under conditions in which people feel oppressed and excluded from decision making and the benefits deriving from state and corporate uses of their resources.

This book offers an account of the quest for justice by the San peoples of Botswana – and of its widely ramifying effects – with a focus on those few people who were forcefully displaced from the Central Kalahari Game Reserve (CKGR) and who became the focus of the

San's justice cause more generally.[1] The San of Botswana (also known internationally as "Bushmen" and nationally as "Basarwa")[2] who were facing numerous forms of discrimination and dispossession, were often compelled to confront their government as an adversary in a context in which the state refused to recognize their legal status as indigenous. And so San representatives reached out to others – to researchers, donors, and NGOs from abroad – who sympathized with their struggles and identified with the way of life they sought to defend. The high-profile justice campaign that resulted from these collaborations is in fact a prominent instance of a wider phenomenon that is occurring in many parts of the world: publicly visible contests between marginalized peoples and those powerful governments and industries with which they are in conflict.

In addition to the more familiar focus on the *pursuits* of activist struggles, with their compelling narrative of displaced peoples using legal tools to fight back against powerful foes, I pay equal attention here to the *outcomes* of these struggles. What happens, for example, when judges render their verdicts, the dust settles, and people continue with their lives under new legal conditions? What are the actual consequences of recourse to justice campaigns, especially for how people come to see themselves as legal subjects? What is the relationship between dispossession, legal struggles, and the formalization of group identities, including their exclusionary consequences and the implications for redistribution? In this book, I provide answers to these questions by refererring to how legal and political processes play out at multiple levels, from the local to the state, and to international forums, reflecting the simultaneous multiple strategies of many indigenous justice campaigns.

The San's social justice activism took on some of the qualities of movements that have formed around a variety of causes, including those of women, children, those who are LGBTQ, and persons with disabilities. It first involved identifying their conditions of oppression in terms of injustice, for which they sought legal and political remedies in multiple venues. To accomplish their goals, they developed collaborative networks with donors, experts, and justice-oriented non-governmental organizations (NGOs). Finally, their activism was largely oriented toward communication, persuasion, and public outreach, in efforts to influence legal and political decision-making through the mobilization of public sympathy and support. As an *indigenous* movement, however, it was different in the emphasis it placed on distinct rights to ancestral territories and to self-determination. This put it at odds with a state striving toward the equal rights of citizenship and a common national identity. The San's indigenous claims of difference also involved framing their rights in terms of their distinct contributions to humanity, as the embodiment of hunting peoples' ethics of egalitarianism, social intimacy, and ecological wisdom in a time of global crisis.

It was unclear at the outset of this investigation whether justice campaigns have the potential to deliver on their promises in ways that actually improve the conditions of peoples' lives or whether they readily become mired in the hegemonic structures erected not only by the powers against which they struggle, but also by those very structures and strategies that they employ of to advance their causes. There is a tendency for legal and governance institutions to assign rights claimants to specific categories. Institutions are regularly inclined toward the formalization of collective selves, creating particular narratives that define group identities, conceived and contested in ways that either further or diminish (and sometimes even eliminate) possibilities for peoples to exercise their distinct rights.

There are good reasons, however, to treat state-centered law and transnational activism not just as one-dimensional, top-down, hegemonic processes, but also as negotiated and malleable resources that claimants are able to use, sometimes effectively, in defense of their interests. The focus on the outcomes of the San's hunt for justice allows us to see more clearly how particular causes and cases can transform the interpretation of legal principles, raise questions about the implementation of legal judgments, and cast light on the conditions in which restitution and redistribution stall or fail, revealing more clearly the obstacles to and opportunities for justice that would not otherwise have appeared.

This book will therefore follow San representatives and activists in a process through which the categories and templates of state and international law are appropriated, incorporated, and resignified in making justice claims. It will also consider how new legal norms are created through these practices (see Wilson 1997, Merry 2006, Parmar 2015). In some ways these dynamics recall points of continuity between the role of law in the colonial period and that of international and state law today (see, e.g., Chanock 1998, Comaroff and Comaroff 2006, Mamdani 2012), including some of the ways in which law has been shaped by the "spaces of resistance, struggles among colonizers, and forms of accommodation by colonized elites" (Merry 2003).

The case of the central Kalahari is a kind of artifact that I examine from different angles and follow in my ethnography, using it to see how the use of formal systems of law does not depoliticize the struggle (see, Eckert et al. 2014), but brings it more actively into a wider political field in which law and politics are embedded in one another. I consider the consequences of the activist campaign with a focus on how justice goes beyond its formal venues to influence claimants' sense of themselves and others, their sense of the seemingly stagnant conditions of injustice in which they live, including its tangible effects on their bodies and well-being, and the imagined possibilities they might have for a just future.

A LAND FILLED WITH *FILES*

While I was visiting Metseamonong, a village in the eastern part of the CKGR, in 2011, I was present at a heated discussion that occurred in the shade of an acacia tree. I had met some of the people involved in this exchange several years earlier in New Xade, one of the resettlement villages that the government of Botswana had developed to relocate over 2,000 San and Bakgalagadi people outside of the reserve in the late 1990s and early 2000s, which they had since left to return to their ancestral home. Their removal had occurred in the name of modernization, conservation, and development, even though many of those who were displaced did not want to be removed from their territory in the CKGR. They knew about my interest in their struggle against the government and they knew I was there to follow up on how life had been for them since they were allowed by the Botswana High Court to go back to their villages in the reserve in late 2006. I had travelled there with Jumanda Gakelebone, whom I had known for many years, then a community mobilizer of the indigenous NGO First People of the Kalahari (FPK). He was helping me out, not only driving me around but also translating between English and Sekgalagadi and G//ana (one of the many San languages).

The people in Metseamonong were fired up by a recent visit from several government ministers that had taken place a few weeks earlier; and wanted me to understand how they felt about this visit and the injustices it invoked with greater intensity than was usual in these kinds of group discussions. One elderly woman recalled how, over the past years, the government of Botswana had tried to convince the people of her village to leave their territories (*ǂkai*) in the Central Kalahari, places where they had lived for generations, and asserted, "They still want to relocate us. They say this is a land for wild animals not for people." A man in his forties reminded me of events I had heard about many times before, when government employees came and loaded people onto trucks and then moved them hundreds of kilometers away. Family members were sometimes split up and taken to different places, without informing anyone of their location. Their homes were burned, their water tanks overturned, and the only water source that they had, a borehole that took water from deep below the sand, was stripped of its gas-powered pump with cutting torches and sealed with cement. Now he was back, but some of his relatives were still in the resettlement villages because they needed permits and a means of transport to reenter the reserve without risking arrest. "We do not trust the government," he said. "When they promise development we end up suffering … The government does not respect its own law." Another elderly man reminded me, "I refused to be resettled by the government. I never left my home." He recalled that, when he was a child during the time of the British Protectorate, the area where he lived had been declared a game reserve. He and his family were not consulted about the decision to create this reserve, and he did not believe it was right for the government to suddenly announce that people could not live there anymore "just because of what they called it."

As they talked about their lives, a pattern, or at least a common theme, emerged. At almost every turn, they were faced with a regulation, a rule, a demand for information that they did not have, or a thumbprint indicating their consent on documents that they could not read. The women who made crafts needed licenses to collect ostrich eggs, which they did not have and were not able to obtain. Crossing the gate to leave the reserve to visit relatives in one of the relocation villages, guards would search their belongings for meat. They were not sure whether this was arbitrary or indicated a new pattern of enforcement of a hunting prohibition that applied to them. In an interview with three young men in Molapo, a village in the Central Kalahari, they made their concern clear. "People are afraid to hunt" and "We do not know what we can hunt," they said (Sapignoli 2012: 14). This was not a casual concern, but was ultimately connected to whether or not they and their families would have enough to eat.

These stories revealed a great deal about the extent to which these peoples' lives, experiences, and emotions have been shaped by the presence of the state, in the form of legislation, gates, permits, political decisions, ministerial visits, meetings, game scouts, and police patrolling the land that they considered theirs. But certainly the state was not the only presence in the reserve, and not the only one interested in its resources and inhabitants. Tourists and tour guides, employees of mining companies, researchers, journalists, lawyers, United Nations and African Union delegates, and representatives of international and national NGOs, just to mention a few of the many kinds of people who have populated the reserve over time to explore the environment, extract its resources, gather information, document human rights violations, bring assistance, or just discover the "true" Bushmen.

In the encroachment of state law and government politics into their lives, however, the San were not mere spectators or passive victims. In collaboration with lawyers and a broad network of support, they have pursued a range of grievances through legal activism and litigation, organizing their struggle with the creation of NGOs, networks, and committees. Largely as an outcome of the San's decades-long public struggles against their dispossession, the Central Kalahari region is now known as a highly political place, the source of a "place-based struggle" (Escobar 2008: 7), rich in diamonds and other minerals, a place where human rights are violated, and where indigenous resistance has occurred – and recurs.

A year later, I returned to the CKGR, this time traveling to the village of Mothomelo to meet Matsipane Mosetlhanyane, a Mokgalagadi (*sing.* of Bakgalagadi), the first applicant, or plaintiff, of a case over water rights that had concluded with a victory for the San in the Court of Appeal a few months earlier. I had first met him in 2006 when he was a witness and applicant in the famous *Sesana and Others v. the Attorney General* case of 2002–2006. He welcomed me warmly and proudly told me that he was happy about the various court cases that they had initiated against their government, adding, "We now have papers; we can show them to the government when they tell us to move again." I asked him how things had changed with the new borehole, and he offered to take me to see it. As we were walking to the borehole site he pointed out some bony goats and donkeys, barely clinging to life. He explained that there was an especially acute shortage of water for the animals, and that the water that was being pumped was not quite enough to sustain even the people from Mothomelo and the other villages with which they were sharing water. "My horses are in Kaudwane because here they will die," he said, "A horse died a few days ago because we did not have enough water. The pump was broken."

While he was talking, I noticed a copper sign erected in the middle of the sparse vegetation, standing slightly out of kilter in the midst of sand

and goat dung, which read: *This borehole celebrates the struggle of the people of the CKGR for survival, and for their right to their ancestral land. It was made possible by thousands of supporters around the world. For tribal peoples – for all our humanity.* This sign had been erected by Survival International, a London-based indigenous and tribal peoples advocacy NGO, to celebrate a court victory that gave the communities of the CKGR the right to drill their own boreholes, at their own expense, to meet their needs for water. It is an artifact that materializes the community's connection with an international justice campaign, representing not only an international NGO's (somewhat premature) claim of victory, but also drawing attention to the village in the Central Kalahari as a globalized space where contestations over human rights and fundamental political values play out. In its optimistic and celebratory tone, it stood in incongruous contrast to the struggles that remained a daily part of people's' lives in the village.

Yet, hope remained in Mosetlhanyane's earlier remark, "now we have papers," almost as though as a source of life the documents had as much significance as water. The CKGR, in other words, had become a place where documents were wanted and needed, as part of the San's and Bakgalagadi's legal engagements with the state. Files, understood in the broad sense of documents, law, and policies, the products of development workers, anthropologists, and bureaucratized struggles, are today used to document their diversity and indigeneity and to assert their identity as hunters. They have been enabling – and disabling – instruments in legal contests, and reference points for rights and formalized identities. Files have also been used to dispossess them, to violate or take away their rights. They have become an essential part of life, among the obstacles to be faced and sources of the will and the means to survive.

As we will see, the San are today "subjects" of law as topics of legal definitions and debates, subjected to law as the state and its courts redefined who they are and what rights they can claim, and at the same time subjects of their own making as they reappropriate legal institutions and standards to assert their rights and represent their core collective values.

JUSTICE IN (AND BEYOND) THE "LEGAL"

This book represents an effort to document the indigenous peoples' engagement with and resistance to dominant normative systems in order to arrive at a more ethnographically grounded approach to justice and injustice. I explore how people practice, experience, and translate notions of rights and justice after many years of engagement in legal struggle, activism, and collaboration with lawyers and organizations, and how this impacts their sense of self as individuals and collectivities. My approach is based on a premise that I share with Falk and Brunnegger (2016: 4), who write, "What is at stake in the anthropology of justice is a deeper recognition of the multiple ways in which 'justice' is understood." The ethnographically grounded approach to questions of justice – including what it is and how best to achieve it – invites us to begin with how it is characterized by individual actors and within activist networks. Our focus should not be restricted to the formal systems, institutions, or processes of law, but should range further, to the aspirations and intimate subjectivities of those whose sense of injustice has been activated and who are acting on justice claims.

An anthropological approach, through its attention to the subjective and the everyday, is especially attuned to the "disjunctions between the demands for justice and 'legal cultures'" (Falk and Brunnegger 2016: 5). The "legal cultures" in question should not be restricted to those of courts or institutions of global governance, but can extend to the very advocacy networks on which indigenous campaigns for justice often depend, and with which they occasionally find themselves in conflict. Human rights networks, Mark Goodale argues, have a tendency to become "imperial" through "the evacuation of alternative discourses on the basis of what the imperial power believes – earnestly or not – is the correct, or morally superior, or economically more advantageous set of perspectives and practices" (Goodale 2009: 108). In other words, in human rights campaigns the appeal to universal moral values runs the risk of evacuating alternative conceptions of justice.

The ethnography of justice activism is able to shed light on observations of the kind made by Goodale by bringing attention to how, and the extent to which, actors are constrained by the authoritative legal knowledge and practice that they employ. But, it can also shed light on their space for institutional manoever as they "talk back" with discourse and action that constitute a critical response to the structures that limit their aspirations to justice. The actors' use of multiple layers of activism translates into different practices and visions of justice that open alternative strategic pathways when dealing with the moral imperialism of dominant discourse and institutional structures.

One of my goals in this book is to come to grips with the changed spaces of justice activism, by depicting a more complete range of legal engagements than has previously been done in the ethnography of the San, to offer a comprehensive discussion of the San people and their claims making through formal institutions. In doing so, I maintain consistent attention to the "law talk" that takes place in response to the encroachments of the state and the opportunities inherent in new indigenous advocacy networks. I focus on the claims-making processes or on the specific sites where claims take place (such as courts or international meetings), as well as on parallel and interconnected forms of activism (publicity campaigns, protests, lobbying, etc.) and the implications these have for the everyday lives of rights claimants and the peoples they work for. In taking this approach, I hope to add substance and detail to accounts of the growing influence of law and its embeddedness into local and international politics and societies. The ethnography I present here thus takes the concept of juridification outside the court and other formal legal venues and into the everyday lives of the people who are engaged in and affected by justice claims and activism. This includes the somatic effects of the sense of injustice, the ways that state-sanctioned arbitrariness and illegality are expressed in bodily experience, the sense of sickness, pain, and uncleanliness that follows directly from, and is associated with, government policies and practices.

JUDICIALIZATION AND JURIDIFICATION

The San's complex legal subjectivity compels us to evaluate the consequences of the increased recourse to formal legal processes, especially for how people come to see themselves as legal subjects. Certain authors in the political science and anthropological literatures (e.g. Couso et al. 2013) see the phenomenon of increasingly frequent use of courts as part of a global transformation in the uses and influence of law, and have referred to it (largely critically and negatively) as *judicialization*, or the "transfer of decision-making rights from the legislature, the cabinet, or the civil service to the courts" (Vallinder 1994: 91). Ran Hirschl considers this transformation on a grand scale, noting a constitution-reforming dimension to the way that national courts and supranational entities are engaging in "the ever-accelerating reliance on courts and judicial means for addressing core moral predicaments, public policy questions, and political controversies" (Hirschl 2008: 94).

The approach taken here builds on these observations by being attentive to a wide range of consequences that follow from growing recourse to state and international law, whether as a source of state domination and control or as an instrument of judicial review. The authority of judicial review represents a significant pathway toward the correction of the abuses of state governments by underrepresented people seeking justice through state courts. The emphasis on what law does in practice is perhaps best represented by the concept of *juridification*, which is fast becoming a key concept of analysis in efforts to understand the changing relationship between law and politics (Eckert et al. 2014, Kirsch 2014a). Yet, the concept itself is unclear, and empirical knowledge of the social implications of various processes that might apply to it is insubstantial (Magnussen and Banasiak 2013: 325). This is where an account of the San's many-sided engagements with law can help. The fact that legal oppression and activism have taken form in so many aspects of their lives provides us with a guide to how the concept of juridification might be unpacked and applied comparatively.

One significant consequence of the increased recourse to law – juridification as legal framing – can be seen in the process by which people increasingly tend to think of themselves and others as legal subjects (Blichner and Molander 2008: 39), a process that emerges with particular clarity in indigenous rights claims. This approach to the influence of law includes a wide spectrum of legal institutions and procedures, with a focus on the experiences and perspectives of rights claimants. It considers law as entrenched in the everyday, as generative, as part of the way relationships are created and identities and expertise developed. Mahmood Mamdani argues that this generative power of law can clearly be seen in the period of indirect rule, when the British preoccupation with defining and managing difference led to the consolidation of racial and tribal categories (Mamdani 2012: 3). However, this is not a process that ends with the rise of anticolonial nationalism and the promotion of a common humanity. Even in circumstances of postcolonial nation building, there is a tendency for group identities to be defined, enumerated, and formalized through legal and administrative processes, with important implications for rights claimants and their causes. In the Kalahari legal cases, for example, the judicial process called for particular formulations of the "applicants" rights and identities, and assigned specific roles to those who pursued their rights through the court and those who did not.

The manner in which the San's pursuit of justice was channeled through NGOs, partly as a condition of having an organized and recognized voice, offers another key example of the formalization of collective action, producing contested visions and insecurity in the relationships between activists and their donors. This has implications ultimately for the survival of San organizations and their ability to act on their rights. The consequences of legal processes and activism therefore must also include how the San have been externally conceptualized and categorized in law – by NGOs, the state, international agencies, and by their own leadership – and the ways that they have influenced and made use of these conceptualizations. Ultimately, I consider how an engagement with law creates a new sense of belonging for a community of legal subjects, as defined by changing understandings of their rights and duties.

I will also consider the implications of juridification for politics. Some scholars focus on the consequences of recourse to courts and describe what they see as a "juridification of politics," in which political mobilization in the public sphere (including in international forums), media campaigns, street demonstrations, and parliamentary debates are increasingly displaced onto, or carried out at the same time as, court litigation in the national and international arenas (Randeria 2007: 39). Colin Hoag, for example, goes beyond the influence of courts and attributes the source of depoliticization to a much wider phenomenon, namely the inherent effects of bureaucracy. Bureaucracies, he notes, base their laws, rules, and regulations on ideals of an abstract, universal kind, without the specificity needed to fit them into a local context. The task of bureaucrats is therefore to interpret the rules for specific applications. Fundamental issues are deferred, and ideals "operate as depoliticizing technologies, masking the exercise of power in the guise of an always emergent – but never attained – perfect order" (Hoag 2011: 82).

Others associate this development toward depoliticization with what they see as an insidious form of hegemony, in which the hope that is placed in courts for reform of the state is misplaced; in other words, the juridification of politics is seen as actually producing the opposite result by narrowing the space for collective action (Magnussen and Banasiak 2013: 332). Arguing along these lines, Comaroff and Comaroff (2006: 25) situate the problem of depoliticization within a wide-ranging overview of the postcolonial politics of coercion, which favors "those equipped to play most potently inside the dialectic of law and disorder" (2006: 31). "Ultimately," they argue, "it is neither the weak nor the meek nor the marginal who predominate" in the rise of "lawfare" in a "culture of legality" that is "infusing the capillaries of everyday life" in postcolonial societies, in ways that "depoliticize" the effects of dissent (2006: 25, 31). This juridification-as-hegemony approach draws attention to how increasing use of courts by citizens to render their governments accountable has the paradoxical effect of shrinking the space for politics within democracies (Randeria 2007: 39). The result, as Olaf Zenker puts it, "quite often entails an emasculation of the transformative potential of political agitation through the self-confinement to 'legal cases' that, in its appeal to laws, ostensibly instantiate rather than transform the existing order" (Zenker 2012: 138). Such a process of emasculation might not be immediately apparent. Zenker highlights the ambiguity of the distinction between law and politics, which makes it almost impossible to tell whether a particular action is actually political or legal, and with the difference being more "a matter of switching between two different and ultimately incommensurable codes than an issue of differential ontology" (Zenker 2012: 139).

There is by no means a consensus on the depoliticizing effects of recourse to law in the context of activist movements. The legalization of rights, Richard Wilson (2007: 355) convincely points out, "may indeed be associated with the rising influence of legal technocratic elites, but this does not preclude their potential contributions to political engagement, in which, borrowing from Clausewitz, law becomes a form of 'politics by other means'." As this book demonstrates, this inseparability of law and politics characterizes indigenous peoples' involvement with legal institutions and extends to their practice of law in the everyday. With this reassessment of the relationship between political and legal action in mind, the processes I describe in this book can be seen as involving an almost hyperpoliticization of (or through) law, whereby recourse to legal remedies in some ways *intensifies* political struggles and becomes inseparable from them. In fact, we might even be more direct and refer to the San's use of law as imbricated with politics, or even as politics *tout court*. In other words, legal activism does not necessarily depoliticize its issues of concern, but can become itself a publicly prominent locus of political struggle (see Kirsch 2014a).

This point comes out more clearly in the period "after judgment," therefore justifying a longitudinal approach to the arc of justice. The experience of collective claimants in courts tends to emphasize the concepts and processes of litigation, and focuses on claims-making and/or the specific legal contests in which the struggles take place, leaving little space for understanding what the recourse to adjudication produces, in particular what happens to people's understanding and activation of their rights. A view to the longue durée offers another way of understanding the stakes involved in the juridification of indigenous claims. By taking into consideration the extended aftermath of key judgments, it becomes easier to see how, in their use of courts, justice claimants became ensnared in repeated legal contests, in "litigation chains," that require them to be constantly "litigating a way of life." It also allows us to see how this recourse to litigation influences their discourse on unfairness or injustice in ways that indicate their growing familiarity with, and readiness to use, the norms and powers of formal legal systems.

BATTLING ESSENTIALISM

The essence and interpretation of the changes to the San's way of life that have accompanied their justice-seeking have by no means gone uncontested. The San have the distinction of being the focus of a series of debates that began with questions about the central qualities of their way of life and spilled over into the vitriolic expression of differences about the trajectory of human history and the nature of justice. The contests that focused on the San are important to briefly consider here because they shape how we see the San's historical relationship with the state and outside societies and institutions, as well as their continuity and enduring identity as an indigenous people. These debates take us from the essence of life in the Kalahari to the consequences of law in people's everyday lives, from digging sticks to documents and lawyers as tools of subsistence.

One of these sets of discussions and exchanges – the one that in effect started it all – is known as the "Kalahari debate." This is in fact a misnomer since it soon spilled over from its focus on the Kalahari to become a key debate in anthropology at large about group identity. The focus of this debate concerns the degree to which – and when – San people began to engage in pursuits other than foraging, and the extent to which they have maintained the values of egalitarianism with which foraging is associated. One set of perspectives, whose proponents are characterized as "traditionalists," sees the San as primarily hunter-gatherers or foragers who were relatively isolated, meaning that they hunted wild animals and gathered wild plants for food, medicines, and other material needs and had a unique culture based on principles of egalitarianism, sharing, and consensus-based decision-making that constituted the basis of political life.[3] Among many San groups, important decisions were a product of extensive consultation, consensus-building, and discussion among the members of the community, with all adults and children, if they chose, having the opportunity to participate. Decisions were made on the basis of public consensus. According to the traditionalist view, the loss of this way of life, where it occurred, was fairly recent. Over time and in different places, San groups acquired different forms of subsistence, including animal husbandry (raising cattle, sheep, goats, horses, and donkeys), fishing, and agriculture (Solway and Lee 1990; Hitchcock et al. 2006). The values that accompany a foraging lifestyle were slower to change, and the San still maintain attachment to the practices of sharing and principles of equality.

The other view, characterized as "revisionist," sees San peoples as having long been part of the larger economy and society of southern Africa, in close contact with other groups, such as the Tswana, Herero, and Kalanga; involved heavily in livestock production, agriculture, and trading; and as an "underclass" dominated, subordinated, and marginalized by their neighbors.[4] Much of this often-contentious debate revolved around basic issues relating to variations in lifestyles and identities of San and their neighbors. Edwin Wilmsen initiated the controversy by amassing evidence (much of it becoming the focus of acrimonious contestation by specialists) to show that the San groups of southern Africa had long participated actively in the diverse economies and political systems of the region. "The isolation in which they are said to have been found," he argued, "is a creation of our view of them, not of their history as they lived it" (Wilmsen 1989: 3). This observation did not remain in the realm of history, but extended into political philosophy, with Wilmsen arguing that it is better to understand the San as an underclass, as part of a much larger system of commodity capitalism, rather than as an ethnic group. He thus called for the use of the concept of citizenship as opposed to ethnicity in dealing with issues of minority rights in Botswana (Wilmsen 2002: 825).

An attempt to find a reconciliatory position in the debate came from an alternative view held by Solway and Lee (1990), who saw a range of variation in the Kalahari in issues relating to livestock ownership, exchange, labor, and autonomy. Susan Kent (1992) and Alan Barnard (2007) similarly proposed a "third way" that took note of the regional variation that exists among San peoples and agreed that San were not isolated and not full-time hunter-gatherers, while arguing that this finding does not mean that they should be considered to be just another class of citizens without a different culture and way of life. The Kalahari debate has not remained stuck in a sterile dualism, but has yielded a body of scholarship that is more nuanced, taking into account the San groups' complexity, diversity, and adaptability.

Even if the San are recognized as the most marginalized socioeconomic class in Botswana, San activists, their organizations, and the people of the Central Kalahari who are the focal point of the CKGR struggle certainly see themselves as far more than an "underclass," more than, in the government's terminology, "Remote Area Dwellers" who need to be uplifted and removed from an impoverished and beggarly way of life. In the years that scholars were debating the essence of their identity, history, and subsistence practices, San activists and representatives from southern Africa were claiming indigenous rights and identity with reference to international legal standards, based on their common history of dispossession, criminalization of their hunting and gathering way of life, and attachment to the land. They emphasized the fact that the Botswana government was using discourses of economic and social development to pursue policies aimed at resettling people far from their land and way of life – which had hunting and gathering as an important social marker.

At the same time, the emphasis on the San as hunter-gatherers as a central pillar of their rights campaign was not shared by everyone, and may even have had the effect of marginalizing many San in southern Africa. Renee Sylvain (2003), for example, finds that the underclass of farm laborers in the Omaheke region in Namibia, who did not conform to the stereotype of the San-as-hunters, were either left out of the indigenous rights claims or forced, despite the farm-based circumstances of their lives, to correspond in some way to the stereotypes that had become part of the process of securing recognition as "indigenous."

This concern points to a situation that becomes even more complex when we consider a more complete range of activist strategies. For instance, the "indigenous idea" in court decisions is sometimes translated into a frozen understanding of tradition and culture, with important implications for the daily lives of those whose rights the court sets out to define. In international law, however, "indigenous peoples" is not a limiting idea fixed to stereotypes, at least in principle, but is the result of complex and changing understandings of belonging, with self-determination as a guiding principle. International forums present the challenges of self-representation that transcend particular issues, sometimes making use of the popular tropes of indigeneity, but also leaving open the possibility for activists to formulate their own visions for the future and to convey aspirations for development on their own terms.

This risk of recognition solely through the tropes of hunting and gathering and the supposedly simple life of survival in the Kalahari has been well expressed by a San national organization, the Botswana Khwedom Council, which observed that "The San are often framed as pristine hunter-gatherers, representatives of some previous human utopia, living close to nature, rejecting the concept of ownership, and needing nothing more than the land. In so doing, they [as well as their issues] are effectively removed from the economics and the politics of the present" (Botswana Khwedom Council 2012: 5). The tension between the popular idealization of the past and the challenges of the present arises at many points in the San's justice cause.

A nuanced account of the San struggles against removal and assimilation is one of my central goals in this book. This can serve to highlight the artificiality of the distinction between essentialist depictions of the San as primordial hunters and antiessentialist depictions of them as having a contingent identity that is readily shaped and put to use in the service of claims-making.

A second, related controversy builds on the Kalahari debate, with a specific focus on the San's adoption of indigeneity and pursuit of indigenous rights claims. In the setting of southern Africa, with the backdrop of Apartheid, and with apprehensive reference to strident forms of nationalism in Europe, these claims of difference were particularly sensitive, and discussions concerning assertions of indigenous rights based on a distinct way of life readily took on an inflammatory tone. This controversy focused on the concerns of scholars who had worked among the San and other peoples of southern Africa, although the arguments they made were meant to apply to claimants of indigenous rights and identity more generally. It was initiated by Adam Kuper's (2003) arguments against indigeneity, which, he claimed, plays on a "blood and soil" nationalism in which the original "primitive" inhabitants of a place have rights on it while the colonists and "second comers" do not. He therefore asserted that the category of "indigenous" leads to new types of racism and to ethnic conflicts and exclusionisms that can have serious political consequences (Kuper 2003: 395).

Other scholars (e.g. Ramos 2003, Kenrick and Lewis 2004) opposed Kuper's arguments with the assertion that indigenous identities have to be understood analytically in a contextual way and not dismissed. Many of Kuper's critics point out that in his attack on indigeneity he is silent on the colonial processes and the relative powerlessness and marginality of those who claim indigenous identity. Anthropology can therefore support those who define themselves as "indigenous" without necessarily promoting "romantic" and "obsolete" notions (Barnard 2006: 12).

As I will show in this book, the resignification of the notions of "indigenous peoples" or "hunter-gatherers" and "culture" by San activists and organizations is not a reproposal of "old images of primitivism." In a recent article, Sylvain (2015) argues that the debate on San indigeneity was based on an illegitimately forced choice between identity politics and class politics, without careful consideration of the implications of social construction. Adding another dimension to the debate, Steven Robins (2003: 399), argues convincingly that denying indigenous rights claimants access to important resources as compensation for past injustices simply because indigenous communities use the "essentialist ideologies" of "culture" and "identity" would seriously damage the tradition of advocacy in anthropology and hamper the cause of those activists who attempt to reconcile a "cultural politics of acknowledgement" with redistributive justice.

The false dichotomies that have arisen in these two debates, with their significant implications for San identity and claims-making, lead directly to Nancy Fraser's arguments in favor of combining claims of recognition with those of redistribution. Fraser (2003) is known for her arguments in support of both the social justice claims to *recognition* – those that promote the distinct perspectives and experiences of, for example, ethnic, racial, and sexual minorities, women, and indigenous peoples – with claims that are oriented toward *redistribution*, that seek a more just distribution of wealth, resources, and government services. She argues against the approaches of such philosophers of recognition as Charles Taylor and Axel Honneth, forcefully making the point that separating these approaches to social justice produces a false antithesis, that justice claims are in reality hybrid, that "subordinated groups suffer both maldistribution and misrecognition in forms where neither of these injustices is an intended effect of the other, but where both are primary and co-original" (Fraser 2003: 19). Indigenous peoples are clearly among those whose justice claims have inclined toward recognition, in which their empowerment as a distinct people is then oriented toward rights of redistribution.

Evidence in support of Fraser's position does not have to be limited to the arguments of moral and political philosophy, but is also apparent in what rights claimants actually do. This point is clearly relevant to the San's quest for justice and the "transformative remedies" (see Fraser 2005) intended to undo the structures of dispossession. San peoples have not only been seeking recognition in the form of rights to self-determination and cultural expression; they are also seeking improvement in the material conditions of their lives and in their access to resources, health, and conditions of prosperity. One dimension of redistributive justice that is particularly relevant to indigenous peoples is that of *restitution*, which can include establishing regimes for the restoration of the resources and territories that have been illegitimaly removed, including acknowledgement of historical injustices. The two kinds of rights are "co-original," in Fraser's terms, with claims to recognition as a distinct people inextricably connected to those that are redistributive, that have important implications for access to land and resources, food security, and equal access to government services.

Fraser later added a significant political dimension to her model that entails the problem of *representation*. The "stages on which struggles over distribution and recognition are played out," she argues, turn largely on the question of "how" claims are to be mooted and adjudicated (2005: 75). This issue can be approached by considering "the nature of the state's jurisdiction and the decision rules by which it structures contestation," paying particular attention to the question of whether, "the boundaries of the political community wrongly exclude some who are actually entitled to representation" (2005: 75). For her, the solution to problems of oppression, marginalization, and injustice therefore turn upon efforts to "democratize the process of frame-setting" (2005: 80). Taking Fraser's model as a starting point, we can see how the San's justice cause involved forms of "misframing" – in the formal structures of state institutions, NGOs, and global organizations – that excluded them from equitable relations among fellow citizens and from the ability to "participate as peers in social life" (2005: 73). At the national level, even those who developed new forms of organized leadership were often excluded from participation in a wider national political community by a state-sponsored assimilationist orientation to group belonging that privileged dominant Tswana politics, language, and identity. The San justice campaign can therefore be seen in part as a struggle to achieve new forms of representation through frameworks that in fundamental ways misrepresented them. Their misrepresentation, in other words, occurred through the very processes in which they were compelled to pursue their claims. Similar to what happens with participatory development initiatives through the "tyranny of participation," indigenous perspectives, far from shaping the planning processes by which their justice causes are reframed, are usually structured by them (see Mosse 2001).

My goal in highlighting this issue of representation is to provide empirical support to an approach to indigeneity that draws attention to the consequences of broad-based justice campaigning for people's lives, and to highlight the opportunities that might arise (or be lost) by making indigenous rights claims against a state that has the capacity to obstruct and dismantle aspirations that accentuate difference. A long-term perspective, which considers the multiple points of leverage in the San's activist campaign, reveals the extent to which this debate actually entered into their struggle. The false antithesis of recognition and redistribution, together with the related oppositions inherent in the Kalahari debate and contested notions of indigeneity – involving claims of standing and representation – were often explicitly taken up in disputes between the San and the state. Advocates of the "dark" side of indigeneity raised concerns about the reification of culture to justify the exclusion of those such as the San and hinder their development on their own terms, even though the San's goals for justice derived from the web of relationships and experience of territory that give their lives meaning.

THE LEGAL AND ECONOMIC INDIGENOUS

The concept of "indigenous peoples" is not only a legal category with implications merely for political recognition, but has significant consequences for the politics of redistribution, since it has become increasingly an economic category. Emerging legal tools such as free, prior, and informed consent (FPIC), which has become the focal point of indigenous activism in the international public sphere, have the potential to bring about equitable sharing of the material benefits that are derived from the lands and resources. FPIC recognizes the distinctive and profound relationship such peoples have with their lands and the importance of their right to own, control, and use their lands and territories, including a requirement that states and industries obtain their consent before beginning development projects involving mining, construction of hydroelectric facilities, logging, or ranching – projects that have often permanently destroyed indigenous lands and resulted in the forced relocation of indigenous communities.

Several UN agencies such as the International Fund For Agricultural Development (IFAD) and the Food and Agriculture Organziation (FAO), as well as development banks, have adopted FPIC as a prerequisite for financing states' development projects that affect indigenous peoples. States, particularly those defined as "developing countries," have had to face the fact that genuine recognition of indigenous rights has become an international standard for the provision of economic support, and failure to observe indigenous rights can (in rare instances) result in the cancellation of projects or the withdrawal of investor funds. Intellectual property rights have also emerged as a significant area of international law, with important implications for indigenous peoples as rights holders and beneficiaries of products based on their knowledge. Even the global network of donors associated with indigenous peoples' rights and development has economic or "redistributive" implications for those who claim indigenous identity.

These developments are not uniformly seen as auspicious. Mark Goodale (2016) recognizes this economic dimension of indigenous rights claims as an essential quality of indigenous identity, and refers to "'dark matter': the ineluctable, constant, and veiled presence of transnational (primarily extractive) capital working not against, but with, policies of indigenous rights." In the concept of indigenous peoples in international law, "the logic of capitalism was hardwired ... from the beginning" (Goodale 2016: 441). In the form it has taken, Goodale argues, indigenous rights mobilization has had little real impact on the underlying political and economic conditions that perpetuate indigenous peoples' vulnerability (2015: 442). Concerns about the capitalist economic rationale built into indigenous rights claims raise an empirical question concerning the actual consequences of the pursuit of indigenous rights and identity. Following the need for empirical observation, this book reveals a more complex reality, in which the mobilization of indigenous peoples' rights can in the long term influence the structural conditions of their dispossession.

If we are to fully understand such economic and political concerns about the concept of indigenous peoples and the ways it is deployed, it is also important to return to the source of what we might call the "legal indigenous": the international instruments and organizations in which the concept and the indigenous movement in which the San took part had their origins. Since the 1980s, the word "indigenous" has appeared more and more frequently at a global level as it became connected to international law (Niezen 2003; Merlan 2009). The word has become an expression of identity, a label carried proudly by indigenous representatives, which often reveals something significant and personal about whoever uses it and the collective identity that it represents. An overview of the most significant developments in this history makes it possible to situate the San's pursuit of justice in the context of a global rights movement.[5]

The term "indigenous populations" was first included in an international legal instrument with the passage of the *International Labour Organization's Indigenous and Tribal Populations Convention and Recommendation (No 107)* of 1957, an initiative aimed at poverty alleviation and political representation. Yet there was at this point no grassroots movement of indigenous organizations and networks to participate in the elaboration of new standards in international law, and Convention 107 was oriented toward the assimilation of the indigenous populations into the states to which they belonged. This prompted the ILO to revise its approach to indigenous peoples with a new instrument, *Convention 169, the Indigenous and Tribal Peoples Convention* (1989), which explicitly acknowledged and overturned the integrationist and assimilationist approach of Convention 107 and, in the process, affirmed the cultural and political integrity of indigenous peoples. So while the ILO introduced the concept of indigenous peoples to the UN system as early as the 1950s, the reconceptualization and active use of that concept, including the formation of identities based on it by rights claimants, did not come until significantly later.

The organization and representation of indigenous peoples in the UN first occurred when the United Nations declared the years from 1973 to 1982 the Decade for Action to Combat Racism and Racial Discrimination, a Sub-Committee of which had as its main task the organization of a series of NGO conferences on racism and racial discrimination. The United Nations Economic and Social Council (ECOSOC) followed up these conferences with the creation in 1982 of the Working Group on Indigenous Populations (WGIP), which quickly became the largest United Nations forum dealing with human rights issues.

From the early 1980s on, the numbers of indigenous NGOs participating in international meetings increased exponentially, together with the extent of the activist networks through which they worked. Indigenous organizations began to make effective use of new media to develop and maintain their international connections. Transnational networks were built into some of the "umbrella" organizations participating in the WGIP, such as the International Work Group for Indigenous Affairs, the Inuit Circumpolar Conference, the International Indian Treaty Council, the World Council of Indigenous Peoples, and the Indigenous Peoples of Africa Coordinating Committee. The formation of these organizations and their alliances into an international movement of indigenous peoples in recent decades reflects a changing alignment of political advocacy. Despite their limited power and resources, some indigenous organizations, representing those who once had little recourse in response to their oppression, have become significant players in the contemporary national and international scenes.

The establishment of the Permanent Forum on Indigenous Issues (PFII), which held its first session meeting in 2002, was without question one of the most significant developments in the global indigenous movement. When the Permanent Forum was created as an advisory body in the UN system, reporting to the powerful Economic and Social Council (ECOSOC), it inherited many of the people who had developed their expertise through previous initiatives such as the WGIP meetings and various workshops on the future of the indigenous agenda in the UN.[6] Every year, indigenous spokespersons at the annual two-week session report on conditions faced by the people they represent, asserting their claims to self-determination and collective rights as distinct "peoples," often making reference to states' violations of treaties and existing international standards of human rights and fundamental freedoms (Sapignoli 2017).

Many of the participants in the Permanent Forum had also acquired experience during the twenty-year process of drafting the *UN Declaration on the Rights of Indigenous Peoples* (DRIP), adopted in 2007. The Declaration is described by the UN in a press release as prohibiting discrimination against indigenous peoples and promoting "their full and effective participation in all matters that concern them, and their right to remain distinct and to pursue their own visions of economic and social development."[7] The Declaration is widely considered the most complete statement of the legal and political aspirations of indigenous peoples, addressing such issues as self-determination and free, prior and informed consent, and envisioning an end to assimilationist policies (Charters and Stavenhagen 2009).

These developments in international law have occurred in a context in which there was no formal "gatekeeper" definition of indigenous peoples by which one could include or exclude peoples and organizations that were the presumed beneficiaries of these initiatives

(Daes 2008). The reports intended to provide clarification on what constitutes an indigenous people offer only guidelines, working definitions, and descriptions of common qualities. The Independent Commission on International Humanitarian Issues (1987) argued that four elements are important in the recognition of who indigenous peoples are: (1) preexistence, (2) non-dominance, (3) cultural difference, and (4) self-identification as indigenous. This last criterion of "self-identification," is also a key feature of the famous working definition by Jose Martinez Cobo in his *Study of the Problem of Discrimination against Indigenous Populations* (1985): "Indigenous communities, peoples, and nations are those that, having a historical continuity with pre-invasion and pre-colonial societies that developed on their territories, *consider themselves distinct* from other sectors of the societies now prevailing on those territories, or parts of them" (emphasis added). An important criterion for "indigenousness," therefore, is the identification by people themselves of their distinct collective identity (see Daes 2008). Most indigenous people prefer to reserve for themselves the right to determine who is and is not a member of their group, but as a feature of a working definition in international law it meant that indigenous rights claims could be made by any people from anywhere with a plausible claim to "indigenous" status. As Ronald Niezen (2003: 6) points out, the use of the term "indigenous peoples" paradoxically arises from the fact that it refers to peoples with a "primordial" identity and a "continuative" affection for a specific area and culture that continued for centuries and millennia, even though it is a relatively new concept.[8]

When indigenous peoples from Africa entered the UN, the idea of indigeneity had already been shaped by the experience of those who had been subjected to European settler colonialism. The ideas of "first comers" and historical continuity with precolonial territories had been central to the understanding of indigeneity in international law. The recently decolonized countries, including those in Asia and Africa, were excluded from this original vision of indigenous peoples. Indigenous peoples from North America and Australasia had been first in becoming organized at the global level entering the United Nations, discussing international law, lobbying and building alliances that led to the creation of an indigenous global movement (Niezen 2003). They were more concerned about self-government and sovereignty, whereas those in Africa and Asia were more concerned with issues of fundamental human rights, security, and cultural difference (Erueti 2011: 109). At the time that the indigenous people's movement first began in the UN, there was no representation by indigenous peoples from Africa. African indigenous participation in the UN began in the late 1980s and the 1990s, with just a few people attending these meetings.

It is important and meaningful for a sociopolitical reading of this situation that indigenous status is reminiscent of oppression under a regime of colonial domination – precisely one of the reasons that African governments have been steadfastly unwilling to recognize it. Opposition to indigenous rights by African governments tends to emphasize the concern that claims of indigeneity promote "tribalism" and could lead to secession efforts, undermining the integrity of the state (African Group of States 2006). African governments have claimed that making a distinction between indigenous and nonindigenous peoples favors one group over another and that differentiating people on the basis of ethnic identification or specific status undermines efforts to create unified states. A more scholarly appraisal of African indigeneity points to the problem of defining an indigenous people in the African context, where no objective criteria exist to determine the concept's boundaries, leaving it open to appropriation through ethnic politics (Ndahinda 2011: 345). This leads to a fundamental questioning of the utility of the indigenous peoples concept as a tool of empowerment in the African context. As we will see at many points in this book, consistent with these concerns about ethnic division, the government of Botswana presented its human rights obligations in terms of citizenship rights, while opposing recognition of the distinct rights, territories, and identities of indigenous peoples, including the San.

In terms of recognition by international organizations, the reluctance to recognize African indigenous peoples was overcome in a very simple way: by having representatives of NGOs attend meetings, and having some key international organizations such as the International Work Group for Indigenous Affairs (IWGIA) promote an African indigenous peoples' agenda both in international and in regional-African meetings. African indigenous organizations and spokespersons took full advantage of this support and eventually participated in UN initiatives in such numbers that it became impossible to ignore the fact that there was a regional dimension to indigenous experience, with indigenous peoples from Africa and Asia asserting distinct claims and identities in different postcolonial contexts.

To some extent the San have been able to position themselves above the fray surrounding indigeneity in Africa. In fact, they have been almost iconic as an African indigenous people, often represented (and sometimes representing themselves) as *the* people whose origins reach back to the primordial beginnings of humanity. Other groups have captured the public imagination – above all the Maasai as the culturally colorful pastoralists of East Africa and the Tuareg as the camel-herding nomads of the Sahara – but the San of southern Africa represent the quintessential hunter-gatherers, an identity that gives them special leverage in indigenous debates and rights initiatives.

This particular quality of their representation is important to bear in mind as we consider the sometimes ferocious dedication of their high-profile supporters (including, on various occasions, Prince Charles, Gloria Steinem, Brad Pitt, Angelina Jolie, Jackson Browne, Colin Firth, Bishop Desmond Tutu, Iman Mohamed Abdulmajid, etc.). The strength of their popular claim to indigeneity is also important to keep in mind as we discuss their relationships with governments for which the idea of distinct rights as "indigenous peoples" is anathema.

METHOD AND THE MULTIPLE LEVERAGE POINTS OF SOCIAL JUSTICE ACTIVISM

In the research conducted for this book, the primary goal was to arrive at an intimate study of the San justice cause. This has involved taking into account its many dimensions and the various strategies and settings that are at the origin (and a reflection) of my own multiple forms of engagement as a researcher. Applying this commitment to engagement toward my research with the San people, who are living in conditions of displacement and making use of various forms of "law against the state," it became clear to me that my work had to be framed in one way or another in terms of a shared project in which my research was ideally to be applied to their advantage.

My research in "the field" started with observations in Botswana's High Court in 2006 and ended with the 2017 session of the UNPFII. From the beginning, my research foci were informed by a number of exchanges I have had, starting with email correspondence and phone conversations with San spokespersons and their supporters, that guided my interest in documenting the CKGR case and the San people's justice concern more broadly. At that time, this case was at a peak of national and international interest, and was a focal point of the San people's concerns about their rights and their future. Thanks to First People of the Kalahari and Survival International, two NGOs that facilitated my introduction to the applicants' legal team, I was able to attend the final argumentation of the *Sesana* case in September 2006 and to gain the trust of the people of the CKGR with whom they were working in support of the case.

It was no accident that my field research began in court. Litigation has been a prominent feature of the San's justice campaign I was following, to the point that one old man, an applicant of the first legal case (*Sesana and Others v. the Attorney General* [2006]), remarked to me, "The only way the government listens to us is when we bring it to court" (author notes 2012). In fact, in the recent past, the CKGR has been the subject of legal cases that have drawn the interest of international lawyers, anthropologists, indigenous organizations, the United Nations, the African Commission on Human and Peoples' Rights (ACHPR), and governments of countries as diverse as the United Kingdom, the United States, Canada, Denmark, Sweden, Norway, Spain, Bolivia, Italy, Kenya, South Africa, and Namibia.

During the decade or so since I began my fieldwork in the Botswana High Court, I followed San representatives as they positioned themselves at three levels: at the local level with communities and politically engaged individuals; at the national level in meetings with government officials; and at the international level in a variety of UN agencies and annual UN sessions relating to indigenous peoples' rights. Within this period, I spent a few months as an intern in Survival International's London office; in the UN Secretariat of the Permanent Forum on Indigenous Issues (SPFII) within the Department of Economic and Social Affairs (DESA) at the UN Headquarters in New York; and in the International Foundation for Agricultural Development (IFAD) in Rome. Over a ten-year period, I also attended the annual sessions of the Permanent Forum on Indigenous Issues (2007–17). In the UN, I paid attention to the place that the African indigenous movement had in the development of international law, in particular the specific place of the San in these events, the way they navigated the UN, struggled with its rules, sought to understand the influence it might have on their government, and strove to achieve consensus among themselves and with other African delegates. Following from this varied experience in international institutions, I was in a good position to understand the processes of making rights claims from several angles, to observe and be part of the creation of an international network of indigenous peoples' supporters.

Taking my work with the San back to Botswana, I was motivated to travel widely: to Gaborone, the capital, where I interviewed government officials and NGO representatives; to D'kar and Ghanzi, the regional centers of NGO activism and administration; to several farms in the Ghanzi district; and finally, but most significantly, to the resettlement villages of New Xade, Kaudwane, and Xere and, inside the CKGR, to Metseamonong, Mothomelo, Gugamma, Gope, and Molapo, where the San and Bakgalagadi people directly involved in the controversies that I was following expressed their views and gave me insight into their lives.

I ended up doing not just a "multi-sited ethnography" (Marcus 1995), but what I call a "multi-positioned-engaged-anthropology," in which the ethnographer takes on different formal roles within the same setting and/or organization (see Sapignoli 2017: 80). I worked with San activists and politicians in their efforts to organize and seek redress for forced removals and other human rights violations occurring in their communities in Botswana. This approach was not without its difficulties: engagement often required me to take side in political contests, enhancing access in some areas and to some people while risking to close off other avenues and relationships (see Hale 2006).

In my experience in Botswana as an engaged researcher, I was involved in making indigenous rights locally relevant in a context in which they were being imported and disseminated; and I realized at times that I was involved in producing the very knowledge that was the subject matter of my research (see Merry 2005: 243). In the United Nations I occasionally found myself (as Secretariat intern, or activist, or expert) in a position of advising newcomers on how to write a statement, what structure should be followed, what kind of narrative would be most effective in reaching the Forum members or their own states, and how to effectively quote policies and laws.

In responding to the tension between participatory engagement and academic analysis, my starting point in "engaged" anthropology is informed by the perspective of Charles Hale, who argues that activist research is "a space of profoundly generative scholarly understanding" (Hale 2006: 98). Ultimately, engagement in activist movements generates insights that would otherwise be impossible to achieve. Along these lines, Shannon Speed, for example, has forcefully advocated for the study of activist movements through a "decolonizing practice in anthropology," to be acted on in part through "the overt recognition of and continued reflection about the differential power relations that exist in the research relationship" (Speed 2008: 7).

One of the difficulties engaged anthropologists face as a consequence of this mobility and multiple positions involves securing a collaborative role. The question I faced in this regard was how to accomplish this goal when my positions as a researcher were, over the years, constantly shifting. It was therefore necessary for me to reframe and in some sense renegotiate the terms of my relationship with the people with whom I was working, to reflect the different power relations inherent in the spaces of engagement and my diverse roles (consultant, intern, student, researcher, expert, and so on). Because of the rules governing my activities during my internship in the Secretariat of the Permanent Forum, for example, I was more limited in terms of what I was able to do with San delegates than when I was attending the session meetings as a civil society representative and "observer."

These difficulties of my multiple forms of engagement were eventually mitigated quite simply as an outcome of the long duration of my work, which, in a sense, blended its flavors. I became known in varying degrees to the key people with whom I was working through relationships based on trust, and these relationships carried over into others. Introductions became easier as time went on; and through my various positions, I was exposed to a greater variety of opinions than I would have had if I had remained in a more secure position and place. In reporting on these opinions, I had to distinguish carefully between spokespersons and leaders with high public profiles, who I could identify by name, and others whose anonymity had to be protected. When necessary in this book, I limit mention of the place names where I did interviews, making general reference only to the regions in which they took place to protect the identities of individuals.

Engagement required a certain amount of care in deciding what to reveal in my writing and what was best left as a confidence. I eventually came to realize that in some ways the difficulties of writing about a story mirrored the indigenous activists' own difficulties as they switched between various roles, in local and regional organizations and international meetings, with demands for information sharing and explanations of their activities to their different constituencies. Most of these spokespersons become friends over the years, and writing this book has, at almost every page, posed for me the dilemma concerning narrating those parts of the story that were the result of our relationships, which can have practical consequences in people's lives. So I decided to emphasize the public lives of activist struggles and what was told to me about daily life in the Kalahari, the things that people wanted to reveal as part of their experiential world of personal knowledge. Taken together, the lives and thoughts of the people with whom

I worked provide an illustration of the structures and dilemmas of new and emerging forms of activism and justice-seeking.

THE PLAN OF THE BOOK

The multiple strategies of San activism are also reflected in the organization of this book. It would of course be inaccurate to describe each of their strategies in isolation from the others; and one of my challenges has been to divide the contents of this book in such a way that the different realms of activism are introduced and discussed in a manner that allows for their inseparability and interconnections to come to the fore.

Chapter 2 presents the government of Botswana's decision to relocate and resettle the San and Bakgalagadi outside the CKGR. Following a historical overview of the establishment of the CKGR during the British Protectorate, its legal status through time and position within a wider debate and understanding on conservation and people, I move to the description of the removal of its inhabitants in the second half of the 1990s into newly established resettlement sites. I will also introduce life in the government-established settlements, pointing to a corresponding variety of experience behind a collective sense of injustice.

The situation of the people of the Central Kalahari can be seen as inseparable from the process through which the San and other minorities were called upon to become citizens of the country, the subject of Chapter 3. Some of these qualities of the political order – and hence the motivations and possibilities for indigenous resistance – can be seen as having their origin in the precolonial and colonial Tswana proto-states and their relationships with subject peoples. The British inquiries into slavery and the postcolonial efforts to overcome the entrenched privilege of chiefs in an effort to establish tribally neutral conditions of equality have shaped current conditions for the assertion of collective rights claims. In this context, the rights of equal citizenship were an ideal that perpetuated inequalities and enforced assimilation to the values defined by the collectivity that controlled governance. Citizenship was associated with the dominant values of ownership and productivity, institutionally realized in land reform, the creation of land boards and districts, the promotion of a cattle-based rural economy and, more recently, conservation policies, including policies of removal and the prohibition against hunting. Activist mobilization occurred in a variety of ways and in response to a variety of conditions. The CKGR case is for this reason inseparable from the claims made by San elsewhere in Botswana (namely, in the Ghanzi District) whose political mobilization occurred in the context of land loss and the encroachments of a large-scale, privatized cattle industry.

In Chapter 4 I focus on the dynamics that are internal and external to NGOs in Botswana, which played significant roles in articulating the rights and identities of those San people who rallied around the cause of the CKGR displacements. The creation of the NGO First People of the Kalahari clearly illustrates how the international promotion of indigenousness translated into the institutional formation of a San organization and how rights claimants in many parts of the world organize themselves into formal collectivities in response to their dispossession – including the far-reaching ramifications that follow from this strategy and structure of organization. The need for NGOs to conform to organizational templates created a demand for new leadership positions and political priorities that did not always correspond to those of the people they represented. It is clear from this exploration of NGO formation that the multidimensional processes of activism have introduced significant changes to San society, creating political divisions between those who advocate different strategies, and social divisions between those who are experienced in the knowledge and networks of activism and those who are not.

International networking and use of the international arena as a tool of action have helped San delegates from southern Africa to frame their struggles for rights and recognition and to engage with international organizations, donors, and other indigenous NGOs, the topic of Chapter 5. In particular, I offer in this chapter an example of the ways people learn how to "be indigenous" and how they can (or cannot) contribute to the development of international law and policies. I consider the African indigenous questions and the San engagement with the global indigenous movement in practice. The practical potential and outcomes of the justice cause turns toward the San's engagement with the economic and legal objectives of indigenous activism and what this produces in their relationship with the state, NGOs, and their constituencies. A key observation in this chapter concerns the development of a new form of leadership, sometimes referred to as an "indigenous élite," among the marginalized peoples of Africa (and elsewhere), as an outcome of the UN's structural preconditions for participation and exchange between rights claimants, UN agencies, and states. The San participation at UN meetings offers an understanding of the power dynamics at play in a space where diplomacy and etiquette shape the interaction between state delegates, international civil servants, and NGOs representing indigenous rights claimants.

In Chapter 6, I consider the San's pursuit of justice through the state courts – and beyond into the negotiation leading up to litigation and the NGOs' activism that occurs throughout the legal process. The focus here is on the landmark legal case, *Sesana and Others v. the Attorney General*, a lawsuit initiated by the people who had been forcibly displaced from of the CKGR. It considers the ways that the court proceedings produced narratives that involved experts and witnesses to create a body of evidence that formalizes the language, collective identities, and framing of rights in sometimes unexpected ways. It also goes outside the courtroom to consider the role of media in presenting the case to a wide public, and in the process shaping the politics of rights-oriented activism.

Chapter 7 considers the consequences of activism, including the period "after judgment" when legal decisions have been rendered, and in the case of the people of the Central Kalahari determine their possibility (or lack of it) to go back to their land. I consider the social life of legal technologies, such as the applicant list, with its significant consequences for peoples' lives, including their political relationships with the state. Legal constructions are more than a form of procedural knowledge, but have real consequences for the claimants' conditions of life. Injustice is "embodied," manifested in symptoms and ailments, built into a physical sense of being that reflects the illegitimate use of power. The discourse and artistic representation (see, for example the cover of this book) through which it finds expression point to the significance of the justice campaign for everyday life in the Central Kalahari. The increased recourse to law in activist campaigns also has consequences for subjectivity. For the people who today live in in the CKGR, engagements with courts, NGOs, and global organizations have activated their sense of themselves as legal subjects and members of a wider, potentially global politically active collectivity.

Chapter 8 includes a discussion of subsequent trials, which indicate how the recourse to courts has become an almost institutionalized form of the San's engagement with the state, sometimes involving "litigation chains" that require claimants to repeatedly return to court to secure and defend their rights. I follow the influence of activism beyond the courtroom, to consider the activity and ideas that surrounded and followed the cases. This includes local controversy concerning the choice of activist strategy to be followed, including use of courts, international activism, and the pursuit of political election and appointments as justice strategies. At the same time, I consider how the state occasionally exercises a form of co-optation that includes employing activists as civil servants or recruitment in the government party, the result being that the political voices of the most effective opponents of the state become muted. This strategic action has its origin in the practices of Tswana proto-states, which, since pre-colonial times, have maintained stability and "harmony" through the incorporation of minorities into the state structure (see, e.g., Gulbrandsen 2012).

Chapter 9 offers a conclusion with a reconsideration of the book's central themes. In the light of the material presented in the book, I assess the relationship between law and politics through processes of juridification. This leads me to consider what indigenous mobilization actually accomplished, as reflected in the lives and ideas of the residents of the CKGR. The generative process of campaigning for justice includes both its material consequences and the production of new ways of thinking about the collective self.

This book brings out the ambiguous outcomes of the San's quest for legal and political redress through social justice campaigning. There is no clear-cut result, no state-respected judgment, negotiated agreement, or legislative reform, that points to the campaign's liberating results; nor is there an inescapable trend toward capture and co-optation by institutions serving the interests of powerful elites. Minorities on the margins of states have long histories of making positive uses of courts – and of being subjected to legal oppression. Delving into the history and ethnography of the San's struggles with (and against) formal legal processes brings out more clearly the widely ramifying effects of legal decision-making and institutions, particularly in the period "after judgment." These effects range from the contested regimes of recognition at the international level to the framing of rights, benefits, and forms of belonging that influenced peoples' lives locally in the Central Kalahari, often in unexpected ways. The structures of legal contestation are in some ways manipulated and imposed from outside, yes, but also creatively imagined, enacted, and resisted in everyday life, in ways that sometimes take on a life of their own.

2

UNSETTLING THE CENTRAL KALAHARI

DISPLACEMENT AND THE SENSE OF GRIEVANCE

On January 29, 2002, twenty-nine heavy trucks and seven smaller Land Cruisers and Land Rovers drove the dirt track to Mothomelo in the heart of the Central Kalahari Game Reserve (CKGR) in Botswana. This settlement was at that time the site of the only borehole that provided water to the residents of the reserve. The convoy had come to bring this service to an abrupt end and at the same time to take the residents away from their old lives and into the new places that had been prepared for them, beyond the gates of the reserve. To get to its destination, the convoy drove along what one observer called "one of the most kidney-jarring, axle-snapping, sand blasted and sun-burned landscapes on Earth" (Workman 2009: 1). Where the track divided, the drivers had to pick a careful route around patches of deep sand that, especially for the smaller vehicles, could result in getting bogged down, a difficult extraction, and delay. Occasionally the convoy would stop for maintenance. Tall grass that accumulated in the undercarriages of vehicles with lower clearance had to be periodically removed before it caught fire from the heat of the engines.

Under these conditions, there had to be a resolute purpose behind the journey. On this occasion, the basic motivation was the removal of the San and Bakgalagadi from what the government explicitly viewed as a backward way of life.

The details surrounding the forced removals of residents from the CKGR in 2002 were (and continue to be) contested, with some government officials maintaining through the years that the removals were consensual, orderly, and the outcome of intensive consultation with everyone concerned. Officials claimed that tables had been set up at the edge of the villages and residents lined up to provide their consent to the relocation with the particulars of their names and places of birth and a thumb print on the documents that made their decision official. According to them, it was all very peaceful and "by the book," and compensation for the inhabitants' losses was paid. Together with assertions of order and consent in the process of relocation, the government promoted a narrative of prosperity and development as a justification for it. The Minister of Local Government, for example, stated:

> May I add here once more that the Government has the interests of Basarwa [San] at heart ... We as governments simply believe that it is totally unfair to leave a portion of our citizens undeveloped under the pretext that we are allowing them to practice their culture. I would therefore urge you ... to appreciate the fact that all we want to do is treat *Basarwa as human, not game*, and enable them to partake of the development cake of the country.[1]

In talking to the San and Bakgalagadi who were the subjects of these removals, however, quite a different story emerged. According to those who witnessed the events, some of whom later provided testimony in court (as discussed in Chapter 6), a large convoy of government and district council vehicles came unannounced into the various settlements in the reserve. Employees of the Ghanzi and Kweneng district councils jumped out of them and immediately set to work destroying people's homes, completely ignoring people's entreaties for them to stop. Goats and dogs were chased down by the government workers and captured, tied up, and thrown on the waiting trucks. Some village residents attempted to reason with the government officials in charge of the operation, but they were rebuffed, and the government workers continued to load people and animals onto the trucks. In some cases, people who attempted to resist were struck or warned that they would be beaten if they did not immediately get onto the trucks. In the context of actual violence, the simple threat of violence was persuasive. Most people did what they were told. Houses were burned, fruit trees were uprooted, and storage pots and other goods in people's homesteads were destroyed. Most devastatingly, the village's source of water was demolished. Workers (some of whom, in circumstances of bitter irony, were former residents of Xade in the CKGR who had been resettled in 1997) were brought in to dismantle the pump on the borehole with blowtorches. A steel plate was welded over the pipe to permanently seal the borehole. The main plastic reservoir was overturned and emptied, with the water spilling out in the sand. Then it was destroyed to prevent it from ever being used again. Other smaller water storage vessels, including ostrich eggs, were crushed.

In some cases, people from the same family were loaded onto separate trucks, with some going to the government-established resettlement sites of New Xade and others to Kaudwane, just outside the CKGR: (see Figure 1, p. xvii). The convoys loaded with people and animals then slowly bumped and jolted their way along the narrow track leading out of the Central Kalahari. When the operation was completed, some of those who were relocated did not know where their relatives were, and some feared that their family members and friends had been killed or had run off into the bush where they might have been taken by lions, leopards, or hyenas. The operation took place in the several villages in the eastern part of the reserve, following the same pattern of destroying water sources, homes, crops, and rounding up animals, and occasionally trying to seek retroactive "consent" from the residents to their relocation. These were not isolated incidents, but underscored a firm and longstanding determination by the government to empty the CKGR of everyone who made it their home.

We will see in this chapter that the relocation of 2002 was a middle phase in the process of removing people from the reserve that started in 1997, when people were relocated mainly from the area of Xade in the western part of the reserve, and recurred in 2005. While NGOs and San and Bakgalagadi activists working against the relocation had already started their activities in the mid-1980s when the government's plans to relocate the people in the reserve were first made public, it was the 2002 events that were at the core of the main legal case, *Roy Sesana and Others v. the Attorney General of the Republic of Botswana* (2006), that finally brought the government to court.

To fully understand the motives behind both the removals and the resistance to them, we need to briefly consider the origins of the CKGR and the shifting ideas about the benefits of a protected area and the human presence within it. The sense of injustice that followed from the forced relocations and the conditions experienced in the relocated communities are connected to their claims of rights (described in the chapters that follow), serving as a motivation for the activism and the pursuit of legal redress that has come to be a new marker of San identity.

THE (POISONED?) GIFT OF THE RESERVE

Covering more than 52,000 sq. km, the CKGR is the largest protected area in Botswana and one of the largest in Africa. The Central Kalahari region is now very well known internationally, thanks to films, popular books, and websites. Flying over the Central Kalahari or venturing into the region by car, it appears at first glance to be a monotonous, featureless, flat grassy plain, dotted with trees and shrubs, where humans would find it difficult to live; but it actually contains a variety of habitats, from open, grassy plains to deep, well-vegetated dry valleys that in the past were sizable rivers. There are areas of thick forest and shallow, streambed-like features known locally as *molapos* (after which the village of Molapo is named), which sometimes carry water during the rainy season (roughly from November to April). In various parts of the CKGR there are pans, low-lying depressions where water accumulates for one to two months a year and that attract wild animals, including a wide variety of antelopes, predators (e.g. lions, leopards, and hyenas), and birds. Because of their seasonal abundance of water and game, these pans have been the focus of human occupation for thousands of years.

Many San and Bakgalagadi never accepted the presence of the CKGR. To them, it either did not exist, or did so only in the abstract. Their focus was on their land and their use of it. The law in the late colonial period excluded them, but at the same time elaborated a regime of distinct rights, even if in an ambiguous, indirect way. The rules elaborated by the British for the governance of the park included measures intended to improve the San's capacity to stay in the park and pursue their chosen way of life. This was accomplished through legislative means, with laws concerning fauna, conservation and, ultimately, the constitutional provision on rights of occupancy.

The creation of the CKGR occurred in the final years of colonial rule. In the late 1950s, the Bechuanaland Protectorate government, realizing that the country was soon to receive its independence, decided that further efforts should be made to assess the socioeconomic status of "Bushmen" since this was a sensitive point in the British Parliament (Silberbauer 1965: 7, 1981: 16–17). In 1958, an administrative officer and anthropologist, George Silberbauer, was hired by the Bechuanaland Protectorate to undertake surveys and come up with recommendations for handling what had come to be known officially as the "Bushmen Problem." He carried out ethnographic studies in Ghanzi District and the Central Kalahari region, and served in the capacity of Bushmen Survey Officer and as a district administration official in Ghanzi District. One of the recommendations he made in the course of his work was the creation of the CKGR, known as *Tc'amnqoo* to the people of the region. In accordance with his recommendation, the reserve was established in 1961.

The CKGR was in part a response to pressures from both inside and outside Bechuanaland to "do something about the Bushmen." One of the original motives behind the creation of the CKGR was the remediation of a situation of inequality, resulting from the fact that most of the San land at the time was occupied by farmers (Silberbauer 2012). Silberbauer told me that some officials in the Protectorate administration felt at the time that it would be useful to have land set aside to protect the habitats and resources for people and wildlife in the Central Kalahari, which had long been under pressure from the expansion of cattle-grazing areas (author notes 2010). Since there were no laws allowing land to be set aside for use by local people, the existing legislation (*The Fauna Conservation Proclamation* 1961), which dealt only with wildlife, was used. In addition, making the reserve specifically for the people who lived within its borders might have upset the farmers residing on the Ghanzi ridge to the west of the Central Kalahari, who were concerned about the reserve being used as a base for people "squatting" on and stealing from their ranches, and at the same time about the loss of labor if people left the farms for the open spaces of a game reserve (Silberbauer 1965: 114–26).

The Protectorate administration (especially the Resident Commissioner, George Winstanley) was concerned about the ethics and criticisms raised by having a "people reserve" in circumstances that could be seen as echoing those of American Indian reservations or the South Africa Bantustan, both of which were seen as having significant social and administrative problems. Allowing hunter-gatherers to continue their traditional lifestyles, the Protectorate administration officials argued, was condemning them to a "primitive way of life." Some officials went so far as to suggest that setting up a "Bushman reserve" was an attempt on the part of anthropologists to preserve people in a kind of "human zoo" where they could be studied. Silberbauer made an important point with reference to this concern:

> The retention of Bushmen in the Reserve would appear to be a reversal of the policy of economic advancement advocated for the rest of the

> Bushmen of Bechuanaland. The resolution of this paradox is that it is not intended to preserve the Bushmen of the Reserve as museum curiosities and pristine primitives, but to allow them the right of choice of the life they wish to follow. (Silberbauer 1965: 133)

Basically, Silberbauer's approach was one of allowing people the right to make their own decisions to choose the ways that they wanted to live. Silberbauer prevailed in the debates about people remaining in the Central Kalahari. However, the final decision of the Protectorate administration was that territory would be called a "game reserve," under the control and administration of the Bechuanaland Protectorate.

The people inhabiting the territories that were gazetted as the CKGR were not consulted at all, which is to this day a source of complaints and protestations, expressed to me in statements such as, "I do not know if this is a game reserve; what I know is that this is my land," "We have not been asked," "It was not our decision," and so on.[2]

The geometric boundaries of the reserve were gazetted in 1962, measuring 52,000 sq. km, surrounded by the tribally owned land of three Tswana *merafe* (chiefdoms) – the Bakwena, Bamangwato, and Batawana – and, to the west, the Ghanzi freehold farms. Silberbauer was fully aware that the boundaries were artificial and that people recognized land outside the reserve as theirs, for their use. For instance, people who lived periodically in Kikao and Gugamma actually had their primary homes in Salajwe in the Kweneng District, while people living in Molapo recognized rights to areas near Kedia and Rakops and other places along the Botetle River in the Central District (Cashdan 1984).

Hunting regulation became a significant issue in the new established reserve. Such regulation was not new to the San but already had a long history, going back to the early period of British rule. Some hunting regulations, for instance, were instituted by the Bechuanaland Protectorate Administration, for instance in the 1891 *Game Law Amendment Act*, which introduced in its Appendix 1 a number of principles, including the protection of such species such as giraffe and elephant, as well as the kinds of hunting and seasons during which hunting could take place (Spinage 1991). The Protectorate Administration retained control and regulation of the hunting and exploitation of wild animals in all parts of the Protectorate. It was considered expedient to let all chiefs in the tribal areas have complete autonomy over the formulation and implementation of rules and regulations applicable in their respective areas (Spinage 1991; Hitchcock 2001).

Since the Central Kalahari region was part of the Western Crown Lands, there were no traditional authorities with the power to issue licenses to hunt; this task was conducted by members of the Bechuanaland Protectorate Administration (district commissioners). There were occasional arrests of people who hunted in the reserve, as occurred in 1964 during the time of the Bechuanaland Protectorate Census that was conducted by Alec Campbell and census officers. These arrests were made by police from Kweneng and Central Districts (Alec Campbell, personal communication, 2010). At independence the people in the Central Kalahari were allowed to hunt as long as they did so for subsistence purposes and as long as they used traditional weapons (bows, arrows, and spears).[3]

The protection of subsistence hunting rights for people both in the Central Kalahari and in the country in general was reinforced in 1979 (Murray 1979) through a universal set of hunting laws that would apply to citizens, subsistence hunters, and safari hunters. Known as the *Unified Hunting Regulations* (Republic of Botswana 1979), this set of regulations included the requirement of a subsistence hunting license, known as the Special Game License (SGL) (Hitchcock and Masilo 1995; Hitchcock 1996). This was the first and only national-level subsistence hunting license ever created in Africa. It was to provide a legal foundation for the San's (sometimes disputed and officially rejected) practice of hunting in the CKGR. Through this license, hunting was not considered a "cultural right," but was oriented to an economy of subsistence. In other words, only those San who depended on hunting and foraging for subsistence and income could apply for a license; formal employment would disqualify an applicant from obtaining a license (Hitchcock 1996: 55). One problem that arose in implementing this policy was how to define who qualified for the license: how could a government wildlife officer or policeman determine who had a right to the license because of their livelihood? As some wildlife officers told the personnel working in the Remote Area Development Programme (RADP) in the 1970s, they looked at the clothing of the individuals – if they were wearing clothing made of wild animal skins, they did not arrest them; if, however, they were wearing store-bought clothes, they would arrest them for violating hunting laws (Robert Hitchcock, personal communications, 2011, 2014).

Creating the CKGR as a game reserve, with a secondary purpose of providing a protected territory for its inhabitants, introduced the problem of how to make it legal for human habitation – or, more specifically, "Bushmen" habitation – without at the same time allowing all manner of people to enter the reserve and deplete its resources. Addressing the specific place of the Bushmen in the reserve, hunt, and deplete called for them to have distinct rights to the territory and its resources. In other words, it called for a legal solution.

This solution was built into both the reserve regulations and, later, the Constitution (1966) of the independent Republic of Botswana. As soon as the reserve was created, regulations governing entry were laid down by *Government Notice No 38 of 1963 of the Central Kalahari Game Reserve (Control of Entry) Regulations*. The section that refers to those who are eligible to enter states: "2.(1) No person *other than a Bushman indigenous to the Central Kalahari Game Reserve* shall enter the said Reserve without having first obtained a permit in writing from the District Commissioner, Ghanzi" (cited in Ditshwanelo 1996: 15, emphasis added). A similar section also found its way into the country's Constitution – Section 14, on Freedom of Movement, which was later to have an important role in the *Sesana* case, both in the lawyers' arguments and in the final verdict. This includes Section 14(3)(c), which allows "for the imposition of restrictions on the entry into or residence within defined areas of Botswana of persons who are not Bushmen to the extent that such restrictions are reasonably required for the protection of Bushmen." This can be understood to mean (a) that Bushmen had the right to live and move anywhere in Botswana and (b) that non-Bushmen could be restricted from entry into specific areas (notably, the CKGR, although this was not mentioned explicitly). In 2005, during the *Sesana* case, the Botswana government announced its intention to remove this section of the Botswana Constitution. This led to an outcry both inside and outside the country. As of this writing, this section is still in the Constitution.

FOR WHOM THE RESERVE WAS MADE

At the time of the establishment of the CKGR, several thousand people inhabited the region or used its resources. Their numbers and distribution fluctuated, depending on environmental, social, political, and economic conditions. The degree to which they engaged in full- or part-time foraging, agro-pastoralism, and other subsistence activities has also varied (Valiente-Noailles 1993: 47, 60, 78–9). Kuela Kiema (2010: 29–31, 83) notes that the G/ui San people in the southwestern part of the reserve raised livestock, cultivated crops, and dug wells, as his father did at a pan south of Xade known as Kg'aukcwe.

In contradistinction to the stereotype of "San, the hunter," those who did subsist on hunting and gathering still had diverse economies, based in communities that had become increasingly concentrated during the independence period. Groups were organized into bands or "camps," co-residential groups consisting of adults and children who were linked through kinship, marriage, descent, friendship, and economic ties. These groups ranged from about seven to eighty people, with twenty-five to fifty being the average number (Tanaka 1980: 79, 117; Silberbauer 1981: 193, 196, 299). Group size and composition fluctuated depending on the resources available and also on group members' decisions to visit other places.

Mobility was a key strategy for people to adapt to the patchy natural and human resources, but it was also a way to avoid conflict with outside authorities and to facilitate resistance. People in these CKGR communities ventured out periodically for long-distance hunting or gathering trips or travelled to various places outside of the reserve in the surrounding districts to see relatives and friends, exchange gifts, seek jobs, or purchase goods. In the dry season – the period between from mid-May to October, which the G//ana characterize as the time of "no water" (*tsao seka*) – people usually spent time living with relatives and working on the farms and cattle posts around the reserve. Some Central Kalahari people also engaged in long-distance labor migration, opting to seek employment in the mines and on the farms of South Africa and, to a lesser extent, Zimbabwe.

The main groups in the CKGR area are the G/ui, G//ana, and Tsila San, who collectively call themselves *Kua*, and the Baboalongwe Bakgalagadi, often refer to as */Kebeì*, many of whom lived in the eastern part of the reserve (Sugawara 2002: 96). One must keep in mind that there have always been shifting identities among the San and Bakgalagadi.[4] Sometimes San referred to themselves as Bakgalagadi, meaning "people of the Kalahari," or indicated that they identified closely with Sekgalagadi-speaking peoples.[5]

The Bakgalagadi have been in the region for generations. Most of them had very close ties to other people in the reserve. They engaged in foraging and small-scale livestock production (goats) and agriculture. The interactions among the San and the Bakgalagadi in the CKGR have always been complex, but generally characterized by cooperation, friendliness, and symbiosis (English et al. 1980; Sugawara 2002: 99).

Some of the Bakgalagadi were wealthier than others in the reserve, with assets ranging from small stock to ploughs to wagons and motorized vehicles. Oral histories and narratives recorded by Sugarawa (2002: 99–100) provide useful insights into the interactions between the groups. G/ui and G//ana both served as hunters for the Bakgalagadi in the reserve, using horses and weapons provided by the latter (Sugawara 2002: 102). G/ui and G//ana also watched over goats, donkeys, and horses of the Bakgalagadi and worked in their fields, weeding, scaring away birds, and harvesting in exchange for a small portion of the harvest. G/ui, G//ana, and Tsila women and children also worked as domestic servants in Bakgalagadi households. Consistent with these narratives, analyses by Japanese researchers of the interactions between San and Bakgalagadi suggest that in some cases, the "former assumed a subordinate position to the latter" (Sugawara 2002: 99; Ikeya 1999; Osaki 2001: 34–8). Offsetting some of the narratives of Bakgalagadi wealth and superiority over the San is the common practice of intermarriage. Both G/ui and G//ana intermarry with the Bakgalagadi, but the G//ana tend to have higher rates of intermarriage (Tanaka 1980: 14; Sugawara 2002: 99–100).

Even among themselves, the San of the CKGR are not homogeneous, and the relationships among San groups vary. Sugarawa (2002: 107–8) observed cases in which some of the G//ana-speaking people expressed superiority over G/ui-speaking people; at the same time he reported cases where in daily conversation the G/ui sometimes made negative remarks on the character of the G//ana. Sugarawa underlines that the logic of discrimination used to differentiate two dialect groups, the G/ui and the G//ana, from each other is basically the same as the logic used to differentiate San from the Bakgalagadi (though the former is not as significant as the latter).

Employing the discourse of environmental wisdom that is common to many indigenous activists, many people in the CKGR I spoke with explained the relationship between themselves and the land through metaphors of human relationships, making such remarks as, "The land is my mother," "The land feeds us" (making a gesture of a woman breastfeeding an infant), and "The animals are my brothers." They would also sometimes emphasize their connections to the land, with statements like, "We are from this land." The San and Bakgalagadi understanding of the concept of territoriality generally incorporated notions of rights to land use and the responsibility to manage the land so as to maintain its resources. There were also generally understood rules or principles about sharing the land and its resources with others based on need (Silberbauer 1981: 95–9, 141–2; Kuela 2010: 30–2). Some people with whom I spoke said that they had a responsibility to take care of the resources in their areas in such a way that, as one G/ui woman put it, "They are not finished." When I asked her to elaborate on this idea, the woman said that from her perspective, they "owned" (*kào-kg'ao*) the land and therefore had the responsibility to "take care of it for ourselves and our children."

Many scholars have picked up on such statements and described the San and Bakgalagadi as closely connected to their "socialized nature" (Descola 1994), and their territories as the spatial expression of their relationship with the natural world (Silberbauer 1981: 95–110). San in the Central Kalahari have what can be called "territories," although there is much debate about the degree to which these areas are marked and boundaries observed.[6] The territory is called a *gu* among the G/ui and *g!u* among the G//ana. In general, their sizes are based on the types and amounts of resources they contain, which, theoretically at least, should be sufficient to meet the needs of a group in an average year (Silberbauer 1981: 99, 141–2, 186–7, 191–4). Around the time of independence, territories in the Central Kalahari were large, averaging from 450 to 5,000 sq. km, with the average being 1,000 to 4,000 sq. km. They appear to have declined in size over time in the CKGR, although expansions also occurred, as for example around Xade in the early 1980s.

The contraction and expansion of territories and ranges (areas within which people moved and carried out social and economic activities) was a product not only of environmental factors, but also social, technological, and political conditions. Edwin Wilmsen stresses the reciprocal personal relationships, above all the entitlements acquired through marriage, which lie at the foundation of San approaches to geographical space and resources. Groups of people with carefully cultivated relationships constituted stable sets of "descendant tenure holders," the *nqore kausi*, "possessors of a place or country," who, Wilmsen argues, "have generationally continuous, inherent rights of tenure in their ancestral land" (Wilmsen 2009: 55). Elizabeth Cashdan (1984) makes a similar observation of personal ties and access to territory among the G//ana of the Central Kalahari, for whom kinship ties served both as a means of "territorial exclusion" and as a way to acquire temporary access to other territories. The need to maintain relationships of reciprocity acted as a disincentive to breaking the rules (which rarely occurred). "In these environments, where reciprocity is important," Cashdan observes, "the short-term benefit of cheating (trespassing unannounced) is outweighed not only by the risk of expulsion if caught (a short-term cost) but by the risk of losing one's 'good name' (a long-term cost)" (Cashdan 1984: 455). People observed rules about how property should be handled, maintained, distributed, and passed on. While birthplace was important in defining rights to an area, one could also acquire rights to other places through various means, including marriage, exchange, relationships, and arrangements made between individuals. Kinship thus played a significant role in forming relationships between individuals and groups that constituted the foundation of the subsistence economy. Groups competed with one another to recruit members, with the aim of increasing productive capacity. Having a larger set of people who could engage in hunting, gathering, and exchange relations enhanced that groups' chances of achieving a better standard of living or quality of life. Wealth, in other words, could be calculated in persons as well as things. (This is important to bear in mind as we consider the consequences of forcible removal and the social divisions caused by the court process.)

In summary, their distinct sense of territory means that people of the CKGR cannot be defined by the borders of that reserve, nor do they wish to be. Their sense of territory is based on the need to live from and manage the resources of the land. The boundaries of belonging among them are similarly complex. The relationships of labor, exchange of goods and resources, and marriage between the San and Bakgalagadi defy some of the stereotypes of San hunters, based on notions of isolation, racial purity, technological simplicity, and exclusive reliance on hunting and gathering. Yet the stereotypes have a significance that goes beyond mere errors or misrepresentations in the ethnological record. They have also served as a reference point for contested ideals of the future, with some of these ideals centered on how to give the San their rights as a distinct indigenous people, and others wanting to guide them toward a better life through development, premised on their equality as citizens.

A WAY OF LIFE WITHIN (AND OUTSIDE) THE LAW

Between the late 1960s and the 1980s, significant changes occurred in the subsistence hunting system in the Central Kalahari (Osaki 1984; Ikeya 1996). At the time of Botswana's independence in 1966,

San hunting and gathering practices had already been affected by the establishment of farms, ranches, and cattle posts around the Central Kalahari. A veterinary cordon fence,[7] the Kuke Fence, planned in the early 1950s and built in 1958, formed the northern boundary of the CKGR. This fence cut off some of the movements of wild animals, including buffalo and, to a lesser extent, wildebeest and zebra. Fence-related deaths of animals contributed to calls by ecologists for changes in the handling and management of wildlife issues in the CKGR (see, for example, Owens and Owens 1981: 30–1).

One part of this change relates to the expansion of the number of horses in the reserve. By the early 1980s, there was a total of twenty horses and seventy donkeys being kept by the people of Xade, then the main settlement in the reserve (Osaki 1984: 52). As Osaki (1984) demonstrated, equestrian hunting was very effective. For one thing, donkeys facilitated long-distance hunting by enabling meat to be transported back to camp. The areas over which groups ranged to hunt antelopes and other wildlife expanded, particularly around Xade. Osaki (1984: 56) reported that mounted hunters moved over an area of some 5,000 sq. km in search of game in 1982–3, and were able to kill considerable numbers of animals, especially gemsbok, usually using mounted hunting techniques. The numbers of group expedition hunts in which people attempted to obtain several large animals at a time also increased significantly (Osaki 1984: 53–6).

The fact that people were hunting on horseback and using traps and other "non-traditional" techniques led ecologists and NGOs such as the Kalahari Conservation Society to call for changes in the laws relating to hunting in the Central Kalahari (see Owens and Owens 1981; Spinage 1991). Concerns were also expressed about the fact that people living in the reserve were keeping goats. The image of the "non-traditional Bushman" engaging in activities other than foraging and using bows and arrows for hunting contributed to calls for the residents of the reserve to be removed from the area (Owens and Owens 1981: 11).[8]

Whereas some ecologists and officials have maintained that the hunting activities of local people have led to significant wildlife losses, the data suggest otherwise. The only large mammals that showed any evidence of having declined were giraffes (Republic of Botswana 1992). Some antelope species, including hartebeest, wildebeest, and gemsbok, increased significantly and, according to the Department of Wildlife and National Parks' (DWNP) aerial census data, overall biomass in the reserve more than doubled between 1986 and 1996.[9]

This seemingly contradictory juxtaposition of effective long-range hunting methods and relative stability or increase in game populations can be explained quite simply by the fact that the residents of the CKGR had concentrated in settlements near boreholes, where the economy became increasingly diversified, including raising small livestock and agriculture, thereby reducing residents' reliance on hunting. The first borehole inside the CKGR was drilled at Xade in 1962 or 1963 (there are no records of the event and collective memory on the exact date is inexact). As Silberbauer (1981: 27) recalls, the borehole had significant impacts: "The constant water supply attracted people from as far away as 160 km, and for a time there was much friction and illness as well as a serious shortage of food, which developed because of the presence of so many people in one territory."[10] In these circumstances, subsistence hunting would be impossible without some form of long-range transport. (Subsistence hunting in the Arctic and boreal forest regions of the north, it should be noted, was similarly facilitated by the use of snowmobiles and outboard motors [Wenzel 2000].) Nevertheless, the changes in hunting methods and the increased effectiveness of hunting on horseback in the Central Kalahari contributed to the growing perception among ecologists, environmental NGOs (e.g. the Kalahari Conservation Society), and the DWNP in Botswana that efforts were needed to stop hunting on the part of the residents of the reserve.

The debate over hunting techniques and their impacts on wildlife populations raged throughout the 1980s and 1990s. SGLs were important for the people of the Kalahari, since the failure to be in possession of a SGL while hunting could lead to arrest and detention, sometimes for extended periods of time (Mogwe 1992; Hitchcock 1997, 2000). Laws that were made to limit an activity and regulate its impact often, created conditions of illegality.

Hunting and collecting of resources by local people was also affected by the passage of special wildlife conservation legislation. The collection and use of ostrich eggshells became a subject of controversy after the passage of the Ostrich Management Plan Policy in 1994 (Republic of Botswana). Individuals who had ostrich eggs and eggshell bead items could be arrested if they did not have a license from the government (Hitchcock and Masilo 1995; Hitchcock 2012). This meant that an important source of income for sizable numbers of households in and adjacent to the Central Kalahari was made unavailable. The sale of these items continued, however, with some risk for the sellers. The sales of crafts dropped off in the 1990s, especially after the first relocation of people by the government out of the CKGR in 1997. By 2002, trips into the Central Kalahari were no longer being taken by craft-purchasing organizations, which meant that residents of the reserve had to leave the CKGR and travel to places outside the reserve such as Ghanzi, Rakops, or Salajwe if they wanted to sell crafts.

In the 1970s and 1980s, district-level government officials were the only continuous state presence in the reserve, yet they were quite autonomous from the central government, which did not have particular interests in the area, leaving room for maneuver in officials' daily practices and applications of law. This situation lasted for about ten years, until the central government began putting pressure on the Department of Wildlife to be more proactive in arresting people for illegal hunting. This policy was already evident in grievances expressed by CKGR residents to researchers sent by the Ghanzi District Council in early 1980. Interviews conducted by members of this research team with people in the eastern part of the reserve, in Menoatse, Kikao, and Metseamonong, reveal a deep sense of injustice, with residents making observations like, "They (the Wildlife Department) don't ask permission to go into houses – is this right?" and, "I am surprised to be chased away from where I was born" (English et al. 1980: 20–1).

One of the first areas where international attention was focused on San issues in Botswana had to do with the treatment of people suspected of being involved in hunting illegally. Hunting arrests picked up in the mid- to late 1970s, and resentment on the part of San toward game scouts in the DWNP increased. From the perspective of the San, as expressed in interview material included in a report commissioned by Ghanzi District Council's Remote Area Development Office, the state was imposing unfair regulations on them and using brutal methods of enforcement: "We killed an eland and then Wildlife Department beat us and left" (English et al. 1980: 20–1). The feeling was that they were being racially profiled; they received higher sentences and fines for alleged poaching than non-San. San people were also concerned about what they saw as human rights violations, especially the use of torture by government game scouts and police in order to extract information about illegal hunting (Mogwe 1992).

Reforms of hunting regulations and their enforcement led to the repression of the San hunting economy in the name of conservation. On July 14, 1999, thirteen men from the settlement of New Xade were arrested for allegedly hunting illegally even though they were in possession of SGLs. Lawyer Rahim Kahn, a board member of the rights-oriented NGO, the Botswana Centre for Human Rights, Ditshwanelo, represented the San. At the trial, two of the charges against the 13 men were dismissed, and in January 2001, the final charge against the 13 men from the settlement of New Xade was dismissed.

Another incident occurred at Molapo in the CKGR on August 29, 2000, when DWNP officers and two policemen descended on Molapo in an operation to enforce game regulations. While details are sketchy, it was reported that approximately a dozen people were detained in Molapo by Botswana Police and DWNP personnel, accused of being involved in a hunting operation in which eight giraffe, eight gemsbok, and more than two dozen other animals were killed. This poaching was allegedly tied to a commercial ring based in Rakops that carried out hunting on contract for wealthy individuals residing outside the CKGR. The group was taken to a remote camp away from the village, where they were questioned over a three-day period. The men were allegedly beaten and tortured in the process. One man, Mothambo Sesana, the headman of Molapo and the brother of Roy Sesana, died of a heart attack after being questioned. Some of the men were tortured for days until they confessed that they had killed an eland and/or a giraffe, which they could not hunt legally (Gall 2001: 246). Another death as a result of torture by wildlife officers was that of Sesana's nephew Gaolikwe Kilo, who died from beatings and torture he received in custody in 1993 (Kiema 2010: 45; Gall 2001: 194–5). No efforts were made to follow up on this or the other deaths allegedly resulting from torture by government officials (Kiema 2010: 45, 47).

Antipoaching activities and their impact on the lives of the residents in the reserve has remained more or less constant over the years, influencing the residents' perception of the government as untrustworthy and potentially dangerous. Many of the complaints about arbitrary arrests and confiscation of meat, weapons, and even hunting licenses by game scouts and Botswana police continue to this day.

BRINGING DEVELOPMENT TO THE RESERVE

From the 1970s through the 1980s Botswana, as an aspiring "welfare state," introduced to the reserve residents its national policy on development, the Remote Area Development Programme (RADP).[11] Several types of infrastructure were built in the area of Xade (in the western part of the reserve) that made visible the presence of the state:

a new borehole was drilled in 1979, government buildings such as a school, a clinic, and houses for government workers, were erected, and an open-air *kgotla* – a multipurpose community council, meeting place for public discussion, or customary court – for public discussion was established. A headman position was created with the aim of effectively disseminating public announcements and handling disputes. The headman was either to be elected by the communities or sometimes appointed by the Ministry of Local Government.

The Ghanzi and Kweneng districts provided all the settlements in the reserve with services such as water delivery, the payment of pensions to elderly people (those over 60), transport for children to schools and the provision of food rations to destitute people and to registered orphans, in part as a response to the drought of 1982–3 as well as to the Destitutes Policy of the Botswana government (Republic of Botswana 2002). People were getting water from two boreholes, one at Xade and the other at Mothomelo and from the water tanks delivered by the Ghanzi district officers.[12] They were also getting food and other goods from the district councils.

During these years the presence of government officers increased. These officers consisted primarily of game scouts, social workers, community development personnel, and agricultural officers from the district councils, who sometimes visited the people in the reserve to provide services such as food rations, health care, water, transportation to school for children, and training. The officers were acting in the name of *botho*, a "benevolent" state that takes care of its citizens and brings social justice (Sapignoli 2015). It is important to underline that these services were not consistently provided, but that nevertheless they accelerated the sedentarization in larger communities in the reserve. By the mid-1980s people in the CKGR were living in a number of different communities, including Xade, Mothomelo, Metseamonong, Molapo, Kikao, Gope, Gugamma (Kukama), Menoatse, Bape, and Serube.

In 1984, the Botswana government, through the RADP, provided goats to households in the CKGR (Tanaka 1987; Sugawara 2002: 96), and increased the availability of cash-for-labor programs, which generated cash income for households in Xade (Ikeya 1996). New services led to a further concentration of the population into permanent settlements. There were several factors that motivated movements of people from the eastern part of the Central Kalahari to Xade in the early 1980s. Once the school and the clinic, or "health post," at

Xade were completed in 1983, more people moved there, some of them children whose parents wanted them to attend the school there. According to Jiro Tanaka (1987: 41), there were 125 pupils in the school at Xade in September 1984. People were also attracted to Xade because of the presence of a clinic with a nurse, and food was available for the patients and for pregnant and lactating women. Another important reason for the aggregation of people at Xade was the availability of market opportunities. Temporary jobs were available (for example, construction of roads and buildings). The influx of government workers provided a market for a wide range of products, including food that could be sold at a mark-up: sugar, yeast, mealie-meal, not to mention the introduction of a market for alcohol, including *khadi* (traditional beer). Botswana Craft, a Botswana-based parastatal organization, opened a shop at Xade where people could sell their goods and purchase food and other items. It also provided employment for a few residents. Other outlets for crafts, including Kuru, Ghanzi Craft, and Maiteko Tshwarago Development Trust, widened the market for products made by the San, which became particularly important to San and Bakgalagadi women as a source of income, even as the regulations concerning gathering ostrich eggs – the staple of San craft production – remained in force.[13]

The result of the growth in the population of Xade, which increased to several hundred in the 1980s, was localized environmental degradation, in part exacerbated by the larger numbers of goats, donkeys, horses, and dogs kept by local residents, in addition to the presence of government officials, wildlife officers, teachers, and RADP personnel. Intergroup tension increased. A 1980 report commissioned by the Ghanzi District Council's Remote Area Development Office depicts an already complex situation in the (then) recently centralized community of Xade (English et al. 1980). There was indeed scarcity of food with the influx of new residents, driven by drought, putting pressure on food resources. Deforestation increased within a 2-km radius of the village, as people constructed homes and shelters. Yet the borehole, as one resident's statement in a report sponsored by the Ghanzi District Council makes clear, was the draw that brought people to the settlement: "Life has improved double. In the old days you couldn't wash for three years, but now we are feeling more comfortable. A long time ago you had to wash your face in urine and even drink it" (English et al. 1980: 47).

There were also wider concerns. Some residents of the CKGR expressed their attachments to the place where their ancestors had lived and to the life that they knew. Some resisted the idea of concentrating government services in one place (see English et al. 1980: 42). There was a practical dimension to this attachment to place: the realization that they could expect no better conditions if they were to move and that, moving to Xade would mean imposing themselves on the territories of others. As one resident of the reserve put it, "We haven't moved to other places because we don't want to steal food at other places" (cited in English et al. 1980: 41). A resident of Molapo looked somewhat further than the immediate difficulties of an expanding village with limited resources, expressing an aspiration toward rights that somehow anticipated the willingness of the San to seek recourse in the law: "Can not the government give us education first so that we also have equal rights?" (in English et al. 1980: 41).

CONSERVATION AND TOURISM

In the late 1970s and early 1980s a number of recommendations were made by ecologists, environmental organizations, and some Botswana government ministries, all pointing to the idea that the people of the CKGR should be relocated outside the CKGR.[14] Government talks and papers foreshadowed some of the justifications of removal by representing nature as a separate world, independent from and other to the world of "culture" and "civilization."

In the mid-1980s, the government of Botswana decided to investigate the status and conditions of the CKGR and its residents. A government commission was appointed in 1985 to make recommendations regarding the future of the reserve, including tourism. The CKGR Commission did not include any representatives who were residents of the CKGR (see Republic of Botswana 1985).

The Central Kalahari Game Reserve Fact Finding Mission recommended that people be allowed to stay in the reserve and to be permitted hunt, gather, and pursue other livelihood strategies in specific parts of the CKGR. Resettlement was not considered a "viable option" by the mission (Republic of Botswana 1985: 41). The report recommended that the DWNP take immediate steps to tap the tourism potential of the reserve. One way of doing this would have been to have local people take part in community-based tourism operations in order to take advantage of their "profound knowledge of their environment and the animals and plants they live with" (Republic of Botswana 1985: 37). The commission recommended the possibility of creating a "Biosphere

Reserve for humans and the wildlife" so that the reserve's inhabitants could both benefit from conservation and facilitate it (1985: 43). The commission saw mining as a significant potential threat to conservation. It was also concerned about poaching, the expansion of the cattle population in the areas bordering the reserve, fences that interrupt the migration of animals, and – the capstone of its apprehensions – the weakness of the Department of Wildlife to develop and implement policies.

The government, however, responded to the recommendations of the CKGR Commission by publishing a circular in 1986 stating that the CKGR should be maintained as a game reserve and that residents should be "encouraged" to move elsewhere to take advantage of "development opportunities" (Ministry of Commerce and Industry 1986). A government lawyer also noted in later court testimony that the thinking at the time was that if local people were relocated to other areas, it would be easier to deal with them administratively (author notes Botswana High Court 2006).

The promotion of tourism and conservation were closely related to the motives behind the relocation. Another possible strategy of reserve management, which the Botswana government eventually elected to follow, was to remove the people and to allow safari companies to bring in tourists who would be able to see what they believed to be the "unspoiled wilderness" of the Central Kalahari (Ministry of Commerce and Industry 1986).

Tourists who visited the CKGR usually were not so much attracted by opportunities for cultural tourism as they were by ecotourism. This was in part the outcome of policy. In the 1970s, wary of the implications of Apartheid and ethnic boundaries, the government of Botswana was very cautious about the idea of promoting "cultural tourism" in which tourists could come to Botswana to see "traditional peoples" engaged in hunting and gathering or traditional dances (Wily 1975: 1; Alec Campbell, personal communications, 2010, 2011). There were governmental stipulations restricting the taking of photographs of local people if they were wearing traditional clothing or were engaged in such activities as hunting with bows and arrows (Wily 1975), precisely those activities that were the quintessential attractions of cultural tourists.

Another important pressure for "fortress conservation" came from some ecologists working in the Kalahari who had suggested that the

San and Bakgalagadi were no longer "traditional" because they "lived in stationary villages, kept domestic stock, and hunted with the aid of guns, horses, donkeys, and dogs," and thereby had a negative impact on the wildlife in the reserve (Owens and Owens 1981: 28–31). Conservationists argued that the reserve would have greater tourist value if it was "pristine," that is, if there were no people living inside it (Owens and Owens 1981: 28–9; Kalahari Conservation Society 1988). Ironically, at the same time that it was promoting conservation, the government was allowing mining companies to seek licenses (which I will discuss later in the chapter) and promoting the (largely unregulated) activities of tourism operators.

While discussions and pressures to relocate the people from the reserve were taking place, representatives from the communities in the reserve together with local NGOs tried to draft a management plan in order to develop community-run activities in the reserve, including tourism, which was then to be discussed with the Ministry of Wildlife and National Parks. Between 1988 and 2002, a series of surveys were undertaken and management plans drawn up for the CKGR. This process was officially approved by the 1986 Wildlife Conservation Policy (Republic of Botswana 1986) (which I will discuss further in Chapter 3). In the first of these surveys, conducted by the Kalahari Conservation Society (1988) the consultant who drew up the plan focused primarily on zoning for conservation and tourism activities. The Second Draft Management Plan for the Central Kalahari and Khutse Game Reserves included zones set aside for local communities and others for wildlife and tourism (Department of Wildlife and National Parks 1998). In the 2000–1 period, an extensive survey and management planning process took place, which saw the addition of areas designated for community use (so-called communal use zones or CUZs) (Department of Wildlife and National Parks 2001: 74–80). The resulting Third Draft of the plan, created after what the DWNP said was "extensive consultation," set out a management regime whereby communities could remain inside the reserve and continue to hunt and gather sustainably, while engaging in some economic ventures such as tourism if they wished to.

This planning process in effect entailed negotiations concerning the future of human occupation and use of the reserve, involving the Department of Wildlife and National Parks, the Ghanzi, Kweneng, and Central district councils, and the negotiation team composed of NGOs and CKGR representatives. The surveys that served as reference points for these negotiations were based on extensive interviews with people in all three districts and in the CKGR itself. CUZs were (ambiguously) recognized by the DWNP.

In 2002, however, the government of Botswana decided to abandon the Third CKGR Management Plan and to remove the rest of the people who remained inside the CKGR to settle them in three resettlement sites outside the reserve. Those who were involved in the preparations and discussions of the management plan were quick to point out that the *volte face* occurred in the context of the campaign by the London-based NGO Survival International (discussed further in Chapter 4), which insisted on granting the San freedom to pursue their traditional hunting and gathering way of life in the entire expanse of the reserve, and which disdained anything oriented toward "development" and economic diversification. Following the government's change of approach, tourists were not encouraged to visit the resettlement sites, and sometimes the *dikgosi* (chiefs) of the resettlement sites would have tribal police in the settlements threaten tourists and researchers with arrest if they visited there without government permits. After the forced relocation of 2002, the government produced its final draft of the Third CKGR Management Plan, which had removed all reference to communities living inside the reserve and restricted use of the reserve to two areas near the resettlement camps of Kaudwane and New Xade. Some fifteen years of research and negotiations were summarily negated as if they had never occurred.

MINING AS THE MOTIVE[15]

One of the hot-button topics of the Central Kalahari removals – brought up on many occasions both in lobbying activities and in academic controversies – centers on the place of mineral extraction in the reserve as the government's central reason for the forcible relocation of its residents. Several NGOs, including Survival International and the San organization First People of the Kalahari (FPK), as well as some academics (cf. Good 2009; Zips Mairitsch 2013), have argued that the CKGR residents were relocated primarily because the government wanted to exploit diamonds in the reserve.[16] The government vigorously rejected this claim, to the point that some scholars attributed the hardened attitude of the government toward the San and their supporters to the offense caused by Survival's campaign (Solway 2009).

(We will return to this controversy at several points later on, as it arose in various contexts of the San's justice claims.)

Tempting as it may be to dismiss Survival's claims as overblown and propagandistic, the presence and potential of mining in the territories occupied by the San in the CKGR are tangible, impactful, and on more thorough examination, not so easy to dismiss. The 1985 Central Kalahari Game Reserve Fact Finding Mission report states matter-of-factly that "mineral prospecting has gone on in the CKGR for some time" and that petroleum and diamond extraction would likely occur within the foreseeable future (Republic of Botswana 1985: 27). The Fact Finding Mission report also mentions adverse side-effects of mineral prospecting including "increasing access for poachers and perhaps also increasing the kill by residents for sale to the prospectors" (1985: 32). Diamond mining in particular has had a significant place in the economic and political development of postindependence Botswana. An outline of the place of mineral extraction in the government's uses and plans for the CKGR will shed light on what become a significant point of controversy and hopefully lay to rest the government's view that mineral extraction has had no place in its policies toward the CKGR residents.

Transnational corporations have played a central role in Botswana's mining sector (Jefferis 2009: 61). As is the case with a number of mineral-led economies in Africa, foreign direct investment has been extremely significant in the promotion of economic development in Botswana. Over half of Botswana's income is derived from minerals. It should be stressed that the nature of multinational corporations' involvement in Botswana has changed over time. Whereas large companies such as De Beers and Anglo American were the key drivers of the mining industry early on, smaller companies have more recently entered the scene. For example, the UK-based Gem Diamonds purchased the rights to a diamond pipe at Gope in the CKGR from De Beers and Xstrata in 2007 for US$ 34,000,000 (Hitchcock and Sapignoli 2012: 57).

Botswana had originally discovered diamonds at Orapa in early 1966, but the announcement of the discovery was held back until the country achieved independence on September 30, 1966. The government then developed a close relationship with De Beers, a global giant in diamond extraction, and formed Debswana, a joint mining company that was half-owned by Botswana and half by De Beers. Debswana was soon effectively producing about one-third of the country's GDP, employing between six and seven thousand workers (Botswana Ministry of Finance and Development Planning data 2014).

The relationship between the state corporation Debswana and De Beers is a distinctive partnership. In other instances, the government derives royalties from extractive enterprises, but Debswana was formed through a government–industry partnership with De Beers. In Botswana, subsurface resources such as minerals belong to the state, not to individuals or communities. There has been a marked reluctance to allow specific communities or ethnic groups to profit directly from subsurface resources. If private companies exploit the minerals, they must pay a certain royalty to the government. This source of revenue has been key to what some refer to as the "success story" of Botswana (e.g. Robinson, Acemoglu and Johnson 2003), making it possible for the government to finance programs that are at the foundation of its liberal national agenda and identity. The revenues from minerals go into the national treasury, in part to be used in broad-based development programs that provide, for example, health and social services and education programs, or that engage in rural economic development – including the Remote Area Development villages for which the San and Bakgalagadi who had been removed from the Central Kalahari were destined.

In the course of several discussions I had with residents and ex-residents in the CKGR, the topic of mining and its connection to the relocation was sometimes raised. They consistently told me that in the late 1980s, government officials came to the reserve to announce the policy of removal, invoking diamonds as a reason for the relocation. Many people recalled that at that time (in the 1980s) they encountered people in the CKGR doing tests for mineral extraction. Researchers for Ditshwanelo writing in the mid-1990s also found that some people they interviewed perceived mining as the real threat to conservation (Ditshwanelo 1996: 7).

Where does this leave us in terms of the removals from the Central Kalahari? What role have extractive industries played in the government's motivation to remove the residents from the reserve? On the face of it, there is nothing that points incontrovertibly to a connection between the removals and mining. At the same time, however, the presence, potential, and profits of mining make it an undeniable presence in the Central Kalahari, factoring into a wide range of policy decisions, including the location of San settlements. The connection between mining and the removals is certainly not as far-fetched as many have supposed.[17]

It is also undeniable that, whatever its complaints about what it saw as Survival International's unfair tactics, the government, in its public statements, has grossly mishandled the issue of mining in the Central Kalahari. It has repeatedly denied that extraction was taking place, only to have its denials confronted with the physical presence of extractive enterprises. Under these circumstances, it is small wonder that its claims that the removals were not motivated by mining interests should be met with skepticism and, more to the point, a redoubling of activist efforts to undo the damage of the removals and to pursue justice for the dispossessed.

REMOVALS

The reasons given by the government of Botswana for moving the San and Bakgalagadi people out of the reserve are various and have changed through time, but they cluster around two main goals: first, to develop the people of the CKGR along the lines of other citizens of the country; and second, to promote conservation of the environment and wildlife and the development of tourism, which were in the national interest (Republic of Botswana 2004).[18] The Office of the President has maintained that the rationale behind the relocation was to administer the inhabitants in a way consistent with the rest of the nation. It noted that if local people were relocated to other areas, it would be easier and less costly to deal with them administratively (author notes Botswana High Court 2006). For the government, the relocation was necessary for the creation of the citizen/human, while for the San and Bakgalagadi activists who opposed it, the relocation was a process of dehumanization and the extinguishment of their citizenship and basic human rights (Sapignoli 2015).

In the period from 1986 to 1997, efforts were made by government ministers and district councils to convince people to leave their places inside the reserve. *Kgotla* meetings were held in the CKGR, with the first taking place in May 1988 when two Botswana government ministers met with residents of Xade (Hitchcock 2002). These *kgotla* meetings were mainly used to *present*, not to discuss, a decision that the government had already made. At the same time, the first stirrings of organized opposition began to occur. In 1989, Survival International entered the fray by publishing its first Urgent Action Bulletin on the CKGR issue, denouncing the government's intention to relocate the CKGR's inhabitants. One of the most significant campaigns on behalf of an African indigenous people began to form even before concrete action had been taken to remove them from their territories.

Testifying in court, Geoffrey Serebolo, the Ghanzi District Commissioner at the time of the 1997 relocation, recalled that the government held a decisive *kgotla* meeting in Xade in 1995 to discuss the possible relocation, at which the "majority of the young people strongly wanted to relocate," while the "dissenting voices" tended to be the elders, including the headman of arbitration. Given a choice of possible sites for a new village, Serebolo recalled, the Xade residents discussed a site some 40 km outside the reserve on the road to Ghanzi. Later the same day, a group of residents travelled with the district commissioner to a place they called *K'gosekane*, meaning "a place with plenty of grass and wild fruit," and which was located near a pan that would attract game. At the residents' insistence, this was later to become the site for New Xade (*Sesana* unofficial transcript, August 16, 2005).

Most residents of the reserve, however, disagree with this portrayal of the relocation. One of their oft-repeated complaints was that "their voices were not heard" in these *kgotla* discussions because, as they noted, they had little opportunity to respond to the statements of government officials. This is a perspective that rings true, reflecting a longstanding pattern of government-sponsored public meetings.[19]

In March 1997, the Minister of Local Government, Lands, and Housing requested from the Botswana Parliament a budget appropriation of P6,000,000 (US $1,320,000 at the time) for the resettlement. Most of these funds were to be used for the development of New Xade, located just outside the boundaries of the reserve in the Okwa Wildlife Management Area of Ghanzi District. People were also to be moved to Kaudwane in Kweneng District and Xere in Central District.

From that time on, various pressures, both subtle and not so subtle, were brought to bear on people inside the reserve to "encourage" them to move outside the reserve. There was a policy of "freezing" development in the CKGR. For example, when the borehole at Xade, the largest community in the reserve, broke down, it took months before it was fixed. Buildings and roads were not maintained except for those related to the DWNP and mining exploration camps, such as those around Gope in the southeastern portion of the reserve. According to several people I spoke to in New Xade who recalled their experience before the relocation, the drought-relief feeding and labor-based work programs were implemented more slowly and less effectively in the Central Kalahari than before (author notes 2006).

The Botswana government also offered incentives to convince people to relocate, announcing that compensation would be paid to households that lost assets such as homes, trees, and livestock during the relocation (which, some people claim, was never, or only partially, paid out). Promises were made to residents of the CKGR, including compensation in the form of land and livestock, additional services, job opportunities, development projects, and expanded facilities for the education of children. According to government figures, compensation totaling 4.4 million pula (at that time approximately US $900,000) was disbursed to 730 households. In addition, 2,300 cattle and 2,018 goats were distributed among 602 people.[20] The government also allocated residential and arable plots to households that were relocated, together with seeds and, in some cases, tools (e.g. ploughs) (Ikeya 2001: 188–91). Information on how to go about planting and harvesting crops was provided by government agricultural extension personnel and an NGO, Permaculture Trust. Some of the families that were allocated fields did not plant crops, and a number of them opted to leave New Xade and move to other places, in part because they wanted to have greater chances of getting wild resources or jobs (Sapignoli 2015).

It is important to stress that the Botswana state is not a coherent and monolithic entity, and that there were different positions on the relocation and the treatment of the San and Bakgalagadi in the country. In particular, opinions differed between people in the central government offices in Gaborone and people working at the district levels in places such as Ghanzi. In the run-up to the removals of people from the CKGR, many local officials went along with the central government, but some officials in the Ghanzi and Central districts councils, along with the regional offices of the DWNP, attempted to support the people in the Central Kalahari and tried to resist the top-down initiatives to remove people from the reserve and establish new settlements. Their efforts were to no avail, and the government went ahead with the relocations in spite of district-level opposition.

A much darker side of the relocation effort soon emerged. Among the daily forms of violence experienced by the San and Bakgalagadi who lived in the reserve was harassment by government officials (for example, Botswana police and DWNP game scouts and occasionally members of the Botswana Defence Force, BDF). These officials engaged in intimidation, arrests, detentions, and mistreatment for alleged violations of the law.

Representatives from Ditshwanelo undertook a "fact finding mission" in the reserve in April 1996 (in part due to the "response of the media" regarding the CKGR) to investigate the situation of the residents of the reserve, particularly to determine whether the relocation was "encouraged" or "forced" by the government. In the report many cases were mentioned of people being pressured to leave by the BDF, a military police, particularly in Molapo and Mothomelo. References to cases "of serious torture in the CKGR were made in different areas" in which people were "allegedly castrated" and a few died after being assaulted (Ditshwanelo 1996: 16–17).

In May and June 1997, the government of Botswana undertook the first large-scale removal of people from the CKGR. The total number of people relocated in 1997 is uncertain, but is estimated to be between 1,300 and 1,700.[21] Some of the people of Xade moved out of the reserve voluntarily in May 1997, although others chose to remain in the reserve, some of them originally from the eastern part of the CKGR.

Among its many effects, the removals exacerbated divisions that already existed in the CKGR villages. There were longstanding struggles in Xade between what Kiema (2010: 135) refers to as the "Western Group" and the "Eastern Group," who came from such settlements as Molapo, Mothomelo, Metseamonong, Kikao, Gope, and Menoatshe. Part of this struggle was based on competition over resources, and part was related to claims to territorial access and leadership positions in Xade (Kiema 2010: 134–45). There were also inter-group and intra-community tensions, some of them involving families and bands.

The Western and Eastern Groups responded in different ways to the government's plans for resettlement. Kiema and some of the members of the Western Group opted to move "voluntarily" out of the reserve, and Kiema sent a letter to the Ghanzi District Commissioner to that effect in early 1995. In April 1995, Kiema and members of the Western Group were called to the *kgotla* in Xade, where they were accused of organizing private meetings of community members to "promote relocation" (Kiema 2010: 48–9). As a result, as Kiema (2010: 49) notes, "The crack in the community widened, and many fingers were pointed." FPK (the organization that is the main topic of Chapter 4) took strong issue with Kiema's actions and asked him to withdraw the letter, but he refused, much to the chagrin of FPK and some of the residents who refused to relocate voluntarily. Kiema, who has since recanted his support for the relocation, discusses the disagreement in a poignant passage in his book *Tears for My Land*:

> Eventually, I 'won' the battle against the FPK. Yes, I was the winner and FPK the loser. I won the loss of my land, the heritage of my forefathers. I won against my will. I won against my soul. I had managed to break away from the presence of my ancestors. Many followed me, and we lost our land. After relocation I tried to reconcile with the FPK but I will remain FPK's enemy number two, on the list immediately after the government of Botswana. (Kiema 2010: 49)

Thus, the debate over the relocation was highly contentious not only between the San and Bakgalagadi and the state, but also among inhabitants themselves. In practical terms, the 1997 relocation was far from complete or permanent. People who had moved to Xade from the eastern part of the reserve chose not to leave and moved back east. Some stayed put, as did a group at Metseamonong and another at Kikao. Some left for the settlements outside the reserve; others returned to the reserve for extended periods or to visit friends and relatives; still others moved back and forth between the reserve and the outside settlements. It was costly for people to move. Only those who could afford it and who had the necessary connections with people who owned vehicles were able to arrange for transport. Those who travelled on foot mentioned the stress that the long trips placed on them, especially the thirst and hunger and fear of predators such as lions, hyenas, and leopards, which were all the more dangerous when herding small livestock and carrying young children.

The people of the reserve experienced the relocation in different ways, which they did not express with a unified voice. However, the vast majority of the relocates, even those who participated in the "voluntary" relocation of 1997, emphasize the emotional difficulty of the decision, which, as one resident put it, they made "with their heads not with their hearts" (Ditshwanelo 1996: 12). Some people, especially in the eastern part of the CKGR, refused to abandon their homes or to accept cash payments offered by the government as compensation (Ikeya 2001: 188).

By January and February 2002, the only borehole with potable water being used by local people in the CKGR was at Mothomelo.

Figure 4 Jumanda Gakelebone at Mothomelo's sealed borehole

Local people were not allowed to have new boreholes drilled, nor were they allowed to equip existing ones, such as those drilled by mining companies.

In acting on its policy of removal, the government used water as a carrot and a stick, offering it in abundance with new boreholes in the relocated communities while denying it within the reserve by destroying boreholes and cutting off water delivery services. The management of water in this sense became a tool of forcible relocation; this seems to have become an established pattern of government relocation actions (see, for comparison, Chapter 8's discussion of the Ranyane case). Water, as an essential source of life, was an instrument of power that the government showed itself ready to use to compel compliance with its goal of removing the inconvenient residents of the Central Kalahari.

Litigation surrounding the forced removals of 2002 did not put an end to government action intended to empty the reserve of inhabitants. Again on September 12, 2005 (during the time the court case that I discuss in Chapter 6 was ongoing), armed police and wildlife officers entered the CKGR and told people living there to leave. Three days later, on September 15, 2005, the radio belonging to the indigenous NGO, FPK, was confiscated. This began another, all-too familiar process of forced removal in which people were allegedly prevented at gunpoint from hunting and gathering or from transporting water, in which dozens of people were loaded onto trucks and removed from the reserve against their will, and in which goats were removed from the reserve or, in some cases, killed. People who were suspected of hunting illegally were beaten, tortured, and in at least one case shot in both legs while standing unarmed with his arms raised.

On September 24, 2005 a confrontation occurred when people attempted to enter the CKGR to bring water and food to their friends and relatives living there. Sidney Pilane, the government's head attorney in the ongoing court case, was present with a group of police and wildlife officers who opened fire on the group with rubber bullets and tear gas. During the violence, three people were hit with rubber bullets, one of whom was seriously wounded and had to be hospitalized. In this incident, twenty-eight people were arrested, including four members of FPK. All those arrested, including the FPK representatives, were eventually charged with unlawful assembly.

Confrontations occurred between government forces and those who resisted the relocation, refused the cash payments offered by the government, and escaped physical removal or returned to the reserve surreptitiously as soon as they were able. It is this small group of a few dozen, living in the villages in the eastern part of the reserve, that eventually drove the story lines behind media campaigns, international lobbying efforts, and cases that reached Botswana's High Court.

RELOCATION IN REGIONAL AND GLOBAL CONTEXTS

Even though the CKGR removals became the most iconic and heavily disputed event of its kind, government-sponsored relocations had happened before and were to happen again. Yet the removals from the reserve became the focal point – or better, the flashpoint – for contests between the residents of the reserve (together with their supporters) and the government of Botswana. The struggles of the peoples of the Central Kalahari came to represent the conditions of all the San peoples of southern Africa. Their removal, rather than drawing attention to a wider pattern, in one sense distracted from it, even if was clearly part of a global pattern of indigenous-peoples-confronting-fortress-conservation. In fact, more than any other similar case, the CKGR relocations inspired the commitments of NGO activists and corresponding flurries of media attention, but similar events have occurred in Botswana and in neighboring countries further from the spotlight to people that were "in the way of development" or "needing development" (Campbell 1973). Their removal also consigned the situation of the majority of the landless San to the shadows, where they have remained, relatively unseen, in a condition of marginalization and discrimination.

Some of the more significant forced resettlements of San peoples involving the creation of parks and national monuments in Botswana include the removal of the "Subiya River Bushmen" from the area designated for Chobe National Park in 1961, in which hundreds of Subiya were resettled in the Chobe Enclave (Hitchcock 2001). The creation of the Moremi Game Reserve in 1964 was accompanied by several relocations of the Bugakwe (//Ani-koxe) San (Bolaane 2013). The establishment of the Tsodilo Hills National Monument in 1992 was followed three years later by the removal of Ju/'hoansi San (the more politically influential Mbukushu people, also resident in the Hills, remained where they were) (Giraudo 2011; Hitchcock 2016). The Tsodilo Hills removal occurred in 1995, when a group of some seventy Ju/'hoansi were told that they had to leave the Hills and move to a new location about 5 km to the south. They were paid approximately 17,500 Pula (about US $1,750 at the time) in compensation for the entire community (Giraudo 2011; Hitchcock et al. 2015). Later, in 2001, Tsodilo was declared a UNESCO World Heritage Site, and soon began hosting a regular influx of tourists to visit the rock art sites and local people (Taylor 2014).

To these forced resettlements we can add the situation in Ghanzi, where thousands of San were dispossessed through the influx of Boer farmers and the development of private ranching (see Chapter 3). The creation of the Tribal Grazing Land Policy in the 1970s, intended in part to protect land from overgrazing, resulted in a condition of "land grabbing" that exacerbated the San's condition of landlessness (Sapignoli and Hitchcock 2013). From the perspective of some San activists from the Ghanzi district with whom I spoke, there was a tension between solidarity with the people of the CKGR, whom they saw as facing similar circumstances of dispossession to theirs, and a sense of resentment, particularly toward the work of NGOs and the national and international attention garnered by the CKGR case where "all the funds go."

The forced removal of San peoples is by no means limited to Botswana, but has also taken place in similar circumstances in other parts of southern Africa. The Tshwa, a San group in Zimbabwe, for example, were removed from the Gwayi Valley after Rhodesia declared the establishment of the Wankie Game Reserve in 1927 (today the Hwange National Park) and, as recently as 2013, were forcibly relocated away from the southern border of the Hwange National Park following several incidents of elephant poaching by cyanide poisoning (Hitchcock, Begbie-Clench, and Murwira 2016).

The Hai//om San of Namibia were removed from their ancestral lands through a variety of processes, including the creation of commercial farms and their recruitment as farm laborers, the establishment of colonial police posts, and the declaration of the game reserves in the early part of the twentieth century (Dieckmann 2007). Although their occupation of the Etosha National Park had been tolerated for more than forty years, the Department of Nature Conservation decided in the 1950s to move the estimated 400 to 500 Hai//om living in the park to places outside the reserve. Nature Conservation officials considered this a necessary change of policy because "the Hai//om begged from tourists and disturbed game and visitors at water-holes" (Berry 1997: 5). Most of the Hai//om who lost their lands ended up working on commercial farms, while some were retained as trackers, scouts and laborers by the Department of Nature Conservation in the game reserves (Dieckmann 2007; Hitchcock 2015). The Hai//om reacted by filing a collective action lawsuit against the government of Namibia and 13 others in September 2015 (see pp. 306).

On a wide scale, ambitious projects intended to generate economic growth and improve general welfare "have left people permanently displaced, disempowered, and destitute," while resettlement plans have been poorly planned, financed, implemented, and administered, to the point that the entire process often produces "development disasters." In Anthony Oliver-Smith's words, "displacement becomes a 'totalizing phenomenon'" affecting virtually every aspect of life (2009: 3), while "the trauma and hardships experienced by the displaced pose critical moral questions about the nature, scale, and ethics of such development models and practices" (Oliver-Smith 2009: 5). Integral to these circumstances of removal and hardship is the use of state law as an instrument in the process. Law has been used, for example in the passage of legislation to protect nature or to effect changes in land policy, producing legal conditions that justify, naturalize, and depoliticize the traumas produced by human displacement.

The displacement of indigenous peoples through the establishment of protected areas, combined with various forms of legally sanctioned "land grabbing" by states and private companies, has resulted in tens of thousands of indigenous people being displaced in the twentieth and twenty-first centuries (Brockington and Igoe 2006; Brockington et al. 2008). These events are a result of the desires of governments, private companies, or NGOs to promote conservation development or commercial activities. In almost all of these cases, indigenous peoples have resisted these actions through legal and political activism.

The tendency for the establishment of protected areas to result in the displacement of indigenous peoples has in fact become one of the key themes in the promotion of the rights of indigenous peoples in the United Nations. The Special Rapporteur on the Rights of Indigenous Peoples, Victoria Tauli-Corpuz, issued a report to the General Assembly in 2016 outlining the rights violations associated with conservation measures and the establishment of protected areas. In her report, she points out that

> The three Special Rapporteurs on the rights of indigenous peoples have, since the creation of the mandate [in 2001], paid particular attention to the human rights violations that conservation measures have caused indigenous peoples worldwide, notably by the expropriation of land, forced displacement, denial of self-governance, lack of access to livelihoods and loss of culture and spiritual sites, non-recognition of their own authorities and denial of access to justice and reparation, including restitution and compensation. (Tauli-Corpuz 2016: para. 9)

The tension between the goals of "safeguarding biodiversity" and violations of human rights associated with removing the human impact on protected areas is, she points out, a worldwide phenomenon and a central area of concern in her work as a Special Rapporteur. It is in this global context that the CKGR removals became a *cause célèbre*, and a focal point of legal contestation and activism.

OPPORTUNITY AND DESPAIR

On first impression, the resettlement village of New Xade does not seem to be a place of hopelessness and despair. It is a place where government officials bring dignitaries to show them the benefits of its development initiatives. Goats, sheep, horses, donkeys, and cattle roam freely on the peripheries of the village where there are more trees to offer shade and possibly a bit of scrub on which to graze. The wide dirt and gravel roads of the main thoroughfare are lined with simple government buildings with plain, purposeful signs indicating their function: a clinic, a primary school, and a *kgotla* indicated by the blue-and-black-striped national colors. Family compounds are fenced off and widely spaced. The Coolway Bar and Fresh Produce keeps its empty beer cans collected in a single, manageable mound near the corner of a fence. It is a typical rural southern African village, with all the basic amenities.

It is only when I spent time with the residents of the village that another reality became apparent, a reality in which people had few jobs and depended mainly on government destitute rations, in which they "do not know what to do" because the land is poor and unfamiliar, and in which they often get arrested while hunting or in possession of wild meat. In 2006 during the last phase of the first CKGR court case, people in New Xade pointed to the problems of alcohol (the number of bars was estimated at nineteen in 2001 [Maruyama 2003]), glue sniffing and HIV infection among young people, among other issues.

A common complaint, which I was not always able to confirm, was the lack of implementation of the government promises of development: "the road to Ghanzi is too dangerous and a lot of people died on that road," clinics were "not working" and "nurses are not around"; the water supply often breaks down and take days before someone can fix it; and recently (2012) "cards are needed to have water" for household water service in a process of privatization. As we have just seen above (p. 49), similar grievances were expressed in reports from the 1970s and 1980s in the village of Xade in the reserve, suggesting that their lives before the relocation were far from paradisiacal, but as one resident put it, "We knew the land before and we felt freer."

The resettlement sites attracted people from areas outside the CKGR who wanted to take advantage of economic opportunities, including the distribution of cattle. New Xade, for example, had expanded considerably by August 2011, with many of the new residents having come from places as far away as Kuke, Rooibrak, D'Kar, Hukuntsi, and the villages around the Okavango Delta (e.g. Tsau, Sehitwa, and Toteng) (Sapignoli and Hitchcock 2014). Illness and mortality rates are high in New Xade, Kaudwane, and Xere, a pattern similar to that existing in other settlements in which indigenous peoples are found today around the world (Samson 2003; Bodley 2015). Nutritional deficiencies and health difficulties plagued the population, and settlement residents frequently complained that they were "very hungry and ill." Social distress found expression in tensions and interpersonal conflicts, especially in situations involving alcohol. In Kaudwane and Xere, the other two relocation settlements, conditions were somehow worse than those of New Xade. There they had fewer facilities and periodically lacked basic medicines like antiretrovirals (ARVs). When Chief Segwaba spoke with me in Kaudwane, he seemed not to want to complain too much and made an effort to add a more optimistic note: "There are drought-relief and labour-based relief activities here. People are cleaning up the settlement. There are no nurses at the clinic, but other than ARVs they do have medicines." When I revisited Kaudwane in 2012, the residents of the village confirmed their chief's reluctant pessimism. The most common theme in what people told me was a sense of purposelessness: "We are here because our children are in school. There is no hostel here, so the kids stay with us. We want to make sure that they are ok"; "There is nothing to do here" (this, from an applicant in the *Sesana* court case who now works tanning hides for saddles); "Life in the CKGR is less difficult than it is here" (author notes 2012).

These arduous circumstances in the new villages were not for want of trying to establish viable lives there. In 2000, eighty-three agricultural fields were planted and crops were harvested, but the next year fewer fields were planted, in part because of insufficient rainfall. Prices for food in the dozen or so small general dealerships and stores were too high for many residents to afford, while at the same time other opportunities for subsistence were limited. The few sustainable economic development activities, found primarily in the large settlements near the CKGR, were heavily subsidized by the government. In New Xade in 2001, for example, of the 1,200 people living in the settlement itself, thirteen had government jobs (as, for example, chief, assistant headman, or member of the Village Development Committee), forty-eight were involved in income-generating projects, and one hundred fifty-eight were being paid for construction work (Maruyama 2003: 229).

Not every young person who had been relocated, however, had a disparaging view of life in New Xade or the other relocation settlements.

New Xade for them is still associated with the CKGR, expressed by the Facebook localization function in their posts, "New Xade-CKGR." One recent high school graduate in New Xade told me that he liked living there and had little desire to return to the CKGR except possibly to run a professional guiding outfit for tourists. It is not that he was unaware of the problems the community faced – he did not hesitate to point out that only around a quarter of the people in New Xade had fields and not all of these were planted. He noted the uncertainty of land tenure in New Xade since people who had been moved there had not been granted land board certificates for their residential plots. In addition, some people lost the cattle and goats that had been provided in compensation for the relocation to theft or loss in the bush, often to predators like jackals, and even if one had livestock it was difficult to increase herd size because there was so much demand from others in the community to slaughter the animals and share the meat. He did not have a job, but his family was doing well selling beer at the local *shebeen* (bar). He had also volunteered on HIV/AIDS intervention with a variety of NGOs as well as the Village Development Committee. He pointed out that the problems had been aggravated by the fact that the first relocation in 1997 corresponded to an influx of government workers, familiar conditions for the spread of HIV, other sexually transmitted diseases, and the breakup of families. For all its problems, this high school graduate saw New Xade as his home, where he wanted to stay and build his future. Even if they were sometimes nostalgic about the reserve and expressed a sense of injustice about the prohibition on travelling there, young people particularly valued the possibility for education that New Xade offered them and the opportunity to achieve a better social status and build a way of life that offered escape from conditions of dependency.

Despite those who find opportunity in the new settlements, one could argue that San have been experiencing a "violence continuum" directed against them as individuals and as communities. They live in conditions of "radical social exclusion, dehumanization, depersonalization, pseudospeciation, and reification that normalize" violence against themselves as individuals and as communities (Scheper-Hughes and Bourgois 2004: 21). They often naturalize their condition, and they see it as the only possible way of living (Scheper-Hughes and Bourgois 2004). The common expressions I heard in the settlements are emblematic: "We gave up hope," "We are always near death," "We are dead."

What gets lost in this poignancy, however, is the ultimate source of the injustice that goes back to the colonial and precolonial periods: the ways that the San were consigned to an inferior social status, including how "Basarwa" has been used as a term of opprobrium, and the misrecognition of the San's own conception and patterns of land use as they were legally overlaid by the ideas and ambitions of the ruling elite. These are the subjects of the next chapter.

3

THE "BUSHMEN PROBLEM"

THE GHOSTS OF THE PAST

Gellner, Hausner, and Letizia (2016), referring to the postcolonial history of Nepal, use the term "ghosts of hierarchies past" to characterize the persistent influence of the caste system in a state struggling to achieve the ideals of equality and meritocracy. Something similar might be said to have taken place in Botswana, but with a crucial difference to be found in the way that Botswana has achieved global legitimacy in its postindependence regimes of governance and national economic development. There is still a sense, however, that Tswana overlordship and the distinct ways in which it was exercised and extended over the centuries before decolonization seem to resonate in the present, above all in the agro-pastoral ideals of development and material prosperity, in the disdain for hunting and gathering as a way of life, and in the treatment of the "Basarwa," who in the present-day state are to be improved and "cultivated." One of the more prominent San activists of the 1990s, John Hardbattle, saw the attitudes of the precolonial social hierarchy continuing to influence political decision-making in postcolonial Botswana. In a speech presented at a 1993 conference on African indigenous peoples in Tune, Denmark, he remarked, "Many among the elite today still consider [the San] no more than serfs since they 'inherited' them from their forebears" (Hardbattle 1993a: 144). The sense among San leaders that they and their people continue to be marginalized as *malata* or "serfs" in the postcolonial order is an important part of the sense of injustice that has inspired their campaign to be recognized as a people with distinct rights.

But this notion of "ghosts of the past" acting in the present tells only part of the story. The rise of San activism in the late twentieth century occurred in the context of a state that was actively striving to establish the institutions of statehood in a durable way that embodied ideals of inclusion and equality, even though these ideals, and the institutions that conveyed them, often took the form of "Tswanification," the promotion of the language and values of the dominant Tswana society. The independent Botswana state strove to establish an economic miracle, from a seemingly inopportune starting point at independence in 1966 as one of the world's poorest countries to rapid development and growth centered on large-scale cattle ranching and diamond mining (Samatar 1999; Mwakikagile 2010). Citizenship was associated with the dominant values of ownership and productivity, institutionally realized in land reform, the creation of land boards, and the promotion of a cattle-based rural economy, mineral extraction, and conservation policies. The state has also made sweeping changes to local forms of governance through the development of district councils, district administration institutions, and village development committees (Egner 1987; Picard 1987).

Whatever might be said about Tswana-centrism in the postcolonial era, state institutions were also a central part of the quests for justice pursued by various minorities. The San, like others who pursue indigenous rights, have navigated and made use of state-sponsored institutions and programs to challenge their conditions of marginalization and assert claims to self-determination. The foundations of the San's contemporary quest for justice are to be found in both the displacements that followed the extended reach of conservation, large-scale development, and private landholdings, on the one hand, and the establishment of new forms of collective organization on the other. The San, in other words, were displaced by government initiatives at the same time that they were afforded new tools of political representation and activism within them.

This chapter presents an overview of these developments in the San's relationships with dominant powers spanning a period of more than a century. The depth of this overview is intended to do more than provide context for a later analysis of contemporary events. As Hardbattle's perspective reveals, the deep history behind the transformation of hunters into "squatters" is inseparable from the more current sense of grievance and the pursuit of legal avenues toward recognition and redress – making it possible to see in the San's response to displacement a struggle against the ghosts of the past.

TSWANA OVERLORDSHIP

The conditions endured by "Bushmen" or "Basarwa" in the Kalahari on the margins of a Tswana-ruled *morafe* (kingdom or proto-state) were sometimes described by European travelers in terms of abject servitude and violence aimed at their elimination.[1] In 1870, the explorer and trader Edward Mohr said of the "Bushmen" in the area of what is now northeastern Botswana and western Zimbabwe, that they were "like hunted game" (Mohr 1876: 156–7). Bryden (1893: 142) reported that the Bushmen in 1890 were "in a state of absolute slavery and of hopeless degradation." He went on to point out,

> Woe betide him if the hunting season has been bad, or if the wild beasts have made havoc with flock and herd. He and his family must answer for it, in such a case, with heavy stripes, not seldom, indeed, a brutal death is the penalty. Even his children and women folk are not his own, but may be and are seized and carried away into domestic servitude or concubinage. (Bryden 1893: 143)

Not all observers depicted them as passive victims of this violence, however. Gordon Cumming (1870: 261), for example, noted that a Tswana chief had sent an army out to destroy "a horde of Bushmen" whose robberies had reportedly become so daring and extensive that they were allegedly the terror of all who dwelt a hundred miles around them.

The San's history of subjection to servitude and violent repression can be seen as inherent in the wider structure the Tswana sociopolitical order, even if, as Isaac Schapera noted (1938; 1970), Tswana polities had their own legislative powers and were diverse, as was the degree of repression of the San within them. It is true that the kinds of interactions that existed between San and other groups, including Bantu-speaking populations such as the Tswana, ranged from cooperative to competitive and from symbiotic to conflict-ridden. Reciprocal exchanges of goods and services among groups were common. In essence, however, the San were disadvantaged by both a tribal hierarchy and by the extension of the reach of Tswana proto-states into their hunting territories.

In the tribal hierarchy of the precolonial (and, later, Protectorate) period, the San in many ways were at the lowest end of the social order, often working as serfs (*malata, bolata, botlhanka*) under "masters" who had complete authority over their work and place of residence. Wilmsen argues that in the early nineteenth century the independent Tswana polities were less well defined and hierarchical than they would later become (Wilmsen 2002: 827).

The most significant dimension of this structure of domination was the system of clientship, or, as some chroniclers termed it, "vassalage," "compulsory servitude," "serfdom," or simply "slavery," with San, Bakgalagadi, Kalanga, Wayeyi and others incorporated into and dominated by an overarching sociopolitical system. Known in Botswana as *botlhanka*, *malata* or *bolata*, this system was a kind of institutionalized dependency relationship between Tswana overlords and a variety of organizationally and culturally distinct subject communities.[2] Serfs quite simply did not have the same rights as other people. As *bolata*, they were excluded from land allotments; they did not have wards under their own headmen and they effectively had no political voice or any rights, simply because they were not recognized as members of a *morafe* (Miers and Crowder 1988: 195; Datta and Murray 1989: 59–60).[3] If San or Bakgalagadi were attached to a Tswana family, they could not transfer their allegiance to another person (Schapera 1938: 251–2, 1970: 89). Not having a voice in the courts and in public meetings, they had little, if any, recourse if they were mistreated by the master for whom they worked. They were also considered racially inferior, as underscored by the testimony of Chief Tshekedi Khama to the Masarwa Commission in 1931, in which he stated matter-of-factly that the Mosarwa are "certainly below the average in intelligence," and that "a Mongwato who marries a Mosarwa woman is apt to be despised" (Tagart 1933: 8–9).

The ethnic composition of the Tswana *morafe* was the product of considerable migration from distant places, variation in processes of incorporation, and differences from one *morafe* to the next. What has been a hallmark of Tswana political development was their capacity to incorporate strangers as "citizens," while allowing for ethnic difference, redefined within certain terms of rank and subjection of those considered unequal (Schapera 1952; Werbner 2002: 680).

Within this variety, certain key common features brought them together to constitute a distinct Tswana society. The Tswana, including the Ngwato, Ngwaketse, Kwena, and Tawana, had a stratified system in which chiefs (*dikgosi*) and their councilors (*bagakolodi*), many of whom were the chiefs' relatives, were in a class at the top; the next class below them was made up of Tswana commoners (*badintlha*); and below them in the third class were members of groups who were conquered by the Tswana or who were foreigners who migrated into the areas claimed by Tswana "tribes" (*bafaladi*). At the lowest levels of the Tswana sociopolitical system were members of so-called servile groups, the *bolata*, including San and Bakgalagadi. In this system, the chiefs had the power to make all decisions, passing laws, allocating land, and punishing those who did not follow tribal laws or customs. Politics and law were therefore inseparably interconnected in a single, hierarchical structure of rule and adjudication.[4]

Another of the *dikgosi's* (chiefs') non-conflictual tools of political control was co-optation. This is one of those "ghosts of the past" phenomena that appear in literature on both the Tswana states and Botswana since independence. It is sometimes pointed out that the contemporary state of Botswana exercises a form of co-optation that includes employing activists as civil servants or recruitment into the government party, the result being that the political voices of the most effective opponents of the state become muted (see Chapter 8). While this strategic action is of course an almost universal phenomenon, in Botswana it has particularly strong roots in the political system. It has its origin in the practices of Tswana proto-states, which, since pre-colonial times attempted to maintain stability and "harmony," "peace" (*kagiso*) or a harmonious environment (*kutlisiswano*) through the incorporation of minorities into the state structure.[5] In Tswana *merafe*, it was common to incorporate an ethnically diverse population in their territories by capturing particularly potentially challenging leaders and individuals from outside communities into the structure of the kingdom (Werbner 2004: 37; Gulbrandsen 2012: 29–63).

The Tswana proto-states followed a settlement pattern in which the hunting territories of the San and Bakgalagadi were on the outer margins of cultivated space, and hence remote from the Tswana values of productivity through agriculture and cattle rearing. The San, by virtue of their hunting practices and mobility in these territories, were seen by their neighbors as part of the bush, as people who "have always been living in the area" (Gulbrandsen 2012: 51), and as "dangerous" in the sense that they were hunters, uncontrolled, part of the wild, even potentially shape-shifters, transforming into lions or other dangerous and powerful creatures of the wilderness. At the center of the proto-state's territory was the tribal capital, which was usually a large town.[6] Surrounding the tribal capital were the agricultural areas, the lands (*masimo*) where tribal members had their agricultural fields. Beyond the lands were the grazing areas where the cattle posts (*meraka*) were located and where people kept their livestock (such as during the growing season in the agricultural areas). In this concentric zone model, the outer ring consisted of the hunting areas, the bush (*naga*), which in many cases was occupied by members of minority groups, including San, Bakgalagadi, Kalanga, Mbukushu, Herero, and Wayeyi. In the peripheral hunting areas, *bolata* were incorporated by the Tswana into hunting systems, sometimes taking Tswana on hunts (Morton 1994; Morton and Hitchcock 2014). In some cases, San and Bakgalagadi in these areas were required by the Tswana to provide *sehuba* (literally, "breast meat") or tribute to the Tswana overlords.

Tswana chiefs appointed local headmen or overseers in remote districts away from the tribal capitals and lands, creating an organized "tribal administration" (Gulbrandsen 2012: 57). These individuals, who were tied directly to the Tswana state, collected tribute from San and Bakgalagadi, pressed them into service on tribal hunts for the chief (*letsholo*), and had them engage in such activities as tracking lions, leopards, or hyenas that were said to have killed cattle belonging to the tribe.

Datta and Murray (1989: 59–60) characterize the Tswana concept of rights within the *morafe* as being "community-based," rather than oriented toward the individual; in other words, those people who were not recognized as members had no rights. Traditionally, the only legitimately recognized members of a *morafe* were Tswana adult males. By definition, therefore, adult Tswana males would be the only group eligible for land grants, and hence the accumulation of wealth, and – most significantly – the privilege of speaking in public meetings. As Ørnulf Gulbrandsen (1987: 218–19) puts it, "A man who has cattle is a man who can speak." Cattle were the essential resource for the development and maintenance of the Tswana tribe, as well as of political power (Gulbrandsen 1987: 1, 247).

An important system of long-term loans of cattle, which allowed members of the tribe to manage livestock for other people, was known as *mafisa* (Schapera 1938: 217, 246ff). Under this arrangement, which was most prevalent in the among Ngwato, Tawana, Kwena, and Ngwaketse peoples, San and Bakgalagadi "serfs" who owned holding "milk-bucket" (*kgamelo*) cattle were supposed to provide the chief with meat and milk and to perform various services for him (Schapera 1938: 67, 248–50). By loaning cattle out, economic and social obligations ensued. The *mafisa* system was an integral mechanism in the development of patron–client relationships, and it was crucial in spreading wealth and reducing risk (Hitchcock 1978; Wilmsen 1989). One of the arguments put forth by the contemporary Tswana leadership is that the *mafisa* system was a means of helping the poor, a kind of welfare system

(Wilmsen 1989: 99, 133, 138). These values are reflected in the popular sayings, *Kgoso o jesa Morafe* ("The chief feeds the nation") and *Yare tlotsa a gogabe* ("When the chief is poor, the tribe suffers").

The ward system and *mafisa* system worked together to organize and consolidate chiefly wealth and influence. This politico-administrative structure was thereby able to incorporate a very large number of people, while giving the *dikgosi* considerable control over other groups. At the same time, the *mafisa* system had the effect of expanding the range of political support directly linked to the office of the chief through personal ties of loyalty (Gulbrandsen 1987: 34; Wylie 1990: 23–4). Servile groups, "immigrants," and large numbers of livestock provided a base that enabled high-status individuals in Tswana tribes to enhance their political support. At the same time, these factors provided for an economic foundation that was useful to chiefs who sometimes needed to provide the members of their tribes with resources (e.g. during drought periods or times of losses due to disease or pests).

These institutions of co-optation and serfdom were not applied in the same way in every Tswana group; because of this the Tswana cannot be considered a homogeneous entity, structurally uniform and in isolation from other influences. To differing degrees and from different origins, there were influential minorities that participated in the *morafe*, perhaps not as equals, but as people who occasionally had a voice and who were able to reach the decision-makers of the tribe. For many years, the San, as *bolata*, were not among those able to exert such influence (Schapera 1938: 31–2).

The center of Tswana political, religious, and legal life (reflected to this day in the government's values and protocols of "consultation") was the *kgotla*. The *kgotla* was the place where public discussions were held. It was also the place where disputes were aired and offences adjudicated with the *kgosi* acting as both mediator and judge. Based as it was on the principles of inclusion and participation, it offered, at least in principle, a way for those on the margins of the state to influence policy. It is important to note, however, that until the 1960s and 1970s San and Bakgalagadi were rarely seen in *kgotla* meetings, in part because they did not feel welcome there. For them, the *kgotla* system was part of an alien power structure, inviting their participation only to the extent that it could mitigate the worst abuses in conditions of their domination. While there are those Batswana (citizens of Botswana) who consider the *kgotla* system to be a kind of democratic system in which all people had the right to put forth their views, in practice, women, the poor, and members of minority groups were regularly excluded from or ignored in *kgotla* meetings (Schapera 1938: 8, 19, 196–8). That is to say, they were denied some of the key attributes of legal personhood. The reality of the *kgotla* system for those on the margins of the state was its service to the ruling elite as a way to communicate decisions that had already been made elsewhere. The "Basarwa" were ruled *through* the law rather than participating in legal process as autonomous agents.

As we will now see, the status of the "Basarwa" as an underclass and the extreme instances of their mistreatment by some of their Tswana masters were to cause a central tension within British rule from the late nineteenth century to the time of independence in 1966, between the goals of establishing an autonomous and largely self-governing protectorate and the will to use imperial power as a tool of human betterment.

LEGALIZING DISPOSSESSION IN THE BRITISH PROTECTORATE

In a peaceful transition in 1885, the region that is now Botswana was declared a protectorate of Great Britain. The territory taken over by Britain as the Bechuanaland Protectorate was organized into a cluster of eight Tswana-ruled *merafe*, variously referred to as chiefdoms, "kingdoms," or proto-states. In this process, the power of the *morafe* became consolidated, encapsulating vast, multi-ethnic communities within their structures (Comaroff and Comaroff 1991: ch. 4; Gulbrandsen 2012: 15). There were a number of reasons for the decision to establish and consolidate the Protectorate, some of them relating to the desire of both the Tswana and the British not to have the area become part of South Africa, to prevent German expansion from the west, and to protect trade and facilitate the northward expansion of British interests while keeping the Afrikaners to the south from encroaching into the region (Ramsay, Morton, and Mgadla 1996: 145, 154–7).

The governance of the Protectorate of Bechuanaland was based on a principle of "cautious overlordship," founded on the injunction "not to interfere with native administration" and in particular to allow chiefs to retain sovereignty over internal affairs (Ifezue 2015: 272). To the extent possible, the colonial government, initially at least, avoided getting involved too deeply in the affairs of the Tswana chiefdoms including the thorny issues related to "ethnic subordination." This principle, however, was eventually violated as the British exerted increasing control over their colonial territories. One of the most significant steps was the 1891 *Order in Council* authorizing the High Commissioner to South Africa to "legislate for Bechuanaland by Proclamation." This granted sweeping powers to the machinery of colonial administration, even as it called for those powers to be exercised in a way that respected "native law and custom" (Ifezue 2015: 272).

Despite the principle of "non-interference" and respect for custom, the British took away many of the powers of the *dikgosi*, such as jurisdiction over cases of rape and murder. Charles Fernand Rey, as Resident Commissioner from 1930 to 1937, was particularly strident in acting on what he saw as a mandate to curtail the powers of chiefs in order to put an end to their abuses. Proclamations were introduced in 1934 to limit the power of the *dikgosi*, and the legitimacy of native laws and customs was guaranteed only if they were not incompatible with the Crown's power and jurisdiction. In other words, if a conflict of laws and values with the Crown occurred, the *dikgosi* should be limited in their jurisdiction.[7]

With their powers defined by the Protectorate, chiefs worked on behalf of the Crown as they administrated the distribution of land and natural resources, exercised political, religious, and juridical power, and collected a newly imposed "hut tax" (Gulbrandsen 2012: 51–7). Many of the *dikgosi* operated as "tribal innovators" (Schapera 1970), that is, those who secured their "societal control by means of legislation." As Schapera (1943: 260) observed, "legislative activities intensified progressively during the colonial era" as a means for exercising authority over the subject communities.

The Protectorate was divided into Tribal Land and Crown Land (see Figure 2, p.xviii). Within the borders of the Tribal Land region in 1900 there were five "Tribal Reserves" occupied by the Bamangwato, the Bangwaketse, the Bakwena, the Batawana, and the Bakgatla, all members of the politically dominant Batswana. In the Tribal or Native Reserves, land allocation was the responsibility of the tribal chiefs (*dikgosi*) and their headmen and headwomen (*dikgosana*). The Tribal Reserves were different in size and composition of the population, with the Bangwaketse, the Bakwena, and the Bamangwato being larger and more powerful (Schapera 1952; Gulbrandsen 2012).

In 1895, when the British decided to identify and demarcate lands for the principal Tswana tribes, an additional objective was to identify lands that could be retained by the administration. Through the Order in Council of 1910, Crown Lands were defined as all other land situated within the limits of the Protectorate elsewhere than in the Tati District. This definition essentially placed the vast territories in the west and north of Bechuanaland in the hands of the Crown and its designate. In this way, the Crown effectively claimed title to land belonging to the San, the Bakgalagadi, the Wayeyi, the Kalanga, and other minority groups. The region that would later be designated as the Central Kalahari Game Reserve (CKGR) was a major part of these Crown Lands.

The British Protectorate essentially institutionalized the Tswana division of the land in the Tribal Land regions, recognizing only the Tswana as having rights to land, not the subject peoples, including the San and Bakgalagadi. The British may have seen the Tswana conceptions of land as being close to theirs: land tenure was recognized only for uses such as agriculture and livestock production. Those groups that were seen as lacking political structure, foraging for a living and moving about the landscape, were not viewed as having a legitimate form of land use and therefore could be ignored in the land allocation process.

Some land in the Bechuanaland Protectorate was also set aside as freehold (private) land – specifically, concession areas for companies, including the Ghanzi farms, the Tati District (now the North East District), and the Lobatse, Gaborone, and Tuli blocks. In the case of the Ghanzi Ridge, much of the land taken over by the Protectorate was allocated to white farmers. The Bechuanaland Protectorate administration, in cooperation with Cecil John Rhodes, agreed to allocate forty-one farms of approximately 6.5 sq. km (5,000 *morgen*) each to Afrikaner and English farmers who trekked out of South Africa in 1898–9 (Russell and Russell 1979: 12–15). The resulting Ghanzi Freehold Farming Block, or simply the "Ghanzi farms," was (and remains) the first of several cattle ranching blocks to be established by the colonial government after it annexed Bechuanaland in 1885. The Ghanzi farms were intended mainly to provide land for European settlers in the region, but also to establish a buffer zone in the west against potential expansion by the Germans out of German South West Africa (Wily 1979b: 13).

The establishment of the freehold farms was a key factor in the dispossession of thousands of San and members of other groups (Wily 1979a,b). This was the case particularly for the San of the Tuli Block and the Ghanzi farms, where some became laborers on the farms and others squatters on (and around) farm property. In some cases, removals occurred later in the colonial period as farms grew in size and took on a greater commercial orientation. Mathias Guenther (2015) argues that through much of the colonial period there was in the Ghanzi *veld* a relationship of "racial paternalism" between the (mostly) Afrikaner farmers and the San, not unlike the *mafisa* system under the Tswana. In the haphazard circumstances of early settlement, this paternalism "developed an intensely personal flavour, of easy familiarity, intimacy and an abiding interest in one another's lives and affairs" (2015: 142).

In these circumstances, the so-called servile groups had little if any say over land issues, and they were usually ignored by traditional authorities and colonial government officials when it came to land distribution. Some San did seek to register their claims to land, going to the chiefs and sometimes to the Protectorate administration, asking that they be given blocks of land so that they could continue to sustain themselves and their families (Hitchcock 1978: 105–14; Wily 1979a: 116–48). There is no indication in the archives, however, that any of these requests were granted by either the chiefs or the Protectorate administration.

Historians have taken a number of different perspectives on the nearly eighty years of colonial rule in Bechuanaland. Some have observed that what had been a somewhat fluid sociopolitical structure was, in a number of ways, frozen. Richard Werbner (2002) makes the significant observation that

> the kingdoms, as in so many parts of pre-colonial Africa, had frontiers, not boundaries. Bounded territories were a colonial invention, which created clearly demarcated units of administration, ended the ambiguities of sovereignty in buffer zones and placed formerly autonomous communities under paramount chiefs. (Werbner 2002: 674)

The powers of these chiefs were also subject to definition and control, against which some resisted. There were occasional clashes between Tswana leaders (Tshekedi Khama of the Bamangwato being a prime example) and the Protectorate administration (Crowder 1985; Wylie 1990: 175–80). Tswana chiefs were not allowed to send out expeditions to punish those who challenged their power (Schapera 1970: 64, 225). Those who advocated "progress" and "development" tended to be favored by the colonial administration, as opposed to those who promoted Tswana nationalism, culture, and chiefly power (Schapera 1943: 268, 270; Ramsay et al. 1996). It should be stressed, however, that in some ways Tswana chiefs continued to have significant influence over their subjects. As Pnina Motzafi-Haller (2002: 90) observed, "The territorial organization associated with centralized political power was, to a large extent, preserved throughout colonial rule." At the same time, the patterns of labor migration that came about in part as a response to the imposition of the hut tax in 1899 saw even greater socioeconomic differentiation among Tswana polities, with the elites staying home and commoners, poor people, and members of "servile groups" or "subject peoples" going to the mines (Motzafi-Haller 2002: 87, 90).

After World War I, and particularly in the 1930s, the British reassessed their method of indirect rule as they reconsidered their involvement, or lack of it, in the administration of the Bechuanaland Protectorate (Gulbrandsen 2012: 69). Interest in the welfare of the San, to the extent that it existed, was largely inspired by anti-slavery sensibilities originating in Britain, with less attention given to the far-reaching consequences of transformations in the economy and society under British rule.

ANTI-SLAVERY AND POLITICAL REFORM

One of the major concerns of the British regarding Bechuanaland was the harsh treatment and possible enslavement of so-called subject populations, including the Bakgalagadi and the San. Pressured by missionaries, humanitarian organizations such as the Aborigines Protection Society, and anti-slavery advocates who had initiated a far-reaching anti-slavery movement in Europe (Parsons 1973; Brantlinger 2003), the British sought to convince the Tswana to reform the ways in which "minority tribes" were dealt with. These concerns applied particularly to the most powerful tribe, the Bamangwato, in which social stratification based on the system of vassalage was particularly pronounced. The League of Nations weighed in on the issue of slavery and mistreatment, as did the Parliament of Great Britain (Miers and Crowder 1988).

The San were fully integrated into a system of serfdom under British rule, and the anti-slavery campaign took note. A surprising variety of voices lay behind the influence of the British anti-slavery movement and the related campaigns on behalf of native laborers, oriented toward reform of working conditions in the British colonies. Early in the Protectorate period in particular, officials tended to approach questions of "native labour" with caution. In one of the first official reports to the colonial government on the status of the Bushmen, issued in 1887, John Smith Moffatt, a Resident Magistrate, said that cases of mistreatment should not be handled "by taking aggressive steps" and that efforts to change Bushman status would "disturb the whole country" (BNA file HC 3/2/71). One of the stronger sources of reformist pressure, influencing opinion both in Britain and in the Protectorate, came from members of the Tswana elite, such as Simon Ratshosa of the Bamangwato, who denounced the practices of his own people and called for major reforms in the ways in which Bushmen were treated.[8] In 1926, Ratshosa wrote a report entitled *How the Masarwa Became Slaves* (Ratshosa 1926), which brought official attention to the issue of San sociopolitical and economic rights. There were often good political reasons for Tswana leaders to take this position, which in the case of Ratshosa involved a bitter power struggle with the incumbent regent-chief of the Bamangwato, Tshekedi Khama. There were also pressures from humanitarian advocacy groups such as the Anti-Slavery Society (Brantlinger 2003: 3, 13, 712), which campaigned on behalf of native laborers. Parliamentarians (for example, those MPs in the British Parliament's Aborigines Committee) also drew attention to the mistreatment of Bushmen and Khoekhoe in southern Africa and to the conflicts occurring there. Missionaries, such as those of the London Missionary Society, brought forth their own expressions of indignation and appeals to their congregations (Brantlinger 2003; Penn 2006: 237–67). Then there was internal pressure from colonial administrators like John Barrow, the private secretary of the governor of the Cape Colony, and from district commissioners in the Protectorate who sought to address the issues faced by Bushmen.[9]

Although the Protectorate administration would have preferred to ignore the San, events overtook them. In the early 1920s, attention was drawn to the status of San and other minority groups in Botswana when the League of Nations conducted investigations into slavery (see BNA file S.34/8). There were numerous reports of severe mistreatment of cattle post employees and *bolata* from the early to mid-twentieth century.[10] *Bolata* or *badisa* (herders) were sometimes beaten because of what was seen as misbehavior, such as leaving a cattle post without permission or allowing cattle to stray. Some of these incidents were denounced by members of the Tswana elite, by missionaries, and by the Bechuanaland Protectorate Administration (Parsons 1973). The Secretary of State, in response, called for an inquiry into "hereditary service" in the Protectorate (BNA file S.43/7).

On August 3, 1926, the High Commissioner, Lord Athlone, made a statement in the Bamangwato tribal capital, Serowe, concerning the status of San:

> It has been said that the Masarwa are slaves of the Mangwato. The Government does not regard them as slaves, but realizes that they are a backward people who serve the Mangwato in return for the food and

> shelter they receive. I understand that for the most part they are contented and that they do not wish to change. But the Government will not allow any tribe to demand compulsory service from another and wants to encourage the Masarwa to support themselves. ... It is the duty of the chiefs and headmen to help these people to stand on their feet. (Statement by High Commissioner, BNA file S.43/7)

This statement reiterated British attitudes about the ways in which San were treated, thus responding to public concerns in Britain about the Protectorate administration's passivity with respect to the slavery and serfdom issues. At the same time, the public statement was a not-so-subtle attempt to transfer the responsibility for taking care of what came to be called "the Bushmen problem" to the Tswana, notably the Bamangwato.[11]

For all the impetus it gave to British involvement in the political affairs of the Protectorate, slavery was but one of the factors in the so-called "Bushmen problem" (others being landlessness, poverty, discrimination, and exploitation). As a first step to addressing the question of Masarwa slavery and subjection to abuses of power, the British formed a commission of inquiry, known as the Masarwa Commission. The mandate of this commission was to inquire into conditions of forced labor and corporal punishment in the Protectorate, particularly as they affected the San or "Masarwa." The inquiry was carried out in the Ngwato district in 1931, led by Edward S. B. Tagart, a former Secretary for Native Affairs in what is now Zambia. The focus of the inquiry was on the conditions under which San were employed by the Bamangwato and their rights to payment and property. Corporal punishment was also a major focus of the inquiry (High Commissioner's Proclamation, July 11, 1931; Botswana National Archives [BNA] file S.204/8; Tagart 1933). One of the issues that had been raised in Ghanzi and in eastern Botswana, as well as in Gobabis and the Omaheke regions of Namibia, was the mistreatment of San laborers, some of whom allegedly were beaten or chained in order to keep them from running away from the farms.

One of the striking features of the Masarwa Commission report is that the Masarwa themselves do not appear as witnesses, never giving their testimony directly to the hearings. The one near-exception occurred when a Tswana master, Mokgowe, offered testimony to the effect that he "would be quite satisfied for [his Masarwa] to leave me" and brought one of them to the hearings for support, who then "intervened" in the record as follows: "I, Chentachwe, am one of them.

I can go away if my master tells me. I kill animals for him. He has many skins I have killed for him in his hut" (Masarwa Commission, August 2, 1931). This sketchy account in itself tells us something significant of the erasure of the San from the record, a circumstance that was also borne out many times in the testimony in relation to the Masarwa's ability to represent their causes in the *kgotla*.

For the most part, the San's experience with legal process was defined by their subjection to the right of their masters to inflict corporal punishment on them as they saw fit. J. W. Joyce, an Administrative Officer "allocated with special duty to the Masarwa," speculated that

> the reason for the summary procedure was the difficulty of bringing the Masarwa to any recognized Court, even when they had been caught [stealing cattle] red-handed. The distance from the cattle post to any recognized Court is usually great and the Masarwa almost invariably manage to disappear on the way. This problem will have to be solved if cattle thefts are to be kept within normal proportions. (Joyce 1937: 69)

Where the *kgotla* was more accessible, as in Serowe where many of the Masarwa Commission hearings took place, the Tswana masters were more inclined (though not obligated) to bring complaints about "their" Masarwa to be heard and decided on by the *dikgosi*. Because the Masarwa did not have the means to pay fines, this often resulted in corporal punishment, a point raised by Captain Almar Gordon Stigland, the Assistant Resident Commissioner at Mafeking: "Generally speaking, I would say that there is only one punishment for a Basarwa, namely flogging, whereas a Bamangwato might pay a fine" (July 15, 1931).

On the question of whether the Masarwa were able to represent their interests in the *kgotla* system, the testimony to the Commission was divided, mainly along the lines of the prominent rivalry over the chieftainship of the Bamangwato. The reigning chief, Tshekedi Khama, attempting to head off British interference in the sovereignty of the chiefs, emphasized the right of the Masarwa to bring their grievances to the *kgotla*:

> Masarwa often bring complaints to me. They know that I am here and open to listen to what they have to say. ... I am satisfied that the Mosarwa has just as good an opportunity as a Mongwato [a member of the Bamangwato] for obtaining redress in the Kgotla for any grievance which he may have, whether against his master or another. (Masarwa Commission, July 21, 1931)

Simon Ratshosa, who clearly supported, and to some extent even instigated, British intervention in the abuses of the chiefs, told an entirely different story:

> The general condition of the Masarwa is that of slaves. They have nothing which they can call their own. Anything which they acquire whether a skin or an animal belongs to their masters. ... In some instances they would be sold. ... I have seen a Mosarwa with one hand, the other one having been burnt by his master. ... I saw another Mosarwa who said his master had cut off his fingers, two of which were missing. (Masarwa Commission, August 31, 1931)

The fact that the British were taking a more active role in enforcing the prohibition on compulsory service and curbing the abuses of cattle owners made the colonial authorities a potential source of intervention for those San who had been mistreated. As Nettleton noted in his testimony, "the Mosarwa is beginning to realize that his complaints will receive a sympathetic hearing from European officials" (Masarwa Commission, July 18, 1931). Assistant commissioners were not only administrators of British rule; they also had judicial powers, sitting as magistrates with wide powers that extended "to the fullest terms of penal servitude" (Bennett 2008: 21). Magistrates with similar powers were located throughout the protectorate. And although their powers, based on the proclamation of 1891, were largely restricted to "European" cases, leaving "Native" cases to the jurisdiction of the *dikgotla*, Nettleton's observation suggests that by the 1930s some San were able to bring their grievances to British magistrates or officials and to sidestep the *kgotla* system from which they were largely excluded.

Tshekedi Khama reacted strongly and disparagingly to the findings of the Masarwa Commission (Miers and Crowder 1988). Like him, some of the chiefs, particularly those of the Bamangwato who were the focus of the commission's work, felt that they had been depicted unfairly by the testimony of the commission and had been illegitimately divested of control over the *malata* through the British policy of promoting free labor. Tshekedi Khama was also incensed that thefts of livestock had increased once it became understood that the British were exerting their authority over the application of corporal punishment, a point that was confirmed in British observations. As J. W. Joyce reported, "the Bamangwato have, in certain cases, so misunderstood the policy of the Administration that they have made no attempt to check the ever-recurring stock thefts by Masarwa, and the Masarwa have not been slow to avail themselves of this misunderstanding and their imagined immunity from punishment" (Joyce 1937: para. 4). These stock thefts were then invoked as a reason for the Protectorate administration to further involve itself in explaining its new policies and in restoring order.

The activities of the Masarwa Commission thus offer not only unique insights into the structures of domination that prevailed during this period of colonial rule, but also a set of findings that was perhaps not directly intended by the British inquiry: the ways that different groups of San (Masarwa), in different circumstances, resisted, accommodated themselves to, and navigated the structures of power wielded by the Tswana chiefs and headmen of the Bamangwato. Their resistance took forms that highlight their relative powerlessness: most commonly escape and stock theft, and only very rarely the use of adjudicative institutions, the *dikgotla* of the Tswana, from which they were largely excluded, and the magistrates courts of the British, which occasionally heard their claims against their masters.

One of the outcomes of the hearings and investigations into labor conditions in the Protectorate was the decision to establish settlement schemes for the San, likely intended as a way to foster their autonomy and provide an alternative to their servile status relative to the Tswana. "Rehabilitation" efforts, as they were termed, including an agricultural and training scheme for the San, was a result of the report by Joyce, who recommended that some land should be set aside for Bushmen who wished to raise crops. The Protectorate government initiated two Bushmen development schemes, one in Olifantskloof in western Ghanzi District and another at Letlhakane in the eastern Kalahari, both ultimately unsuccessful. A school was also started for Bushmen children. This scheme lasted for two years before it was abandoned and the infrastructure taken over by other groups.

By the end of the 1930s, the nature of "master–Mosarwa" relations was changing well beyond the scope of any planned intervention. In the expanding and increasingly commercial cattle economy, San were being displaced at the same time that ties of clientage and patronage were being replaced with salaried labor. The consolidation of power in the hands of an elite few in the Protectorate, Wilmsen (2002) argues, was an outcome of new mercantile relations – the outcome, in turn, of closer ties to Europe – which created incentives for greater control of people who were a source of labor. The result was the restructuring and reconceptualization of the wider Tswana political entity in political, social, cultural, and geographic terms in a way that resulted in the increasing disenfranchisement of those on the margins (Wilmsen 2002: 827–8). Herd owners found it more profitable to pay their workers a marginal salary than to be responsible for them and their families as hereditary servants. Under these circumstances, the San were subjected to increasing labor demands, with low salaries and without the usufruct rights to land and access to the meat and milk of the cattle they herded (Motzafi-Haller 1994: 544). Together with changes in the economy and social order, the San underwent a social transformation from serfs to members of an underemployed underclass, living in new conditions of economic and political marginality, with the central element of continuity being their stigmatized status as "Sarwa."

In cases where there were commissions of inquiry, such as the Masarwa Commission of 1931, the San, although they were the subjects of the discussions, had little opportunity to register their views. Instead, other people spoke for them. Their voices are almost eerily absent from the record, with others – those with power over them – speaking on their behalf, defining their essence, their needs, and how their needs might be met. They were spoken "about" and "of," but rarely given the opportunity to speak for themselves. Even the reports supposedly addressing their problems and issues do not give them voice except through their masters.

INDEPENDENCE AND THE "BUSHMEN PROBLEM"

Tswana nationalism was on the rise in the early 1960s, with the first political parties in the Protectorate forming in 1960–1. In 1962, the Botswana Democratic Party, which has remained in power since independence, was formed with support from Seretse Khama, the chief of the Bamangwato, later to become the first president of the independent Republic of Botswana.[12] A constitutional review took place in 1963, following which it was announced that the Protectorate would be granted a form of self-government that would facilitate the transition to independence.

This transition, from the Bechuanaland Protectorate to the Republic of Botswana, produced a transformation that went beyond the transfer of power from colonial authorities to an African national leadership. Seretse Khama ushered in a new constitution that promoted the liberal notions and institutionalized principles of separation of powers, a bill of rights, and the rule of law in an independent judiciary (Fawcus and Tilbury 2000). All of these new foundations of national governance were antithetical to the elite powers and politics of the *dikgosi*. Khama was therefore faced with the formidable challenge of nullifying the traditional rule of hereditary chiefs, while establishing the principles and mechanisms of a new constitutional dispensation (Ifezue 2015: 280). As a progressive leader who looked to both African and European models for inspiration, Seretse Khama concluded that the chiefly system of the Tswana was ill suited to the task of nation building. It was, in his view, autocratic, outmoded, and antithetical to accountable governance. Under the new constitutional design, and through the *Chieftainship Law* of 1965, the local powers of the *dikgosi* were taken over by district councils, and the chiefs themselves consigned to a new House of Chiefs, with their authority limited to such matters as tribal membership, tribal ceremonies, and the reporting of crimes committed in tribal territory (Ifezue 2015: 281–2). At the same time, Khama adopted a strategy that was common in the precolonial times in Tswana *morafe*, to incorporate an ethnically diverse population in their territories by capturing potentially challenging leaders and individuals from outside communities and bringing them into the hierarchical structure of the kingdom (Gulbrandsen 2012: 12–63; Werbner 2004: 37). Under his postindependence government, many Kalanga, the most educated minority group, were recruited to serve in the newly established parliament and in government and judicial posts, ending up in certain cases outnumbering the Tswana in key positions. Through this strategy, Khama brought the Kalanga elite under his control and co-opted them in the state apparatus and bureaucracy (Gulbrandsen 2012: 123), while, at the same time, dispersing the power of potential Tswana opponents. This strategy was, naturally enough, often questioned by other Tswana, who saw it as threatening to have Kalanga representatives in decision-making positions. As Werbner underlined, these were unfounded concerns, and the Kalanga as a whole have remained loyal to the state (Werbner 2004: 108).

For the San, the transformations that came along with independence were not fully consistent with the narrative of progressive and enlightened reform. In the transition from being *malata* under the rule of chiefs and headmen in the Protectorate to citizens of an independent state, they certainly had more individual constitutional freedoms. But in practice their liberty was framed in terms of the projects of the state. They were subjected to the development designs of the economic "miracle" of postcolonial Botswana, in which their mobility and attachments to a foraging way of life were understood and acted upon as indications of "poverty," while their territories were subjected to the designs of large-scale cattle ranching and mineral extraction operations. The San went from dependency on Tswana elites, who ideally had the San's interests at heart, to dependency on the designs and benevolence of an independent government set upon making better (mainly commercial) use of their territories while "civilizing" them on the national model of Tswana language and values. In a sense, what seemed a revolution from the perspective of liberal constitutional and economic values translated for the San into a simple change of masters.

Things did not start off that way. Seretse Khama was widely seen as sympathetic to the San. As president, he agreed with some of the well-intended (though not consistently successful) initiatives on their behalf, including the establishment of the Bushmen Development Programme (BDP) in 1974. He also went along with the concept of "remote area settlements," which were established in Ghanzi and several other districts (e.g. Central, North West, Kgalagadi, Kweneng), and "communal service centres," which were set up as the more "progressive" part of the implementation of the Tribal Grazing Land Policy (TGLP), launched in August 1975, which I will discuss shortly. President Khama agreed with the principles of compensation for lost lands and resources under the TGLP. He had had extensive interactions with Kua and Tshwa San at his cattle posts in the western sandveld region of Central District (Hitchcock 1978). When, more than forty years later, his son Ian Khama become president of the country, many San with whom I spoke were excited and optimistic, thinking about the legacy of his father and comparing it to the difficult years of the presidencies of Quett Masire and Festus Mogae, under whose leadership the forced resettlements from the CKGR took place. Their hopes, as it turned out, were to be disappointed.

In the transition to a newly independent state, a significant shift took place in policy-oriented ideas about the San. Where once the central problem was to inquire into the conditions of their lives and, if need be, protect them from slavery, the focus of concern after independence was to assimilate them into the nation as fully participating "citizens." The problem for the new Botswana Democratic Party (BDP) government was that, in the terms of the new ruling class, the San were most definitely not participatory citizens, not equals, but were on the contrary, "backward and inferior, and would only be equals when they became culturally, economically and socially, Tswana" (Wily 1979a:165).

A 1966 report filed with the Ministry of Home Affairs outlined the San situation that had been inherited by the new government, recalling the main theme of the Masarwa Commission of the 1930s by giving this situation the title of "the Bushmen Problem."

> In recent years serf labour has come to be regarded as something of a liability in that the serfs' consumption of food and other resources outweighs their productivity. Because of their peripheral position in the life of the villages and the low regard in which they are held by their masters, these Bushmen are not exposed to effective acculturation processes. These factors, combined with their own backwardness and poverty, deny the Bushmen virtually all opportunity for advancement. (cited in Wily 1979a:19)

The "Bushmen Problem" was situated in the context of ambitious plans for economic expansion. At the time of independence Botswana was concerned with enhancing rural development and promoting economic opportunities for all of its citizens. Like other newly independent states, it presented itself as ethnically neutral in order to claim its legitimacy in postcolonial Africa. In this case, however, ethnic neutrality was ultimately pursued not through the suppression of all tribal markers, but through promoting the supremacy of a dominant identity. The status of minorities was articulated in a project that can best be described as the creation of a "melting pot" under Tswana domination. Marginalized groups were called upon, in the interest of national unity and prosperity, to subsume their languages, politics, and practices within the dominant, national model of Tswanadom.

The new nation of Botswana wanted to protect its sovereignty and at the same time promote localization, expand the economy, and strengthen its political position in the complex environment of southern Africa. In order to do this, it had to address some of its complex internal issues, not least of which was the status of groups like the San and Bakgalagadi and other "minorities" such as the Kalanga and Wayeyi. As Hitchcock and Holm (1993) have pointed out, one of the means by which the nation-state secured its control over minority groups was to establish an administrative bureaucracy and extend its reach to communities in the remote areas.

It is instructive to consider how the hopeful beginnings of independence, particularly the elaboration of policies intended to empower marginalized communities, ultimately had the effect of displacing, disenfranchising, and disaffecting many San. This discussion of the San's configuration as an underclass in independent Botswana and their mobilization as justice claimants would be incomplete without considering those policies of the independent government that, in promoting the commercial economy, worsened San's conditions of landlessness and left many without a secure means of subsistence.

At the same time, however, some development policies had the paradoxical effect of facilitating the San's capacity to organize in relation to state institutions, develop familiarity with formal structures of power, and prepare avenues of legal resistance. I want now to provide overviews of two of the most significant of these development initiatives, the Remote Area Development Policy and the Tribal Grazing Land Policy, each of which, one way or another, enters into the story of the San's pursuit of justice.

From Bushmen Development to Remote Area Development

In its 1966 Annual Report, the Anti-Slavery Society urged the British government to do something to safeguard the Bushmen's rights prior to granting independence to Bechuanaland. It was particularly concerned about land rights (Silberbauer 1981: 14–15; Guenther 1986: 296). This then led to Silberbauer (1965) recommending several ways to enhance San development, among them a number of suggestions on how to resolve the "Ghanzi farm problem." Settlement schemes and development plans aimed to "train the Bushmen" to undertake diverse activities such as farming, carpentry, and animal husbandry were recommended, together with the suggestion that anthropologists be employed as government consultants.

Ghanzi farms had been set aside in the 1890s for use by Afrikaner[13] and other European farmers, when Cecil John Rhodes and the Bechuanaland Protectorate Administration offered Boer settlers blocks of land,[14] in part as a buffer against potential expansion by the Germans from the west (Russell and Russell 1979: 12–13). In the process of establishing the farming blocks, sizable numbers of San were displaced, eventually leaving them impoverished and working as farm laborers on the commercial farms of other people (Guenther 1986). The San worked on these farms until the 1960s, when they were told to leave the farms and congregated in Ghanzi Township.[15]

In 1966, the Ghanzi farms were a major source of discussion among members of the Batswana elite who were about to take over the country. In the 1970s the problems affecting the San in the Ghanzi District, including the racist behavior of certain farmers, were often raised in parliament, particularly as reported by development workers and civil servants working in the area (Guenther 1986: 303). A survey of the situations of Ghanzi San was carried out by Gary Childers, who recommended a resettlement program for San living in the farm to four designated places in Ghanzi District (Childers 1976).

In 1974 the government of Botswana created a program called the Bushmen Development Programme (BDP), aimed, as its title declares, at assisting Bushmen. This program was targeted toward a set of people, principally the "destitute" Basarwa of the Ghanzi farms, who were seen as highly marginalized from the mainstream of Botswana society. Liz Wily, who had been teaching San children at Bere settlement in the Ghanzi District, was appointed as the first Bushmen Development Officer (BDO). In this capacity, the focus of her concern was that "less than .001% of the national rural development budget was being spent on San, who comprised, however, some 6 percent of the rural population" (Wily 1979a: 76–7). Wily made considerable efforts to reason with government officials in her reports and communications with them, sometimes pleading for the development of an approach to integration on the Bushmen's own terms, including accommodating a hunting economy alongside the support given to agriculture and the cattle industry:

> What is required to ensure their easiest integration with modern society ... is a framework which fosters their self- reliance ... in a gradual enough way to prevent their entry into ... beggarly dependency by withdrawing their present sustenance (wildlife, wild foods) or by demanding of them an immediate transition into agriculture, which they cannot make, and will therefore fail to adopt. ... Their own aspirations centre around regaining those assets they once fully had; a place WITH WATER where wild foods grow, and to hunt game. (Wily 1979a: 119)

Her efforts were to no avail, as BDP officials consistently defined the success of the program in terms of "the degree to which San spoke Setswana and were sedentary agriculturalists" (Wily 1979a: 164).

The Tswana concept of *boipelego* (self-reliance) was a reference point for the government's efforts to encourage the San to abandon their "primitive" and "unproductive" way of life and adopt a more "progressive," settled livestyle. This was accompanied by another key concept, *botho*, which implies recognition that being human involves engaging in actions, words, and feelings that have effects on others, and that being human entails certain responsibilities over others (Livingston 2008: 294). Proper state governance is therefore characterized by responsibility for citizens. The government believed not only in the rights of its citizens, but also in the responsibilities of the state. Combining these two terms we see the outlines of the government's approach to the "Bushmen problem." The San were to be brought toward self-reliance by a government acting compassionately and responsibly toward them as citizens. This conception of progress, however, was usually understood in a narrow sense, with reference to Tswana preferences for agriculture and cattle rearing. Wily (1979a: 166) reports that visitors to her office would often ask, "Are they ploughing yet?" and express disappointment that the "lazy" Basarwa were so resistant to change.

At least in the early period of decolonization, this drive toward development mainly took the form of small, locally managed projects. In the early 1970s the government provided district councils with generous amounts of money to build classrooms, clinics, health posts, roads, etc. around their districts. It also gave life to the district council as an operational development agency in the rural areas, which the Bushmen Programme was quick to exploit. By the end of the 1970s, almost the entire BDP (with its 50-plus sub-projects) was being implemented by district councils, which Wily, perhaps overenthusiastically, characterized as "Champions of San" (Wily 1979a: 86–9). But even with such champions in local office, little was done to alleviate the displacements and landlessness that was at the root of the "Bushmen problem."

The BDP was to come to a close in 1978 with a change of name and a reorganization of priorities toward infrastructure development. The change of title followed simply from the programs use of the term "Bushman," which raised concerns about using ethnic identification as a basis for "separate development" through the allocation of special programs and facilities (see Saugestad 2001). The government instead chose an ethnically neutral approach in its policies toward minorities and indigenous peoples in an effort to distance the country as much as possible from neighboring South Africa, which was emphasizing Apartheid (and with it, separate development for "inferior races"). It therefore shifted the focus away from "Bushmen" and established what was termed the Remote Area Development Programme (RADP). The target group for this program was Remote Area Dwellers (RADs), a group that was not defined in ethnic terms, but mainly according to poverty indicators.

The period from 1978 through the early 1990s thus saw the establishment of more than sixty Remote Area Dweller settlements, each with social and physical infrastructure including a borehole, school, health post, a meeting place (*kgotla*), and housing for government workers such as teachers, nurses, and tribal police (see Figure 3, p. xix). Support for these settlements was provided by outside donors, especially the Norwegian Agency for International Development (NORAD) (Chr. Michelsen Institute 1996; Saugestad 2001).

Although the RADP was not, initially at least, supposed to be a "settlement program," the effect of establishing water points and social services at specific locations encouraged landless people to move there. The infrastructure attracted people to the settlements, many of which exhibited density-related social and economic problems (competition among individuals and groups, social tensions, alcohol addiction, and dissatisfaction). Many of the elders I interviewed in the settlements of East and West Hanahai indicated that they wished they were still living in their home areas, where "now the farms are," but at the same time they stressed that they really do not know where their "home" is because they "have always been moved" (author notes July 2011, Ghanzi District). An old blind man (who presented himself as one of the original founders of First People of the Kalahari), after proudly explaining how he was able to fence his garden and house, changed his expression when I asked what he thought about the newly established settlements for the people who had been relocated from the reserve. He put his hand around his neck in a gesture of strangling himself and told me vehemently that people there feel like dogs chained to a tree. There was an often-expressed sense of sympathy and solidarity between the San displaced by the Ghanzi farms and those of the CKGR based upon an understanding that they shared many of the same experiences.

From the outset, as in the RAD villages established for the people of the CKGR, there were a number of problems with these settlements, including lack of sufficient land to allow for hunting and gathering, relatively few employment and income-generating opportunities, and the presence of (mostly) powerful outsiders who saw in the new villages opportunities to realize their own ambitions, many of them non-San people, who often took over the water, grazing, and arable land of the settlements. This situation can be seen most vividly in Ghanzi District, where none of the remote area settlements was large enough to support even a group of fifteen full-time foragers (only 400 sq. km of land was allocated per settlement, whereas 1,000 to 4,000 sq. km of land is needed for mobile foraging in the central and western parts of Botswana). In some cases, people living in the settlements were supplied with food and other goods, especially if they were considered "destitute" or people without visible means of support (see Hitchcock 1988; Seleka et al. 2007). There were, however, several more fundamental problems with the government's approach, not least among them the encouragement of dependency on the state and the tendency for support to be withheld if communities did not follow governmental dictates.

Once in the RADP villages, the new residents often found that the infrastructure and services they had been promised had not yet been put in place. Government officials tended to be oblivious to the harshness of daily life in the villages, offering a "pull-yourself-up-by your-bootstraps" solution to the entrenched ills of displacement and the loss of purpose that comes with unemployment and dependency. A particularly telling *Daily News* article in 1988 reports on the visit of a Kgalagadi district MP, Lesedi Mothibamele, to a gathering of his constituents in Phuduhudu, during which he exhorted them to "send their children to school and to stop them from taking alcohol," with a promise that "some remote areas would be provided with schools and clinics in due course" (Maphangela 1988).[16]

One of the ways that administrative centralization was approached in practice in the RAD settlements was through the imposition of local leaders on the San by government. A common attitude among government officials in Botswana was that San communities did not have formal leaders and that the "Basarwa," as they preferred to call them, did not have organized political institutions (Hitchcock and Holm 1993). Successive Botswana governments chose to ignore the existing San leaders in the remote settlements and instead appointed people with the requisite literacy skills, often non-San, to chair *kgotla* meetings and oversee community affairs. Some headmen also sought to simply take power without governmental or community agreement. When young, educated San were appointed, they often lacked leadership experience and did not have community support. In the CKGR resettlement site of New Xade, for example, the appointed headman was seen by some of the residents as not having the background to serve in that position when he was appointed. The appointment of people who were not local or who lacked authority or recognition at the local level had the effect of undermining the social and political integrity of San groups.

Discussions with San, on the other hand, indicate that virtually all communities had respected people whose suggestions they tended to follow. At the same time the idea of representational leadership, that is, having one person speak on behalf of others, was anathema to many San, including the G/ui, the G//ana, and the Ju/'hoansi (Silberbauer 1981: 167–71; Biesele and Hitchcock 2013: 181–2). In the politics of San communities, the expression of individual opinions was not only tolerated, but was even, in fact, much admired (Biesele and Hitchcock 2013: 181).

Robert Paine (1977: 3) has called the domination of indigenous peoples through a political system that creates relationships of dependence on the state "welfare colonialism." The RADP, from the perspective of many of the "targets" of the initiative, was aimed at assimilation and promoting a kind of compliant dependency.

In the last few years a new category has appeared: "Remote Area Communities" (RACs), under the recently announced Affirmative Action Framework of the Botswana government (Republic of Botswana 2014b). The fact that they are no longer "settlements" but "communities" excludes them from the National Settlement Policy (Republic of Botswana 1980, 1998), which was aimed at assisting villages with 500 or more people in an area of 15 km which would be gazetted – that is, officially recognized by government. The new terminology of "communities" has significant legal implications in that it gives the government the right to dispossess and resettle people living in existing villages because they are not formally recognized as inhabiting "settlements" with rights. It is a strategy not just of nonrecognition of indigenous rights, but also of absolving the government of responsibility for providing basic social, economic, and cultural rights. Rights to government benefits and security of place can be contingent upon a single word, which, when changed, introduces a new reality, preparing conditions for the "community's" subjection to the will of the state.

The Tribal Grazing Land Policy (TGLP)

Once established as an independent nation, Botswana decided to change the basis of land tenure in the country, passing a *Tribal Land Act* in 1968, which came into effect in 1970 (Picard 1987; Peters 1994). Initiated in part as a means of allowing for the commercialization of "tribal land," it was also a way of taking power away from the chiefs, thus reducing their authority over land allocation. It transferred the allocation rights of the chiefs to land boards composed of people drawn from the district's population. The chief became an *ex officio* member of the land boards.

In the late 1970s a national policy was implemented that was arguably to have the most significant consequences for the San of any policy since independence in 1966. This was the Tribal Grazing Land Policy (Republic of Botswana 1975). This policy aimed at dividing the tribal land into (a) commercial leasehold ranches, which would be further divided into ranches leased out to individuals and groups of livestock owners, (b) communal land, where customary land tenure rules would continue to prevail, and (c) reserved land, which was aimed at ensuring the rights of the poor.

At the heart of this policy was a central contradiction: on the one hand, it aimed to safeguard the interests of the landless poor, expressing what could even be seen as a commitment to social justice with the goal of ensuring that every individual and family had enough land to meet their basic needs. The TGLP white paper makes this goal of economic equity explicit, stating that, "Planning will aim to ensure that land development helps the poor and does not make them worse off" (Republic of Botswana 1975: 2). In addition, the policy underscored what it believed to be the basic principle of the traditional land tenure system in Botswana: "the right of every tribesman to have as much land as he needs to sustain him and his family" (Republic of Botswana 1975: 4).

At the same time, however, the TGLP aimed to encourage the expansion and commercialization of the livestock industry through the enclosure of grazing lands that had long been communally owned (Cullis and Watson 2005; Peters 1994). This commercial aspect of the policy eventually came to the fore, as the primary focus of the TGLP turned toward ranch establishment (Bishop 1998; Sapignoli and Hitchcock 2013b). The major consequence of this was an eventual increase in the numbers of landless rural poor and their further dispossession. What is more, hunter-gatherers' land use simply did not feature in the new grazing lands policy. What happened, in effect, was that San and other rural people were incorporated into commercial leasehold ranches in the tribal lands, where they had no rights; many of them were then told to leave those areas and had to move off of the ranches onto communal lands. In some cases, San and other former cattle post residents moved to communal service centres, which were set up in the late 1970s (Wily 1979a; Hitchcock 1988). Some San moved into towns and cities where they became part of the underclass of the urban poor.

Little thought seems to have been given to the possibility that the San might be adversely affected – after all, allocating grazing lands was supposed to be geared toward their development. No one expected – or at least no one made the expectation clear – that the reform of grazing lands would lead to more Ghanzi farm situations, more "squatters" on the margins of land that provided wealth for a few. As it turned out, no land was "reserved for the poor"; instead, those areas were later defined as Wildlife Management Areas (WMAs) through the Wildlife Conservation Policy of 1986, which eventually comprised more than 22 percent of the total area of the country (See Table 3.1 below; Sapignoli and Hitchcock 2013b: 136).

The Wildlife Conservation Policy (Republic of Botswana 1986) was aimed at promoting both commercial and noncommercial use of wildlife, and it argued for the involvement of WMA residents in conservation and wildlife utilization (Republic of Botswana 1986; Poteete 2009: 290). One of the problems with the WMAs was that they were not gazetted (that is, legally defined) by the government. As a result, many people moved into them with their livestock without bothering to get district land board or central government approval. Often the only way to maintain control over the land for many poor communities was to form a community trust, develop a management plan, and obtain a wildlife quota from the Department of Wildlife and National Parks for the community-controlled hunting areas (CCHAs), under the government's Community-Based Natural Resource Management (CBNRM) policy, which was introduced formally in 1990 (Republic of Botswana 1990).[17] The characteristic feature of some of these community trusts was that local people were able to get some control over their land and some cash income, employment, and, in a number of cases, meat from animals that were obtained in their areas. Local communities could contract out their rights to wildlife to private companies, which paid them for permission to bring in hunters or tourists. The only areas in the country where these kinds of programs could not be established were in the freehold farm areas and in the state lands, including national parks and game reserves such as the CKGR. However, as we have seen, the CKGR was an exception, the site of several (thus far futile) attempts to establish a CBNRM plan, with the negotiations that were integral to this process being the source of considerable hope, and ultimately, disillusionment for the people of the reserve.

By 2000, the government of Botswana and the district councils and land boards had solidified a set of land use categories (see Table 3.1). The only portions of the tribal land (71 percent of the country) that were set aside for Remote Area Dweller settlements, settlements predominantly populated by San people, constituted less than 0.6 percent of the country (3,523 km^2). Furthermore, in an effort to offset the dispossession of people who had been residents of cattle posts that were turned into ranches, a small amount of land (1,058 km^2) was designated for Communal Service Centers in leasehold areas of the tribal land. The service centers were small segments of what were called Commercial First Development Areas. Approximately 3,000–4,000 people occupied

TABLE 3.1 Land zoning categories in Botswana

Type of land	Land zoning category	Amount of land (km²)	Percentage of country
Freehold land	Freehold farms	32,970	5.7
State land	Parks and reserves	101,535	17.4
	Other	32,455	5.6
Tribal land	Communal	173,432	29.8
	Commercial	51,094	8.8
	Wildlife Management Areas	129,450	22.2
	Leasehold ranches	3,351	0.6
	Remote Area Dweller settlements	3,523	0.6
	Other land	53,910	9.3
Total	All land	581,720	100.0

Note: Data obtained from the Ministry of Lands and Housing, the Ministry of Local Government and Rural Development and the Ministry of Environment, Wildlife and Tourism, government of Botswana. The category "other" includes land in towns and land set aside for government purposes (e.g. trek routes, quarantine camps for livestock).

these areas, many of them San (Robert Hitchcock, personal communication, 2010). One of the problems with the service centers was that the resettlements of people into them were carried out without much care or concern. These centers, like the RAD settlements, were not gazetted, and as a result cattle owners and other people had the legal space to move into them with their animals to take advantage of the grazing and the subsidized water. The long-term outcomes of these processes included overcrowding of the service centers and settlements in or adjacent to the commercial ranching areas; the loss of livelihoods and decline of well-being of many of the residents of the settlements and of communal service centers; and increased problems related to disease, poor-quality water, and lack of wild foods in the people's diet (Hitchcock 1978; Wily 1979a, 1981). This form of dispossession did not stop with the setting aside of sizable amounts of land for leasehold ranches under the Tribal Grazing Land Policy, and it has continued most recently with the 2015 decision of the Botswana government to initiate a new land policy (Republic of Botswana 2015; see also Chapter 7, p. 278).

Overall, the TGLP benefitted white ranch owners and Tswana elites far more than it did the residents of the areas where the ranches were established because it provided ready access to land and the cheap labor from the populations that had been displaced. As one San in Central District who was dispossessed by a TGLP ranch in the Western Sandveld said, "We were sacrificed for the interests of wealthy cattle owners."[18] By the 1990s, San had been dispossessed of nearly all of the land that they saw as theirs and that their ancestors had occupied for millennia.

EMERGENT ACTIVISM IN THE GHANZI FARMS

The San groups living in Ghanzi District were in many ways uniquely disadvantaged because they were generally poorly paid farm laborers on freehold land from which they could be evicted at any time, according to the whim of the owner. The Ghanzi situation was, from the perspective of some Batswana, a serious problem that they tried to address through various development plans. The Ghanzi farms were held under individually owned freehold tenure, with the disastrous consequence that, "The 4500 local hunter-gatherers now have no legal right to use or live on that land. They are squatters who may legally be removed" (Wily 1982: 292). The leasehold farms that proliferated with the TGLP's support for commercialization created a condition of illegality for the people living in what they considered their land.

These problems continue to this day, with high unemployment and uncertainty regarding the future of the livestock industry in the face of international competition, disease (foot-and-mouth disease in particular), and declining prices and market access for livestock. San who have been working on the farms for years are threatened with replacement by other workers (for example, Zimbabweans), cutbacks on the number of farm employees, and greater skills being required of farm workers (e.g. the ability to drive or operate heavy equipment).

Among the farmers I spoke with (2012), there were a few who were very sympathetic to the needs of their workers and their families. A few farmers had developed schools, including, if needed, transportation from the neighboring villages, offering workers the possibility of keeping their livestock on the farm, and trying in some cases to protect the graves of the workers' families from the impacts of development. But there were many other farmers – by far the majority – whose thoughts were limited to complaining about the unreliability of their workers and expressing their sense that too many people were living on their farms. They sometimes explained their disdain through explicit and racist references to sexual promiscuity.[19]

One of the qualities of the San noted by many observers from the time of the proto-states to the period of decolonization was their reluctance to come forward to talk about their grievances, to react outwardly and publicly, even in response to extreme suffering. A Ministry of Local Government and Lands memorandum on tribal grazing land allocation circulated to all district commissioners, district councils, and land boards in 1975, for example, remarks that "Basarwa are a 'silent' sector, notably unvocal about their land needs" (in Wily 1979a: 140). From the government officials' perspective, it would be far better that they clamor vocally for the benefits being offered them than remain silent about their conditions of landlessness and poverty. The inferior status to which they were consigned, reinforced by attitudes of racism, was not taken into account as a possible source of their silence, producing a circular judgment that, in turn, served to explain and justify their marginality. In other words, they were *politically silent*, which further reinforced the ruling elite's prejudices against them. Their silence, however, was the *result* of their legal and political marginalization, not a cause of it. It should be noted that until the 1970s, San did not speak up much in *kgotla* meetings. When I asked about this, some said this was because nobody would listen to them anyway, and they did not feel comfortable speaking in what they saw as meetings that were called by outsiders, notably government officials.

The San people living in Ghanzi District in some ways became an exception to this trap of political quietism. Although they retained what Guenther (1977: 196) describes as "cursory social ties with free-roaming, band-organized hunter-gatherers who live at and beyond the periphery of the farms," they also included those who were more organized and resistant to the predominant, longstanding "serf-like attachment to Bantu-speaking villagers" and Afrikaans-speaking settlers.

The Ghanzi District was, in essence, the cradle of San activism, providing both an acute sense of injustice over conditions of displacement and imposed conditions of poverty and an organized network consisting largely of those who had been educated in missions and RAD schools[20] and were engaged with the work of development workers and anthropologists (Barnard 2006: 113–27).

One of the reasons for the politicization of the San in the Ghanzi district was related to the fact that it was the scene of the Bushmen Development Programme (led by Wily starting in 1974) and researchers working there. After Wily terminated her appointment as Bushmen

Development Officer, she wrote a highly informative reflection of her activities, stressing that the role of the Liaison Officer was that of "animator, basically politicizing the San" (Wily 1982: 297). For her, liaison was a euphemism for "conscientization" (Guenther 1986: 303). During the time that the BDO was in full swing, workshops and training sessions were held to teach such practical things as how to file a complaint with the police or the land boards and how to apply for hunting licenses, land access, and water points permission (Childers 1976).

Wily reports on a workshop in which the San's problems with the farmers were discussed through a "theatrical performance," at the end of which a San commented, "We have sat on the sand so long doing nothing, never speaking up. We have been oppressed ... and we have been waiting for Government to end our oppression. Now today I have seen that it is in our own hands" (Wily 1982: 305). An officer in the Ghanzi District Council reported how government officials needed to be prepared when they met San in *kgotla* meetings "because questions will be raised and now they have the guts to bring out their grievances against the headman and that the District Commissioner was taking action based on their complaints" (Botswana 1978: 120, cited in Wily 1982). Wily noted with some satisfaction that "Self-reliance is not quite the controllable quality it may appear. In being given the means for self-reliance, San are being given the key tool for self-determination" (Wily 1982: 306).

Our first glimpse of these outspoken San in the Ghanzi District is, typically, second hand, in the newspaper articles reporting on their protests. In one such article, a *Daily News* piece titled "Basarwa demand social justice" (Letshwiti 1981), the central issue was framed as a need for "more social integration and equitable distribution of the national development projects in Botswana." Of course, we cannot be sure of the extent to which journalistic license is being applied to the San's claims. They are surely centrally concerned with the fact that they were not benefitting from the government's development initiatives, but (and this is not mentioned in the article) their concerns go much further, to the fact that they had been displaced by those very initiatives. The central point to take away from this piece, however, is the evidence it provides of a nascent, organized activist movement. An advisor to the sub-chief elect is reported as saying that the Basarwa "have decided to organise themselves because for too long they have not been taken seriously. They were treated badly and paid low incomes by the farm owners ... who only visit the farms occasionally to choose the beasts for sale to the Botswana Meat Commission." Another man, identified simply as "a tribesman," is quoted as saying, "Let our voice also be heard throughout the country so that we could be known as an organized community who would like to integrate with other tribes in the country" (Letshwiti 1981: 2).

Whether or not "integration" was a common priority of the Ghanzi farm workers, conditions on the farms began to emerge as a topic of public discussion in the 1980s. A "Basarwa" reported to a journalist the shocking information that when a farm was sold, the workers were sold with it. As part of their duties, farm workers were required to trek more than 600 km over a period of a month in extremely hazardous conditions in order to bring cattle to market. A herd boy might be paid annually with a calf, and those with salaried positions were often not paid for more than a year (Mooketsi 1989). Even these occupations were precarious, as increased use of vehicles and mechanization made manual labor on the farms obsolete, and workers coming from other parts of the country or Zimbabwe and South Africa were prioritized, consigning even more San laborers to the status of "squatters." In other words, the sorts of conditions that had long been part of San life in the farms began to be felt more widely and to emerge in the 1980s as part of a public narrative of injustice.

The San's political quietism was to change, most notably with the public appearance of a small cohort of politicized San and charismatic San leaders who began their activist careers lobbying against the dispossession and conditions of desperation found in the Ghanzi area. They were particularly concerned with the problems facing landless and exploited farm workers and widespread poverty, and they started to be more vocal in local and national discussions. D'kar village and some of the surrounding farms constituted the center of most of the San's organized activism in the 1970s and 1980s, especially with the development of several NGOs (Chapter 4). Chances are, these leaders had been educated in a mission farm (D'Kar) in the Ghanzi Block, which had been established by missionaries for the San in 1964 by a branch of the Dutch Reformed Church in South West Africa (the Gereformeede Kerk Aranos) (Mathias Guenther, personal communication, January 2017). In this settlement, local structures were sometimes co-opted for purposes of faith-based development. For example, church councils became the primary focus of the community rather than the band system that had existed previously. The church also provided assistance in the form of education, health, training, and employment. Within two years of its establishment, the school enrollment had expanded to 39 San pupils. The most notable feature of this mission project was that at the time of Independence in 1966 it was the only nongovernmental project in the country that acted counter to the goals of Tswanification by being oriented specifically toward the benefit of the San (Wily 1979: 22). For this reason alone, it was central to the development of an activist consciousness that went against the grain of national discourse and assimilationist policies.[21]

The mission became predominantly secular through the formation in 1986 of Kuru Development Trust (KDT), a community-based organization (LeRoux 1996). A series of trusts specializing in various project areas were later formed, all of them becoming part of what was called the Kuru Family Organizations (KFO), with several projects directed at empowering the San throughout the Ghanzi and North West (Ngamiland) districts (see Bollig et al. 2000). Kuru was the home of a number of activist figures, whom we will later find working in other organizations dealing with the rights of San peoples and who became involved in fights over development agendas, the distribution of decision-making powers, and accountability (see Chapter 4, p. 119).

The connection between these mission-based education initiatives and the emergence of San activism in the Ghanzi district is not accidental. D'kar was and remains a focal point of San-oriented development initiatives that ran counter to the government's ostensibly "ethnically blind," Tswana-centric policies. Together with this awareness came resentment of its denial. Writing in the mid-1970s, Guenther observed that "the Bushmen in the farming block are becoming increasingly resentful towards the whites whom many have come to depict as oppressors and exploiters who have illegally taken their land. ... Most of the new generation of farm Bushmen exhibit sanguine anti-white attitudes" (Guenther 1977: 198; see also Guenther 1997).

Another issue that emerged in this early resistance was the imposition of government-mandated local leadership. When, for example, local authorities appointed their own man as headman of the D'Kar community without consulting its residents, the San from D'Kar did not hesitate to protest to the Ghanzi District Commissioner. His response was to warn them about the dangers of "tribalistic tendencies"; he refused to take the matter any further, keeping "the outsider" in place as the official leader of the community. When a delegation of San travelled to the capital of Gaborone to meet with officials in order to raise the issue and to propose the establishment of a national council of San that could "benefit the country as a people capable of creating our own development plans in co-operation with the government" (Hardbattle 1993a: 141), they were given a stern lecture by Pelonomi Venson, the permanent secretary for the Ministry of Local Government, Lands, and Housing, who castigated them for following "the indigenous minorities fashion." According to a journalist who followed this event, Venson told the Bushmen that Botswana is a signatory to international conventions that commit the state "to develop and integrate the Basarwa by improving their standards of living" (Kelso 1993: 51; see Chapter 5, p. 234, for further discussion of this meeting). John Hardbattle, who led the San delegation, later reflected on what this form of representation meant for his people:

> The first thing [the representative] does is to get a hawker's license (to help his constituents) and he physically moves to the settlement. Instead of selling his goods [at] reasonable prices, his prices are quite often the double of the shops in the nearest town. He also sells alcohol, which is illegal. ... [H]e gives credit easily, but is ruthless in collecting debts. Very quickly he is a livestock owner in the settlement. All the cash from drought relief programmes ... goes directly to him on pay-days ... These same exploited people are then called apathetic, lazy, useless drunks, when the development programme fails, by those who exploit them. (Hardbattle 1993a: 145)

The imposed headman remained in place despite the delegation's entreaties. If this was the response they consistently received from making personal appeals for reform and redress to officials, it is small wonder that the first formally educated San activist leadership looked to their own organization and to the "outsiders" who supported it to address their concerns rather than putting their trust in government.

The government's rejection of their distinct political identity could well have been, paradoxically, a central source of motivation for the rediscovery of who they were as a people, starting with the revival of trance dancing, involving all-night events in which healers go into an altered state of consciousness in the process of curing sickness. During a trance dance, as many as 300 people from a wide area converge on the dance site and interact intensely for hours on end. The San of the Ghanzi District accorded some power and prestige to the dancers, to the point that they became a "rallying symbol of the Bushman people and their culture" (Guenther 1975: 165). With the revival of trance dancing on these terms, "Bushmanness" became a positive and assertive trait – and a source of emerging political awareness and leadership.

The "Ghanzi revival," as I will discuss further in Chapter 4, became a focal point of distinct San identity and activist organization. It was later to form the foundations of the first San NGOs, First People of the Kalahari, which was to become actively engaged in outreach to those people, mainly Europeans and Americans, who were sympathetic to the San people, their way of life, and their causes, and resistant to the government policies oriented toward their assimilation into Tswana society.

MINORITIES AND INDIGENOUS PEOPLES

In the view of some analysts, the Botswana Constitution, which came into force on September 30, 1966, and other Botswana legislation such as Section 2 of the *Chieftainship Act* and the *Tribal Territories Act*, essentially permitted discrimination on the basis of ethnicity, language, and culture.[22] The "eight Tswana tribes" in the country were recognized officially, while the other groups had no such recognition and were marginalized socially, politically, and economically. The idea behind independence, from the perspectives of many Batswana, was "One Botswana, One Nation." The Tswana-oriented foundations of this national slogan can be found in a more subtle, yet deliberate blurring of the distinction between being a citizen of Botswana (*Motswana*) and being a member of the dominant Tswana tribes (also labelled *Motswana*). These two meanings of the root *tswana* tend to be conflated in everyday discourse, so that if you are a *Motswana* (citizen), you should embody Tswana values and the Setswana language. This conflation of an ethnic identifier with national identity, I found, can actually shape subjectivity.

The attitude of becoming a Motswana (as we will relate in Chapters 4 and 6) is seen very differently by the San youth involved in the work of NGOs and international and national politics, for whom their indigenous and San identities are proudly asserted. Outside the circle of activists, however, it was more common for people to privilege a national narrative as Motswana, citizens of Botswana, rather than underline their ethnic origins.

At the same time, it is possible to find what Jacqueline Solway describes for the Bakgalagadi as a process of "ethnogenesis," an awaking of ethnic pride, also taking place among the San (see Solway 1994). For Solway, trust in the bureaucratic process is the critical condition that "provides people from stigmatized groups with the confidence that enables them to perceive their disadvantage and, more importantly, to act on it" (Solway 2002: 717).

Minoritization was clearly not a uniform process, and was not consistently based on the experience of racism, but varied across the country, from ethnic minority to minority, with some asserting "difference-blind" equal rights and others claiming recognition of distinct minority status (Werbner 2002: 673). The assertions of minority status were a significant challenge to the "one-nation consensus," leaving greater room for "difference politics." These had significant implications for a wide spectrum of political action.

It is important to briefly consider some of the most important challenges to the state's approach to collective rights and their implications for the San's pursuit of recognition as indigenous peoples. Writing around the turn of the millennium, Richard Werbner (2002) noted a transformation in the public consciousness toward the status of minorities in Botswana, in which new human rights discourse, tied to advocacy in favor of multiculturalism, was posing a significant challenge to the one-nation consensus. Under the slogan "unity in diversity," the minorities were oriented toward upholding their distinct cultural rights (Werbner 2002: 676). They engaged in a wide-ranging, multi-strategy campaign geared toward gaining the backing of global opinion and ultimately involving the courts and human rights NGOs and agencies. Once they had acquired a base of international support, minority activists made known their intent to bring their case to the United Nations and call into question the government's reputation for good governance if it failed to respond to their demands for group rights (Werbner 2002: 672). This is precisely the way that the San approached their efforts to gain rights from the Botswana state.

The focal point of minority claims was the issue of equal participation in the House of Chiefs. These claims were led by the Wayeyi, a Bantu minority group that had been marginalized as *malata* under Tswana rule in the precolonial and colonial eras. Demanding equal inclusion in the House of Chiefs, the Wayeyi and their Kamanakao Association led the movement, which became the major focus of the minority identity struggle, calling for the amendment of articles 77, 78, and 79 of the Constitution regarding membership in the House of Chiefs (Nyati-Ramahobo 2009). This struggle went on for several decades. In 1995, a motion in parliament asked the government to make the constitution of the country "tribally neutral" by revising its sections 77, 78, and 79 (Republic of Botswana 2000b: 1–2). A Commission of

Inquiry into the Constitution, known as the Balopi Commission after the name of its chairperson, was appointed in 2000.

The Balopi Commission held hearings from early August until late October 2000 in many of the major villages and towns across the country. The commission was flooded with a deluge of oral and written submissions, many richly reported in the media. Live radio broadcasts brought the commission's activities into households even in the remote rural regions of the country. A vast outpouring of opinion took place, manifested in articles, letters, and exchanges in the press.

One result of the work of the Balopi Commission was a push for constitutional reform, though one that balanced the entrenched interests of the Tswana chiefs against the calls for sweeping reform. According to Lydia Nyati-Ramahobo, a professor at the University of Botswana who founded the Kamanakao Association and led the Wayeyi claims against the government, the amendments to the Constitution did not alter its discriminatory nature in practice (personal communication, 2013). The Tswana and their *dikgosi* continue to be members of the House of Chiefs and remain secure in their positions as chiefs in tribal territories in which there are actually many minorities. The constitutional reform allows candidates for elected office to be recruited from ethnically mixed zones, but with temporary mandates and diverse constituencies that make it difficult for them represent specific ethnic groups (Gulbrandsen 2012: 218). Werbner affirms that in the ultimate outcome of the Balopi Commission, "There was no radical reintegration of tribes; rather, it was more a shift in idiom to avoid old appearances, especially in now disdained colonial language" (2004: 45).

More significant were the changes in political consciousness that swept the country. Above all else, the Balopi Commission opened a space for long-silenced voices, for expressions of dissent and resentment, and for a process of "political learning" among minorities struggling for recognition and rights (Werbner 2004: 44). It widened the recognition not just of minorities, but of the activist strategies that they employed to assert their rights and to seek a new dispensation of recognition and collective dignity.

Aside from its effects on activist collaboration, there is another hopeful outcome of the minority struggle in Botswana. As the group at the forefront of minority rights in Botswana, the Wayeyi continued to pursue their quest for recognition, and in particular for a place as equals in the House of Chiefs. In 1999 they elected their own chief and asked for recognition, which was refused. From this point, they took their struggle beyond the campaign that led to the Balopi Commission. When the government rejected their attempt to elect a chief, the Kamanakao Association decided to bring their claim to the High Court. Werbner (2004: 61) describes the resulting landmark case, *Kamanakao and Others v. the Attorney General and Another* (2002), as putting "assimilationist nationalism ... on the retreat" in Botswana. The court ruled in the Wayeyi organization's favor, denouncing the discriminatory nature of the *Chieftanship Act*. The legal action led to policy reform, particularly to the *Bogosi Act*, which replaced the *Chieftainship Act* and which allows recognition of non-Tswana tribes and their chiefs (Nyati-Ramahobo 2009: 2). As an outcome of several decades of social justice activism, the Wayeyi were finally granted permission to have their own chief in June 2016, and at the time of writing were engaged in the process of selecting a chief.

San representatives have been resistant to asserting their identity as a minority. The mechanisms of exclusion and systemic prejudice that are associated with San or "Basarwa" identity do not apply equally to Bantu minorities, and go some way toward explaining the San's marginal position relative to other minorities. San activists have underscored that they represent the most dispossessed among the minorities, not only discriminated against by the Tswana, but also by minorities such as the Herero, Bakalagadi, and Kalanga. In making this argument, they assert the fact that they represent constituents who are not *minorities* but *indigenous peoples*, knowing very well the difference that this assertion makes in international law, particularly since indigenous rights have been globalized (see Anaya 2009).

This link between rights violations and indigeneity, for example, was articulated in a 1992 report by Alice Mogwe (later to become the first head of the rights-based advocacy organization Ditshwanelo), entitled *Who Was (T)here First? An Assessment of the Human Rights Situation of Basarwa in the Gantsi District, Botswana*. This report had far-reaching impacts on rights consciousness, particularly with respect to the treatment of San who were accused of poaching and who were tortured and mistreated in order to extract information (Mogwe 1992: 12–15). The graphic description of mistreatment resulted in calls for investigations into the allegations from the international community, states, and local NGOs. The report also raised questions about the ways in which San were treated by government institutions, including land boards, schools, and farm owners. Perhaps most significantly, it raised these human rights issues in the context of the "indigenous rights" and "indigenous identity" of the San.

At the same time, however, a number of their grievances and ambitions are shared with those who advocate on behalf of minorities rights. Almost all, for example, want to see their language and leaders recognized and to see the national census take ethnic identity into consideration, something that has not happened since the 1936 and 1946 Bechuanaland censuses (Schapera 1952; Alec Campbell, personal communication, 2011). Interviews with some members of NGOs in Botswana indicated that at least a few of them were concerned about the emphasis that some San placed on promoting indigeneity instead of their minority status in the country, which they felt would be more inclusive and acceptable to the government, a vision that is often shared by many NGOs operating in Africa.

As I will show, however, indigeneity has remained the centre of San advocacy organizations and their activities. It was their participation in emergent legal entities – the NGOs and other registered organizations – that represented another key step in San movement toward legal personhood and capacity for activism. The development of NGOs with San or, more broadly, indigenous people's interests at the center of their agendas – the subject of the next chapter – is one of the most significant events in the San's quest for justice.

4

GETTING ORGANIZED: THE SOCIAL LIVES OF SAN NGOS

CIVIL SOCIETY AND NGOISM

The proliferation of non-governmental organizations (NGOs) is one of the most notable recent changes that have occurred globally, and particularly in the developing world.[1] This can be seen in the growing number of registered organizations, the thousands of NGOs attending international meetings, and the increasing involvement of civil society and NGOs in world politics and in development, human rights, and governance. In the process of this development, NGOs' relationships with states, international donors, and organizations have had profound impacts on globalization and on local lives (Fisher 1997: 441).

In Botswana, the development of NGOs was marked by relative autonomy from the state. In contrast to "the typical African corporatist system" of authoritarian governments in which NGOs are "creations of or captured by politicians" who use them to mobilize support for their regimes, Botswana's civil society was based more on the struggle of organizations that were part of social movements to establish themselves, independent of capture by politicians (Holm, Molutsi and Somolekae 1996: 58). In the 1980s and 1990s in particular, organizations established by groups advocating for a wide variety of causes, including those relating to San interests, rapidly multiplied. One of the many effects of this proliferation, which I discuss in this chapter with reference to San activism, was the introduction of new legal and political discourses, together with the forms of leadership with which these discourses were associated.

International NGOs, state administrations, and global organizations each have their own, often broadly shared requirements, expectations, and languages for engaging with those marginalized communities that are seeking a better future. They call for local forms of leadership and organization to be legible and legal in their terms, for new organizations to be bureaucratized and political relationships *juridified* (see Chapter 1). Local agencies and their representatives are not powerless in this process, but are called upon to navigate new structures and languages of political representation, while meeting local demands for familiar forms of reciprocity and personal ethics of "leadership" responsibility. As we will see later in this chapter, meeting these very different demands is no easy matter, and failure to do so can lead to the collapse of an organization.

NGOs are often discussed as a uniform kind of entity, sometimes under the vexed rubric of "civil society." In the case of indigenous activism and many other similar justice movements, it is important to recognize the variety of activist organizations. Kirsch distinguishes between "horizontal" and "vertical" forms of organization. Simply put, horizontal organizations draw their leadership from among autonomous local organizations, which have deep wells of legitimacy and participation but limited communication or coordination among different parts of the campaign. Vertical NGOs, by contrast, are those more hierarchical forms of organization that facilitate decision-making but offer less in the way of commitments and broad-based participation (Kirsch 2014b: 225). Of course the two forms of organization are not mutually exclusive: there are aspects of vertical decision-making even in the organizations with participatory ideals, and there can be differences in the extent to which advocacy-oriented NGOs are "vertically" or "horizontally" structured, sometimes even within a single organization over time.

These differences were particularly far-reaching in the San justice campaigns, bringing out basic contradictions not only between different forms of activist organization, but also between the community-based NGOs and the forms of leadership and expectations of the communities that these organizations were intended to serve. In a cacophonous social movement there were often discordant voices and, at the risk of oversimplification, there was at times a fundamental disconnect between the personal relationships and systems of reciprocity and obligation that tend to govern San organizations (their "traditional" politics) and the depersonalized forms of responsibility and accountability that underpinned the wider networks and structures of NGOs. In San activism, those organizations representing local interests and popular participation were often economically reliant on donor organizations, usually based in Europe or North America, which emphasized formal structures and rules of accountability as conditions of support and for which the struggles of the San were one cause (albeit in some cases a significant one) among others.

Botswana is recognized for the extraordinarily rapid development of civil society that occurred in the 1990s. This NGO boom is celebrated by Terrance and Barbara Carroll, who emphasize the "literally hundreds of functioning ... nongovernmental organizations (NGOs)" that emerged in a single decade, "most of which had regular direct or indirect interaction with the state" (Carroll and Carroll 2004: 334). In contrast to most African states, they argue, Botswana can be seen to have an active and influential civil society. It is worth noting, however, that many of the NGOs that feature in this optimistic assessment, particularly those that worked in and represented rural regions, might typically "consist of a founder, and handful of friends and enthusiasts and – if they have succeeded in getting funding from a foreign aid donor – an office and an employee" (Carroll and Carroll 2004: 349). Even though some NGOs are seen to be inclined toward minimal "capacity," there is a common thread of (sometimes undue) optimism in some of the literature on civil society in Botswana, which compares it favorably to that of other countries in Africa and which occasionally makes explanatory reference to the deliberative traditions of Tswana politics or to a "cultural predisposition toward consultations between state and society" based on a supposed Tswana tradition of consulting citizens on important decisions (Carroll and Carroll 2004: 345).

Dissenting from this optimism, Gulbrandsen (2012: 251) emphasizes the importance of recognizing "the extent to which these organizations have been captured into the state structures of control and surveillance." Taking note of the autocratic aspects of what Gulbrandsen refers to as Botswana's "authoritarian liberalism" leads us to qualify the "success story" narrative and to look at the often subtle (and occasionally not-so-subtle) means employed by the government by which the influence of NGOs is rendered politically neutral. As I note at several points throughout this book, the ethic of consultation is readily set aside when the government takes issue with points of public dissent and sometimes reacts in ways that are hostile, uncompromising, and at times explicitly repressive.

Focusing on the state's "capture" of grassroots initiatives or ways that political life is attenuated with reference to Euro-American political values and forms of organization, however, will lead one to overlook some of the key features of activism and political life in Botswana (as elsewhere). There has long been a variety of public spheres in Botswana, including voluntary associations, commercial interests and churches, which have cumulatively prevented the Tswana chiefdoms from securing a monopoly on power and political legitimacy. Deborah Durham extends this observation to certain informal political engagements, such as women's activities in arranging labor for funerals, forming purchasing associations for securing bulk cloth, and protecting their market activities at a busy train station. "It is simply false to assume, as is so often done," Durham writes, "that prior to the rise of ... Western-modeled women's rights groups ... local politics had been restricted to contests for male authority" (Durham 1999: 197). The point can, of course, be extended to our consideration of the contemporary qualities of NGO-based activism; moreover, in addition to the San's struggles with the structures of donors and the state, we should be alert to the political activism that takes place away from the precariousness of funding and infrastructure, that is to say, in the informal realm that NGOs produce through their sponsorship of ideas and relationships. In conditions in which it has acquired deep legitimacy, an NGO can exist with little more than a reputation, continuing to have influence beyond its apparent demise as an organization.

It is sometimes difficult to find the specific sources of the development of civil society in Africa, but in the case of the San NGO First People of the Kalahari (FPK), we can be reasonably sure that it is closely connected to the international movement of indigenous peoples, which I will discuss in more detail in Chapter 6. Augusto Willemsen Diaz, a UN diplomat who was active in the representation of indigenous peoples in international forums in the 1970s, advised all the indigenous leaders with whom he was in contact to form NGOs in order to meet the requirements of the UN on access to the meetings it sponsors (Minde 2008: 55). To achieve this NGO status, many nascent indigenous organizations reached out to donors and situated themselves in networks of activist organizations. The micro-politics of NGOs are thus embedded in larger contexts, and they depend on connections with national and transnational forces.

What are the consequences, intended and unintended, of an international agenda relating to the promotion of indigenous peoples' rights and the creation of civil society organizations? International donor organizations have selectively assisted certain groups, organizations, and causes, depending upon the utility of specific local issues for furthering their own wider agendas. On the one hand, they may offer local NGOs more autonomy and leverage in their struggles with national governments, while on the other hand they can expose those NGOs to risk and loss of autonomy, with direction and control taken over by dominant networks. The process of NGO-based activism also creates dependency on donors (including, on occasion, states), in which local NGOs become accountable more often toward funders than to the groups' grassroots constituencies. Their international connections often become a motive to question the local legitimacy and representativity of "grassroots" organizations.

In attempting to create a locally based organization, its organizers often have to conform to international models of development and accountability. Before it can come into existence, an organization has to create a board of trustees, have a constitution, develop a formal organizational structure, establish a bureaucratic apparatus, network with other organizations and donors, raise funds, and register with the state. For communities with limited budgets, training constraints, and sometimes a pool of nonliterate staff, these first steps can end up consuming most of the time, efforts, and budget of the organization. As we can see in the case of FPK, self-identified as the first indigenous NGO in Botswana, these steps are often only partially completed.

SAN NGOISM

The San of Botswana are in some ways a bellwether for NGO involvement in indigenous and minority issues in southern Africa. The list of organizations that have worked with them and on their behalf is astonishing in its length and variety, and includes the following (which I invoke at length to complete the picture): the International Work Group for Indigenous Affairs (IWGIA) (based in Denmark); Survival International (SI) (based in the United Kingdom); the Minority Rights Group (also based in the United Kingdom); Cultural Survival and First Peoples Worldwide (both based in United States); the Forest Peoples Programme (based in the United Kingdom, the Netherlands, Italy, and Spain); the Saami Council (based in Norway); the Indigenous Peoples of Africa Co-ordinating Committee (IPACC) (based in South Africa); the Open Society Initiative for Southern Africa (based in South Africa); Land is Life (based in the United States); Vox United (a water organization based in Michigan); Plenty Canada (based in Ontario); Permaculture (based in Australia, with a locally based satellite organization working with San and other rural peoples in Botswana), as well as several Botswana-based organizations such as the San Studies Centre at the University of Botswana; Reteng the Multicultural Coalition of Botswana; Ditshwanelo, the Botswana Centre of Human Rights; and the Botswana Council of Churches (BCC). The list could go on and on.

Various other San-related organizations were founded in the 1970s, 1980s, and 1990s, internationally, nationally, and regionally. These include the Kalahari Peoples Fund (KPF), founded in 1973 and based in Austin, Texas, which grew out of the Harvard Kalahari Research Project of the 1960s and early 1970s (Biesele 2006). In 1986 the Kuru Development Trust (KDT), a multipurpose development organization targeting San people, was established, with its main base at D'kar in the Ghanzi District (LeRoux 1996; Bollig et al. 2000). Also significant was a regional San advocacy organization, the Working Group of Indigenous Minorities in Southern Africa (WIMSA), later to play an important role in San litigation, with a WIMSA-Botswana office set up at D'Kar in the late 1990s. This list does not include the other San organizations in South Africa, Namibia, Zimbabwe, and the many community trusts.

To this panoply we can add several organizations created by and for the San, based on models provided by the organizations with which they were already working. The San Council (Khwedom Council), Teyamasi, Tane Ko Teemahane Women's Foundation in Khwai village, the San Youth Network, and FPK (of which I will have more to say later in this chapter) were all based on human rights activism, premised on local leadership and service to local constituencies.

Despite this impressive list, the actual *effects* of NGO advocacy – in terms of achieving their stated objectives – are relatively negligible, at least from the perspective of affecting the government's policy and politics toward the San. Many of the San organizations I have just listed have in recent years either folded and ceased to exist entirely or have pulled out and moved their operations elsewhere. Others continue to exist in a kind of limbo, with a mere business-card existence, mentioned occasionally as a source of professional identity but without funding, office space, or regular meetings. This leaves a number of organizations that continue to operate and new entities still occasionally coming into being, with important consequences overall for the lives of the San.

The great amount of international attention and NGO advocacy that the San have received calls for some explanation. In this regard, it is important to note that they are one of the most researched people in anthropology, popularized by the many nonfiction books and films produced since the 1950s.[2] Added to this is the significant scholarly interest in the San as hunter-gatherers.[3] The poor treatment of San and the human rights violations that they have had to cope with was another important reason that many scholars and NGOs paid attention to them, again contributing to raising their public profile.[4] Finally, the fact that the San have been one of the first African indigenous peoples to attend international meetings and to speak out about their issues and ask for support outside of Botswana made them politically visible on a global stage. In some cases, San have been portrayed as representatives of the archetypical other, those whose qualities are "good to think with." They also fit the discourse of the first peoples, those who are among the possible saviors of the future of the humanity by virtue of the extensive knowledge they possess that can be helpful in dealing with the challenges of climate change, environmental responsibility, and resource sharing – all qualities of indigenous peoples that have been central to the development of the NGO apparatus based on indigeneity.

All of these complexities of structure and representation can be seen in one example, FPK, on which I now want to elaborate. In doing so, I do not intend to present a historically balanced portrayal of NGO activism in Botswana. In particular, in relative terms I give short shrift to WIMSA, which was another regionally active NGO in its support of the Central Kalahari Game Reserve (CKGR) cause, including their preparation for litigation. My goal in focusing on FPK is to provide a more detailed portrait of a single NGO than could be achieved if I were to give each organization its due, and in the process to bring into relief the constraints and challenges of building an indigenous organization, as well as the social relationships (including their tensions) that are produced in the process. FPK perfectly captures the conundrums and opportunities facing justice claimants as they navigate the far-flung networks of NGOs. It will offer some insights into the ways that local causes can become translated and transformed into much wider networks and common interests – which, as we will see, also serve as the background for occasional conflicts and rivalries.

FIRST PEOPLE OF THE KALAHARI

In the late 1980s and early 1990s, San activists in Botswana began to speak out more forcefully about the need for greater recognition of their rights and their desire to participate as equal partners with state and regional institutions in decision-making that affected their lives.[5] Several events in 1992 brought the issues of indigenous rights in Botswana to the world's attention, including statements made by San delegates at national and international conferences, troubled (and troubling) meetings between San and government officials, and calls for San representation and rights made in the media and in discussions with a variety of organizations.[6] Roy Sesana's clear message during one of these meetings was, "We want back our land which has been taken and we want representatives at the House of Chiefs" (*Mmegi/the Reporter*, 1992).

D'kar was the main center of San advocacy in Botswana at this time (see Chapter 3, p. 101). Most of the San spokespersons and organizations such as Kuru Family of Organizations (KFO), WIMSA, Teyamasi, and FPK came out from discussions initiated in this small, heterogeneous village a short drive from the regional district headquarters of Ghanzi. There were several reasons for this. First, there was the presence of charismatic leaders, who emerged out of a formally educated cohort of people. The Dutch Reformed Church had long been involved there, starting in 1973 with the missionary couple, the Jerlings, who put in place a set of training and outreach programs that produced a formally educated base of former students. This put a distinctly religious stamp on the style of leadership that emerged, with those who were to become activists beginning their training by reading the Bible in church. This was fully consistent with the Christian ethic, where prayers are said at the beginning of public meetings and Christian discourse is publicly pervasive (Lawy 2016: 81). Through their participation in church activities, youth leaders were nurtured as those who could take on, and be recognized for, public speaking roles (Lawy 2016: 297). At the same time, the association with the church also divided San spokespersons, some of whom were very critical of those activists associated with churches, as a vestigial form of colonial domination.

The formally educated youth cohort, beginning with those who went to school in D'kar, was to play a significant role in the rise of San activism and in its ability to meet the sometimes complex demands of donor agency priorities and state regulations. The San have typically recognized leadership in terms of specific talents (Biesele and Hitchcock 2013), and in D'kar it was therefore fairly easy for educated youth to take on active roles in organizational activities, without having to accommodate an established, conservative leadership structure, even with the presence of the elders who usually sit on the boards of these organizations. This does not mean, however, that it was always easy for them to accept the legitimacy of a new youth leadership. Michael Taylor (1997: 61) emphasizes that this is a widespread phenomenon, and that there are often conflicts in the villages when the power of representativeness has been given to the youth: "There seems to be some resentment that this is given to 'boys' only because they have education. Perhaps this is a frustration with the wider system, that demands education in order to participate in formal political process."

The new leadership roles extended to women who had education and training and who were able to make significant contributions to the establishment and activities of NGOs, even though they still sometimes had to overcome assumptions from male colleagues about their role being limited to behind-the-scenes work. As educational opportunities increased, so did the numbers and presence of those who were prepared to take on active roles in NGOs. This rise of a formally educated cohort was later to become a notable aspect of NGO activism among the San. The link between formal education and activism is common to other cases, not only the church in D'kar, but in all circumstances in which activism was facilitated by schooling.

At the same time, some of these youth and their families were seeing and experiencing the sense of injustice from some of the Ghanzi farmers. The Naro people of the Ghanzi farms and surrounding areas, one of the largest San groups in the country, were heavily affected by the presence of the farms and by government policies that favored commercial livestock production over other kinds of activities such as small-scale economic enterprises and agriculture, in which many San wanted to make their own livelihoods. Some of the most outspoken people were children of San and European farmers, as was the case of the Hardbattle family.

The early phase of the San movement, of what we might call the institutionalization of the movement, reveals the extent to which the government was concerned about the development of civil society organizations and was willing to intervene in their efforts. State intervention in civil society first occurred in the origins of the KDT (later part of the KFO), originally founded in 1986 at D'Kar with the sponsorship of an independent Reformed Church council comprised largely of Naro San.[7] It described itself as a development organization, not an advocacy organization, intended for the benefit of the San and to have San on its board. Its establishment was obstructed when the government declared that Braam LeRoux, a British citizen who had spent twenty-seven years working on development initiatives in Botswana and South Africa, was declared a "prohibited immigrant." This was done in part because of Kuru's complaints about remote area farms that in 1991–2 were supposed to be set aside for Remote Area Dwellers (i.e. San) but were instead being taken over by high government officials (Chr. Michelsen Institute 1996: 31–2). Eventually, after the intervention of the South African, Danish, Dutch, and Norwegian governments, the Botswana government backed down and allowed LeRoux to stay in the country. With these events marking the organization's early years, some of Kuru's leadership cannot have had anything other than a wary, if not hostile, approach to the ruling elite of Botswana.

As with Kuru, the establishment of FPK received a jolt of indignation and unintended impetus from government opposition. When Komtsha Komtsha, John Hardbattle (whose biography I present in more detail below), and two other San travelled to Gaborone in May 1992 to meet with then MLGLH Permanent Secretary Pelonomi Binns (now Pelonomi Venson-Moitoi) to discuss issues of San leadership, they were greeted with a phalanx of officials, including two assistant ministers, the Member of Parliament for Ghanzi, three councilors from the district, and others. There were immediate clashes over issues such as the San representatives wanting the meeting to be conducted in English, a national language, rather than, as the government officials were insisting, Setswana, in which John Hardbattle was not fluent. After a short recess to assess their position, the San delegation handed the officials a statement that they had previously prepared, expressing the desire of their people to have political autonomy and recognition of the issues surrounding representation in the Botswana Parliament and House of Chiefs. The statement was rejected. Some government officials claimed that the San were attempting to obtain self-determination (expressed in terms of "self-rule") and that they were seeking to secede from Botswana (Reporter *Daily News* 1992). Pelenome Binns was reported in the media as saying, "[the Basarwa] will never be allowed to walk around in skins again" (Reporter *The Gazette* 1992).

As Hardbattle later recalled, "It seemed that all they wanted was to find out which foreign agencies had put these wild ideas into the heads of the N/oakwe [San]." One of the assistant ministers remarked, "You think that these outsiders will always help you (meaning the donor agencies), well, one of these days they will be gone and there will only be us, and we own you and we will own you till the end of time and you will not achieve what you want" (Hardbattle 1993a: 143). Hardbattle remembered this encounter with bitterness, noting that, "many among the elite today still consider [the San] no more than serfs since they 'inherited' them from their forefathers" (Hardbattle 1993a: 145). At this time, under the impulse of this meeting in which "all went sadly wrong," the San leadership felt more strongly than ever the need to create an indigenous organization with real political influence.

The coalition of San leaders wrote a letter to the MLGLH presenting themselves as *kgeikani kweni*, the first people of the Kalahari, and asking the government "to acknowledge us as one people, recognizing the diversity in terms of language and territorial ownership." They proposed an initiative "to set up a national council and ask Government to recognize this council as a legitimate negotiating partner" (cited in Saugestad 2001: 178–9). This manifesto made explicit the San's problems of invisibility, marginality, and lack of recognition as "one people" with their own legitimate leaders, way of life, and culture. To this impassioned statement, the deputy minister replied curtly, "there would never be a Basarwa [San] Council" (*Botswana Gazette* June 3, 1992).

Despite (or perhaps because of) resistance from some officials, the idea of a new organization began to take hold. But responding to injustice through the creation of an indigenous NGO was not easy. As a first step, the organization had to be registered with the state, following the bureaucratic pathways of approval required of all NGOs. The state closely monitors NGOs, which can operate only on the condition that they have been given a permit and registered in accordance with the *Societies Act* of 1972 (Guldbrandsen 2012: 221). Once an organization has been named and registered, indigenous rights activists are, through the requirements set out by the state, formally initiated to the bureaucratic and administrative field of the NGO. Activism thus becomes bureaucratized, moved in the direction of formal structures, methods of work, and expertise.

Some of this formalization can certainly be seen in FPK. It was registered officially with the Botswana government on October 11, 1993. Some of its founding members had previous (and ongoing) experience with Kuru.[8] It had a constitution, a deed of trust, and a board. It opened an office in Ghanzi in April 1994. There were several difficulties the organizers faced right away in trying to get the new NGO accredited. It was registered as a charitable organization under the guidelines of the Botswana government. For some time the organization was considered a sub-partner of KDT. The original application for NGO status as a San organization was turned down because the Botswana government would not allow the formation of an ethnically based NGO. For this reason, FPK in its Constitution (1993) states that it is an "advocacy organization working with the Ncoakwe (San)," but its members could be any citizen of Botswana. In practice, however, it positioned itself as a "San indigenous-run-organization" and representative of the San people. During the CKGR court cases, the organization expanded its mandate to include the Bakgalagadi people living in the reserve, creating a coalition that brought together people from different backgrounds under the category "indigenous peoples." It was one of a number of indigenous and minority organizations in Botswana and was the most vocal about the rights of indigenous peoples. Unlike KDT, whose board was composed primarily of Naro San, FPK drew board members from several San groups, including G/ui, G//ana, Tsila, and Ju/'hoansi. This diversity was important because it gave the organization links to a broad set of San communities in Botswana. At the same time, because of this broad spectrum of representation, the organization was faced with problems of legitimacy, with a membership that was not known to its various communities of constituents. What is more, in order to function and be seen as accountable and representative, the organization had to have its board meet periodically. This was made difficult by the fact that the board members were scattered across Botswana, and when funds eventually became short they were unable to travel and assemble.

FPK began modestly. Early support was provided by small grants from individual donors (e.g. from the academic community in the Harvard Kalahari Research Group and its KPF), but the bulk of its funds were channeled through Kuru because FPK did not have a bank account. Even though there were obstacles to its formal organization, the San leadership was still able to use FPK as a gathering point for mobilization. When the Second Regional Conference on San Peoples was held in Gaborone in October 1993, FPK emerged as a major player, showing itself to be an effective advocacy organization that brought people together and that was representative of the San people of Botswana.[9] The main aim of the San attending this meeting was the "right to the land" on the basis of priority, which implies freedom of access to resources such as wildlife and wild plants and land restitution (Saugestad 2001: 89–91). Another important goal was the right to speak to the government and to represent themselves as a distinct people.

It was from this beginning that FPK began its work of San advocacy. We can now turn our attention to those individuals who were most visibly influential in the struggle for rights in the CKGR and the relocation villages, and who together embody the transitions in leadership (while emphasizing that they are "followers" of their people) from informal reliance on exemplary individuals toward formal structure and internationalism. Here I concentrate my analysis on three people who have arguably had the most publicly prominent roles in the FPK and indigenous politics at several levels of governance, and who were particularly significant in the activist movement that I discuss in the next chapters.

INDIGENOUS SPOKESPERSONS

The struggle for the rights of the San, and in particular the people of the CKGR, was given impetus through the activity of a small number of significant public personalities, three of whom I briefly introduce here. These are people who were able to perform the delicate double task of communicating with their constituency through local knowledge and effectively representing the San cause and its place in a wider sense of the "indigenous" to sympathetic observers. Their basic common talent, expressed in their own idiosyncratic ways, was to embody what it was to be San and at the same time to "mediate" (in part through media) the injustice experienced by the San to wider public audiences.

John Hardbattle, Roy Sesana, and Jumanda Gakelebone had each personally experienced the discrimination, assaults to dignity, and denial of rights and distinct cultural identity that the San as whole had suffered. They incorporated different forms of indigeneity, and they exemplified the complexities, ambiguities, and dissimilarities of San identities. Like all prominent indigenous spokespersons, their personalities and public activities came under close scrutiny, becoming the focus of debate and controversy. All three were effective brokers, expanding the networks and strategies of advocacy and conceptual translation. Over time they became symbolic individuals, representing the San movement as a whole and the San's resistance to the Botswana government's decisions and policies in particular. John Hardbattle, the visionary original founder of FPK, was considered an individual of "two worlds," growing up as San but receiving a British education and serving in the British military. Roy Sesana was a "realist" who had the constraint of not being able to speak English but who nevertheless represented the grassroots indigenous face of the movement, having been born and raised in the CKGR. Sesana also had extensive experience abroad, including working on a tobacco farm in what was then Southern Rhodesia and in the mines of South Africa. Jumanda Gakelebone, who was much younger than his two mentors, was born in the Central Kalahari, attended boarding school and received a formal education in Ghanzi and in Kweneng districts that allowed him to move easily in national and international contexts.

Hardbattle, Sesana, and Gakelebone were the main public faces of FPK over time. Yet the stereotypical expectations of activist leadership went against their own understanding of their roles, as expressed by Gakelebone, who once told me that they are "not leaders, because they do not take decisions for their people, but they follow what people ask them to do" (author notes 2015). Robert Hitchcock, an anthropologist who was closely involved in the activities of FPK, spoke about the question of leadership among the San in an interview with the *Washington Post*: "People who are the most powerful in that culture are the most generous and the quiet ones, not the bombastic ones." Then, referring to John Hardbattle as FPK leader, he added, "He is the first among equals" (Boustany 1995).

I never met Hardbattle before his death in 1996, and have based what I say here on his own written statements, newspaper coverage, and what others have told me about him. I was, however, fortunate enough to be able to follow Roy Sesana and Jumanda Gakelebone in different settings, from their home villages to Ghanzi Council meetings, from the High Court of Botswana to offices in the capital of the country, and in international NGO and UN meetings. It became clear to me over the years that their roles and images changed over time, especially as they became more influential and increasingly involved in national and local-level politics.

John Hardbattle

John Hardbattle, like many other indigenous leaders, was a man with a very atypical past: son of a Naro woman or, as he put it, "of a stolen child," and a Scotsman who, after being a policeman in South Africa, moved to Ghanzi and built a farm. He usually expressed his complex mixed ancestry in simple terms: "I am one-quarter Naro – the rest of me is white, I guess. I grew up as a Bushman until I went to school" (Hardbattle 1993b: 1). He spent his first sixteen years in

Ghanzi, on the family farm, where he was educated by his mother. Being part of the Ghanzi farms, which were often associated with a powerful minority, did not protect him from experiences of racism or prevent him from acquiring a strong sense of San identity. He explained one of his formative childhood experiences to a reporter from *The Guardian* as follows: "I remember as a child running away from an anthropologist who came from Wits University (Johannesburg) to measure me and look at me because they could not believe that white people, 'real people', could breed with the Bushmen" (Taylor 1996).

In 1959, Hardbattle was sent to England to attend school, and remained there until 1972. Afterwards he joined NATO forces, taking part in activities in Germany. He returned to Botswana in 1975, where he resumed working on his family farm, and where, as he put it, he "started to become a farmer really" (Hardbattle 1993b: 2). He returned at a critical time. The government was opening up land that had previously been occupied by the San for commercial cattle ranching (under the Tribal Grazing Land Policy, see Chapter 3), and settlements were also being created by the government to resolve the "Bushmen problem," transforming semi-nomadic peoples into sedentary groups, often classified as "squatters."

Hardbattle spent a major portion of his life fighting for the rights of the San, some of this through FPK. He developed local and global alliances with NGOs, anthropologists, politicians, foundations, international institutions, and other indigenous leaders to fight for the respect and rights of the San. He created ties with international NGOs such as the First Nations Development Institute (FNDI)/First Peoples Worldwide (FPW), IWGIA, and KPF.

In 1992 Hardbattle was asked by Komtsha Komtsha[10] and several other San to set up an organization to address human rights violations. He described the birth of FPK as follows:

> After the greetings and the drinking of tea, Komtsha Komtsha said: "John, we have come to ask you a question. You are the son of the N/oakwe so perhaps you can answer this question. Whose land is this?" I [Hardbattle] replied, "This land is the land of the N/oakwe." And then he asked me, "And Ghanzi, whose land is that?" And I replied: "Ghanzi belongs to the Nharo for they have never sold it. Just as the deep sand places belong to the G/wikwe for they too have never sold it." "That is what we wanted to hear" he said. "Will you show us the path and will you open doors for us so our voices can be heard?" And I said, "Yes."

> And he said, "That is all right then." And that was how it started for us. (Hardbattle 1994: 6)

Hardbattle used the same storytelling language to describe how in this organizational meeting he was prompted to look for "someone who could talk," and was pointed in the direction of Roy Sesana. The path was thus shown and the doors opened to two men who were to became key players in an internationally prominent indigenous rights cause.

One of the most important reasons Hardbattle was chosen to be a spokesperson was that he was seen as being on the border between "two worlds," the "San and the Whites." This characteristic is common to many indigenous leaders, who must have the talent to make their discourses recognizable and their voices heard in a dominant and unequal context. In Hardbattle's words,

> As they [San] told me, I can sit at the fire of my mother's people and get up and sit at the table of my father's people, since *I am a man of two worlds .... I am not promoting myself as a leader*. It is not like here when you tell people vote for me and I will set you free. It is more complicated. What has happened to our culture? Now they can give them food, and when they take it away, our people have nothing. What else can they do to our people? Just put a gun to their heads. ... This is my mission, my whole life. It is all that I have known, all that I believe in. If I have any ambition, it is that my people should live. (Cited in Boustany 1995, emphasis added)

With regard to the San who lived on the farms and those living in the bush, Hardbattle once remarked, "Although my own immediate family on the N/oakhwe side had dresses and shirts and stuff, they were *real Bushmen* as we can say, because they hunted. There was no restriction on hunting in my dad's land" (Hardbattle 1993b: 2). It is clear from these words that hunting and gathering is a key aspect of San identity. This ethic of closeness to the natural world was something Hardbattle was able to convey effectively to the press, as in a 1995 article based on an interview by Nora Boustany: "He [Hardbattle] has *always* lived at one with *nature*. He climbed trees before he learned to walk, and ate resin from their trunks in time of drought." The image presented here fits completely with the ideal of the "indigenous," representing the people who belong to the world of nature. This representation was not without its flaws, however. Saugestad (2001: 196) reports that when Hardbattle's image was on the front page of the *Washington Post*, he was criticized because he did not look like an "authentic Bushman," and

Botswana government spokespersons questioned his ability to represent the San.

Even if he sometimes unavoidably tapped into popular ideas of the savage hunter, Hardbattle had a much wider agenda, which also occasionally made its appearance in the press. In an article in *The Guardian*, Michael Taylor (1996) reported Hardbattle's response to being asked what he would like to say to the president of Botswana: "I would ask him to give the Khwe people the respect that they deserve. Respect is the (basic) thing Khwe people feel they are not getting as citizens of the country." This was the essence of the agenda to change the San's relationship with the state.

Hardbattle and Sesana attended a number of international meetings together, including one in 1994 of the UN Working Group on Indigenous Populations in Geneva. On February 20, 1996, Hardbattle and FPK received a request from Roy Sesana for assistance and legal representation to stop the removal of people from the CKGR (Hardbattle, 1996). In March 1996, they went together to visit the Human Rights Commission in Geneva. At these meetings the two men spoke out forcefully on the need for Botswana to recognize the rights and identity of the San. They stressed the importance of their ancestral territories, the wide-ranging roles of wild plants and animals, the value of reciprocity and sharing to San peoples, and the crucial significance of San custom and tradition. Hardbattle spoke about "culture," "tradition," "indigenous identity," the "egalitarianism of hunter-gatherer society," and "rights," borrowing anthropological and legal categories and repurposing them as "authentically" indigenous and local. They based some of their statements on research that had been conducted mainly by anthropologists and geographers, over several decades in the Central Kalahari, and some on their own interviews and discussions with residents of the region. (Hardbattle often remarked on the importance of research as a means of providing the basic data upon which development initiatives and land claim efforts could be based [Hardbattle 1996].) This illustrates how indigeneity is formed out of ideas intended for export, a globalized discourse, in which spokespeople fit their people's experience into values and conceptions of human difference that are recognizable to their audience.

Alongside these experiences in international meetings, their priorities were sometimes taken on tour, in what might be seen as organized campaigns of public outreach. In June 1996, John Hardbattle, Aron Johannes, and Mathambo Ngakaeaja visited the United States (including Alaska) and Canada (where they met representatives of the NGO Plenty Canada). The visit was sponsored by FNDI of Fredericksburg, Virginia. Hardbattle's visit coincided with an official visit of the president of Botswana, Quett Masire, at the Botswana Embassy in Washington DC. Hardbattle took this opportunity to directly address the president, saying that greater attention should be paid to the Bushmen's rights and especially the rights of the CKGR people. The fact that he addressed the president abroad instead of trying to meet with him at home was much criticized in Botswana, but should be seen in light of the many aborted attempts the San had made to engage in a dialogue with the government and with the president. It is very often the case that marginalized groups have better access to their national representatives abroad than in their own countries.

John Hardbattle died of cancer on November 12, 1996. San across the country mourned his passing. He had laid the foundations for the Bushmen's continuing political struggles. His loss was not the only one suffered by the San in the early years of their movement. Since it began in 1993, FPK has lost five of its founding members (including Komtsha, Hardbattle's uncle, who died only a few weeks before he did), leaving Roy Sesana as the central spokesperson from the older generation of FPK activists to represent the cause.

Roy Sesana

Roy Sesana has been discussed more than any other figure in the context of the San's pursuit of justice. He is a G//ana San who was born just before World War II in the Molapo area in what is now the northeast part of the CKGR. His name in G//ana is Tobee Tcori, which means "peeling off hair." In public meetings Roy often wears a headdress consisting of ostrich eggshell beads and a portion of the head of a steenbok (*Raphicerus campestres*) with a pair of horns, and a jacket also made of steenbok skins with ostrich eggshell ornaments. His clothing choices have changed over time. When he appeared in court he wore "traditional" ornaments. When he appeared before political bodies such as the Botswana National Front, he often wore a suit. As he explained to me, "When I wear the antelope horns, it helps me talk to my ancestors and they help me. They represent my tradition, people, and ancestors" (September 2006, Lobatse). Unlike other groups, hunter-gatherer groups often do not have an easily recognizable "traditional dress" (see Hodgson 2011). Sesana thus "invented" a mode of attire to provide a striking and visible affirmation of his identity.

As a young man, Sesana spent some time outside of Botswana, working in the mines of South Africa and on a tobacco farm in Zimbabwe. Later, as a representative of the San he made a number of trips to Europe, the United States, and Canada, trying to stop the Botswana government from evicting his people from their land. In the United Kingdom he met with members of Parliament and with Prince Charles; in the United States he met with diplomats and members of Congress; and in Brussels and Vienna he met with members of the European Parliament and UN officials.

Sesana personally experienced the government's violence toward the San and Bakgalagadi and the effects of the relocation, with the deaths of several relatives, including his brother, Mathambo, the headman of Molapo and a member of WIMSA, who died after being tortured by Department of Wildlife and National Parks officials in 2000 (Gall 2001).

Another death as a result of torture by wildlife officers was that of Roy's nephew Gaolikwe Kilo, who died from beatings and torture he received in custody in 1993 (Kiema 2010: 45; Gall 2001: 194–5). No efforts were made to follow up on this or the other deaths allegedly resulting from torture by government officials (Kiema 2010: 45, 47). This event was formative in Sesana's career, helping to explain the determination with which he struggled for the his people's rights

In an interview with the *Mmegi/The Reporter*, Sesana, speaking about his right to be in the CKGR and his resistance to being relocated, repeated something he had also said to me:

> I told him [the President of Botswana] that our creator gave us this place [CKGR] and that the lion and I are brothers and I am confused that I should have to leave this place and my brother the lion can stay. How can it be that the lion has more security than we do? ... They say that we will be moved to live in the settlement but the life in those places has turned our people into thieves and beggars and drunkards. I do not want to live this life. First they make us destitute and then they say we are nothing because we are destitute. Where I am I have the seasons, the game, the earth – no matter what day of the year it is I know where to go to find food.[11]

Whereas Hardbattle was able to express the hunting ethics of the San by effectively using key concepts, Sesana had the rare gift of capturing this ethic in poetic words that even in translation lost little of their power to evoke the perceptions of the people of the Kalahari.

In spite of his efforts, Sesana's family was evicted from their homes and land in 2002 while he was "in Ghanzi campaigning in support of my people" (2006). Three years later, he was arrested with twenty-eight others as they attempted to enter the reserve with food and water for members of their families, who were desperate after having been prevented from hunting and gathering by the police and game scouts. He and the others were imprisoned for four days. Sesana sang loudly while he was beaten by the police, so that others could hear. When he was thrown to the ground and had his face rubbed in the sand, he said, laughing and singing, "This is my land, you give me my land" (author notes 2013). Just days after his release, he discovered that he and his organization FPK had been awarded the Right Livelihood Award, touted by some as the "Alternative Nobel Prize." The award statement acknowledged Sesana "for resolute resistance against eviction from their ancestral lands, and for upholding the right to their traditional way of life."[12]

A short while later, when I first interviewed him, Sesana elaborated on his people's connection to the land, which he had famously expressed under torture, explaining to me what he meant when he claimed to be indigenous:

> We are different from the others, we have a different culture. We have the knowledge of the land and we live in the land, we occupy it. We are as Adam and Eve, the first on this land. ... The land is our Eden. The land is important. It defines our identity. Through the land you know where you are from. We know our land. We were born in this land as our parents and our ancestors. They have taught us how to live in this land. We know what to do. The relationship with the land allows us to practice our culture and makes us what we are. The land is our mother, it is our breast-feeding, it gives us food. If we can live in our land, hunt there, make her offers, respect her, we are happy and healthy because we have everything. (Author notes, Lobatse 2006)

Roy Sesana was a key figure in the trial that was given his name as first applicant (*Sesana and Others v. the Attorney General*, 2004–6) and the negotiations with the government preceding and succeeding them (which I discuss further in Chapters 6 and 7). Although he was the first applicant, he was not called as a witness during the trial. He did, however, provide considerable advice to the lawyers and also made statements in public outside the court (some of which, as we will see in Chapter 6, were viewed unfavorably by the judges of the High Court). He was at the same time the public face of SI and its campaign efforts on behalf of the San. In this capacity he eventually combined deep local knowledge of the people of the Central Kalahari and a sophisticated understanding of the power of public outreach to global audiences.

Saugestad (2011: 48) describes Sesana as a "classical trickster," a "figure that is the embodiment of ambiguity and moral ambivalence."[13] In keeping with this observation, there are differing views on Sesana at the local and national levels (see, for example, Kiema 2010: 96–8). Some felt, possibly enviously, that he become "too proud of himself" because of his role in the CKGR struggle, in FPK, and because of his receipt of the Right Livelihood Award. Others felt that he had done a tremendous service for his community of Molapo, for the people of the Central Kalahari, and for the San in general. In the simple words of a representative of Teyamase, a San organization based in D'Kar: "I support Roy Sesana because he is one of the few that speak out for the San people. He is not afraid and I respect him" (author notes, D'Kar 2011). Sesana's role in FPK has been questioned, as has his involvement in the CKGR negotiating team. His commitments were seen by some as being too narrowly focused on the CKGR. His participation in the negotiations with the government that followed the first court case was also called into question, not so much with reference to his personal capacities but by questioning the utility of negotiating with a government that, as his critics saw it, could not be trusted (Chapters 8, p. 321–23). He often responded to this kind of criticism by saying that his struggle for the rights of the CKGR people and for San in general has been part of a broad-based effort, and that he was part of a large group of individuals and organizations that sought to enhance the rights of the peoples of Botswana (author notes 2011).

When I visited him in New Xade in 2015, he and his wife introduced me to their newborn daughter Xg//oakgo, whose name roughly translates as "I am taking her back," a reference to the family's commitment to tradition and their ultimate goal of returning to the land. He told me, "We usually give a newborn a name related to something important that is happening." The name expressed nostalgia not only for the life on the land, but his role in the struggle in its defense.

Jumanda Gakelebone

Jumanda Gakelebone (X/laebor, meaning "the reporter") can be situated somewhere between the San elders of Sesana's generation and the younger generation of college-educated San leaders. He has had the benefit of a wide-ranging formal and informal education, and is equally competent in making arrow poison and using a smart phone and social media. As a child, he closely followed the examples of his elders and learned the hunting way of life, including its hardships. I had known him for several years before he began to open up tell me stories about his childhood, including his terrifying and heartbreaking experience of losing a brother to the bite of a black mamba. He was out on a trail in the reserve with his brother and a group of friends when the snake suddenly leapt out of the bushes, sinking its fangs into his brother's ribs and killing him within minutes. He and his friends brought the body home on a mule.

Gakelebone is one of the few of his generation in the CKGR who completed school and can speak and write fluent English, Setswana, and several San languages. He was born in 1974 in Menoautse in the Central Kalahari, the son of a Mokgalagadi man and a San woman, and spent much of his early life in Metseamonong. He attended primary school in Ghanzi and in 1993 went to Molepolole to attend Kgari Sechele secondary school. In 1997 he decided to become a policeman and went to the Botswana Police College, but soon quit when he took on the role of an activist, working in support of the people in the CKGR. He also received additional training as, for example, a tourist guide through the Department of Wildlife and National Parks. Gakelebone was interested in the activities of FPK from the time of the creation of the organization. He had many discussions with John Hardbattle, Roy Sesana, and other members of the organization, who "told me the organization's goals, and I was impressed with what I heard." In 1998, when he returned to Ghanzi, he joined FPK officially, becoming a "community mobilizer." He had all the right connections for taking this step: Gakelebone's father had been a member of the FPK board, later also the councilor of New Xade, and Roy Sesana is, as he put it, "my uncle from my mother's side."

Gakelebone's formal education helped his work as a representative and activist for the San movement locally and internationally. He explained his decision to work for FPK as follows:

> When I went outside [the CKGR], to the school in Ghanzi, we [San] were treated in a bad way. I studied the industrial revolution, and I compared this situation with our land dispossession. We have been dispossessed, our land taken away. I wanted to understand why we were treated so bad. I read books, I spoke with my grandfather and they said we are the first, from the beginning. We are from this land and we have to protect it; we have the right to live in this land, it is our mother. I have decided to do this for my people, my parents, my son. (Author notes Ghanzi, 2006)

He thus compares the injustice his people experienced with the dispossession inherent in the division of the commons during the industrial revolution. This is a different language of activism, one that reflects his combination of bush experience and formal education.

When it comes to the language of indigeneity, however, Gakelebone is consistent with others, not only among the San but in the global movement of indigenous peoples. For example, he explained the name "First People of the Kalahari" to me as follows: "Batswana says that all people are the same, that there is only one culture, the Tswana. But the San are different. ... We call ourselves *Kgeikani Kweni* because it shows *we are the first to be there*" (author notes, Ghanzi 2006). His activism is thus premised on (and motivated by) a conception of his people's priority of occupation in their territory and on the distinctiveness – and distinct rights – that follow from that priority.

Throughout his career as an activist, Gakelebone has worked effectively with a wide network of friends and allies. In the 1990s he participated in the ethnocartographic mapping of the CKGR with Arthur Albertson, a consultant and, later, expert witness in the *Sesana* case. He also assisted the lawyers in the preparation of the data for several court cases, gathered applicants' signatures, and served as interpreter between the lawyers and the San and Bakgalagadi during the court cases.

Gakelebone was living in Ghanzi in the early part of the new millennium. Part of his family now lives in New Xade after their relocation, and some returned to the CKGR after the 2006 High Court verdict. His family was relocated from Xade in 1997, but he was already outside the reserve at that time so he was never directly subjected to the forced displacement, and he was not among the applicants in the 2004 court case. (Nevertheless, his grandmother had been taken to Kaudwane, while her two daughters were taken to New Xade in 1997. They were not consulted, and the resettlement split up their family.) Years later, however, he was added to the list of applicants who could enter the reserve without a government permit. This occurred following his arrest for "illegal" entry into the reserve in 2011 while accompanying the lawyer Gordon Bennett. Government officials told him that he was supposed to pay US$ 692.00 (5,000 pula) or go to prison for five years. After a long argument with the wildlife officials and police prosecutors in Ghanzi, during which he affirmed his right to belong to the territory inside the reserve from which he was "never relocated," he was added as an applicant and as a resident of the reserve, probably as a way to avoid the publicity that would inevitably follow from prosecuting him. The rationale behind this step still remains mysterious; as he put it with a shrug of his shoulders, "I don't really know how."

Gakelebone experienced the marginalization and mistreatment that are features of life in the San villages, from his childhood to the time that he was in school, to his activities as an adult and as a member of FPK, and through the stories his grandfather told him. During one phase of his youth and activist activity, particularly in the years of the *Sesana* case, he often received anonymous death threats, experienced several home invasions, and developed concerns about witchcraft. This variety of stresses eventually manifested themselves in bouts of alcohol abuse, which became particularly critical during the time of the court case. He was able to quit, along with a turn to Christianity, when he saw how much his drinking was limiting his activity as an activist, particularly because his opponents used it to call his leadership into question.

Despite these personal struggles, Gakelebone acquired a solid understanding of the most effective political and legal strategies. Because of his association with FPK and the documentation of the applicants for the affidavit of the court case, as well as his involvement in demonstrations, meetings, and workshops on the CKGR and on wider issues affecting the San, he is now widely recognized as an indigenous spokesperson, even though some persist in questioning his leadership, focusing on doubts that remained in their minds from his younger days.

Gakelebone's main tool throughout his lobbying and political activity has been the media. Over the years he has written numerous letters to local and international newspapers to describe the situations his people have been facing and to clarify FPK's positions regarding government decisions. He also enters media discussions indirectly, in part by serving as a guide to the CKGR for a global network of journalists, diplomats, NGO representatives, UN experts, and anthropologists (myself included) who visit the region. He has met with government representatives and opposition political parties, and discussed the situation of the CKGR inhabitants with them, eventually inspiring him to publically join the Botswana National Front in 2013. He followed Sesana in many of his activities abroad, helping him in the delivery of his statements, translating them from G//ana to English, making familiar the words and concepts of NGO activism and global governance that are difficult to understand and almost impossible to translate. He has travelled to England, Norway, Italy, Switzerland, Germany, Sweden, Canada, and the United States to meet with members of international organizations, other indigenous leaders, and government and UN representatives, and he has attended a number of international meetings.

Despite the controversy (which I discuss below) that has followed him, he has also been one of the main local contacts with SI, an NGO that makes use of controversial, combative strategies of global "consciousness-raising." Because of this, he has often had to respond to attempts to delegitimize his work by those who accuse him of representing SI interests rather than those of the San:

> People accuse SI of everything. They do not ask why it acts, intervenes. SI has a mandate from the people of the CKGR. Government and many Batswana think that we cannot think or speak for ourselves. But like the three chiefs who went to Britain in the 1890s, we have spoken out. We speak out by ourselves. (Author notes, CKGR 2011)[14]

Gakelebone can also be seen as replying here to those who try to silence or discredit him by attributing his remarks to an outside organization that lacks legitimacy in Botswana.

Having followed his career as an activist for many years, I have witnessed several transformations in his status and the strategies he has employed in the San struggle. The first was acquiring a separate political identity from that of his mentor, Roy Sesana, even though they continue to collaborate. I also observed over the years the passage he underwent from "radical" and confrontational activism to a more "diplomatic" approach in which he engages directly with the government through political dialogue and involvement in opposition parties, leading to his election as a councilor for New Xade in 2014 (Chapter 8). Through these personal transformations, however, his values have remained constant. He has turned down offers of government employment that he saw as attempts to "shut my mouth" and has always been oriented toward the promotion of human rights, the importance of the land and of hunting and gathering to San identity, and of the recognition of the San as an indigenous people.

John Hardbattle, Roy Sesana, and Jumanda Gakelebone are good examples of "globalized" indigenous spokespeople and activists. They have all been engaged in the political struggle for self-determination at the international, national, and local levels. They have had a clear sense of the importance of stressing the San indigenous identity. They have all been involved in peaceful social and political mobilization. They are seen by many of their people as well as international agencies as playing key roles in the efforts to promote the rights and wellbeing of San peoples. They attended international UN meetings and conferences, written position papers, given presentations, taken interested parties into the Central Kalahari, and sought funds to help the people of the CKGR. Each of them witnessed and learned about the larger patterns of structural similarities between their situations and those of the Saami, Australian Aboriginals, Native Americans, and other indigenous groups. They also gained a better understanding of the range of relationships between indigenous peoples and national governments, and the kinds of rights (principally human rights) that indigenous peoples should have. In part through this experience and their ability to communicate it to donors and to national and international supporters, they were able to obtain resources to support FPK activities, at least initially. Sesana and Gakelebone have also worked closely (some would say too closely, as we will shortly see) with international organizations like SI. All three men worked with anthropologists, development workers, and lawyers. And although from different backgrounds, they each came to the conclusion that they had to use state institutions – notably, the courts – and international connections to achieve their objectives.

INSTITUTIONALIZATION AND DIVERGENCES

With FPK established as an idea among a core group of like-minded activists, next came the phase of establishing a formal organization. One challenge faced by many organizations, from which FPK was initially spared, was that of funding. In its search for international donor funding it was at the outset supported with funds and technical assistance by the IWGIA, starting in 1993 with a seed grant of 30,000 DKK (approximately US $5,000) (Dahl 2009: 133–9). Soon after that, and for its first eleven years of existence, FPK received substantial funding from IWGIA and other donors such as the Open Society Institute (George Soros Foundation), KPF, First Peoples Worldwide, the Saami Council, SI, and influential individuals such as Prince Charles, Sir Laurens van der Post, and the Danish writer and filmmaker Jens Bjerre.

IWGIA was actively involved in "exporting" indigenous peoples' rights to Africa and, as part of this goal, in the promotion and protection of San rights, including through the development of FPK. The first major IWGIA project grant in the mid-1990s ("First People of the Kalahari: Creation of the First Bushman or N/oawke Organisation" was for 2,334,502 DKK (approximately US $400,000 at the time). The main objective of the project was, as the donor put it, "to establish a logistic frame and to build up FPK's institutional capacity in order to enable the organization to carry on with its awareness-raising program, organize the Khwe people [San], and link up internationally with other indigenous peoples to exchange information and share experiences" (IWGIA 2000: 15). This was to be accomplished through "capacity-building" and "human resource development."

For a people with little experience using the tools of bureaucracy, however, the skills and practices associated with administering a formal organization were difficult to put into practice. This difficulty was characterized by one director of an international NGO, in an email correspondence that went the rounds of the San-supporting community, as "time wasting" efforts to transform "Bushmen into bureaucrats." There was an unwanted emphasis on auditing, meetings, accounting, reporting, and documentation. Members with whom I spoke said they preferred to be indigenously controlled, and they considered IWGIA's legitimate role to be solely as a provider of funds and infrastructural support. Any other role for IWGIA was often understood as unwanted interference in FPK affairs. Many people on the board preferred to focus on limited objectives, addressing the challenges present in their own villages, lobbying, creating awareness of human rights issues relating to the San, rather than long-range goals that overlapped with such government responsibilities as poverty reduction and AIDS intervention.

This sense of autonomy was not only expressed in words, but occasionally in actions (and omissions) that brought the organization into direct tension with their supporters. In ways reminiscent of the concept of "ordinary resistance" (Scott 1985), there were numerous instances in which FPK staff members made decisions about hiring of staff (e.g. the hiring of a coordinator), financial expenditures (for example, on daily allowances), trips and activities undertaken with project vehicles, and the purchase of materials for the office without the permission or approval of IWGIA. There were problems with lack of keeping receipts and of failure to provide reports to the supporters, including an absence of logbooks on their vehicle, which was allegedly being used as a source of transport for friends and family of staff members (IWGIA internal reports 1998, 1999, 2000). In somewhat essentialistic terms, the ethics of sharing and redistribution that prevail in a hunting society came into conflict with the ethics of bureaucratic accountability.

IWGIA, in turn, was being pushed hard by *its* donor, such as the Danish International Development Agency (DANIDA), to institute reform of the organization. Requests were made to FPK to change its office management systems, but with little effect. In its attempt to improve the organization's institutional capacity, IWGIA carried out numerous monitoring visits to Botswana (without charging either FPK or DANIDA for the airfares, hotels, per diems, or vehicle rentals needed to undertake field visits to Ghanzi and to the Central Kalahari). In addition, in an attempt to gain greater administrative control, especially over the management of the budget, IWGIA appointed a temporary outside advisor, a social anthropologist from the University of Copenhagen, to work closely with FPK staff (this was particularly because FPK staff and board did not want other, non-San Botswana groups having decision-making positions in the organization, fearing that they would then take over the leadership and redefine its priorities). This was an unprecedented step for IWGIA, which as an organization preferred to have local staff in the indigenous NGOs that it supported. However, after some work on Central Kalahari mapping and documentation, the advisor had to leave his position in FPK because of dissatisfaction among some members over having an "expat" in a managing position.

Why was FPK not more responsive to the donors' insistence on the mechanisms of accountability? There were several reasons. At the most basic level, there was an issue of "capacity" – some of the members of the board and staff of FPK were nonliterate. Because of this, there was a lack of institutional responsiveness to the functional requirements of bureaucracy. This had consequences for the day-to-day administration of the organization, and occasionally for more serious matters: checks from donors would sometimes sit in the office for months before finally being taken to the bank to be cashed (if ever). The constitution of FPK is in English and runs to nineteen detailed pages, but it was not readily available to the board members until 2004, when it was translated for them by an evaluation team member during a training workshop she facilitated in connection with a board meeting (Norwegian Church Aid 2007: 43). But the problems went much further than this. With a limited staff, members of FPK were so busy lobbying and creating awareness of human rights issues relating to the San that they had little time for writing or compiling financial or administrative reports. They also did not see the urgency to do so. There was already documentation in the form of reports done by members of the donor agencies that provided support to the organization; as a result, the staff of FPK saw no reason to write additional reports. Some of its members who were in place in the 2000–7 period indicated to me a strong dissatisfaction with the donors' emphasis on auditing, meetings, accounting, reporting, and documentation (even if they recognized the importance of accountability), saying that they did not like how long it took to get things done. Because they were in a structural position of financial dependency, however, they could not, even if they had wished, organize themselves as they saw fit or even, without risking the loss of funding, pursue the causes that they had consensually identified as priorities.

There was also a need early on for the organization to deal with expectations of equal gender representation. FPK was accused by some observers of being male-dominated (see, for example, Kiema 2010: 98), which might seem to be confirmed by the fact that the three prominent leaders I discussed earlier are men. In fact, however, some of the key players in the organization's management, board, and administration have been women. Mama Rampadi, a San from northeastern Kweneng, for example, was appointed as the office manager and coordinator of FPK in Botswana in January 1999. In the first years of her appointment she spent much of her time attempting to improve the management and capacity of the organization. She oversaw the staff of FPK, which at that time consisted of nearly a dozen people, the majority of them G//ana, Naro, and G/ui San. A primary emphasis of her work was on gender and the empowerment of indigenous women. Under Rampadi's leadership, FPK held meetings on women's issues, and the organization went through gender-mainstreaming training, just as a number of other Botswana-based NGOs did in the 1990s. Other San women also played important roles in the organization, serving as office administrators and managers, members of the executive committee, and members of the board. The head of the board in 2012 was a Naro woman from D'Kar, and several other women on the FPK board have been outspoken about the need for FPK to engage directly in promoting women's and children's rights in addition to indigenous rights.

Mama Rampadi attended numerous conferences, representing FPK both in Botswana and internationally, where she raised awareness of San issues, including land rights, rights to political representation, and gender equity. Her career reflects attention to the importance of combining local and international expertise. She undertook several trips to the CKGR in 2000, 2001, and 2002, worked closely with the WIMSA, and spent a year in Geneva on an ILO scholarship.[15] One consequence of these efforts has been that the issues affecting San women have entered into the discourse of San activism, which, as the report of a July 2015 conference of the Khwedom Council in D'Kar reveals, is centered on their experience of "double discrimination," first "as indigenous San people and secondly as San women"[16] – those whom the justice system leaves vulnerable to unpaid child support, who are commonly victimized by rape that goes uninvestigated and unpunished, and who live in imposed conditions of poverty "in barren land which they had been relocated to from their rich and fertile ancestral land" (Botswana Khwedom Council 2015: 6).

In 1996, the residents of CKGR called upon FPK to assist them in claiming their rights in the reserve. FPK engaged in consultations about the potential relocation process and facilitated the selection of two delegates from each village to conduct negotiations with the government regarding its relocation plans. These delegates then formed a committee representing the reserve as a whole, known as the "CKGR committee." This committee and FPK, in response to the first large-scale resettlement in mid-1997, approached a number of San-related NGOs, and together they established a consultative group – the CKGR negotiating team[17] – to carry out negotiations with the government of Botswana on the future of the people living in the reserve (Hitchcock 2002). This team held its first meeting at D'Kar, Ghanzi District, on June 16 and 17, 1997. FPK was the nominal leader and coordinator of the negotiating team.

The negotiating team's mandate was "to seek to negotiate with Government to develop a plan suitable to both the Basarwa/San communities within the CKGR and the Department for Wildlife and National Parks' aims for the CKGR and Khutse Game Reserve" (Ditshwanelo flyer). Roy Sesana, together with other NGOs representatives, met with the outgoing president of Botswana, Ketumile Masire, in Gaborone in March 1998 to discuss the framework of the negotiations and to ask that the negotiating team be recognized as the legitimate and authentic representative body of the residents of the CKGR. The outgoing president took no action.

Despite this high-level request and the subsequent successful efforts by FPK to facilitate elections of village representatives, the Minister of Local Government, Lands, and Housing, Daniel Kwelagobe, announced in September 1999 that the negotiating team did not have a mandate and was not able to represent the people of the CKGR. In a meeting, with the negotiating team in September 1999, Kwelagobe stated that the government of Botswana would not recognize rights to land in a game reserve but would only grant ownership of land to "Basarwa who moved out of the CKGR" and into the resettlement villages of New Xade and Kaudwane. This was only one example of the many disappointments the San and Bakgalagadi experienced as the CKGR negotiating team attempted to consult and negotiate with Botswana government officials from 1997 to 2002 (Hitchcock 2002).

A second phase of the organization was that of *activism through the organization* (1996–2006), which involved a specific justice cause. In support of this phase, IWGIA initiated a capital-infusing project, entitled "Recognition of the Bushmen's Land Rights, Human Rights, and Cultural Rights in Botswana," which lasted from 1997 to 2000, with an investment of 7,742,293 DKK (roughly US $1,200,000 at the time). One of the main aims of FPK's 1997 proposal to IWGIA was to empower the CKGR communities "through training and consultancy" to stand up for their rights and determine their own development (IWGIA 1997: 11). The plan mentions a possible legal claim for recognition by the government of the "rights of the communities in the CKGR to the lands they occupy and have occupied for centuries" (IWGIA 1997: 12) as a "last resort" if negotiations with the government failed. In this phase, the organization was concentrating on activism and support for a specific justice cause, that of the people of the CKGR. In fact, already in 1997, FPK and the NGO coalitions were preparing the basis for a legal case through conducting legal and historical research in preparation for a land claim; selecting expert witness and arranging expert evidence; organizing workshops in the CKGR to inform and train people and discuss a legal strategy; and preparing and filing pleadings with the registrar of the Botswana High Court. IWGIA, along with other international, regional, and national-based NGOs, also provided advice and substantial funds for the lawyers, consultants, and other personnel working on the documentation for the first CKGR legal case, which was finally filed in 2002 after the second major relocation occurred. SI, which was to have an important place in the CKGR campaign, entered the scene in this second phase of activism.

FACTIONALISM

Tensions arose not only between the organization and its donors, but also in the organization itself, between the board and the field staff, and between the organization as a whole and its constituents. As with many organizations struggling with diminished economic capacity, one of the complaints of the FPK board was that the staff did not attend meetings and were not present for many of the training sessions. There was a case in which the coordinator used the organization's resources for personal benefit, which did little to raise the credibility of the board. For their part, the field staff were concerned about board members not showing up for meetings or questioning staff about vehicle use and subsistence funds (daily allowances) (FPK files, Ghanzi, Botswana). Some of these issues were outlined in a scathing report by the Saami Council, which conducted a review of FPK in 2004 as part of a NORAD-sponsored initiative promoting the development of "indigenous to indigenous" collaboration in Africa:

> The board members of FPK have a clear vision of the kind of rights-oriented organization they want to have, but the board plays a fairly weak role. Currently, the chairman is the only one who actually fulfills the functions of the full board. Low education levels have historically led to difficulties for the board to assume the functions of controlling and instructing the staff. ... Probably FPK is relatively well known, but there is undoubtedly a need for more systematic organization of communication, including regular board member elections as prescribed in the constitution. (Borchgrevink 2004: 4)

Clearly, while FPK was focused on the rights and welfare of the people of the CKGR, it was unable to engage with other issues that some members of its board were pressing for regarding other areas of Botswana, as the organization's original mandate stated; furthermore, it was difficult to meet the donor demands of "capacity building" for expanding collaboration with other indigenous NGOs, both within Africa and overseas. Closer to home, FPK became caught up in a set of dilemmas and problems that are common to indigenous organizations, including limits to the legitimacy of speaking for others, the difficulty in combining the requirements of international travel and outreach with local demands for accountability oriented toward a circumscribed mandate. The organization also faced chronic shortages of funding, which resulted in reassessments of priorities that took the various rights-oriented NGOs that were promoting the San cause in different directions.

One of the qualities evident in those who took leading roles in the early years of the San's justice movement was an ability to combine knowledge of the leadership values of their constituents with those of the dominant society. The combination of strong leadership with a rejection of personal ambition, expressed in the words of Hardbattle "if I have any ambition, it is that my people should live" (cited in Boustany 1995), however, is usually not enough to fend off prejudices from two sources: from non-San society, which readily expresses (racialized) doubts about a leader's education, expertise, and qualifications; and from their constituents, who are inclined to express resentments about the supposed benefits of leadership (income, travel, etc.) that are not shared, and particularly to resent the power that comes from "secret knowledge."

The San people often wanted their representatives to stay within a circumscribed mandate that called on them to act in ways that could be seen as consistent with their recognized special abilities. One way that the San leaders used to avoid being seen as self-promoting was through the idea of "revolving leadership" (Biesele and Hitchcock 2013: 137–9, 161–2), in which no one individual stays in a position of power for an extended period of time. This may have met local expectations of egalitarianism, but at the same time presented obstacles to continuity and organizational capacity. To be effective, activist campaigns need an identifiable spokesperson who speaks for others and receives recognition and prestige for doing so, which was not always consistent with local expectations. On occasion, the representativeness and efficacy of the actions of the San NGOs' spokespersons were called into question by other members of their own communities, in part for the simple reason that the constituency resented others taking on wider authority and gaining personal recognition while speaking for them.

The qualities of an effective indigenous leader that Hardbattle represented were all but impossible to realize in the context of the San's justice cause. The San are made up of a number of diverse groups, and they do not all have the same agendas. Most San groups, like those in the Ghanzi farms, are in areas where the vast majority of their lands have been taken away through a long history of land reforms and promotion of the commercial cattle industry. The CKGR was an exception to this history of removal, at least for the majority of its fifty-five-year-long existence. People living in the CKGR were above all aggrieved over the shock of more recent displacements. These differences in the sources of the sense of injustice and the issues to be prioritized were inextricably connected to the values of consensus politics and the avoidance of "speaking for others."

Not only do the structural requirements of activist organizations encourage particular kinds of expertise, their leadership itself is practiced in a way that rewards "personal empowerment," using one's voice to be recognized by others, to emphatically advance an agenda. This leadership style, favored among those whom Lee (2006) refers to as "modernizers," tends to be rejected by the those San who are uncomfortable in institutional environments, and for whom "speaking up" and "speaking out" represent a form of self-assertion that is inconsistent with their way of resolving conflicts (Lawy 2016: 285). For many San, "speaking for others" should ideally only take place within limits, defined by specific issues and circumstances rather than broad mandates of representation within official positions. Individuals who speak for others are often seen as attempting to promote their own agendas at the expense of the group, and as a consequence these individuals face social pressures from kin, friends, and other members of their groups. The idea of having representatives who speak for the community is complicated, never mind having representatives from other San groups with other languages and concerns speaking for the San as a whole. This is particularly manifested in the San movement – comprised of several peoples, NGOs, and individuals from southern Africa and their supporters – where a cacophony of voices and strategies is not surprising, particularly given the varying contexts in which San activism developed and the fact that the various organizations that arose did not share the same strategies or priorities.

Organizations also had to respond to other kinds of demands: the informal standards of accountability applied to their activities from their local constituencies, which called on NGO representatives to make regular personal visits and communicate. The difficulty of accomplishing this was compounded by the government's attempt to discredit the organization. San delegates who travelled to places far from their communities to attend NGO and government meetings were sometimes accused of benefitting personally from such opportunities. These kinds of complaints are very common in indigenous organizations that have sent delegates to international meetings as part of their agenda (cf. Brysk 2000; Hodgson 2011). These views often arose from the fact that some community members saw little short-term benefit from the activities of their spokespersons. This was an issue, for example, during the awareness and fund-raising tour by FPK members in the USA in October 2004, during the first CKGR court case. The Botswana government used photographs of FPK staff on the beach in Malibu, California, as a way to discredit them. Given the wariness of some San toward their representatives, the ruse may have worked. Staff members – who often receive salaries, houses and cars, wear relatively nice clothes, and travel internationally – are often viewed with jealousy and suspicion by other members of their communities, both young and old.

Added to the tendency toward envy of those who are seen to personally benefit from their positions as spokespeople and the difficulty of "speaking for others" was the increasingly common problem of chronic shortages of funding, which produced difficulties both within and between organizations. One consequence of the situation of limited resources has been for the imposition of various kinds of co-optation. As they fight for their rights and struggle for resources, indigenous peoples are often culturally transformed as they take part in the discourses and procedures of the state: "They are required to adopt a particular view of themselves and of the world that fits with the rights-conferring political machinery of the state" (Samson 2003: 228). "Cultural sameness," Colin Samson argues, is not only assumed, but is required in the extension of rights to indigenous peoples.

Another common response to lack of funding was for organizations to narrow their mandates and to focus on particular issues. With different agendas being pursued by various NGOs, an inevitable result was contests over priorities, over the allocation of effort and resources. Collaborative efforts did take place, but many advocacy organizations formed in conditions of meager resources developed inherent differences of agenda that, in turn, became sources of factional division within the San justice movement as a whole. The different vision of rights claims, sometime introduced by personal interests, made it nearly impossible for the San organizations to coordinate their activities and set a common agenda. These differences have led to tensions among NGOs, their leaderships as well as among activists more widely. For instance the relation between some people with a long history of engagement in San political activism in D'kar and FPK deteriorated though time, particularly over the fact that FPK took on the CKGR removals as a defining cause while paying less attention to conditions of displacement in other parts of the country.

The structures of organizations require permanent positions of leadership, sometimes with (from the perspective of those living in conditions of deprivation) significant material benefits, which gives rise to competition. At the same time the mere existence of these coveted positions in the wider context of economic insecurity has been a recipe for infighting. Another example is the KDT, which became "unbundled" in the 1999–2002 period when there were internal power struggles, some of them arising from an effort on the part of Naro in the D'kar community to gain greater control of the organization (Dekker 2002; Kuper 2003; Lebotse 2009: 29–35). Some D'kar families who had played significant roles in Kuru in the past opted to leave and move to other villages such as Groot Laagte, Qabo, and Kuke. Others sought to ally themselves with Bakgalagadi in D'kar who were seeking leadership positions in Kuru. The power struggle eventually became so intense that the government sent in the police to help allay any potential conflict. A government minister from Ghanzi District who had worked for the Remote Area Development Programme was called upon to assist in negotiating the future of Kuru. This struggle was one in which kinship affiliations with specific political parties, membership in faith-based institutions, ethnicity, and tensions between traditionalists and modernists all played roles.

Outbursts of infighting have even been discussed in the press with reference to the country's local NGOs, as when Bihela Sekere, originally from New Xade and a government employee in the Ministry of International Affairs based in the Botswana embassy in London, commented to a reporter about a leadership struggle in a newly established organization, "If I knew that this [Khwedom] Council was for some individuals, I would have not wasted my energy ... to work on the constitution. I thought this was for Basarwa irrespective of their geographical location in Botswana. But now it's clear that this Council has owners" (Letsididi 2011). This severe kind of factionalism should not be overgeneralized. There are criticisms within and among NGOs, temporary fights and repacification, as community workers express animosities, distance themselves from one another, and then (usually but not always) get back to work together again.

The possibilities for overcoming some of the dilemmas of indigenous leadership and for finding a common agenda are evident in an emerging youth movement. Of course, the San youth are by no means immune to the disorders of organized activism. Youth activists in particular are called upon to navigate networks, secure commitments from donors, and create organizations that meet specific requirements in order to be registered with the state and recognized as a legal entity, apply for national and international funding, and attend international meetings through their own organizations and not through others. And in the course of doing all of this, the knowledge they possess and the activities they pursue are largely beyond the reach of the marginalized people they represent.

Differences in technological expertise can also be a source of knowledge differentiation, prestige and an avenue of leadership. Youth spokespersons have from the mid-1990s onward continually applied new skills in computer literacy to networking and dissemination of information. This was part of a much wider phenomenon of indigenous activism and networking through new media (Niezen 2005; Landzelius 2006). There is a certain freedom from editorial censorship and a high degree of distant cooperation involved in the use of the new media to produce of legal and cultural artifacts. This is part of an unmistakable global trend toward "sharpened boundaries of community identity and intensified pursuits of autonomy" (Niezen 2005: 546). To this we can add that the growing influence of algorithms in the preferential selection of material on Facebook is encouraging connections between people sharing similar convictions in online communities, while possibly engendering consistency within their chosen parameters of thought, the phenomenon that Eli Pariser (2011) refers to as the "filter bubble." This by no means prevents discussion and dissent among the youth cohort of San activists, but it can be seen in their overall loyalties to San identity and promotion of indigenous rights online.

There is an emphasis on consensus-building as the youth leadership seeks to formalize its existence in a recently nascent San Youth Network, a regional network based in D'kar, oriented toward "capacitating programmes" that emphasize the importance of education as a foundation for political empowerment. This network is rallied by the slogan, "Because we matter, we make change that matters."[18] To the new technology-literate youth, it has been easier to see possibilities in networking widely with other activists and making connections, both personal and intellectual, which largely transcend local interests. The youth cohort is engaged in an institution–building project which emphasizes their San traditions while drawing energy from the wider picture, making connections to the plights of various groups of San across Botswana and southern Africa and to indigenous peoples worldwide. This is reflected, for example, in a presentation at an international conference at McGill University by Job Morris, a Botswana University-educated San activist from D'kar, founder of the San Youth Network, and son of James Morris, a strong political figure and activist among the founders of FPK and Kuru. To be effective at the international level, Morris argues, a San organization "should identify and *reflect cultural values and integrate traditional knowledge and practices into its management*" (Morris 2011).

(IN)CONVENIENT ALLIANCES

At the beginning of the 2000s there was a gradual detachment of FPK from other local and regional NGOs working on San issues. Part of the reason for this was that FPK's members felt it had more legitimacy in "speaking for the San" than did other NGOs that were not seen as "full San." In addition, during this period, the close collaboration between FPK and the London-based SI led to a breakdown in relations with other organizations that did not share what they thought were Survival's confrontational advocacy strategies concerning the people of the CKGR (Kiema 2010; Saugestad 2011; Solway 2009, 2011). This factionalization was manifested in the fact that each NGO pursued its own agenda, creating a more salient lack of coherence and common strategy in the San movement as a whole.

The agenda pursued by SI was oriented toward defense of those "vulnerable populations" that represented the last "tribal" people of the world. The widely disseminated ideals and images of the San fit perfectly with SI's mission of defending those who represent a form of humanity that had existed for many thousands of years, before the advent of agriculture, states, civilization, and industrialism.

Survival International did not get closely involved in "tribal" issues in Botswana until the latter part of the 1980s. The Africa coordinator for SI, Virginia Luling, who had had extensive experience in Somalia and other parts of Africa, began visiting Botswana at that time. At first she confined her visits to Manxotae, a small community on the Nata River in Central District, but later she expanded her travels to other parts of the country including Maun and Ghanzi. She attempted to engage with government officers in the Remote Area Development Programme in the Ministry of Local Government and Lands, but received little cooperation. She worked with the then director of SI, Marcus Colchester, and several informants in Botswana on an urgent action bulletin on the issue of the CKGR, which was published in April 1989. The government quickly took action against people who were identified as having provided information, including a researcher, Jeremy Perkins, whose name appeared (mistakenly) on the cover of the Urgent Action Bulletin, and Robert Hitchcock, both of whom were questioned by Botswana Police Service personnel and officials from the Office of the President (Robert Hitchcock, personal communication, 2017). SI was asked to issue an apology to the government for its publication of the bulletin but refused to do so, standing by its statement.

As for its methods of intervention, SI favors the use of media aimed toward mass persuasion, such as a film depicting Xoroxloo Duxee, a San woman from Botswana whose death in the CKGR soon after the film was shot was widely attributed to government actions that prevented the San from accessing water. The lobbying campaigns of SI on behalf of the San were driven by a very simple principle: "Oppression continues until the public stands with the oppressed; then it begins to fade" (Corry 2011: 302).

As soon as the removals took place in 2002, SI kicked into high gear with a multiple-strategy offensive. Email message-writing campaigns were organized through links on SI's website, in which participants were directed to the addresses of (then) President Festus Mogae. At the same time, in a series of press releases, SI highlighted the Botswana government's "vigorous campaign of harassment" to drive the Bushmen out of the reserve, emphasizing the violence of the removals. Dozens of press releases were sent out in rapid succession, sometimes only days apart, some covering the theme of violent dispossession under headings such as: "Botswana tortures Bushmen, then prosecutes them"; "Botswana: government plans to destroy Bushmen"; and "Botswana leaves Bushmen in desert without water." Survival even used its own strategy as a "handle" to attract media coverage, with press releases that announced the spread of its slogan, "Diamonds mean despair."

As an international advocacy-oriented NGO, SI was different from other organizations working on San issues, both in terms of scale and strategy. It was connected to a wide network of celebrity sponsors and spokespeople, and had the ability to fund-raise and campaign at levels that were quite unlike other organizations working on indigenous issues. It was able to draw on (and in the process to elevate) the charisma of both its Hollywood connections and the "tribal people" it represented.

In 2002, for example, the organization replaced an advertisement for De Beers on the corner of London's Piccadilly and Old Bond Streets that had featured a diamond-studded top model, Iman Mohamed Abulmajid, with an image of a Bushman woman, accompanied by the caption "Bushmen are not forever." Survival then reported that Iman had "become a Bushman." This was soon followed by action and expressions of opinion on the part of Iman herself. In 2004 she officially ended her contract with De Beers. Her decision was soon picked up in global news coverage, including an article in *The Guardian*, in which Iman explained her action in the following terms: "It was clear that the Bushmen were being destroyed – you take people from their element and you end up with AIDS, drugs and alcohol in the guise of advancement" (Meldrum 2004). Other celebrities, including British actor Colin Firth, chose direct endorsements of the Survival campaign. Speaking at a London preview of the 2003 film *Love Actually*, Firth commented on the CKGR evictions with the remark that the Bushmen have "been shifted off to relocation camps where the lives they've known are basically over".[19]

Survival's 2002 media campaign had almost immediate results, with candlelight vigils outside the Botswana embassy in London and questions about the treatment of the San in the House of Lords. One of the effects of this publicity was the obvious one of raising public awareness of the removals and exerting pressure on the Botswana government to change its policies.

SI at this time was recognized by many people, both inside and outside the reserve as a legitimate and effective ally of the San's cause, even though voices of dissent were not entirely lacking. In the San communities, the relationship with Survival has changed through time, but a basic line of support has remained, which was evident to me over the years in my conversations with the residents of the reserve. The first time I travelled to Botswana in 2006, while I was attending the Kuru Dance Festival (an annual gathering of San from all over Botswana performing traditional dances and songs), to my surprise, I was followed nearly everywhere I went by children smiling, dancing, tugging on my clothes, and chanting "Sur-vi-val! Sur-vi-val!" assuming incorrectly that I was there as a representative of the organization.

At the same time, however, Survival's campaign arguably had the effect of creating a "war" with the state by provoking high-ranking officials and politicians (including the president) and making them intolerant to criticism. For many years, anyone found to be a member of SI was declared a "prohibited immigrant" and refused entry into the country. The government's draconian approach to SI reflected a current of popular opinion in Botswana, which drew attention to what they saw as the organization's "colonial approach" of interfering in local matters.

Through all of this lobbying and NGO fundraising, the area that raised the most ire among Botswana government officials had to do with SI's claims about diamonds being the reason for the removals of people from the CKGR. Some of the anti-Botswana, anti-diamond campaign was focused on De Beers, which initially had an interest in the Ghagoo (Gope) diamond mine (southeast CKGR). In the middle of the SI campaign, it decided to relinquish this interest to another company, Gem Diamonds. Encouraged by this partial victory, Survival continued to make use of its slogan, "Diamonds are for death" (Solway 2009).

There were debates within FPK and among other NGOs as to the best tactics to be followed; for example, whether or not to claim that diamonds were the major issue in the relocation of the San was discussed at length. Members of FPK, even if they were united in the opinion that the Botswana government had a variety of unjustified arguments for relocating people out of the CKGR, identified diamond prospecting and diamond mining as one of the main reasons for the relocation. Ditshwanelo and other national organizations, on the other hand, were not convinced that diamonds had been the cause of government decision-making, "as the Government of Botswana has the right to explore and mine diamonds in any part of the country and any diamonds found would belong to the State no matter who resided on the land – the CKGR is no different."[20] What is more, focusing on the diamond issue could alienate those very government officials and ministries needed to respond to the urgent needs of those in the CKGR (Mogwe 2011).

Survival International's later shift of attention to tourism was something else that deeply concerned the government of Botswana, with much of the national economy reliant on the influx of tourists drawn by the opportunities to see (and sometimes illegally hunt) Africa's wildlife. It should be noted that SI did document the role of tourism fairly effectively, especially the Kalahari Plains Camp of Wilderness Safaris, pointing to the poignant disjuncture between the construction of a luxury tourist lodge and swimming pool in the CKGR and the struggles of the Bushmen nearby who were desperate for access to water. (Recall that their well had been sealed and capped in 2002 at the time of the evictions from the CKGR.)

Survival International's involvement in the San cause has been a central matter of debate in Botswana, both among NGOs and the people involved in the case, with particular attention to the ways in which SI was campaigning against Botswana through confrontational tactics and making claims that were viewed as inflammatory.[21] In particular, some Botswana-based organizations such as Ditshwanelo and Kuru, disagreed with the spirit and tone of SI's campaigns against the Botswana government. There were debates, for example, over the use of the term "genocide" by SI to describe what had occurred in the CKGR (Kenyon 2005). Kuru criticized "the destructive and often untruthful way in which the international NGO SI has tried to give support to the CKGR San and Bakgalagadi" (Kuru Position Paper on the CKGR).

In July 2001, Ditshwanelo likewise issued a press statement distancing itself from the SI campaign, particularly regarding the allegation that government officials tortured CKGR residents. Ditshwanelo saw the "confrontational" intervention of SI as problematic, resulting in "negative effects on the work being done locally," adding pointedly, "We believe that the current Survival International campaign risks reversing progress already made in the protection of the human rights of the Basarwa peoples."[22] Ditshwanelo preferred lobbying sympathetic people in the government to gain their support, and contrasted the idea of "confrontational advocacy" with the Tswana tradition of "talking through problems," particularly during the first phase of the work of the CKGR negotiation team (to be discussed in the next chapter).

In the first week of February 2002, at the same time that the details of Community Use Zones (CUZs) inside the CKGR were being discussed in the negotiations over the Third Draft of the Management Plan, the government suddenly decided to stop all services that had been provided to the communities (See Chapter 2, p. 53–4). Some analysts connected this drastic decision of the government with the effects of SI's public criticism of the Office of the President (Solway 2009; Zips-Mairitsch 2013: 237, 312ff, 324ff). In a private meeting with the vice-president of Botswana at the end of November 2001, Glyn Williams (a lawyer), Alice Mogwe (Director of Ditshwanelo, also a lawyer), and Arthur Albertson (a consultant for FPK) reported that the vice-president "privately confirmed that Survival International's campaign, and particularly FPK's vocal support of it, had hardened attitudes within the government, which has probably led to the decision to cut the services inside the reserve."[23] Perhaps SI's statements and actions did offend key officials and push the government toward a hard line. Perhaps the policy was in place from the beginning, and the government's reactions to SI's tactics were a smokescreen. What we can be sure of, however, is that it was not SI that inspired the government policies of forced resettlement and the violence that followed from its implementation, as well as the development of mining and tourism in the reserve, events that added fuel to SI's "Bushmen are not Forever" campaign.

Even if most of the Botswana-based NGOs objected to SI's tactics, FPK representatives often agreed with the position of SI that local NGOs were too dependent on the government and that a more "radical" intervention was needed. FPK argued that it had to take a hard line because the government was not moving in positive directions with respect to the people of the CKGR. Its leaders entered the public debate several times, supporting the position of SI toward the San.[24]

Indigenous organizations are often accused by their opponents of representing the interests of "outsiders." This was also the case with FPK, which government officials and a few journalists tried to portray as "a tool of Survival International." This was repeated many times, not just in efforts to call SI's priorities and strategies into question but also, it could be argued, as an attempt to delegitimize the voices and actions of the San, relegating them to a state of powerlessness and passivity vis-à-vis other international NGOs with which they work, as well as to discredit them in the eyes of their own people. When questioned about this, FPK staff members defended their actions, pointing out that they were providing SI with the same kinds of information that they were giving to other organizations, including the government of Botswana.

It is clear that Survival's campaign had some effect, even though much of it lay in an intangible influence on opinion, indistinguishable from wider media interest. Even without a direct connection to any of SI's celebrity endorsements or other campaign strategies, the general public in Europe and North America followed the case through articles published by major newspapers such as the *New York Times* and *Washington Post* in the USA and *The Guardian* in the UK. The BBC released several documentaries on the case, and several YouTube videos were posted. Information and opinion was also released by international organizations such as the United Nations and regional institutions such as the European Union and the African Union.

POSTMORTEM

The CKGR thus become a *cause célèbre* and, because of this, a way to raise money. Many NGOs in Botswana and in international programs aimed to help the people of the CKGR, even if they did not often concretize their ambitions on the ground. The CKGR, in other words, became a "commodity" to sell to donors.

The money, however, did not last forever. Under the circumstances of reduced funding and internal tensions, the status of the FPK in terms of its capacity to function is ambiguous, leaving it with a spectral, partial existence. Some people say it has ceased to be effective while others claim that it is still active (2017). It has in fact for a long time been one of the only NGOs whose staff regularly visited the CKGR to consult with the residents. Most recently, FPK, having lost much of its donor support and staff and facing opposition from other NGOs and the government, has not been a part of the team of NGOs visiting the CKGR for purposes of consulting with local communities and engaging in community mapping. In place of FPK, other NGOs, including Kuru, Ditshwanelo, and the San Studies Centre of the University of Botswana, have been involved in that work, which has taken place from 2009 to the present.

From the standpoint of the state, FPK might still be registered as an association and it is mentioned in the press and on the radio and television as being active on San issues. Recently it has focused attention not just on the CKGR issue but also on the dozens of San communities in other parts of the country that have been told by the government or by district councils that they have to move. To take an example, FPK and the Botswana Khwedom Council both played roles in working with the people of the community of Ranyane in the southern Ghanzi District after the government told the people of Ranyane that they had to relocate and shut down their water point. Despite these acknowledgements, the FPK board has not met for the past several years, and most of its efforts come from individuals who represent the organization in their own account without a coordinated plan.[25] Wikipedia sounded an official death knell by reporting that "FPK had dissolved as an organisation by 2013."[26]

In its active years, FPK had been a vehicle for individual leadership and an organizational venue for the expression of grievance and dissent. At the same time, the state had a key role in its decline, by publicly discrediting its activities (such as referring to it as a terrorist organization), and – so some engaged people reported – engaging in arrests and intimidation. FPK was thus reduced further in its connections and capacities to maintain a local focus.

Even though many local constituents of FPK were uncomfortable with some of the formal aspects of NGO activism, the process of "getting organized" continues, with wider networks of participants and greater familiarity (one is tempted to say "comfort," but that does not quite hold true) with the formal structures of activism. Botswana's Khwedom Council, which identifies itself as a national indigenous people's organization oriented toward human rights, has taken up the goals of informing people "of their rights as a people and as women," and of equipping them "to stop abuse of any kind against San people and women".[27] These newly established organizations were built on the energy of some of the youth who acquired their expertise working in FPK and Kuru. Their network has been central to the development of

San participation in the UN and other global organizations, using and influencing the language of indigeneity.

In retrospect, FPK was a kind of transitional NGO, a first effort serving as a starting point and source of experience for others to build on. Like its individual leaders, it had certain chameleon-like qualities. It presented itself as an NGO, meeting the requisite formal criteria, and it also presented itself as an informal representative body to local constituents who needed an advocate in their relationships with the state. In this latter sense, FPK was more than an NGO, as is shown by its struggles in formalizing according to organizational rules. It was also an informal vehicle for the political and justice aspirations of a distinct community of rights claimants. Ultimately, its core convictions were allied to those of the people it represented. In this case it was not a social movement that gave impetus to the creation of NGOs. Rather, organizations like FPK have contributed to the rise of a network of committed activists, who now comprise the San movement. They translated global norms among people for whom they were previously unfamiliar, and through them the San activists have come to share some of the values and convictions of other actors operating in transnational and global networks associated with the human rights movement.

What happens to an NGO when it ceases to exist in the formal sense of the term, when donors have all ceased to fund it, and when the state has stopped receiving reports and soliciting annual payments? What happens when meetings are no longer held, the lights go out in the office and people go home? Does the organization cease to exist in an absolute sense? Or does something continue to happen in an almost spectral, postmortem way, emerging out of people's hopes (however misplaced) and understandings (however mistaken) of what an organization can do after its demise? Just as the medical understanding of death is not self-evident, as is demonstrated in Margaret Lock's (2002) examination of "brain death" and organ transplants, so too might we think of the supposed demise of an NGO as a formality that might conceal other, compelling and potentially problematic, forms of existence.

In March 2011, when I visited Botswana on an assignment for First Peoples Worldwide, there were divided opinions about FPK (unrelated to my sponsoring organization, despite the similarity of the name). Some ex-employees of the organization as well as some San activists told me that FPK no longer existed because it did not have an office or a budget. Others traced its demise to the time a few years earlier when one of its coordinators ran away after being appointed headman of a village elsewhere in the country, stealing computers and other property from the organization's office on his way out, leaving the organization with no funds available to replace them.

Roy Sesana said different things at different times when questions arose about whether he was attending negotiation meetings, that took place after the *Sesana* case, as a representative of FPK, a community representative of Molapo, or as a private individual. FPK's former representatives were no longer invited to negotiation meetings. By these criteria it had ceased to have a pulse, or at least continued to live only in the formal sense, as a registered association or trust in government records, which was no longer asked to make annual payments for that registration.

When I spoke with people who were struggling to eke a living in the communities of the CKGR, a different kind of existence was attributed to FPK, one that gave it a more concrete existence, even if in people's imaginations. "We want FPK to read us the court judgment," one elderly man said. Others, men and women alike, made similar remarks, pointing to a particular human rights-oriented NGO as "serving the government's interests. They are not representing us. We want our own people in the meetings"; and "We feel that the government is not allowing FPK to participate in the negotiations" (author notes 2012, 2015). Here FPK was very much alive, pulled into the conversation as a possible source of effective intervention with a government that was not listening to them, that was pursuing its own agenda at the cost of the lives they had lived and wanted for the future. The practicalities of the budget and the formalities of recognition had little importance for the people of the CKGR. What they saw in FPK was what it had done in the past. The demise of the organization was inconceivable to them, when those who had once spoken for it were living and active. The NGO, in other words, was personified in the people and relationships to which they had once given their trust. The idea that it could exist – or cease to exist – apart from those relationships was meaningless.

FPK was in some ways not unlike some of the other NGOs involved with indigenous and minority peoples in southern Africa. Most of these organizations have as their objectives the promotion of civil, political, social, economic, and cultural rights. The expansion (and later contraction) of donor resources channeled to NGOs that were identified with indigenous causes facilitated the growth of the movement and the bureaucratization of the indigenous protest. At the same time, it increased the dependency of NGOs like FPK on donors and their agendas. All indigenous NGOs face funding constraints, and some of them are contending with issues relating to leadership, representation, and questions regarding the equitable distribution of benefits from the activities of community trusts and associations.

In the next chapter, I turn to the period in which FPK, together with what become a "San movement," represented the interests of the CKGR residents in the United Nations. Many of the tensions inherent in the San's adoption of NGOs as an avenue of rights representation were manifest in their lobbying activities in the UN, where formal organizations are given access and "voice." The forms that this access took inside the palaces of international law and diplomacy are among the most important features of the San's justice cause, situated within the global indigenous movement.

5

THE SAN IN THE UNITED NATIONS

ENTERING THE PALACE

When the San from southern Africa entered the United Nations (UN) as part of their justice strategy in the late 1980s, the battle lines shifted. In the UN people are called upon to represent wide constituencies. They may be there as indigenous delegates to talk about their people's experience of violence and exclusion, or as state delegates to defend the national reputation and promote a particular view of the government's ambitions, but at some point everyone is required to expand their vision, to at least act on the pretense that they represent the interests of a region or hemisphere or, better yet, all of humanity. Only rarely will a specific cause capture global attention and stand out alone as a priority for intervention. With the UN's limited resources, the ears of its officials are tuned to big issues, where intervention and change have the potential to influence the lives of many. Experienced delegates have learned this and have adapted by working in coalitions, caucuses, or more informal regional blocs or alliances.

For the San delegates, the leverage they had in the UN to influence the behavior of states was a major draw, one of their central motivations for attending. Jumanda Gakelebone, during the first time that he attended the two-week session of the Permanent Forum on Indigenous Issues in 2016, remarked after listening to a speech by UN General Secretary Ban Ki Moon: "It is the body of government of all the world. If they [governments] hear us [indigenous peoples] and take steps, I hope there's going to be changes. ... It is the union of nations, not an

NGO talking, so the government will listen more carefully" (author notes 2016). But this hopeful view of the UN's broad influence went together with a corresponding requirement to collaborate and express ideas that matched the UN's ideals of universal good. The issue that activists often faced with donors – of having to bend to wider agendas that are not always of their choosing – was concentrated at the UN. One of the central challenges the San spokespersons faced in accomplishing this effort at accommodation was that the regional caucuses and umbrella organizations within which they had to work were also largely formed in their absence, and they often had difficulty working within yet another power structure that had priorities that differed from theirs. While it is true that working within regional caucuses can bring attention to wider issues that some indigenous delegates may not have been aware of – and thereby create a sense of common cause among delegations – it can just as often bring out differences among delegates and cultivate a sense that the people with whom they are collaborating do not represent them or their people's interests. Particular visions and strategic goals sometimes come into tension with the requirement to work together and to be guided by ambitious visions.

At the end of the 1980s, when the indigenous rights discourse entered Botswana as a result of the work of NGOs (both local and international), the media, scholars, and people participating in international meetings on indigenous peoples' rights, the San as a people found themselves in a position to adopt this language and occupy the "indigenous slot" (Li 2000; Karlsson 2003). The San, along with the Maasai, are iconic among the indigenous peoples in Africa, yet this in itself did not give them a place at the UN and a prominent public voice as "indigenous people." Their participation in the global indigenous movement had to be worked for.

It is easy to assume that grassroots indigenous organizations found their way into the UN entirely on their own accord, on the basis of their own grievances, their own people's suffering, and the legitimacy of their own claims, which then captured the sympathy and attention of the leadership of UN agencies. This assumption, however, would lead one to overlook the very significant impact of larger intermediary organizations and individuals (often anthropologists) that connected, networked, and put forward local claimants, while often remaining in the background.

The way that indigenous spokespersons, political leaders, and organizations from the Americas, Australia, New Zealand, and northern

Europe first found their way into the UN in the late 1970s was through the active intervention of several influential NGOs. The World Council of Indigenous Peoples (WCIP) was prominent in organizing planning meetings, and the Women's International League for Peace and Freedom (an internationally influential NGO first established in opposition to the carnage of World War I) was active in promoting the first indigenous peoples' NGO meetings at the UN Headquarters in Geneva.[1] This development of the indigenous peoples' agenda would likely not have been possible, or would have been long delayed, without the commitment of the International Work Group for Indigenous Affairs (IWGIA), which was also formative in promoting FPK and the San movement in Botswana (see Chapter 4, p. 137). With a professional base of anthropologists behind its efforts, IWGIA made a policy decision in the 1980s to "go global" and promote indigenous organizations and representation worldwide, including in Africa where postcolonial politics tended to be oriented toward securing a national power base and where there was much stronger resistance than anywhere else to granting influence to anything "ethnic" (Dahl 2009: 65). IWGIA began sponsoring African delegates to UN meetings in the early 1990s, making choices about the peoples and issues that seemed to best represent indigeneity in Africa. IWGIA also hosted a 1993 conference titled "The Question of Indigenous Peoples in Africa," co-organized by the Centre for Development Research in Denmark and sponsored by the Danish Foreign Ministry, which contributed to the conceptual reality and institutional momentum behind the participation of African peoples and organizations in the international indigenous peoples movement (Veber et al. 1993). This meeting had been carefully planned and the groundwork prepared for years, with the first discussions about it taking place in a board meeting in 1985 (Dahl 2009: 66). Through such efforts, IWGIA was instrumental in promoting (and developing) the work of African NGOs, encouraging them to connect their struggles to the international indigenous movement, and expanding the concept of "indigenous peoples" to include their positions and claims (Hodgson 2011: 30). In other words, IWGIA was instrumental in transplanting the "indigenous peoples' model" to Africa.

From the beginning, IWGIA was diplomatic in its approach. By inviting both activists and state representatives to the meeting on the outskirts of Copenhagen, it began its efforts with a clear understanding of the unique challenges facing those who identified as indigenous in Africa and the governments who resisted that identification. The San speakers from southern Africa and the spokespersons for the governments of Botswana and Namibia helped to express these contrasting positions with particular clarity.

John Hardbattle, Aaron/Art/wa Johannes, and Komtsa Komtsa represented First People of the Kalahari at this meeting. Hardbattle (1993a) gave a particularly hard-hitting statement in which he recounted the obstacles he encountered in bringing his people's grievances to the attention of the government, situating his indigenous identity in the context of an encounter with officials who refused to hear and who callously promoted a policy of assimilation based on an assumption of the San's "backwardness." He pointed to the impossible demands placed on his people to implement development plans for which they had never been consulted, noting that a N/oakwe (San) "is expected to forget and to discard one of the oldest and gentlest cultures on earth." To Hardbattle's statement, Aaron/Art/wa Johannes and Komtsa Komtsa added the perspectives of ordinary San who experienced discrimination, as in Komtsa's observation that "A lion that eats an eland does not go to prison. But I, when I eat an eland, I do go to prison" (Johannes and Komtsa 1993: 151).

Ulitala Hiveluah, Namibia's permanent secretary to the Minister of Lands, Resettlement and Rehabilitation, contributed to the meeting by expressing the position of African states on the nascent African indigenous claims and identities: "The Indians and Eskimos are indigenous to North America, the Aborigines to Australia, [but] [t]he Namibian scene is different. Here we see a heterogeneous population divided into ethnic groupings, that were ... discriminated against by the colonial system which had oppressed them for more than a century." This is the background to a young republic that is "faced with the great challenge of building one nation out of a highly divided people." In meeting this challenge and the particular obstacles to "integrating" impoverished groups into the nation, "we do not want to give nourishment to the myth that Bushmen should cling to their old way of hunting and fruit gathering. Or to the suggestion of separate development independent of the larger society in which they are to function as individuals" (Hiveluah 1993: 133–5). The governments from southern Africa thus placed an emphasis on individual rights, the "rights and freedoms of all citizens," and the assimilation of distinct peoples into the projects of the states. This was a refrain that was to be repeated in different forms again and again in public statements from this formative meeting up to the present. The lines of contestation between states and African indigenous peoples were clearly drawn from the beginning.

Following from these early efforts to put African indigenous peoples on the international agenda and to, in effect, globalize indigeneity, the Khoi[2] and San from southern Africa were among the first indigenous groups from the continent to attend UN meetings, but it was only in the second half of the 1990s that they started to participate in these encounters with some regularity. In 1994, representatives from Kuru Development Trust and First Peoples of the Kalahari appeared before a meeting of the Working Group on Indigenous Populations (WGIP) in Geneva and made a statement describing how their "people's land had been taken for the establishment of game reserves and national parks."[3] The government of Botswana did not have representatives in the room and, on the surface at least, the statement seemed to have little political effect.

As part of the strategy to stop the removal of the Central Kalahari Game Reserve (CKGR) inhabitants, First People of the Kalahari began to increase its presence internationally, with one of the main objectives being to bring what was happening in Botswana to the attention of the United Nations, and from there to the international media and its global audience. In 1994 John Hardbattle went on a fund-raising tour of the United States, where he hoped to find financial support for FPK. His first stop was Washington DC, where he met with members of the First Nations Development Institute and where he presented a formal proposal and budget to the World Bank, an effort that eventually proved futile. He also solicited funding from the World Wildlife Fund (WWF) US, which was engaged in a Social Science and Economics program that provided support to community-based natural resource management programs in Namibia, Zambia, Uganda, and Zimbabwe. The meeting with WWF also did not lead to any funding for FPK. He had better results, however, when he made funding requests in the international arena. A later visit by Hardbattle to the United Nations Working Group on Indigenous Populations (WGIP) meeting in Geneva, Switzerland did result in donor support from several sources, including Denmark, Norway, and Sweden.

The United Nations soon became a focal point for funding, political support, and media exposure. In 1996, Hardbattle, together with Roy Sesana, travelled to Geneva where they spoke before the UN Human Rights Commission on the situation of the San and met with the UN High Commissioner for Human Rights, José Ayala Lasso. They also met with Julian Burger from the Secretariat of the WGIP, who suggested that Sesana and Hardbattle attend the next Working Group meeting in Geneva, which they did. Their visit to the UN Human Rights Commission in 1996 was covered by the *New York Times*, which referred to them as "two members of a dwindling tribe facing eviction from a Botswana game reserve," followed by a description of their lobbying efforts in the UN (Crosette 1996).

After their 1996 visits to the Working Group and the Human Rights Commission, and above all following their several press statements, many UN agencies and states started to show interest in the CKGR situation. A few months later, delegates from Norway, Sweden, USA, and the European Union visited Ghanzi and the reserve. These visits had the immediate effect of making it clear to the Botswana government that the UN lobbying by San spokespersons was producing results, getting the attention of at least some members of the international community, including the country's important allies. This quality of embarrassing the state in its relations with important allies was both a strategy and an unintended consequence of the lobbying activities of San activists. It was not only in making human rights claims in international arenas, but also in the context of court cases (as we will see in Chapter 6) that the San leveraged the public fascination toward their way of life to press for their rights.

There are certainly the ingredients of a good story here: a people who, for many, represent the last vestiges of "man the hunter" and the living representatives of humanity's ancestry, find their way to the United Nations to protest to the international community about their displacement and the loss of their way of life. This was what captured the attention of the global media outlets and the curiosity, emotions, and sympathetic sense of injustice of their audiences. It gave the San a foothold from which to raise wider awareness of their plight.

But the immediate story of their justice campaign is only a small part of what is interesting about the San's efforts to lobby for justice in the UN and other international agencies. There are other lessons here that can be pulled from the story that have much wider significance, that are symptomatic of indigenous peoples' justice campaigns and advocacy more broadly, that indeed represent shifts in the ways that peoples on the margins of states are engaging with new discourses of human rights and humanitarianism. We can see in this process not only the widely recognized effects of what Sally Engle Merry (2006) has termed "vernacularization" – the adaptation of human rights to local institutions and meanings – but also a related phenomenon sometimes discussed in a literature that emphasizes "upstream approaches" (de Gaay Fortman

2011), in which the emphasis is on local "rights from below" advocacy, a process of "talking back," of small, cumulative influences on the structures and conceptualizations of UN agencies and, ultimately, perhaps even the content and direction of international law and policy.

Here we are also entering territory navigated by Samuel Moyn (2010), who argues persuasively for the very recent emergence of the most significant qualities of the human rights movement, and leaves an open field for understanding just how and under what impetus this global coming-into-prominence of human rights and humanitarianism has occurred. As one of many participants in UN meetings and processes of reform, San activists have played a part – albeit as few among many – in this development, connecting their story to global transformations, making their activities in the UN part of wider developments in global governance and its relationships with local institutions and ideas.

In their efforts to influence international and national law, indigenous peoples face a basic dilemma in which people on the margins of states are required to develop high levels of expertise and administrative capacity, which they are often prevented from achieving by their conditions of marginalization. There is a dimension of the struggle for representation that involves various kinds of co-optation. Perhaps most significantly, they are called upon to seek their political autonomy in state-centered structures that limit their scope for effective action. With reference to the people she studied in Asia, Tania Li is among those who find that indigenous rights claimants "must fill the places of recognition that others provide ... even as they seek to stretch, reshape, or even invert the meanings implied" (2001: 653). This is much the same dilemma that Elizabeth Povinelli refers to as "the political cunning and calculus of cultural recognition in a settler modernity" (Povinelli 2002: 39).

A number of questions follow from these observations, which bring us back to the issue of the social lives of the law. Given the limits imposed by the structures of global governance, what kinds of expertise are required for the promotion of recognition and meaning-making in the UN? And what are the consequences of this expertise for the people who acquire it and for the people they represent? What are the implications of the fact that the training and expertise needed for activists to effectively navigate legal institutions like UN agencies are remote from the communities of the represented, creating distances and divisions that need to be overcome? And how do indigenous experts reconcile their professional skills with their identities and loyalties as indigenous persons? These were particularly acute challenges for indigenous delegates like those of the San, for whom the inhibitions against "speaking for others" made the processes of drafting statements for UN meetings particularly delicate, fraught with potential for disagreements among delegates and loss of community support at home.

All of this occurred within the structures and priorities of UN agencies, with their own qualifications and procedures of participation, their own language concerning what it means to be indigenous, and their own conceptions of humanity and human rights. This institutional and ideological structure formed the backdrop of knowledge acquisition and dissemination for those San delegates who wanted to bring the plight of their people to the world's attention. Yet, far from being an unwanted imposition, some San delegates with whom I spoke were inspired by what they learned and were required to do in the UN. To them, it was often a revelation to find that they faced many of the same problems that other San delegates from Namibia, Zimbabwe, and South Africa faced – and that indigenous peoples more generally from other parts of Africa and the rest of the world were experiencing. The UN was in this sense not a place of futile struggle but of a kind of fragile hope, contingent on at least some victories in a long-term struggle. This hope was based, as we will see, not only in empty rhetoric, but above all in a global sense of belonging, together with economic and political opportunities that incentivized delegates to keep coming back.

INTRODUCING INDIGENEITY IN AFRICA

In many parts of the world it is fairly easy to determine those who are the descendants of a settler society and those who are descended from the original inhabitants.[4] In some countries like Canada, the United States, and Australia there are tangible histories of treaties and legislation, and sometimes even registers that assign identity cards and a distinct status to every individual of "Indian," "Native," or "Aboriginal" origin. Claims of indigenous difference can readily be attached to these forms of history and identity. But in Africa making an indigenous rights claim is much more difficult. In the African postcolonial context, in the absence of dominant settler societies and among people with complex histories of migration, how does one determine who is a "first-comer"? The difficulty of this question means that indigenous rights claims in Africa are situated in complex regimes of diversity within the state. It also means that indigeneity is based largely on conditions of political neglect (Daes 2008: 17). There is in Africa a dimension of indigenous identity that has a great deal to do with political marginalization in the context of recent national independence. What this means is that before any indigenous rights claims are discussed, the indigenous status of the claimants is contested. In response to indigenous rights claims, some African states present the argument that all of their citizens are indigenous, that there is no remaining legacy of a dominant settler society that makes it possible to identify a people with prior occupation of a territory, and that if one group of people can claim distinct indigenous rights to traditional territory, it does so at the expense of the rights of others.

It is into this complex ideological and institutional space that the San took their rights claims. Regional and international networking and use of the international arena as a tool of action have helped San organizations and delegates from southern Africa to bring their concerns to a wider public, to materialize the San movement, and to develop common goals and discourses.

When indigenous delegates from Africa first began to attend meetings of the WGIP – following the path-breaking address by Moringe ole Parkipuny, Maasai activist and member of the Tanzanian Parliament, on August 3, 1989 – the conditions for African indigenous peoples' participation in the UN were anything but optimal. Regular participation of indigenous peoples in UN meetings had begun a decade or so earlier, starting with the 1977 International NGO Conference on Discrimination against Indigenous Populations in the Americas. When the WGIP was established in 1982, the focus of concern was solidly on those indigenous peoples from North and South America, from recognized settler states such as Australia and New Zealand, and the Saami from the Nordic countries of Europe. Indigenous peoples from Africa and Asia were not at this point a highly visible presence.

Part of the reason for the absence of African NGOs from the early years of the Working Group was not only an outcome of the difficulty of claiming indigenous status in Africa. It also had a great deal to do with the late development of civil society in Africa. There was the practical limitation inherent in the fact that, at that time, there were relatively few delegates who were formally educated and multilingual, and who could therefore usefully take part in international meetings on indigenous peoples. From the perspective of southern Africa, activists had more immediate political struggles to contend with, facing the intransigence of their own governments, which were opposed to their participation in meetings involving indigenous rights. In addition, in many parts of southern Africa, San were caught up in the anti-Apartheid struggle, the process of decolonization, and movements toward independence. Some San scholars were in the throes of the Kalahari debate that began in the mid-1980s and by 1990 had become particularly intense (see Chapter 1, p. 13–7). San spokespersons were involved in the debate, occasionally even attending meetings such as those of the American Anthropological Association in the United States.

The reasons for this absence also became clearer when delegates from Africa came to the UN and met with resistance. Surprisingly, some of this resistance came from those indigenous delegates, mainly from the Western hemisphere, who were already well established in the UN system. They argued that the defining issue for indigenous peoples was displacement by alien, invading powers, not marginalization as an outcome of colonial independence struggles at the hands of compatriots with equally deep ties to national territories (Niezen 2003: 74).

States had their own reasons to push back against the recognition and rights of African indigenous peoples. Neither Botswana nor Namibia ever attended WGIP meetings;[5] but the point was made by Morocco, among others, such as in its 1985 statement to the WGIP, with an argument that was (and continues) to be repeated many times by a variety of African states in the UN: "In Morocco the problem of the protection of indigenous populations does not arise. Everyone enjoys the right to life, physical and mental integrity and security in all areas" (1985: 3). That is to say, there can be no distinct rights for those claiming indigenous status, since the state is premised on the same undifferentiated rights for all citizens. Indigenous rights introduce a dangerous form of tribalism to African politics, the argument goes, which can only be overcome by emphasizing constitutional uniformity and equality.

Finally, one of the main reasons why African indigenous groups found it difficult to be part of the indigenous movement arose from a prevalent attitude of resistance within the United Nations itself, in particular through the influence of Alfonso Martínez, for many years the coordinator of the WGIP. Martínez developed a critique that he referred to as the "indigenous *problematique* in the African and Asian context" (1992, 1995, 1999), in which he argued, quite simply, that in the cases of Africa and Asia there are no indigenous peoples. The groups that claim to be indigenous should be considered minorities, he argued, and should therefore bring their problems to the Working Group on Minorities (1999: para. 90). Interestingly, he identified two possible exceptions to this position, the San in Botswana and the Maasai in Kenya (Martínez 1999: para. 78, 165). Since "indigenous peoples" is a concept that reflects the relationship between settlers and first-comers, the use of the term in the context of postcolonial states was particularly sensitive, implying accusations of neocolonialism against states whose reference points of history and identity were situated in their colonial liberation. In terms of political principle, it opened a Pandora's box (as some saw it) of claims of self-determination in regions that had already been liberated from the yoke of colonial occupation and oppression. How could there be legitimate and manageable demands for liberation from states that were already liberated from colonial rule? This was the main challenge posed when IWGIA "went global" and started supporting indigenous delegates from Africa, who began to make regular appearances in Working Group meetings. To have a secure place in the UN and international law, the African indigenous movement thus had to develop a different understanding of indigeneity, one that was not related to settler societies or first-coming but based more on their structural position of marginality and experience of discrimination.

Part of a solution to this challenge came from a regional body inside the African Commission on Human and People's Rights (ACHPR), which took on the challenge of dealing with indigenous rights in Africa. The ACHPR had been debating issues relating to indigenous peoples since 1989 (Crawhall 2011). In its 25th Ordinary Session, held in Bujumbura, Burundi in 1999, Barney Pityana, a member of the commission, introduced the delegates in the room to the report from the First Conference of Indigenous Peoples from Central, Eastern, and Southern Africa, which had taken place in Arusha in Tanzania the same year. In doing so, he affirmed the existence of indigenous peoples in Africa (Thornberry 2002: 260).

The issues being faced by the San in Botswana factored into the African Union's interpretation of indigeneity in Africa. The ACHPR Working Group on Indigenous Populations/Communities (established in 2001 by the ACHPR) visited Botswana in June 2005, when it questioned the government's approach to the issue of indigeneity and pointed out the complex situations facing indigenous peoples in the country, including, in particular, the CKGR (ACHPR 2008).

From this starting point, a variety of law making initiatives began. At the beginning of the twenty-first century, the ACHPR (2005, 2006) tried to translate a global understanding of "indigenous peoples" in a way that would be applicable to the African context, out of which a different translation of indigeneity in the African regional institutions emerged.

The ACHPR was involved in elaborating new human rights standards and took a strong position in favor of the *UN Declaration on the Rights of Indigenous Peoples* (UNDRIP). During its 41st Ordinary Session (Accra, Ghana, May 16–30, 2007), the ACHPR debated the issue and, on the recommendation of its African WGIP, passed a resolution that addressed and endorsed the concept of "indigenous populations" on the African continent. In that same session, the ACHPR presented an Advisory Opinion on the various concerns expressed by African states regarding the UNDRIP (ACHPR 2007). The position African states took against indigeneity was one of the major stumbling blocks affecting the adoption by the UN General Assembly of the Declaration in 2006–7 (ACHPR 2007; Barume 2010; Crawhall 2011). These concerns, which had been outlined in a document produced by the dozen or so African states that took issue with the Draft Declaration (see African Group of States 2006), were addressed systematically. The Advisory Opinion (ACHPR 2007) discussed each of the issues raised by the African groups of states (e.g. concern over the lack of a definition of indigenous peoples and over the right of indigenous peoples to self-determination) and provided an explanation and justification for why the UNDRIP contained the articles that it did. After considerable discussion and lobbying, and after some agreements were reached, Botswana and the other states withdrew their objections. Eventually, on September 13, 2007, Botswana joined many other African states in voting in favor of the declaration.

Despite states' opposition to the concept of indigenous peoples in the African context, in the past decade something within the African Union (AU) has changed regarding indigenous peoples' issues. Specific to the African case is the fact that the term "indigenous populations" in Africa does not mean "first inhabitants" in reference to aboriginality as opposed to non-African communities or those having come from elsewhere. While self-identification remained a central criterion, the position of "first peoples" was rejected as a defining principle and replaced with the people's "structural position" and their "livelihood practices" (ACHPR 2005), which in the case of Africa are primarily pastoralism and hunting and gathering.

These developments in international law initiated by the ACHPR ultimately had less impact on the concept of indigenous peoples in Africa than the participation of indigenous delegates from the continent in UN and AU meetings. Their presence at meetings *was* the argument that they were indigenous. It should also be noted that there were attempts to organize and mobilize an African indigenous movement with the creation of regional indigenous organizations such as the Organization of Indigenous Peoples in Africa (OIPA), supported by IWGIA, and the Indigenous Peoples of Africa Coordinating Committee (IPACC). Indigenous peoples from various parts of Africa attended the early meetings of these organizations and had varying degrees of investment in them. Eventually, however, IPACC prevailed, and it is now the main organization representing indigenous peoples in Africa today (Crawhall 2011; Dahl 2012: 236).

African indigenous delegates strongly opposed their exclusion from relevant UN meetings in their statements to the WGIP, suggesting that "the Working Group would be incomplete without the participation of indigenous peoples from Africa and Asia."[6] In July 1999 a firm stand in this regard was taken by a San delegate, Kxao Moses=Oma,[7] the head of Nyae Nyae Farmers Cooperative (then Nyae Nyae Conservancy) in Namibia, and member of Parliament (Biesele and Hitchcock 2013: 179–80), when he took the floor on behalf of the Working Group of Indigenous Minorities in Southern Africa (WIMSA) at the 17th session in Geneva and stated,

> with respect to Professor Martínez, we reject totally the conclusion of the Martínez report, which is to the effect that indigenous peoples of Africa (such as us) do not belong to this forum ... We, as first peoples of Africa, are indigenous to Africa in every way ... We belong to this forum, and do not intend to go anywhere else![8]

WIMSA started to attend the WGIP in 1997 and since then has participated in WGIP and PFII meetings almost every year. In 1998 its official status found its way in the final report of the WGIP, which states that it "was created to address the needs of indigenous populations in Angola, Botswana, Namibia, South Africa, Zambia and Zimbabwe, where governmental action combined with evangelization policies of the past had put the survival of local cultures at risk."[9]

First People of the Kalahari was another early entrant in the African indigenous movement. A few years after Hardbattle and Sesana travelled to the UN, at the 17th session of the WGIP (1999), the office manager and director of FPK, Mama Rampadi (Chapter 4, p. 140), a Kua San from northeastern Kweneng, stated that the mission of the organization was to assist the CKGR people, adding,

> It appears to us that our Government respects the rights of animals above those of the Bushmen. It also appears to us that our Government does not understand the rights of Indigenous Peoples, as are accepted in the world today ... indigenous peoples know how to coexist with conservation ... we appeal to this forum for support in our struggle for our people's land and dignity.[10]

In that same session, Rampadi worked closely with WIMSA, which denounced the situation in the CKGR and drew particular attention to the plight of a closely related people, the Hai//om, who were dispossessed of their land with the creation of the Etosha National Park in Namibia (Chapter 8, p. 306).

These interventions, indicating the active participation of indigenous peoples' organizations from southern Africa in the 1990s, were made possible not so much by developments in the law, but by a space where law was absent. "Self-definition" is a major part of what made it possible to globalize a concept that was originally focused on the "settler states" of the Americas, the South Pacific, and the Nordic countries of northern Europe. The original "working definition" of indigenous peoples from a 1986 report by José Martínez-Cobo is notably free of any criteria that could be used (particularly by states) to block an indigenous people or organization from participating in the UN's initiatives:

> Indigenous communities, peoples and nations are those which, having a historical continuity with pre-invasion and pre-colonial societies that develop on their territories, *consider themselves distinct* from other sectors of the societies now prevailing in those territories, or parts of them. They form at present non-dominant sectors of society and are determined to preserve, develop and transmit to future generations their ancestral territories, and their ethnic identity, as the basis of their continued existence as people, in accordance with their own cultural patterns, social institutions and legal systems. (Martínez-Cobo 1986: 5, para. 379, emphasis added)

The idea that they *consider themselves* distinct, as indigenous peoples, opened the door to the inclusion of indigenous NGOs from Africa and Asia in UN meetings. This lack of a "gatekeeper" definition has extended to all other UN initiatives, including the 2007 *Declaration on the Rights of Indigenous Peoples*. The absence of a definition, combined with the distinct rights that were being developed, created powerful incentives for NGOs to adopt an indigenous political identity in order to benefit from its terms (Chapter 1, p. 19; Macklem 2015: 157).[11]

This important element of self-definition, however, does not mean that all peoples who represent themselves as indigenous are recognized as such. In fact, to be indigenous in international forums, indigenous leaders and the organizations to which they belong have to be recognized by the UN institutions and by other members of the global indigenous movement. This happens in practice through the process of accreditation at the meetings led by the interested UN agencies, and more informally by the response of the global indigenous community to "newcomers." For instance, in 1994 there was a case in which indigenous peoples refused to recognize a group attending the WGIP as indigenous: many indigenous delegates formally complained that the Afrikaner Volksfront (South Africa) and the Rehoboth Baster Community (Namibia) should not be allowed to participate because of alleged racist backgrounds. These groups, descendants from former European colonists and some African groups, sought autonomy because, they claimed, under the governance of newly independent states they suffered discrimination and threats to their cultures and languages. The Boers of the Afrikaner Volksfront had no problem in asserting that they were the former undisputed masters of South Africa and architects of Apartheid, while the Basters claimed that they were an indigenous people in the Republic of Namibia (Escarcega 2003: 297). Both groups referred to their historical links to the territory. When they took the floor, however, many of the indigenous delegates in the room walked out as a sign of protest. In subsequent WGIP meetings, these cases were invoked in conversations in UN hallways and cafeterias to exemplify the absurdity of such groups' claims to indigeneity and the continuation of neocolonial and imperialist attitudes in southern Africa.

The aborted effort by the Boers to find a place as "indigenous" illustrates one of the most important qualities of indigenous peoples' participation in UN initiatives, which has to do with an informal process of finding shared experiences and common cause among other delegates. In this the San peoples have excelled. They had much to say about their experience that resonated with other indigenous delegates from elsewhere in the world, and their experience in international meetings reinforced their sense of place in the wider politico-legal community of indigenous peoples.

ACCREDITATION AND THE DEVELOPMENT OF EXPERTISE

The now-defunct Working Group on Indigenous Populations and the ongoing Permanent Forum on Indigenous Issues established in 2002 were, despite their different mandates, comparable in terms of the experience they gave (and demanded of) indigenous delegates. The processes of accreditation, travel, collaboration, training, making statements, and engaging with the discourse of states were essentially the same in the sessions of both the Working Group and the Permanent Forum. Through the years that I have attended the UNPFII annual sessions, as well as during the internships I had in the UN Headquarters in New York and in the Indigenous section of the International Fund for Agricultural Development in Rome, it was possible to see how some indigenous delegates acquired broader experience in the UN, sometimes becoming international civil servants and experts in their own right. Although my experience is based on participation in a variety of UN agencies between 2006 and 2017, I am applying my ethnographic experience more broadly to consider how the participation of African indigenous delegates to the UN has taken form, how the rules of procedure to be followed can impose constraints, and how these are overcome in various forms of "talking back," of (re)shaping and introducing to the UN indigenous ways of seeing the world and defining their rights within it. I therefore situate the San activist movement and the struggle for the rights of the people in the CKGR in the wider field of international agencies that the activists were called on to adapt to and navigate.

African delegates to international meetings face particular obstacles that, in turn, impact the selection of those who are able to participate and the ways they are able to strategize. The rights claims of African indigenous peoples are enmeshed in particular postcolonial legacies and in relationships with states that are based in differing perspectives on diversity, development, and visions of the future. First, there is a *practical side* to the processes of indigenous self-definition and self-representation, with obstacles built into the way that indigenous peoples and organizations appear as such in UN meetings, and from there make their presence known to others. The practicalities of participation may seem routine (as in fact they are), but at the same time they have far-reaching consequences. The registration requirement for participation in UN meetings, for example, is at first glance an entirely normal bureaucratic procedure, but in fact it determines the individuals and organizations that are authorized to participate and who become legitimate spokespersons. It gives or withholds the official letters and badges that delegates need to pass through the security gates into the UN meeting rooms. For many people from remote localities this often presents difficulties that follow, first from access to the online forms, the lack of means to pay for computer equipment, and wider conditions of limited communication infrastructure along with the level of formal education, knowledge of a UN language, and computer skills needed to correctly complete the forms. Some delegates do not even know of the procedure and simply arrive in New York without credentials. Others simply "forget" to do it and say something like, "It is not an indigenous way of working."

The accreditation process selects those people who are affiliated with organizations that have recognized institutional elements such as a formal mission statement and an office with an address. If the organization seeks ECOSOC status, which greatly increases its profile in the UN system, the requirements are even more stringent than those to attend meetings such as those of the PFII and Expert Mechanism on the Rights of Indigenous Peoples. This is a problem for many indigenous representatives, as one of them remarked during the 2015 PFII session: "Indigenous peoples are not just NGOs but they have their own institutions and they are not recognized by the UN" (author notes 2015). One result of the accreditation process is that the breadth of indigenous representation able to attend the UN meetings is limited to those who own the technical knowledge, education, and resources to participate. This is a clear example of how international institutions, through bureaucratic procedures, shape the meaning and structures concerning what it is to be indigenous and who can be part of the indigenous global movement.

The practical difficulties do not end there. Influence in international law for indigenous delegates (and states as well) is contingent on having the economic capital to send delegates to the meetings. Once delegates are approved, they need to have the funds to travel to the UN meetings. The cost of airfare, hotels, ground transport, and food for this travel is such that those whose livelihoods are based on subsistence practices in remote regions (common qualities of indigenous peoples) are often unable to travel to UN meetings held in the USA or Europe. It should also be noted that some NGOs play gatekeeper roles in the

United Nations. Umbrella organizations and international NGOs often control the financial resources to bring people to meetings, and therefore have the authority to select representatives and influence their priorities once they arrive.

It became essential to have "donors," to build alliances with regional and international NGOs such as IWGIA, the Indigenous Peoples of Africa Coordinating Committee (IPACC), or the Open Society Initiative for Southern Africa (OSISA), or to be familiar with grants that the UN offers through the UN Voluntary Fund for Indigenous Peoples, along with their deadlines and procedures. The latter is usually the route that people prefer because it gives them independence from sponsoring international NGOs and networks with their own agendas and – not to be underestimated – often offers a better per-diem rate, necessary for surviving expensive capitals and for saving a bit of money to bring back home. Sometimes, blurring the boundary between indigenous activists and states, San, like other delegates, are invited by their own government to attend meetings such as those of the Permanent Forum (as was often the case with Namibia and the San Development Office, now the Division of Marginalized Communities in the Office of the Vice-President of Namibia).

The technological, educational, and financial conditions that have to be met before indigenous delegates can attend UN meetings and appear as representatives of an indigenous people create a basic reliance on NGOs as the vehicles and facilitators of indigenous representation. Among African indigenous peoples, there is a significant degree of international collaboration that accompanies their NGO representation. In contexts as different as the San struggle against removal from the CKGR and the Tuareg struggle for subsistence and autonomy in the Central Sahara of West Africa, NGOs and experts, mainly from Europe and North America, have worked together with African indigenous spokespersons to make their claims known to a wider audience and to make effective use of legal opportunities in international law and in state courts to further their claims. Public audiences in Europe, North America, and "back home" have become significant for the effectiveness of justice lobbying, for the strategies used in making a cause known and applying pressure on states to change their actions and policies. It is in a sense ironic that the isolation and limited resources of African indigenous peoples would lead in some cases to the need for greater international collaboration of the efforts to redress their grievances.

THE PERMANENT FORUM ON INDIGENOUS ISSUES

Since its creation in 2002, the two-week session of the Permanent Forum on Indigenous Issues has been the focal point of indigenous activism in the United Nations. Despite the difficulties faced by representatives of marginalized communities in registering for Forum sessions and travelling to New York, it is still one of the more accessible meetings in the UN system. With its comparatively loose requirements for access (similar in this regard to its predecessor the WGIP), it does not necessarily require NGOs to have consultative status with the ECOSOC. Consequently, it is one of the largest forums in the UN system that invites civil society participation. Indigenous peoples' organizations (IPOs), states, UN bodies, and governmental and NGOs may participate in the Forum as "observers."[12] Although these observers have no formal voting rights, they can be invited to report on their activities regarding indigenous peoples and are entitled to present their point of view and make recommendations during the main session (Sapignoli 2017). The Forum has a mandate to discuss indigenous peoples' problems of economic and social development, education, wealth, environment, and human rights. Unlike its predecessor, the WGIP,[13] the Forum's mandate is not (as many delegates mistakenly assume) to develop human rights norms, but to prepare and disseminate information, raise awareness and develop cooperation (mainly within the UN system), and submit recommendations and expert advice on indigenous issues to ECOSOC. The Forum also has the authority to receive and investigate complaints and to address governments, UN agencies, and international and regional institutions in the attempt to monitor the implementation of the *UN Declaration on the Rights of Indigenous Peoples* (UNDRIP).

The main sessions of the PFII, in which short speeches known as "interventions" are heard, are (like its predecessor the WGIP) a place of human rights activism, learning and networking, making knowledge public, and ideally educating or changing the minds of those who are uninformed about or obstructive regarding the distinct identities, forms of dispossession, and rights of indigenous peoples. Once in the UN meeting room, making a statement is the goal on everyone's minds, the way to make oneself heard, one of the main reasons for being there.

Most of the San delegates participating in the Permanent Forum today are long accustomed to attending UN meetings, but there are always those who are attending for the first time. Some, as we saw, started their experience with the UN during the years of the WGIP in the 1980s and 1990s, others as invited fellows in Geneva at the International Labour Organization (ILO) and Human Rights Council (HRC) trainings and internships. They often participated in the UN meetings as delegates of their own organizations, as was the case, for instance, with First People of the Kalahari and the Working Group of Indigenous Minorities in Southern Africa (WIMSA), but also through other national, regional, and international organizations.[14] There is also a cohort of youth from Botswana that started its international activism in the PFII and who now have become regular participants.

The session is more than a place of activism, contestation, and lobbying; it is a site of encounter, knowledge production and learning, a place for the acquisition and application of expertise, where people share experience and promote knowledge on indigenous peoples' rights and identities.[15] Seen in a wider context, it is a place that has developed conditions for the formation of indigenous elites, those professionally trained representatives or employees of formal organizations whose criteria for leadership are usually entirely different from those of the communities they represent.

Aside from those who fill recognized positions as "independent experts" on indigenous issues, such as member of the Permanent Forum and Expert Mechanism,[16] the Special Rapporteur on Indigenous Peoples Rights, and so on, the UN produces another kind of expertise. This occurs when the activists who are periodically able to attend UN meetings and training sessions related to their chosen cause learn to be "experts" more generally, acquiring familiarity with the UN's working procedures, etiquette, and language to the point that they are able to take on a variety of roles in the UN system, and develop professional expertise on specific topics such as education, cultural heritage, climate change, and so on (see Sapignoli 2017).

This expertise has to start somewhere. First-comers to the Permanent Forum annual session already have at least some scraps of knowledge of the UN, which reached them in their local communities though the work of NGOs, but it still remains quite an abstract and confusing place for most of them. A Khoe-Nama woman from Namibia remarked on her experience as a newcomer to the Forum: "Everything is strange to me. I need to learn everything step by step"(author notes 2008). Most do not have any idea of what they will encounter once they arrive in New York. They soon end up doing all the things that tourists do: wandering around Manhattan and being impressed by the tall buildings, the lights, and the many stores and restaurants, doing some shopping, buying presents for family and friends, taking "selfies" in front of monuments and landmarks, and taking other cellphone pictures of food to post later on Facebook or Instagram.

Then there is work to do. Their initiation to the PFII session comes in the form of indigenous caucuses, meetings of indigenous delegates that are held every year in the World Council of Churches building in front of the UN Secretariat on the weekend before the main session. This is where newcomers first encounter the experience of other long-term indigenous delegates, PFII members, and UN officials from the Secretariat. Here, various consultations take place, often informally, among indigenous networks and caucuses on particular themes or issues. In the regional and issue-based caucuses (particularly global, youth, women's, and African caucuses), they learn about the Forum's limitations and possibilities, their expected contributions to the session, and how to register for the "speaker list," write statements, and talk about their grievances. Here they exchange information with other indigenous participants and become part of the global indigenous movement, a community of people – indigenous and not – who share similar goals and the sense that "they are not alone."

The most widely recognized caucus is the Global Caucus (Dhal 2013). In the collective indigenous Global Caucus statement, the voices of inexperienced individuals often go unheard because their agenda is not a priority for those with more experience in the UN. San spokespersons generally appear to have little interest in the Global Caucus, seeing it as dominated by a few well-established groups (mostly those from the Americas), which tend to control the narrative. They do, however, usually join their regional caucus, the African Caucus.

The African Caucus was created for enabling African delegates to collaborate in UN meetings more effectively, being better able to point to their common concerns and goals for change than if they were drafting statements with delegates from other regions (author notes, African Caucus 2009). After the regional caucuses determine the person with major experience of the UN and better language skills – in other words the "rapporteur" of the delegation – he or she begins to take notes on the several issues discussed. One of the aims of these gatherings is to come up with a strategy regarding their participation in the two-week meeting that is to follow, particularly on the ways the statements should be written. Several issues often emerge, such as the importance of being accurate, the kind of government actions that should be highlighted, but above all (as I will discuss further below) the issues of representation and speaking for others. A key role in the African Caucus is played by IPACC, the main organization behind its creation and the participation of African delegates in UN meetings (Hodgson 2011).

Some San have attended most of the meetings of the African Caucus since its inception. Pastoral peoples have tended to have a more prominent role in the African movement, with Tuareg and Maasai delegates taking leading roles, possibly because of their ready familiarity with hierarchical structures of leadership (Hodgson 2011). The San, by contrast, have tended to be more quiet and retiring, leaving the spotlight to others. These differences in influence were, until recently, manifested in the fact that it was often difficult for the San delegates to insert their comments into the caucus statements. In the last few years (after some open criticism), however, hunter and gatherers delegates have become more active spokespersons for the movement, and have managed to push their issues to the fore in caucus statements, often even being the person to deliver the statement in the conference room in front of the microphone. San delegates attempted in 2012 to informally create their own San Caucus and did present one intervention under the auspices of this new caucus (see below), but it had a short life owing to the fact that the UN's rules of registration do not allow the creation of specific new caucuses.

Indigenous delegates have to be trained by their colleagues and members of the Secretariat on how to play a "diplomatic game." In fact, to make a difference politically during the meetings, indigenous peoples must in short order become experts: they have to learn how to address government officials in ways that maximize their chance of being heard and that do not cause trouble for them when they return home, and they must learn to use cultural and political frameworks that are comprehensible within their own nations and by international experts. They do this most directly through the production of "statements."

DRAFTING STATEMENTS

One of the first lessons learned by new indigenous delegates is their place in the production of documents.[17] To be effective, or even legible, in the terms of global governance in the UN, indigenous representatives' sense of injustice has to be presented in an "intervention" before the microphone, which involves reading a "statement," the document that then, ideally, becomes part of the record of the meeting and finds its way into the final report. One of the key activities through which San delegates are directly initiated into the customs of international diplomacy is therefore in statement-making and delivery. Statements are just one component of the UN's production of a vast corpus of documents that includes reports by UN agencies and forums, thematic studies, country visit reports, NGO reports, and the final reports of sessions.

For indigenous delegates to the UN, the passions and indignation that results from the injustice they experience are channeled into three- or five-minute interventions, contained by the requirements of diplomacy, in the hope that the issues raised will be taken up by the Forum in its report and passed on to other levels and other audiences in the UN system. The statement has to follow a specific format, with formalized greetings, reference to national and international law, and recommendations, ideally using "indigenous markers" expressed in key words like "mother earth," "stewardship of nature," and often introducing and concluding their statements in the delegates' native language, presenting through a few words of salutation the vitality of their ongoing way of life.[18] An example of this narrative can be found in the San Caucus statement presented to the 2012 session of the UNPFII: "The San are known for the reverence in which we hold land, and for sustainability managing and nurturing the earth since time immemorial ... recognized as the stewards and custodians of the earth" (author notes 2012). The language of stewardship and sustainability is often then conjoined with rights in a way that makes the two inseparable.

As a form of discourse, the statement represents an instrument of diplomacy, with structures to be followed as a condition of being heard. It often happens that indigenous delegates deliver deeply emotional statements to the floor of the session, including personal stories of suffering and loss, told with tears, unsteady voices, and trembling hands. The audience usually responds sympathetically, the room applauding loudly, and other delegates sometimes approach the speaker afterwards to express sympathy and solidarity. The global networks of the indigenous peoples' movement seem to converge on these moments of emotional connection.

None of this emotion and sympathy, however, finds its way into the report of the meeting, which strips away all reference to or invocation of poignant sentiments. If the reports ever do describe the failed responsibilities of states, and occasionally their counter-claims, they do so in the most neutral terms possible. Information is selected for wider

Figure 5 Drafting a statement, UN Headquarters, New York

communication in the UN system, with a preference for "facts" and bare, unadorned reporting of events over the experiences and emotions that accompanied them (see Wilson 1997).

Training on how to write and deliver influential statements is organized by NGOs and the PFII Secretariat. As a result of this institutionalized preference for collaboration, indigenous representatives often lobby other NGOs and caucuses to persuade them to include their case in a joint statement because they have more chance of being called by the session chair to take the floor. This lobbying and networking activity will often serve to strengthen alliances and commitments between groups. The joint statements have greater impact because they express broader collective interests. The more times a specific case is mentioned and the more voices are explicitly behind it, the more likely it is to attract the attention of the experts and thus to be included in the final reports with the hope (perhaps distant) that it will ultimately impact international policymaking.

Indigenous delegates' ability to negotiate the order in which they will make their statements, and the inclusion of their case in other statements, often reveal gendered power relations and differences between recent and long-term participants and those from different geographical regions. Some of the more experienced indigenous delegates – usually men – acquire gatekeeping roles and can decide who gets to talk, what is mentioned, and when. For those indigenous representatives with less experience, it is crucial not to be overlooked, to actively participate with the "gatekeepers" and others who know the system.

Locally based indigenous peoples' organizations often deliver their statements through the name of the organization that invites them to the meeting or the umbrella organization of which they are a part at home. They can speak as representatives of their individual communities, as San in their respective countries (e.g. Botswana, Namibia, or South Africa), or as San of the southern Africa region. The San delegates often prefer to make their own statements, as a San people, with their specific issues addressed, where the aim is not so much to enter the final report as to simply have their voices heard.

For indigenous delegates, talking about their problems through caucuses or joint statements is a good mechanism to avoid government pressure and harassment when they return to their home country. Delegations with less experience can also "piggyback" on the work of more seasoned NGOs. For instance, in 2007 First People of the Kalahari made a joint statement with Native American groups because of the latter's extensive experience and involvement in a networking process that had started years before.

Struggle with the statement as a diplomatic form of discourse was clear in the times that I was present during the drafting process. One of these drafting meetings took place in April 2008, when I met some representatives from southern African in the UN Headquarters cafeteria in New York. They, like me, were there to attend the seventh session of the UN Permanent Forum on Indigenous Issues. The people at the table were San and Khoe from Botswana, South Africa, and Namibia. There were three men and three women who averaged around thirty to forty years of age. They represented various Khoekhoe and San groups such as the Nama, Griqua, Tse'xa, ǂKhomani, Bugakhwe, and Hai//om. One of them, a Hai//om man from Namibia who was then living in South Africa, had had extensive experience at the UN. He had attended the WGIP in Geneva in the 1990s and the UNPFII for the past several years. He was offering advice and explaining the activities of the Forum, its dynamics, and the roles that indigenous peoples are supposed to have:

> You should present a statement and speak about San problems and make recommendations. It is important you register your speech with the Secretariat; otherwise you will not be able to talk. You should also

> contact your country mission here in the UN; they can be helpful to you. And you will meet a lot of people that want to help you and that are interested in what you have to say. (Author notes 2008)

Gathered at the table with their laptops, they were talking about the various problems their people were facing and more generally about the attitudes of their governments toward indigenous peoples. They had pages in their laptops linked to the just-approved UNDRIP, a report on South Africa by the Special Rapporteur on the Rights of Indigenous Peoples, Rodolfo Stavenhagen, and a variety of other UN documents. Their goal was to use these reference points of international law to make their statement more effective in terms of the criteria set out by the Secretariat of the Permanent Forum.

Before the drafting of the statement started, the San and the Khoi delegates formed two distinct groups because they felt that their issues were different and that they were "not the same people." Some San delegates, in particular, saw the Khoi people as more politically powerful and not like them in significant ways, having a lifestyle based more on cattle herding than hunting. These tensions between Khoi and San groups were not always present, but if it is true that Khoi organizations often denounced the discriminatory actions against the San of the southern African governments in their statements, the opposite was not true. The San delegate felt little sense of reciprocal support. Most likely, the significance of the distinction follows from the fact that the hunting and gathering way of life as a foundation for indigenous identity is tremendously significant for the San as a source of their recognition as an indigenous people. In this case, combining themselves with "cattle herders," with groups that they saw as more powerful, dilutes the authority of their claims to a "deep" indigeneity, connected to their recognized place in popular and professional narratives.[19]

Despite these divergent identities and interests, it was soon clear that everyone at the table was interested in what was happening in the CKGR after the recent legal case (the *Sesana* case, which is the subject of the next chapter) and wanted to include information on the case in the statements they were writing on behalf of the southern African San. One woman remarked, "I know about the Botswana case and we think that it was a fake victory!"[20] The San delegate from Botswana was a young man from the Okavango area (northwest of the CKGR) who had never even visited the CKGR, was not very familiar with the situation of the people of the reserve, and was therefore, reluctant to talk about issues related to places he did not know well.

The group, in addition to seeing me as a researcher interested in indigenous peoples' issues, considered me an expert on the Central Kalahari. Because of this, I was part of the conversation (a situation that put me in the position of participating in the creation of the very phenomenon that I was setting out to describe as an ethnographer). They asked me for information, which I provided, on what was occurring in the Central Kalahari, the lack of services inside the reserve, including water and medical supplies, the prohibition of hunting, and the restrictions on movement in and outside the reserve. (There were also digressions, such as when they wanted to know how to get around in New York other than by taxi, which was too expensive for those on a fixed budget.) After everybody expressed their concerns, the more experienced representative from Namibia and South Africa decided to include the *Sesana* case and its aftermath in the statement because they thought it was important to speak about all the cases regarding San. They were concerned about speaking for others on things with which they had no direct experience, but at the same time clearly felt that they shared some of the same problems as the San of Botswana: lack of water, loss of land, obstacles to political representation, and the need to have a voice at the national level. Despite the considerable effort that they put into it, their statement never reached the session floor. They were not called upon to speak by the session's chair, who decided to prioritize other interventions on the list. This is something that often happens to indigenous delegations; as a consequence they often register for many agenda items throughout the session. Then, if they are given the microphone, they will slip in some part of their previously prepared statement.

The inexperienced delegates also have to learn patience. For those who come to the Forum session thinking that they will be able to vent their sense of injustice and be listened to, that their cause will be heard by an agency ready to intervene on their behalf, it can be a bitter disappointment. Every year it is possible to see the frustration in some of the less experienced delegates. A common piece of advice they are given by those with more experience is that success in international forums comes with playing "the long game."

A San woman from northern Botswana who had attended UN meetings for some years, had participated in several African regional meeting on the rights of indigenous peoples, and had won a UN fellowship in Geneva, talked to me about her experience in the Permanent Forum in its annual session in 2016. She noted that despite the fact that it takes time to solve the issues of indigenous peoples, the process for her had its benefits:

> [It] was about sharing of knowledge and ways to use the United Nations' treaties and conventions to combat the violations of human rights, and indigenous people's rights, and the networking even was useful ... [O]ne can make connections and fight for the rights of the San. I want to join the indigenous women's caucus, connect with other women and their experiences, as a San woman. (Author notes 2016)

For San women, meetings like these in the UN also gave them the possibility to build alliances with gender rights-oriented NGOs and to push for another set of issues and rights specific to indigenous women, as those who are often the "most discriminated against" by other groups and by their own people.

Despite such collaborations and constructive networking, however, there are personal rivalries and animosities that occasionally find their way into the dynamics of participation in international meetings such as the Permanent Forum. It sometimes happens that particular individuals can disrupt the process of finding common cause with other groups, and even with members of their own organization, by single-mindedly pursuing their own interests and agenda. This occurred, for example, during one session when several San delegates were unable to present a statement that they had collaboratively drafted because the spokesperson who took the floor simply decided to represent what he thought were the priorities for his organization. The San delegates who were sidetracked in this way did not raise any protest that I was able to see, most likely respecting what they saw as the speaker's higher education and deeper knowledge of the UN, or possibly avoiding conflict because of his powerful position at home, and quietly went about their business for the remainder of the meeting.

As this example shows, coming up with a common agenda is difficult at best, and there is a wide diversity of opinions even among individuals from the same group. Indigenous delegates are compelled to collaborate by the rules and structure of the meeting itself, by the time constraints, and by the need to condense their crises and injustices into bureaucratically legible and institutionally manageable forms of expression. The statements that result from these drafting processes are therefore the products of discussion among delegates with differing interests, origins, and forms of expertise. Many, particularly the relative newcomers, struggle to translate their emotion-laden experiences of dispossession and their visions for a better and just present and future into common grievances expressed in the preferred neutral concepts and categories of the UN. This diversity is both healthy and problematic, in that it involves intensive collaboration but at the same time takes the groups an enormous amount of time and effort to come up with an agreed-upon statement. These discussions do not end with the drafting session in the UN buildings. The process of collaboration that I was part of in the UN cafeteria and corridors went further than the delegates who had been present in the room. It extended to organizations and supporters back home, mainly through texting and exchanges in Facebook and WhatsApp groups. Ideas travel among the delegates, with the draft statement being tweaked and adjusted right up the moment when the chair of the session calls on the speakers to take the floor.

TECHNOLOGY AND EXPERTISE

The priorities of San delegates to UN meetings have an independent presence online, with various sources of information and opinion feeding inspiration to one another as the meetings unfold. The use of the Internet is a key aspect of the development of indigenous movements and a tool for the circulation of information among people who are unable to physically gather together. Consistent with this development, many San NGOs and networks have established a presence on Facebook and have been actively reporting on San issues through these and other social websites and blogs. In the UN meeting rooms indigenous representatives share photos, statements, and discussions with their social network friends. At the same time, they are in continuous communication with what is going on at home, and they often share last-minute information in their statements to the Forum. For those with the requisite education, equipment, and connectivity, the Internet offers a way to organize without the costs and consequences of formal organization (at least when it does not involve an officially registered website).

At the same time, however, many San continue to be excluded by this process. Botswana has one of the lowest rates of connectivity in the world, with the Internet used by 27.5 percent of the population (ranked 144th worldwide),[21] and just a small number of people in Remote Area Settlements have access to it. In fact, a San "educated elite" that lives in the capitals or cities and towns is often limited to those who are able to read and write and to have access to the Web.

Usually they are members of the younger generations. Even though antennas are visible in Remote Area Communities and the resettlement villages outside the CKGR, very few people have the possibility of owning a smartphone that will easily allow them to connect to the 3G network. Besides, one of the thorny issues is the fact that some of the elders, those leaders with the most local legitimacy, are not literate, do not speak English, and do not have access to computers. The people who went back and are living in the CKGR after the 2006 verdict – those who are the central topic of many statements delivered to the UN – are the most excluded from the process of statement production. This is mainly due to conditions of isolation and government efforts to cut them off from outside communication, for example by taking away their radios. Few NGO representatives have visited them since the 2006 *Sesana* verdict (Chapter 7), and in the reserve there is no phone connection and no easy means of transport to facilitate their movement outside, where the closest resettlement village (with its own issues of isolation) is at least a full day's walk away.

This means that, like many other indigenous delegates to the UN, the younger San spokespersons, who are best able to navigate the UN's bureaucracies and rules of diplomacy, face a heavy burden of responsibility. They are asked to speak about experiences they do not necessarily have, represent people they do not always know, and explain things they do not fully understand – and to do so in a way that is persuasive and passionate, in three minutes or less, with the red light on the microphone blinking as they reach their conclusion.

The participation in the Permanent Forum of indigenous leaders who do not have the requisite language and technological skills to participate actively in UN meetings illustrates the restrictive effects of some UN structures from another direction. This includes, for example some San delegates from Namibia, who attended the Forum as part of the state delegation form the office of the San Development Program, Division of Marginalized Communities. These indigenous representatives included the elder Tsamkxao=Oma, the son of =Oma who figured prominently in the films of John Marshall (e.g. *The Hunters*) and a recognized Ju/'hoan Traditional Authority (TA) based in Tsumkwe. Tsamkxao and the Ju/'hoansi had been involved in a legal case in the High Court of Namibia concerning the invasion by Herero and their cattle from /Gam in April 2009 (see Biesele and Hitchcock 2010). When I met Tsamkxao in New York it was very difficult to talk with him without the presence of government officials who acted as mediators and translators. Tsamkxao, for his part, found it difficult to follow the discussion during the session since he does not speak any of the UN recognized languages in which the meetings are simultaneously translated, and he was not able to take the microphone and make a statement. The state delegate who loosely translated our conversation reported that Tsamkxao considered the meeting to have been useful. He was intrigued to see other San at the meeting and said that in the past he thought that the only San were the Ju/'hoansi ("the true people").

It should be noted here that being part of a state delegation was not limited to elders who were unable to effectively navigate the Forum, but included others who were more fully part of state policy implementation. In the 2016 Forum session, for example, Kxao Royal Ui/O/oo, a San delegate working as Deputy Director in the Division of Marginalized Communities in the Office of the vice-president, praised the Namibian government for its handling of San and minority issues, and argued that Namibia represented a success story (author notes 2016). The fact that the government of Namibia has decided to invite indigenous representatives to the UNPFII session every year shows that these individuals are recognized as Traditional Authorities or leaders and as indigenous representatives even if the government does not recognize indigeneity as a valid descriptive and legal category in the African context. But it remains unclear what is expected by the Namibian government, by their local communities, and the by the head of the San Development Program from their participation in the Forum. Questions remain about the extent and consequences of the government co-opting the San movement in Namibia. Alternatively, is the Namibian government serving as a "benevolent benefactor" by giving San and Nama a chance to go to international meetings?

As my conversations with them revealed, the Namibian indigenous representatives were not trained before coming to the UNPFII meeting in indigenous peoples' rights or the UNDRIP. Tsamkxao's was not able to listen what was going on during the session without the interpretation of the government official, and was therefore unable to navigate the structure and discourse of the Forum or to make his voice heard. Nor was he able to create alliances with NGOs or other indigenous representatives. On the other hand, his presence at the international level was useful for the government – and by extension the other governments of southern Africa in their "regional" approach to San issues – in helping to showcase Namibia's relations with its indigenous peoples in a positive light.

Despite Tsamkxao's impressive experience and credentials as a leader among the Ju/'hoansi, his skills did not translate readily to the United Nations. The language proficiency, technological aptitude, and legal knowledge needed to effectively participate in the Permanent Forum and other UN meetings belong more to the younger generation. Yet even as these youth leaders find a place in these meetings and networks, they may find it difficult to achieve Tsamkxao's level of recognition and effectiveness as a local leader. The distinct roles of local and "networked" leaders are far apart, presenting a challenge for communities pursuing rights claims from the margins of states to accord a legitimate place for each.

The challenges that San representatives face in their organized activism (discussed in Chapter 4) are particularly acute when the focus of their efforts is international and, therefore, far removed from the experience of the people they represent. The fact that activists spend a great deal of time in conferences and meetings in other countries poses a challenge to their representativeness, to the point that their authority and legitimacy at the local level can be called into question. This was the case of FPK leaders portrayed by local newspapers as "in vacation in the US."[22] In places such as the UN sessions, other indigenous organizations, experts, and scholars, also challenge the representativeness of full-time activists, expressing themselves not just in academic papers and reports, but in small talk and gossip. This problem has been aggravated as indigenous peoples carve out more and higher-level political spaces within intergovernmental organizations. Even though education, professionalization, and participation in national organizations seems to distance an indigenous "elite" from the communities and the "bases," San activists are increasingly able to take their struggles from the local to the national to the international and back to the local, while maintaining connections at all levels.

CONTESTS WITH THE STATE

On session days, indigenous delegates and any others who wish to participate rush to the registration table, where the Secretariat includes their names and the name of the organization with which they registered at the meeting on the list of speakers (some new rules are developing, which provide that indigenous delegates can register well in advance online). Of course, the effort it takes for indigenous delegates to get behind the microphone does not matter as much as what they say when they get

Figure 6 Taking the floor at the UN Permanent Forum on Indigenous Issues

there. Over the years, several recognizable indigenous narratives have emerged, common forms of discourse and lines of argument that almost make the indigenous statement a distinct genre in the UN system.

Several statements made by San representatives from southern Africa denounced cases of dispossession and relocation. Other issues that have been reported include the lack of education in their mother tongue, violations of intellectual property rights (for example, in statements on hoodia and FPIC), and the lack of recognition of their institutions, laws, and above all, of their status as indigenous peoples. All of these complaints revolve around the San's central claim to legitimacy as an indigenous people: "Our ancestors are the ancestors of all the people in this room" (Festus 2004b).

As time went on, the statements on the Central Kalahari situation became more strident. In 2004 (May 10–21), in the 3rd session of the PFII, Joram /Useb, a Hai//om from Namibia, under the agenda item "human rights," very concisely combined the accusation of cultural genocide with a material motive for it, the fact that the Botswana government had developed a partnership with De Beers to promote diamond mining in the CKGR:

> The Botswana government forcefully wants to integrate the San into the mainstream society, which might have negative impact on the San, for example [from] displacement, loss of ancestral land, cultural

> genocide and non-recognition of San identity. It is also a well-known fact that the Botswana government is in partnership with De Beers mining company. This partnership brings in the bulk of income for the Botswana government. De Beers has also secured prospecting rights to mine diamonds in the area of land belonging to the San community. (Useb, UNPFII 2004)[23]

If this were not enough, the conclusion of this paragraph invokes the idea of "land belonging to the San community" almost in a taken for granted way, a point that was almost certainly not lost on the state delegates present in the room.

If we pay close attention, it is also possible to see that the statements reveal differences within the African Caucus and in African regional NGOs. In the 22nd session of the WGIP in Geneva in July 2004, a Masaai woman, speaking on behalf of the regional umbrella organization the IPACC, made an intervention in which she refuted a key point in the statement that Joram /Useb had just presented in the meeting in New York:

> Some powerful international campaigns have linked the aggressive behavior of the Botswana government to the presence of diamonds in the game reserve. IPACC is closely associated with the legal team supporting the San, and believes that the current displacement of San peoples has nothing to do with diamond mining. The insistence of foreign NGOs on the diamond issue is confusing the already difficult negotiations in Botswana. (IPACC, WGIP 2004)[24]

This indirect invocation of Survival International's "Bushmen are Not Forever" campaign against De Beers reveals some of the tensions that existed within and between indigenous delegations and their organizations. The position on diamond mining in the statement by IPACC is in clear contrast to the statement sponsored by WIMSA. In this context, it is worth noting that WIMSA was directly involved in the negotiations with the Botswana government on the Central Kalahari relocations and in the preparation of the first court case, and IPACC was not. The WIMSA delegation, composed of San from southern Africa, therefore, likely felt more poignantly the depth of government resistance to the claims of the CKGR residents. IPACC, for its part, clearly felt the need to distance itself from SI's link between the removals and diamond mining, above all from the "foreign NGO" waging an "international campaign" on behalf of the San (see Chapters 2 and 4).

In the same session of the WGIP, another representative of WIMSA, Baba Festus, a ǂKhomani woman from South Africa, made a statement in which she denounced Botswana's conservation policies, stating:

> In Botswana, San communities in Nata Valley, the Western Sandveld, the Central Kalahari Game Reserve and Ngamiland have had to cope with the imposition of "*coercive conservation*" strategies pursued by the government of Botswana. If you are not a cattle culture in Botswana, the government is not interested. The San are currently taking the Botswana government to court over their expulsion from the Central Kalahari. The view of development held by San peoples and the government of Botswana is very different at this stage. (Festus 2004b)[25]

The ideas of forced removal based on "coercive conservation" and the promotion of "cattle culture" are almost directly parallel to the statement of Joram /Useb, invoking a gross violation of human rights (forced removal), for all intents and purposes tantamount to cultural genocide, motivated by the profit interests inherent in the promotion of cattle. The violation of rights and the profit-seeking hypocrisy behind it are essentially the same in both cases.

Roy Sesana and Jumanda Gakelebone, as representatives of First Peoples of the Kalahari (FPK), met the Secretariat of the Permanent Forum in New York just a few months before the *Sesana* case was to start in Botswana's High Court to petition for support and to discuss the issues with which they were concerned. The Secretariat of the PFII gathered their concerns about the Botswana government's treatment of the people from the CKGR, and then facilitated a closed-door meeting with the Botswana delegation, hoping that the two parties could benefit from more direct dialogue. According to a UN staff member, the meeting was "highly problematic" because, as she put it, "the San openly attacked the government for its actions, which did not create a good climate for starting a dialogue, and the UN had to apologize to Botswana's delegates." In this case, officials became frustrated when the indigenous delegates did not make best use of the opportunity to address their government in a "constructive way" (author notes 2009). Very likely the tone of this meeting was influenced by the fact that preparations were already in place for the trial to take place in Botswana's High Court. Besides the breach of diplomatic etiquette, the failure of this meeting also stems from the lopsided power relationships in global organizations that favor states – influence that, in turn, shapes the way state representatives can and cannot be addressed.

The direct, confrontational approach of FPK was not followed by all San delegates attending international meetings. Indigenous delegates cannot openly discuss their grievances because they are in a position of vulnerability. Those who want to describe their people's situation accurately and poignantly are often worried about presenting information that their government might see as harmful to its reputation. In the words of an indigenous representative from Botswana, "The people that make these statements have to pay attention to what they say, because once at home they can have problems with their own government ... They have to act in a very diplomatic way also for this reason and not just because it is the UN system that requires this" (author notes 2008). Several indigenous activists told me they would feel more comfortable if they could speak only to indigenous peoples, the Forum and the Secretariat, and not have to worry about government representatives monitoring what they say.[26] A San representative from Namibia once pointed out to me that he felt intimidated by the Botswana delegates who were "following him around" and then invited him and other San for dinner, where they said they would reveal "the true facts" about what had happened with respect to the CKGR, apparently hoping that he would withdraw any reference to the Central Kalahari from the statement on which he was collaborating. As it turned out, the San delegates did not withdraw the statement in spite of the pressure nor, on this occasion at least, did they accept the dinner invitation.

Others, on the contrary, hope that, with the presence of their government in the room, they would be better able to challenge and embarrass it in front of those present. Sometimes they will leave papers outlining circumstances of rights abuse on a display table at the back of the room, or they will distribute papers or pamphlets directly to delegates at their desks, the key being to do so quietly and without attracting undue attention. For example, at the time of the 11th UNPFII meetings in May 2012, the Special Support Group (SSG) of the Botswana Police entered the CKGR in an effort to coerce the people who had returned to the reserve after the legal case to stop hunting (Chapters 7 and 8). This incident was not reported by the San in the room because they were worried about its possible implications for the future of individuals in the delegation, and because some of them wanted "to be secure about the information." Despite these concerns, First People of the Kalahari sent a statement by email asking for it to be printed and circulated inside the room. The effect of this was that some NGO representatives and UN officials began to ask the delegates in the meeting room about the SSG's acts of coercion, sometimes throwing them off balance, unprepared to answer questions on a new development about which they had not yet been fully informed. This illustrates the complexity of the tension indigenous delegates face between caution (at the risk of losing the opportunity to make a forceful point) and being forthright (as representatives of FPK tended to be) and risking causing offence among the state delegates. The San, like other indigenous delegates, have had to be strategic in terms of what they present, and they have to think carefully about the implications a statement can have for them personally, for their communities, and, ultimately, for policy reform.

Although these public denunciations may not be taken up for consideration in the final report of the Permanent Forum, they do raise awareness among NGOs, governments, and UN experts, and they may provoke responses from governments. These dynamics make the Forum a unique open space where national and global politics are played out and human rights can be invoked in challenges from "below" to incorporate the concerns and rights of indigenous peoples.

REPETITION

Everyone engaged in justice lobbying recognizes the importance of putting a message out to the public more than once, with public audiences receptive to repetition, as a strategy toward persuasion, and the corresponding public pressure on governments coming from presenting a claim again and again (Niezen 2010: 26–66). Yet, with more than a decade of repeating similar messages in UN meetings without notable change in the situation of the recognition of San as indigenous peoples, the San spokespersons' feelings have been divided between losing their patience and keep trying "because changes take time"; the strategy of filling any slot that opens for advocating their people's rights in several forums and through different languages and media has continued with persistence.

One of the things that has surprised me over the course of my long involvement in indigenous rights campaigns and lobbying in the UN has been the durability of their engagement, despite their experience of disappointment and disillusion. One way that they have overcome this disillusionment and attempt to exert influence in the long term is through "repetition." Repetition takes the form of delegates who year after year attend UN meetings, delivering narratives that are replicated.

These efforts take different forms. Indigenous peoples, for instance, engage in a form of discursive struggle through repetition, following from a need to promote alternative values and create a new narrative on indigenous peoples' rights and perspectives on human relationships with the natural world. This form of repetition has been in some ways "generative" – through the influence of these narratives over time, people, including state representatives and UN officials, have begun to talk in a different way. An official in the Secretariat once situated this strategy within the context of the eventual success of the *Declaration on the Rights of Indigenous Peoples* (UNDRIP) after more than twenty years of negotiations. He explained to me that states may at one point have opposed the Declaration, but over time they took up the language surrounding it. The UNDRIP process gave a platform to activists over a period of two decades from which they created a common language through repetition. "They started to talk about indigenous peoples' vision, holistic approaches to rights, mother earth, sacred sites, and so on without realizing it"; and again, "The twenty years of negotiations made this possible; it gave people who participated in the negotiation meetings the time to learn, repeat, reengage, cultivate belief, and encourage participation" (author notes 2013).

Repetition is not just generative, but also a form of oppression and violence. The "violence of repetition" is one of the techniques used by states to protect their reputations. It involves the practice of reiterating a story of the state's record of rights compliance, repeating particular words, phrases, and arguments to the point that they produce a widely accepted, standardized narrative. It is form of "strategic temporalization" in diplomacy that creates reality through reiteration, in which a powerful actor repeats words and arguments again and again over years and even decades as a form of institutional persuasion, creating a truth that in many respects lacks empirical foundations.

The violence of repetition is part of the backdrop of persistent obstacles in the UN that have long obstructed efforts to situate the rights of indigenous peoples on a sound footing. Whenever measures intended to secure indigenous rights and recognition reach the back channels of diplomacy, the violence of repetition manifests itself.

The capacity for indigenous delegates to influence international law depends largely on their financial means, and the same is true for states. Participation in UN meetings is costly, and for many developing countries it is difficult to find the wherewithal to send delegations.

Botswana's government officials (as an African exception) have been attending UN meeting in numbers that are growing every year. Botswana's presence was particularly notable in 2010, when state delegates presented comments about remote area education, and in 2014 and 2015 when representatives from five different ministries flew directly from Gaborone to attend the meeting and present statements on human rights and "remote area communities." The participation of Botswana reached its peak in 2016 when not just the usual government delegates attended the session, but also the Minister of Local Government and Rural Development, the Honorable Slumber Tsogwane. The government was clearly attempting to present its own views on the "San's problems" and of the CKGR situation in the UN, in part as a way to counterbalance what San spokespersons had said (see Chapter 8, p. 311).

The statements made by state representatives in the session (and Botswana is no exception) commonly assert the state's rights to constitutional and territorial integrity, their duty to further the equal rights of all citizens, and their positive records of human rights compliance and development, which (so they claim) meet the broader aspirations of the international community. Although the governments of a number of countries, such as Canada, the US, and Bolivia, have changed their positions on policy toward indigenous peoples and the scope of indigenous rights that they are willing to recognize (Sapignoli 2017), this is not true for most African countries, from which the same claims and objections are raised in slightly different form year after year. After more than twenty years of participation in UN meetings on indigenous peoples, and ten years after the ratification of the UNDRIP, none of the southern African states have accepted the terminology of indigenous peoples, maintaining national forms of classification that do not do justice to the aspirations and recognition of the claimants. There are also some states that do not shy away from projecting an oppositional image. For instance, Namibia and Botswana, in line with many other African states, have repeatedly talked about "marginalized communities" or "remote areas communities" instead of "indigenous peoples," thus undermining the San claim to differential regimes of rights (Sapignoli 2015). It is also commonly remembered among NGO participants in the Forum that Namibia and Botswana led an African bloc of states in opposition to the adoption of the UNDRIP in 2006 (ACHPR 2007; Crawhall 2011).

In the 2014 session, during the agenda item "human rights," for example, Botswana delegates referred to a visit to the country by Special Rapporteur James Anaya,[27] and underlined that,

> As a general principle, we do not describe ourselves in ethnic terms. Botswana government's position, therefore, is that ALL TRIBES AND ETHNIC GROUPS ARE INDIGENOUS TO THE COUNTRY. However, we are cognizant of the fact there are some segments of our population that are disadvantaged, marginalized and deserve special attention.[28]

This position has remained constant since the San first presented themselves as indigenous peoples in the early 1990s. This is a common attitude of the African states, as emerged particularly from several statements presented by groups such as the Masaai of Tanzania, the Twa of Uganda or Congo, the Tuareg of Mali, and so on during the two half-day discussions on the African region that occurred in 2006 and 2013. In 2013 Botswana stressed its efforts toward the development of the "remote area communities" through the launch of its Affirmative Action Plan (2009), stating:

> The Affirmative Action Framework also recognizes that a majority of the *remote area communities* were at one stage living a nomadic life and therefore they have not accrued any assets to fall back on in times of shocks and vulnerabilities in their livelihood systems; such as drought and natural disasters.[29]

To understand the sources of Botswana's statements and their uses of terminology we need to shift our gaze from the higher principles of human rights and consider local policies and legalization of development and the official definition of the Botswana development target group – in other words, the image of the San that informed the policy.[30]

The Botswana delegates' rejection of the category of indigenous peoples in their interventions has often provoked reactions from the San delegates in the room, who, if given a chance to speak, restate their claims of indigeneity and distinct rights. An example of this comes from a San delegate who was already registered to take the floor and used the occasion to revise his speech in response to the statement made by the government:

> I am an indigenous representative from Botswana and not a representative of "remote area communities," as Botswana prefers to call us. ... Assimilation-oriented policies and practices are consistent with the terminology that would deny us our rights as indigenous peoples.[31]

The war of words between the Botswana government and the San delegates to the UN (separated by the San's need to submit a statement rather than deliver it from the floor) focuses on several key words: justifications of removal in the name of "equality" on one side and assertions of the distinct rights of "first people" on the other. This terminological battle, which has gone on for decades, has profound implications for people's lives.

We can therefore see from these various interventions by the San and the state of Botswana the outlines of diametrically opposed approaches to rights and prosperity. The concepts employed by the San delegations with reference to their rights place emphasis on collective rights and cultural diversity. Invoking the idea of "indigenous peoples" is in itself a collective rights claim, in which the notion of a "people," with distinct rights to self-determination, places the San on the same level as the state of Botswana, in line with the 1945 Charter of the United Nations with its resonant opening words, "We the Peoples of the United Nations ..." As an indigenous people of the United Nations, the San, like all the indigenous delegations attending the meetings of the Permanent Forum, are invoking their status as a political and cultural collective entity with distinct rights, not those of a minority or of an impoverished "community" in need of tutelage and improvement, but those of a people with its own values and decision-making powers, whose needs for services from the state are premised on self-determination.

It is easy to imagine that Botswana, wanting to protect its reputation as a successful democracy in a continent known for its despotisms and civil wars, would be offended by the San delegates' approach to its development policies, and their denunciation of state's violation of the basic rights of the San people. This is indeed what appears from the statements delivered by Botswana to the session floor, but in an indirect way. Diplomats' interventions stress the benefits of the state's program of "remote area communities" where the provision of government services is easier, more cost effective, and able to reach a greater number of those who are living in conditions of isolation, underdevelopment, and poverty. State delegates argue that a positive human rights record can be seen in the fact that "all human rights structures in Botswana do not discriminate on the basis of gender or ethnicity" (SPFII 2015: 10). In these terms, forced relocation serves only as one of the means toward a positive goal, not even worth mentioning in the country's interventions at the United Nations. The essential thing is that the state is fulfilling its human rights obligations by targeting for special treatment those who live marginal lives in conditions of remoteness from the sources of prosperity. "Remoteness" in this case implies its opposite, a center, a source of wealth and well-being, in other words, the Tswana-dominated country, the source of national identity and unity. Pluralism in these terms still exists, but with disadvantaged minorities receiving the benefits of state largesse, conceived in terms of food rations, nursing stations, and schools – the basic necessities, in other words, for living and learning the language and values of an enlightened, beneficent Tswana people. Botswana could not have more perfectly expressed the ideologies and policies of a well-intentioned, assimilation-oriented settler state, an image that is anathema to the international movement of indigenous peoples.

THE ECONOMIC ENDS OF INDIGENOUS ACTIVISM

The San, along with other indigenous delegates to the United Nations, are not only seeking recognition in the form of rights to self-determination and cultural expression; they are also, perhaps above all, seeking improvement in the material conditions of their lives, their access to resources, health, and conditions of prosperity. These two kinds of rights are "co-original" in Nancy Fraser's (2003: 19) terms, with claims to recognition as a distinct people inextricably connected to those that are redistributive, that have important implications for access to land and resources, food security, and equal access to government services. Even the informal processes of networking with donors in the hallways and cafeterias of the UN Headquarters can result in funding for local initiatives, the creation of community-based organizations and NGOs, with corresponding flows of money, not to mention the development of "cultural capital," the networks and forms of expertise that bring about further opportunities. The adoption of indigenous identity is not just a legal claim or assertion of cultural distinctiveness; it is also an economic strategy, one that goes well beyond the eco-tourism and "branding" associated with the commercial uses of ethnic stereotypes (see Comaroff and Comaroff 2009).

This redistributive quality of the claims and lobbying practices at the UN offers another angle from which to assess the possibilities and limits of indigenous peoples' participation in UN initiatives. An emphasis on the development of standards in international law does not take into account the opportunities that arise through the *process* and *consequences* of making claims based on those standards. The involvement of indigenous delegates in drafting legislation and reports offers them an avenue to make their experiences and aspirations known to a wide audience, including those in power who are answerable for their human rights records. When we include a wider range of the dynamics of justice activism in our field of vision we see more possibilities for political influence – above all more possibilities for material benefit in both the long and short terms. In other words, we cannot properly assess the consequences of making indigenous rights claims without taking these other potential benefits into account. It is true that indigenous rights lobbying occurs in the absence of "actionable law," yet it can have other effects than state compliance with international law, certainly enough to make this influence a source of motivation for some of those who attend year after year.

The central pillar for the redistribution of the benefits of development in the global indigenous movement is the principle of free, prior, and informed consent (FPIC). As a reflection of the widespread impact of large-scale projects and displacements around the world, FPIC has increasingly become a (if not *the*) central source of indigenous rights claims in global governance processes. Whether or not it is realized in practice, the ideals behind FPIC are to ensure that indigenous peoples are not coerced or intimidated into accepting a project; that they have complete and accurate information on the scope and impacts of proposed developments; that their consent is sought and freely given prior to the authorization or start of any activities; and that ultimately their choices to give or withhold consent are respected (Ward 2011: 54). Ideally, displacement, if it is to occur, should be so attractive that it is generally accepted, in conditions in which the displaced would become "project beneficiaries" (Goodland 2004: 66).

Since the 1980s, the World Bank has been aware of the need for a safeguarding policy toward indigenous peoples as a guiding principle of project development, largely in response to evidence of the catastrophic results of its absence, in the uncompensated and uncoordinated displacement that had been the norm in World Bank-funded projects. Despite the obvious rationale behind it, however, the World Bank has not unambiguously furthered the concept of FPIC. A new "Operational Policy 4.10" oriented toward poverty reduction and sustainable development affirms that before financing a new project that affects indigenous people, the Bank would require the borrower to engage in a process of free, prior, and informed *consultation* with them.

The dilution of the term "consent" with the less stringent notion of "consultation" was not accidental. As Mauro Barelli points out, "the very decision to replace the commonly used and more rigorous expression 'free, prior and informed *consent*' with 'free, prior and informed *consultation*' speaks volumes of the intention of the drafters" (Barelli 2012: 8).

In other areas of international law, FPIC has advanced without such dilution of its meaning. As a result of effective lobbying by indigenous organizations in the UN, FPIC became a reference point for the protections built into the 2007 *Declaration on the Rights of Indigenous Peoples*. With this instrument in place, it is on the agendas of a number of organizations, including the *Convention on Biological Diversity*, the World Intellectual Property Organization (WIPO), the International Fund For Agricultural Development (IFAD), and the World Trade Organization (WTO), which now conduct their work with awareness of the support behind access and benefits-sharing of biological resources and traditional indigenous knowledge (Cariño 2005: 19).

These developments in international law are not mere words on paper, but can spill out into reality through the way that the benefits of projects are distributed. With indigenous peoples acquiring more tangible rights to their territories and intellectual property through FPIC, the conditions are there for a corresponding shift in the redistributive practices of large-scale development projects.

An example of the economic implications of the principle of FPIC with a focus on the San can be found in the set of claims surrounding the hoodia plant and (separately) the devil's claw plant that followed from the 1993 *Convention on Biological Diversity*. These claims were based on the Convention's provisions relating to the equitable access to and benefit sharing from the biodiversity and knowledge used for commercial innovation. Hoodia is by far the better known of the two controversies, involving the San in one of the most famous cases of biopiracy that resulted from the Convention. The hoodia plant, a low-lying cactus, had long been used by the San and other peoples in southern Africa for a wide variety of purposes, including staving off thirst and hunger. Their use of the plant was observed by colonial botanists, and these observations were later the inspiration for the South Africa-based Council for Scientific and Industrial Research (CSIR) to identify the specific source of the plant's effects as an appetite suppressant. Without consulting the San, the CSIR identified the plant's active constituents and patented them. Then began a chain of corporate agreements, first a licensing and royalty agreement between CSIR and Phytopharm, then between Phytopharm and the "big pharma" corporation Pfizer.[32]

The San, meanwhile, were blithely unaware that commercial applications of their knowledge of hoodia were being exploited and that they had been excluded from the lucrative deals to develop those applications. CSIR had, in fact, gone so far as to inform Phytopharm that the San of southern Africa, who numbered some 100,000 individuals, no longer existed (Wynberg 2010: 22). WIMSA coordinated a legal challenge, which received support from a range of indigenous activists and NGOs. The issue was also raised in the UN, with Baba Festus stating to the 2004 meeting of the Permanent Forum on Indigenous Issues, "The hoodia case is a typical example of how bioprospecting companies have abused the Intellectual Property Rights of indigenous peoples" (Festus 2004a: 3).[33] Ultimately, it was the media pressure following this case that was more decisive, including as it did "contrasting images of emaciated San and obese Americans," and reinforcing "popular notions of 'bio-piracy' by large pharmaceutical companies" (Wynberg 2004: 860). This media coverage captured the public's imagination, and seriously embarrassed CSIR and Phytopharm.

At this point, the San and their supporters were faced with an important choice. Rather than challenging and thus extinguishing the patent, the San decided to negotiate a benefit-sharing agreement so that they would be assured of material compensation for their intellectual property. In 2003 a benefit-sharing agreement was finalized, which gave the San a 6 percent royalty on all future sales emanating from the patent, with money to be paid into a trust established jointly by CSIR and the South African San Council, with the objective of raising "the standard of living and well-being of San peoples of southern Africa" (Wynberg 2010: 23). With dietary control estimated to be a $3 billion per annum industry in the US alone, this promised to be a very lucrative agreement for the San.

The vagaries of pharmaceutical development proved to be the agreement's undoing. Pfizer put an end to its clinical development of the drug and returned the rights to Phytopharm. When the pharmaceutical giant Unilever took interest in the product, the results were no different. A large-scale cultivation program was developed, clinical safety trials were set up, and a US$100 million extraction facility was planned, but ultimately the hopes that had been pinned on the agreement and its potential revenues came to nothing. Ultimately, the

Hoodia Trust garnered only around $100,000, with no mechanism for distributing the money to the various San organizations in southern Africa.

The failure of the hoodia case to bring any significant benefit to the San of southern Africa should not distract us from its wider significance. A number of features stand out. First, the media were quite possibly the most significant source of leverage in bringing the pharmaceutical corporations to the negotiating table. While the UN may have served as a backdrop to the San grievance, and while the courts may have eventually acted as a potential source of compulsion to change the behavior of the corporations – probably after many years of litigation, which the San could hardly afford – what really counted were the reputational costs associated with an egregious example of "biopiracy." The media, with their use of simple, contrasting images of obese Americans and starving Africans, acted as a more direct channel to "redistributive" justice than the long-term campaigning at the UN, even if in the end the royalty-sharing agreement did not lead to the intended economic benefits for the San. This recourse of indigenous delegates to the media was the ultimate source of leverage in UN initiatives, with more immediate consequences for the behavior of states and corporations than had been achieved over many years of human rights standard setting.

The hoodia case also reveals the economic benefits that can derive from engagement with international law. The broad public support for new standards protecting the intellectual property of indigenous peoples was at the origin of the negotiations that were aimed toward royalty sharing in a massive pharmaceutical initiative. Similarly, the standards associated with FPIC that are built into the *Declaration on the Rights of Indigenous Peoples* (Articles 10, 11.2, 19, and 32.2) are clear in their potential to bring material benefits to indigenous rights claimants. These benefits have already started to accrue to those indigenous NGOs that have been most effective in making use of international law as a reference point for justice lobbying.

The material benefits that follow from indigenous peoples' engagement with UN initiatives are of course not always accompanied by such spectacular potential as that inherent in the hoodia controversy. The economic opportunity afforded by attending meetings with international donors is clearly another aspect of the benefits that accrue from participation in the indigenous peoples' movement and the global identity with which it is associated. We should not, however, be led by this observation to the conclusion that activism is motivated by mercenary goals in priority over the pursuit of rights. Rather, it highlights the material need at the root of indigenous rights claims and the corresponding place of redistributive justice as the ultimate reference point of what is really at stake in indigenous activism in the UN.

GOING HOME

In 2008, when I asked Jumanda Gakelebone what he thought about his first meeting with the diplomats from the Botswana government that had taken place a few years earlier and about the role of the UN, his answer was, "The UN is good in that it lets people know about what is happening, changes public opinion, and puts pressure on the government, but if you want to resolve problems you have to stay at the local level and take the government to court" (author notes 2008). In 2016, after he had participated for the first time in the two-week session of the Permanent Forum, and after many years of legal battle at home (see Chapter 7), his perspective had shifted. Having seen the attention given to the meeting by the Botswana government and other state delegations, having performed the magic of printing a business card for First Peoples of the Kalahari and distributing it among other NGO delegates and donors, and having listened attentively to the closing speech of Ban Ki Moon, who stressed the global nature of the struggles of indigenous peoples, his attitude changed. Whether temporarily or in a more lasting way, he had become convinced. "I think I learned a lot," he said. "It gave me an impression that it is not only us. There are other people around the world who have the same problems as us. It gives me an encouragement to talk about indigenous rights ... The state will be encouraged to comply" (author notes 2016).

When indigenous delegates return home, they meet their obligations to the donors who sponsored their attendance at the UN and act on this incentive to "talk about indigenous rights" in several ways. They write reports, organize local meetings, speak on the radio or television, do interviews with journalists, and use social networks and blogs to share photos, comments, and information. They also directly report to their constituencies on what they learned at these meetings.

This is a process that corresponds to what Sally Merry (2006) refers to as the "vernacularization" of human rights concepts and forms of discourse. When Jumanda Gakelebone addressed his fellow council members in Ghanzi holding a copy of the *Declaration on the Rights of Indigenous Peoples* printed from an online source, with its articles on

FPIC underscored, and when he contextualized their obligations and activities in the light of a speech by Ban Ki Moon that stressed the common global struggles of indigenous peoples, he was acting as a "translator" in Merry's terms, as one of those who "refashion global rights agendas for local contexts and reframe local grievances in terms of global human rights principles and activities" (2006: 39). San delegates bring the ideas and experiences of the indigenous peoples' movement home with them, and in the process transmit the language – the way to engage in "rights talk" and more specifically to "talk indigenous" – to new places and to other levels of discursive habituation.

From the perspective of many San and others in Botswana, these efforts are not enough. There is a widespread sense that the information gained by the representatives who attend meetings such as the UNPFII is not always shared broadly with people at the grassroots level, despite their efforts to spread information and participate in community meetings on their return. As one delegate expressed it, the ideal is for them to "go around the country after their return to share the lessons that they learned as a means of stimulating discussion and action at the local level" (author notes 2013). The expectation is that they go on speaking tours, organize meetings, and answer any and all questions the community members might have. Given their limited resources, however, the expectations placed on even the most diligent of San delegates are largely beyond their capacity to fulfill. These travels are often a source of resentment and envy, fueling suspicions that the trips to the far-away USA or Europe are just an excuse for delegates to enjoy undeserved luxuries as they travel with the justification of speaking on behalf of the poor and downtrodden. Some, compelled by other responsibilities, the pressures of daily life, or the desire to avoid the minefields of envy and overblown expectations, do not report to the communities at all when they return from UN meetings. In some cases, their reporting remains confined mainly to posts on the Web, where it does not reach far beyond those who are already part of their online networks.

Overall, though, this negativity is not common enough to be crippling, and the general view among the San and other indigenous peoples of southern Africa is that they have benefitted from sending delegates to attend the UNPFII. Among the participants themselves, this was true in a number of different ways, including learning more about how to go about pressing their case for rights, networking, making contacts, and learning from other indigenous groups who were involved in the UN and other international forums. Whatever doubts we might have about the effectiveness of indigenous rights for their lack of "actionable" law, it is certain that the ideas associated with the promise of these rights continue to circulate widely. The San's omnivorous approach to activism has given us a glimpse into how and why the legitimacy of indigenous rights continues and is, if anything, feeding into wider notions of what it means to be human, with rights.

6

THE COURT

GETTING TO COURT

The court was not the first choice of the residents of the Central Kalahari Game Reserve (CKGR). The San activists and their legal advisors saw it as a last resort, an unknown quantity, something that had never been tried before, at least not at the national level in Botswana. Taking the government to court was inherently risky. Their experience with the legal system, with San receiving disproportionately longer prison sentences in criminal cases, made them suspicious of courts (see Egner and Klausen 1980; Güenther 1986; Maxwell and Mogwe 2006). In these circumstances, it seemed particularly dubious to use the state's own courts to address the harms of the state. There was an uneven balance between concerns about costs and the risk of an uncertain outcome. The negotiating team, which had been formed to reach agreement on a plan that would be acceptable to both the government and reserve residents, was divided. Some members wanted to continue with the negotiations, not wanting to antagonize the government by going to court, while others argued that the negotiations had been ongoing for more than a decade, with nothing to show for it. It was time to do something different, even if it was more risky.

The negotiators (and the people they represented) did not arrive at their decision all at once. It took years for them to make up their minds, but meanwhile they hedged their bets. They realized early on that they needed legal representation to press the case for rights to their land and resources. A workshop that was held in D'kar on February 10–13, 1998 on CKGR issues arrived at the decision "to pursue legal action as a strategy in parallel to that of negotiations and direct action" (negotiating team's unpublished minutes). Glyn Williams, a lawyer from Chennells Albertyn, a South African firm that had experience in arguing several cases relating to San land and resource rights in South Africa, agreed to take the case.

Williams was then instructed to prepare the "Particulars of Claim" for a land claim to be instituted in the High Court of Botswana. The next five years were spent preparing the basis for a legal case. These preparations involved interviewing residents, mapping the communities and their areas, carrying out surveys, working with the Department of Wildlife and National Parks on a management plan that included the people in the reserve, creating a registry of people in the reserve and the resettlement communities, and, at the same time, continuing with meetings with government and district officials.

With negotiations taking place simultaneously with the looming possibility of court action, there was an increasingly urgent need to determine with as much precision as possible the number of people who were affected by the Botswana government's decisions about the CKGR, where they were living, and how they were using the territory. According to the CKGR negotiating team report (unpublished minutes 2001), FPK and the negotiation team represented approximately 850 persons with rights to land in the CKGR, including members of the G//ana, Tsila, G/ui, and Kgalagadi ethnic groups who had been resident in the CKGR "from time immemorial."

In the talks with the government most of the debate centered on the development of a Management Plan for the CKGR and Khutse Game Reserves, which would enable sustainable use of natural resources and wildlife inside the CKGR by the communities. The government consistently promised that they would not force people to leave who remained in the reserve after the May to June, 1997 relocation. At the same time, some members of the Ghanzi District Council and the Kweneng District Council, as well as the regional offices of the Department of Wildlife and National Parks, attempted to support the people in the Central Kalahari, and they tried to resist the top-down initiatives to remove people from the reserve and establish new settlements (see Chapter 2). Approximately a dozen of these negotiation team meetings were held with government officials in the period between 2000 and 2002 and continued also during the *Sesana* case. However, it soon became clear to the members of the negotiating team that the results were only empty promises and their efforts were to no avail.

On February 19, 2002, two weeks after the second large-scale relocation, the lawyers for the people of the Central Kalahari, John Whitehead, Roger Chennells, Glyn Williams, and Rahim Khan, filed a legal case in the High Court of Botswana, which became known as *Sesana and Others v. the Attorney General of the Republic of Botswana*, with Roy Sesana, as the first applicant, representing 241 other applicants when the case began. In the founding affidavit for the applicants Sesana presented himself as an employee of FPK, "a non-government organisation that represents and campaigns to protect and enforce the constitutional rights of the indigenous San and the Kgalagadi people of the Central Kalahari region of Botswana" (*Sesana* 2002: 1).

The motion sought orders from the court that the termination of essential services to the CKGR was unlawful and unconstitutional and that the forced removal of the applicants after the termination of services amounted to "despoliation" and unlawful dispossession. A supplementary motion, filed on March 4, 2002, sought additional relief from the fact that the Department of Wildlife and National Parks refused to issue Special Game Licenses (SGL) and to allow the residents to enter without a permit, which were also connected to the removals and were similarly unlawful and unconstitutional (Ng'ong'ola 2007: 104).

It is noteworthy that the 1997 removals were not included in this lawsuit. A number of reasons lay behind this decision. In practical terms, too much time had passed since the relocation in 1997; in addition, the process in the 1997 removal had been different, with more evidence of consultation and more divided opinion in the affected communities. Nevertheless, some people who had wanted to go to court following the earlier relocation were frustrated by this decision, and even today there are those who feel that the decision to focus only on the 2002 relocation constituted an unjustified narrowing of the claim.

Before the case could be heard, the Attorney General of Botswana (named as defendant or "respondent" in the case) raised objections to Sesana's authority to represent the 241 applicants, arguing that he was resident in Ghanzi and therefore had no *locus standi*, that is to say, no direct connection to the harms that took place (this despite the fact that two of his wives were forcibly relocated). Justice Dibotelo agreed with the state's lawyers and dismissed the case as originally filed, confirming the claims of hearsay in the founding affidavit, which, he pointed out, arose from the fact that Sesana did not himself witness the events of the forced removal and emptying of water tanks at Mothomelo. Dibotelo also took issue with the fact that Sesana could not read or write English (in his deposition he acknowledges that he can only speak several San languages, referred to collectively as "Sesarwa," and Setswana) and that his lawyers had not followed the necessary procedure in this circumstance, which called for the deposition to be read aloud in the presence of an officer of the court, who would then confirm that the deponent had understood it before making his or her mark or signature. Dibotelo dismissed the application, but gave the applicants leave to begin new proceedings. Rather than file new proceedings, however, the applicants took their case to the Court of Appeal, which, in turn, referred the case back to the High Court. It was not until January 23, 2003, nearly a year after the original "urgent" deposition, that the High Court, invoking the contradictory accounts of the facts and serious disputes in the affidavits of the applicants and respondents, decided to hear oral evidence. With this decision the original motion led to a full-scale trial that was to last three years, producing 19,000 pages of official transcripts, ultimately becoming the most expensive and longest-running case in Botswana's history.

Before the trial began, the southern Africa team of lawyers for the applicants was joined by a highly experienced London-based litigator, connected to Survival International, Gordon Bennett, described in the online journal *The Lawyer* as the "go-to tribal rights guy," who "acts for indigenous peoples in developing countries who find themselves caught up in land disputes" (*The Lawyer* 2010). Bennett later (starting in November 2004) worked alongside Gideon Duma Boko from Botswana, a Harvard-trained lawyer, who in the early 2000s was active in one of the opposition parties the Botswana National Front, later (in 2010) to become leader of the main opposition party, the Umbrella for Democratic Change.

Sidney Pilane, representing the Attorney General of Botswana, was one of the administration's highest-paid officials (after the Permanent Secretary to the President and the Chief Justice). He was appointed in 2001 as an "in-house lawyer" to the Office of the President, and acted as the President's "general purpose adviser," or "spin doctor," with broad responsibility for domestic issues and legal matters, including, as it turned out, the CKGR case (Werbner 2004: 91).

The cast of central characters in the case was therefore highly political, with the opposing legal teams representing much more than just the parties in a dispute. The case that the San and Bakgalagadi brought to court was played out by three strong personalities: a "hired gun," a political "up-and-comer," and a "spin doctor," each vying for advantage in an effort to redefine the legal limits of the state's politics of "development" and "equal citizenship."

The case officially started in July 2004, with the case for the applicants led by the South African legal team. During the preceding months Roger Chennells, a lawyer for the applicants, travelled to the villages of the reserve and of the resettlement sites to prepare the residents for the case to come, and particularly for the imminent visit by the High Court judges in their "*in loco* inspection" preceding the opening of the trial. He consulted with the residents of the CKGR and the resettlement villages, explaining the court's adversarial system, how each side would be preparing arguments, and how they need to be able to respond to questions. Chennells posed hypothetical questions that could be raised by the judges or government's lawyer to undermine the applicants' main arguments in the founding affidavit, such as why the government should spend so much money to bring schools and clinics to the CKGR, and why the people should not relocate to make things easier, to which Letsema Tshotlego in Kaduwane answered curtly, "I will not relocate. They will have to kill me right at that spot" (Wicksteed 2008: 21 min. 23 sec.).

When Gordon Bennett later took on the assignment, he noted disapprovingly that the team had not arranged for an anthropologist to act as an intermediary, a person who could discuss the implications of the relocation with the Bushmen, and serve as an "expert." Nor did they prepare an expert opinion concerning whether the lead applicant, Roy Sesana, was truly representative of the people who had been relocated, an issue that was to potentially compromise the case for the applicants (author notes 2016).

Several months later, a few days before the beginning of hearings, some members of the High Court, including the judges, lawyers, applicants, and state officials, travelled to the game reserve, finding their way along the bone-jarring road in a convoy of four-wheel-drive vehicles, followed by a retinue of journalists, to observe the abandoned settlements and the remaining residents. In the villages, the lawyers had already begun to argue their case, off the record and outside the official court setting. Gordon Bennett (in the presence of the judges), for example, stopped to speak to a man in Molapo who was carrying a root, effectively making him a witness outside the box.

BENNETT:	Can you tell us what that is called?
MOLAPO RESIDENT:	This is known as "bee." Sometimes when I am thirsty I am used to eat this. I am also used to digging "gaba" and "gaa."
BENNETT:	[to the translator Jumanda Gakelebone] Are these things he has always done?
MOLAPO RESIDENT:	I have always been doing this. (Wicksteed 2008: 41min: 45 sec.)

During the field visit they also went to Mothomelo, one of the villages that had been the target of the 2002 relocation. There they visited a borehole that had been capped. Bennett later recalled that when he asked a government official why the well had been capped, the official replied that it had been done to prevent children from throwing stones into the well, a reply that came across as deeply disingenuous (author notes 2016).

This kind of exchange was ultimately influential. The judges' visit to the CKGR communities and the new settlements outside the reserve was described in the court's final judgment as having provided "an impression of the physical location of the settlements and the difficulties which confronted the residents which otherwise we might not have known" (*Sesana* 2006c: 19); in other words it provided a form of *living proof*.

The first phase of the trial took place in New Xade, the village to which many of the San and Bakgalagadi had been relocated, selected as the venue so that they could attend the proceedings. However, the proceedings were suspended after only ten days, in which four witnesses for the applicants gave testimony, and temporarily moved to Ghanzi, then moved again to the High Court in Lobatse, where the trial resumed in November 2004. According to Gordon Bennett, this change of venue was requested by the legal teams because of Lobatse's relative convenience and the discomfort of living and working in New Xade, which was seen by the legal team as a "remote and disconsolate settlement." Bennett, reflecting on his experience with this case some ten years after the verdict, recalled his outrage at this decision by the lawyers for the applicants.

> I personally knew nothing of the application [to move the trial to Lobatse] until immediately before it was made, and was startled to discover that the clients had been told nothing about it at all. In the few minutes left before the Court sat, I explained the position to them as

Figure 7 Gordon Bennett consulting with his clients

> best I could and asked whether they agreed to the application. They did, of course, "because the men in black robes knew best." At a stroke, hundreds of Bushmen were denied the opportunity to watch a trial which would directly affect their futures. It was not my proudest moment. (Author notes 2016)

The increasing complexity and rising profile of the case introduced the problem of money to pay legal fees. Even with their combined resources, FPK and the other Botswana-based organizations could not afford a potentially lengthy legal process. Before the case started in November, the representatives of several organizations in the CKGR negotiating team were taken aback when they heard that FPK had chosen to ally itself with Survival International (SI). SI did decide to provide support to the legal case after disagreements erupted over the ways in which the South African team of lawyers was handling the case. It was in this new setting in the High Court in Lobatse that Gordon Bennett took full control of the case.

By the time of the reopening of the CKGR case in November 2004, Ditshwanelo stated that the organization would step back because the negotiation strategy had failed and because they did not support SI's advocacy positions. Alice Mogwe, director of Ditshwanelo, frequently emphasized the importance of "talking through problems" instead of going to court in an adversarial system, underlining the importance of resolving local matters locally rather than listening to international organizations. Hers was a Tswana-oriented "cultural justification," in which the adversarial court system was seen as being "far removed from our cultural understanding of conflict resolution" and international organizations "are located within a completely different cultural context" (Ditshwanelo 2002: 34–5). Kuru similarly decided to leave the negotiating team and the lawsuit, citing "the vast numbers of unsupported San [elsewhere] who are losing land every day, and whose stories are not as widely published." It objected above all to "the way ... our sister organisations have been side-lined and diminished by the present court case and SI's micro and personal focus on a small group of individuals rather than a representative group of San" (Kuru flyer 2004). One of the lawsuit's first effects, therefore, was to exacerbate divisions that already existed between various organizations with differing agendas and relationships with donors and the state.

THE TECHNOLOGY OF IDENTITY: WHO WERE THE APPLICANTS?[1]

The process of legal definition and inscription begins with the basic requirement for precision concerning membership, and for this reason I address here the surprisingly thorny question of the "applicants," the plaintiffs or claimants, the significance of certainty in their numbers and identities. Unlike many legally defined categories of belonging, that of the applicants had nothing to do with the strategic essentialism of the categorized group. Rather, it remained a strictly technical/legal category used to register the claimants in a case, both during the legal process and extending into its effects in the period after judgment; it was an empty category that had to be populated by the people signing onto the case, a way to create and number the legal subjects inside a courtroom to whom the eventual verdict would apply. Paraphrasing Merry and Coutin's observation about indicators in another context (2014: 2), a technology for producing "justice" shaped the way that people were managed.

Among all the social categories translated and reconceptualized by the legal process, this was perhaps the easiest to overlook, even though it arguably has the greatest implications for the people of the CKGR region. Understanding the significance of this concept begins with the fact that not everybody who was relocated was part of the applicant group that went to court. Hence the first, immediate outcome of the framing of the case at the time it was submitted in 2002 was the creation a community of applicants with the possibility (and later actuality) of rights that were distinct from those who did not participate in the legal case (Ng'ong'ola 2007; Sapignoli 2017).

For the case to proceed, those who experienced the harms of the removals and denial of services in the CKGR first had to be identified and, literally, sign on to the case. This proved particularly difficult among people with little or no literacy or knowledge of the judicial system. Many were unaware of their constitutional rights or of the bureaucratic and legal procedures and had to be informed about what they entailed. Others were reluctant to involve themselves in a process that brought with it the risk of retaliation by a government that had already shown itself to be ready to use force in exercising its will. There was, therefore, an effort involving active outreach involved to develop a list of individuals – or in some senses, a "community" – of applicants. Representatives of First People of the Kalahari and Working Group of Indigenous Minorities in Southern Africa met with them individually or in small groups to explain the planned case, record names, gather signatures (with many signing with a fingerprint), and take the portraits needed for the forms. Birth records and proofs of identity had to be collected among people for whom such documents were only sporadically available. One member of FPK recently recalled that, "The word 'applicant' was something we battled with, because there is no concept of applicant. But we tried to simplify it." In an attempt at translation, the closest approximation to the concept of the applicants was a compound phrase: "Those who have been part of the court case, being written down on court papers" (author notes 2016).

Before the trial, some 650 documents were assembled. For reasons that remain unclear, nearly half of those who signed up as applicants were not included in the final list of applicants when the case entered the court. This was possibly because they lacked one or another (from the perspective of the lawyers who prepared the case) key piece of information or lacked a necessary criterion for being included in the case, such as being provably subjected to removal in 2002 – the removal that was the focal point of litigation – and not in 1997, even though in the earlier relocation the same policy was at work with many of the same consequences.

For the state, the issues of the applicants and the number of people still resident in the CKGR after the relocations were particularly significant because by reducing these figures they would be able to minimize the significance of the case and the possible costs of any judgment that went against them. When Bennett tried to submit an expanded list of applicants based on revised documentation, the government's lawyer Sidney Pilane rejected it, telling the court that if another list were submitted, he would have to query each new applicant, in effect threatening to delay the trial and increase its costs beyond the means of the applicants. On many occasions during the trial, Pilane called into question the adequacy of the preparation of the case, not only questioning the integrity of the list of applicants and the procedures by which it was arrived at, but also, by extension, the awareness of the applicants of their rights and obligations as plaintiffs in the case. The tempo of these challenges to the list increased as the trial went on as it became increasingly clear that the applicants had a solid case. The government's lawyers thus insisted on the figure of 17 to represent the number of people living in the CKGR who had not (yet) been relocated. This did not include those who had been removed, who were considered to have gone through a formal process of relocation that (as the argument went) extinguished their rights, and then returned to the reserve. Another issue raised by Sidney Pilane concerned the possible existence, and need for removal, of applicants in the case who had been relocated in 1997, not, he claimed, in 2002 during the relocations that were the subject of litigation.

The numbers of applicants varied as the case was being argued in response to the various inclusions and exclusions that occurred as the lawyers battled over the list. The judges hearing the case were uneasy with this uncertainty, prompting Bennett at one point to offer (yet another) reassurance to the judges that he was acting to resolve the issue.

BENNETT: [...] I will make sure that any uncertainty or obstacle is removed because clearly the Court is to know precisely who the applicants are.

JUSTICE DIBOTELO: Because *there will be consequences at the end of the day*. I mean, the decision is going to affect certain people. We know that the respondent is the Attorney General.

BENNETT: Yes. (Unofficial court transcripts May 10, 2005; my emphasis)

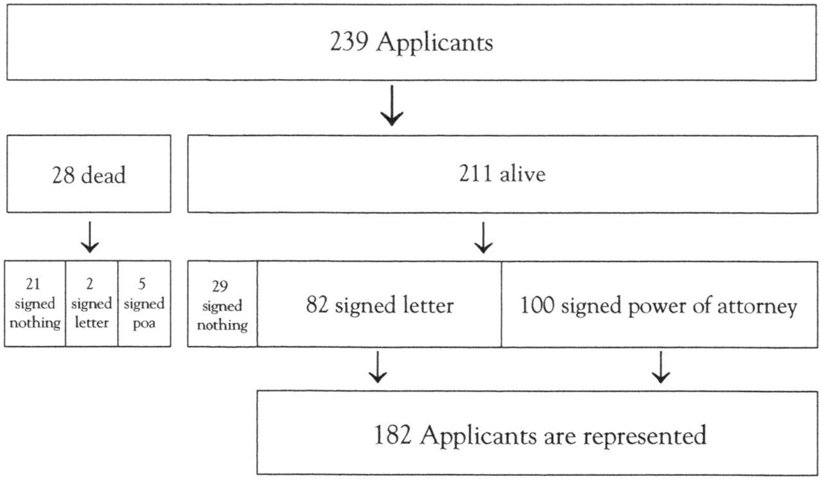

Figure 8 Gordon Bennett's diagram, presented in court, of the numbers of applicants

Gordon Bennett did what he could to clarify the issue at several points during the trial. He pointed out that some of the applicants did, in fact, relocate in 1997, but that they had subsequently returned to the reserve, from where they were subjected to a second relocation in 2002. The 1997 relocation, he pointed out, was perhaps worthy of some future investigation, but "is not a part of our claim in these proceedings" (*Sesana* 2006a: 34–6). Adding to the confusion were typographical errors that occurred in the court transcript as the case went along, resulting in inconsistencies in the number of applicants. Bennett took pains to rectify these in a presentation to the court during his closing arguments, offering a diagram of the changing numbers of applicants and their status from the time the case was submitted through to the end of the hearings (see Figure 8 above).

In the final submission to the court, Bennett returned to the topic of the applicants, claiming that, in spite of the number of 182 that he arrived at, they should not be limited to this figure, but that those who successfully signed on to the case "have made their application for the benefit of all persons with the same interest" (*Sesana* 2006a: at para. 3: 2).

One of the most important "consequences at the end of the day" was simply the creation of a list of CKGR residents with rights that followed from the judgment, which distinguished them from those individuals who did not register as applicants. While the court sought an unequivocal number and description of the claimants, the reality of life in the Kalahari region was anything but well defined, especially in terms of the movement of people and the identity and attachments of individuals who shift between San and Bakgalagadi, between hunting and agro-pastoralism, between communities in the Central Kalahari and government-sponsored remote area settlements, and sometimes between the Kalahari region and life in cities. Courts find it difficult to tolerate this ambiguity. Even when judges recognize the changeable nature of reality, they have to in some way reconcile it with the need for certainty, a demand that requires images, artifacts, practices, and life histories to be chosen with a view to their legibility and translatability. (I further explore the consequences of the applicant list in the period after the verdict in Chapter 7.)

EXPERT TESTIMONY FOR THE APPLICANTS

Botswana has a complex juridical system based on a combination of Roman-Dutch law, British common law, and constitutional and customary law. Its procedural law draws heavily on common law, in which witness testimony plays a crucial role in presenting evidence. By means of the hearsay rule, the reporting of speech by anyone who was not an eyewitness is normally not accepted as evidence (Quansah 2007). The result in the *Sesana* case was that it was important for the lawyers to choose the right witnesses, those with direct experience and knowledge, whose testimony could be transformed into admissible evidence.[2]

The witnesses and their lawyers presented several narratives, which emerged clearly as I was listening to the final pleading in September 2006. The most clear was a story of cultural survival and resilience through time, similar to other indigenous peoples elsewhere. It was a story based on the right of people to choose their own way of life based primarily on hunting and gathering, and of land ownership based on continuity of occupation and aboriginality to the area. The plaintiffs' lawyer emphasized the "right to choose" one's way of life as a fundamental issue. Bennett's arguments revolved around the applicants' "continuing connection" to their land and the continuity of their way of life, with unbroken connections between past and present. Bennett argued that both the San and Bakgalagadi are indigenous to the CKGR, and that there was no need to make a distinction between them because both are "Bushmen people." In addition, he underlined that the suspension of services (particularly water, healthcare, and food rations) in 2002 and the suspension of delivery of Special Game Licenses (necessary for collecting food) were actions clearly intended to force the San and Bakgalagadi to leave the reserve and against Botswana law (High Court of Botswana 2006, author notes). The applicants had to produce evidence that they were forcefully disposed from that land and still had links to that land, which involved using it in a "traditional way."

In the absence of titles of deed or any other formal markers of ownership, one of the main sources of leverage for the distinct rights of the San and Bakgalagadi was the concept of "Bushman." This term had significant potential legal value because it was legally recognized in the 1966 Botswana Constitution, where Art. 14.3 lays out the "freedom of movement in Botswana," particularly the right of the Bushmen to be in the reserve. Article 14.3c restricts certain freedom of movement to Botswana's citizens, but creates an exception for the Bushmen by making provision "for the imposition of restriction on the entry into or residence within defined areas of Botswana [i.e. the CKGR] of persons who are not Bushmen to the extent that such restrictions are reasonably required for the protection or well-being of Bushmen" (Republic of Botswana 2007b: 17) (see Chapter 2, p. 40). So a key point of the debate in court was whether the two different sociolinguistic groups (the San and the Bakgalagadi) that were relocated from the CKGR were both there when the reserve was created and, if so, whether both can today be considered part of the understanding of "Bushmen" to which the 1966 Botswana Constitution's Art. 14(3)(c) refers. Following from the legal significance of the term "Bushmen," several questions were raised in court: Who are the Bushmen present in the Constitution? Do they exist today? Are they part of the peoples who have been recognized internationally as indigenous? Are they indigenous to the CKGR?

To answer these questions, the applicants had to demonstrate their status as the "Bushmen" of the Constitution. Their lawyer, seeking to substantiate their argument, referred to the legal reasoning typical of similar cases in the common law, based upon the related concepts of "continuity" and "native title," even if Botswana, with its dual legal system, is not compelled to apply the common law doctrine of aboriginal title. In common law, "aboriginal" or "native title" is a form of collective title based on the *doctrine of continuity*, which favors the continuation of preexisting customary land rights. This ties in with the idea that colonization did not affect their rights if these rights were not explicitly extinguished by government legislation (Gilbert 2007: 592). This line of argument was supported by the applicants' two expert witnesses, based on reports and studies that they had conducted in the area and, in the case of George Silberbauer, also on his personal experience with the creation of the reserve.

In this trial "the facts" did not speak for themselves. The foraging way of life, to be seen as such, had to be included in a plot characterized by continuity, told as a coherent tale in which the protagonists of the past had to be the same as those in the present. This was accomplished in part through the testimony of the anthropologist George Silberbauer, who had been involved in the original planning of the Central Kalahari area as a place for both people and wildlife (Chapter 2). He was not called in court only as an expert witness, but also as a witness of fact, with each role calling for a different kind of evidence. As a witness of fact he spoke first about his role in the establishment of the reserve, and then why he thought the CKGR had been created. In fact, in his position as former Bechuanaland Protectorate colonial officer, Silberbauer (described in the Botswana newspaper *Mmegi* as "the pipe smoking scholar" [Tutwane 2004]) testified to the fact that the creation of the reserve *did not "extinguish the inhabitants' title"* over their land, but, on the contrary, that the reserve was created to protect its flora and fauna and the people who depended on them: "The main motive behind the declaration of the CKGR was to provide a haven (a place of safety) for the resident Bushmen and for the game animals and other resources on which the Bushmen depended for their living" (unofficial court transcript, July 13, 2004).

Switching roles to that of an expert, Silberbauer had first to deal with questions concerning his legitimacy, his qualifications to be considered an expert. Then he was called upon to confirm the validity of anthropology as a "science" (Sapignoli 2009). Drawing upon his professional knowledge, he presented information on who the "Bushmen" were and tried to document the territorial continuity of the applicants in their occupation and use of the CKGR, emphasizing their knowledge of food plants, their hunting techniques, and the distribution of languages across the area. He was asked for information about the history of the CKGR inhabitants before the colonists' arrival, the relationships between groups, their practices, and about the changes in lifestyle that these populations had undergone. He talked about the spiritual connection that the Bushmen have with the land and their ideas on territoriality.[3] Further, he offered a description of "Bushmen" that tried to resolve the problem of inclusion of the Bakgalagadi in the "Bushmen" identity-category:

> In many cases Bakgalagadi allied themselves with Bushmen groups and there was intermarriage between Bushmen and Bakgalagadi and many of the Bakgalagadi became to all intents and purposes Bushmen themselves while I believe still maintaining links with the Kgalagadi heritage. (Unofficial court transcript, July 12, 2004)

Silberbauer asserted that this category did not have any "racial connotation"; on the contrary, he said, "it indicates a kind of practice" and "a people living in a specific place." To sustain this point, Bennett referred to other anthropological studies (i.e. those of Ikeya, Osaki, Sugawara, and Tanaka) that describe the interrelationships, intermarriages, and shifting identities among these groups over generations. Bennett further supplemented Silberbauer's testimony with his own observation, made factual through the photographic evidence in the anthropologist's book cover:

> The youth standing on the left is ET, who has a Kgalagadi father and a /Gui mother. He is a skillful bow- and-arrow hunter, while his father hunts with a gun but cannot use a bow and arrow. He learned the skills of bow-and-arrow hunting from his sister's husband, who was a /Gui ... In recent years many Kgalagadi have come to regard themselves as San, and both San and Kgalagadi, claiming to be the descendants of the original inhabitants of the Reserve, are opposing the Government's policy of resettling the inhabitants of the Reserve in other areas. (*Sesana* 2006a: 339)

Anthropological knowledge was also used by the government lawyer, Sidney Pilane, to discredit the applicants' claims that their identity differs from the country's other inhabitants, presenting a narrative of "Bushmen assimilation." In the process he drew heavily on Edwin Wilmsen's (1989) perspectives, discussing the Bushmen as the "poor part" of Botswana society in need of development, taking a strong position on the side of the "revisionists" in the Kalahari debate (see Chapter 1, p. 13). He argued against the idea of indigeneity and Bushmen identity, taking the position that the Bushmen were "no longer authentic" because they were not hunting and gathering full-time, as they had in the past, and were involved in agriculture, livestock production, and migrant labor. He pointed to evidence in the literature to the effect that they had come late into the Kalahari as refugees (e.g. Kuper 1970: 5, 7), and that they had been pushed into the region by "stronger Tswana tribes." He also compared the Bushmen patterns with the Tswana agro-pastoral pattern, which involves a central town where people live, surrounded by agricultural areas and, further out, cattle posts. Everyone among the Tswana has a connection to a village. The fact that the Bushmen did not have such a connection was proof, he said, that they did not have land rights. Consistent with the notion of *terra nullius* (the concept used to describe a territory that has never been subject to the sovereignty of a state and which can therefore be acquired by a state through occupation), Pilane argued that there was no evidence of San and Bakgalagadi customary law over land due to their past hunter-gatherer way of life – in contradiction with his position of the San as an underclass – and their lack of a sense of territoriality, an argument that implies the legitimacy of occupation and removal by the state.

In order to counteract the *terra nullius* argument and to assert their claims of native title the applicants called another expert witness, Arthur Albertson, a biologist and land use planner who had worked with the NGO coalition on the development of the CKGR management plan. On the stand for approximately two months, Albertson was asked mainly to testify on the use and creation of a map of the Central Kalahari, using ethnocartographic technologies, which he said he drew on indigenous knowledge (Albertson 2000a, b). This map indicated the distribution of flora and fauna and the communities' borders and use of the territories in the CKGR. It was originally developed with the aim of facilitating negotiations with the government over natural resource use in the CKGR under the Botswana Community-Based Natural Resources Management system; but in Albertson's hands it became a tool for making the CKGR inhabitants' territorial rights legible and understandable to the legal system.

Albertson testified that he was looking at "traditional boundaries" between groups and territories. He sustained the applicant's position of territorial rights and continued occupancy of the land and traditional use:

> Traditional territorial-based land use/conservation principles are still in effect today in resident CKGR communities. Despite external pressures to adopt a sedentary lifestyle, they are still mobile and accordingly make use of dispersed resources within their respective territories. As they are still dependent on veld product they rely on access to these resources. (Unofficial court transcript, February 15, 2005)

As an expert witness, he interpreted the maps in court, explaining the places where people engaged in hunting and gathering, the hunting techniques employed, and the sustainability of foraging. He had to testify on the impact on the wildlife that the residents had, for instance looking at the relationships between animal density and numbers of the population through time. He spent several days presenting the inhabitants' traditional territorial borders, and the techniques he used to determine them.

Throughout the course of his testimony, the judges criticized Albertson's expert report, the way it was done and how it was structured:

JUSTICE PHUMAPHI: But you were aware that you had not written it in a manner that was suited for court?

ALBERTSON: Yes, I appreciated that though.

JUSTICE PHUMAPHI: So you could have then written it for court?

ALBERTSON: This is of course my first time in court.

JUSTICE PHUMAPHI: I see?

ALBERTSON: So there are a lot of things that I am learning as I go along.

JUSTICE PHUMAPHI: Although it's your first time you were aware that if you had written it for court you would have written it differently?

ALBERTSON: Yes, had I, while I was writing it, had I known it will be presented in court I would have written it differently. He [the applicants' lawyer] suggested that I include this document as part of my evidence and I said okay fine. (Unofficial court transcript, February 15, 2005)

The experts were used to substantiate the factual evidence provided by the applicants. Pilane attempted to discredit Albertson's expertise, saying that as a biologist he was not using a "traditional" method of obtaining information. He took this further and criticized the fact that the biologist had utilized, without qualification, an anthropological method, based mainly on hearsay, for the creation of the map and its interpretation. For Pilane, the methods used by the anthropologist as well as by the biologist to gather the information on the history of the CKGR inhabitants and their use of resources were not based on direct observation and the evidence was, therefore, inadmissible. During the presentation of evidence in the courtroom, the two experts were themselves transformed into "evidence." And as "evidence" they were closely examined, like objects from a crime scene, situated in context, measured, publicly presented, and assessed for their consistency, logic, and truth value.

SAN AND BAKGALAGADI KNOWLEDGE

The San and the Bakgalagadi who were called as "witnesses of fact" were only allowed to speak about strictly defined matters, structured in direct examination and cross-examination by the lawyers, each of whom wanted to present the strongest possible case. As "factual witnesses," the applicants had to give evidence that conformed to the narratives of their lawyers and experts. They also had to prove the fact that they had lived as indigenous peoples in continuity and in a sustainable way on the land that they call theirs, and from which they were relocated without their consent. This they did in their own way, using the skills of persuasion that led one writer to refer to them as "the owners of argument" (Megan Biesele, personal communication, 2015). Seated in the witness box or in the gallery, the applicants embodied the very notions of "Bushmen" that were being argued in court. In this sense, they presented evidence without speaking a word.

When they did speak, the CKGR inhabitants selected to serve as witnesses by their own communities in consultation with lawyers testified regarding their life histories, their ways of making a living inside the reserve, and how they had experienced the relocations. They could cite facts about the suspension of the services, about the relocation, and about the resistance toward the government plans and actions. They could not, however, intervene as "experts" in an environment where they and their ancestors had lived for untold generations. For the court, it was only the formally recognized, professional experts and not the San and Bakgalagadi themselves who could speak with authority about their way of life.

Kuela Kiema, a G/ui from the CKGR, who, in 1997, had chosen to be relocated from Xade to the new settlement of New Xade, describes in his book *Tears for My Land* the pain he felt when he was asked during the court case to interpret the proceedings from G//ana and Tsila into English and from English into G//ana and Tsila to enable the residents witness to be interrogated and cross-examined by the lawyers and judges (Kiema 2010: 109). This choice of translator, in many ways, was highly problematic. The witnesses had to rely on him as the source of their voice in court, yet Kiema was at the time a highly polarizing figure, identified as the one who had "given away their land." In his memoir, published four years after the *Sesana* trial, he regretted his support for the relocation, describing himself as feeling pain because his people had been wrongly pushed from their own land and for the fact that now they had to justify in front of an unfamiliar court their ownership of the territory where they and their ancestors had lived for centuries. He emphasized that for his people "the court was an alienating system, and often the government lawyers were trying to discredit them, creating doubts as to their credibility and honesty because they could not read or answer questions on their ages and places of birth" (Kiema 2010: 24). The stories most of the witnesses knew about themselves and their families were part of an oral history which they had learned from their parents and grandparents, and which sometimes did not correspond to what was written in their *omangs* (Botswana identity cards) or in textbooks and that were, therefore, often questioned as hearsay.

The San vocabularies and linguistic systems tend to have no equivalents for dominant legal concepts, so for the interpreters it was often difficult to translate the questions of the lawyers and the judges to the witnesses, and in the translation the meaning was often lost. As Kiema (2010: 109) reported, for the San and Bakgalagadi, it was difficult to understand what was being asked in their own languages. It was even more difficult to translate their ideas into the concepts used by the court. They were required to answer the questions by lawyers and judges in a "factual way," particularly on matters related to their life history and territorial rights.

Even if the San and Bakgalagadi were advised by their lawyers about the kind of evidence they would likely be called upon to produce in court and the rules of proceeding, their reactions to the objections and to the cross-examination questions suggest that they were not aware of or had little patience with the rules of the courtroom. For instance, some witnesses under cross-examination often expressed frustration and refused to answer questions that they thought were childish or disrespectful.

On several occasions, before the judges entered the room and the case started, Sesana, who was not called to the witness box, engaged in a kind of pantomime in which he imitated the distinctive way of walking and other habitual gestures of Sidney Pilane, the state's lawyer, and Kathleen Alexander, a biologist who testified at length as an expert witness for the state. An uninformed observer might not have understood the reason for the hilarity from the gallery, as Sesana, during recesses, deftly imitated their distinctive mannerisms. This kind of humor can be seen as the classic weapon of the court jester, the trickster, the one who mocks the pretenses of those in positions of power. Sesana's pantomimes can also be understood as an expression of disapprobation that is widely recognized as typical of San society, in which relationships of cooperation cannot normally be interrupted by putting oneself forward or by expressions of anger or open dispute. In this sense, Sesana was engaging in the same kind of mockery that regularly acts as an informal corrective to faults and misbehavior in San society, of refusing the "one who boasts, for someday his pride will make him kill somebody," of using ridicule to "cool his heart and make him gentle" (Lee 1969: 63). Seen from this point of view, Sesana was acting on the applicants' collective disapprobation of those who represented the "arrogant" authority of the government, engaging in pantomimic ridicule as a form of "correction" of behavior considered inappropriate.

At the same time, those applicants who did sit in the witness box did what they could to support the case. During cross-examination, the CKGR inhabitants were asked some questions on possible inconsistencies concerning their claims of a Bushman identity, of cultural difference and typicality, and of their continuity of living in that territory. Despite the fact that most of the time Bakgalagadi people are not considered "Bushmen" in the sense of "Basarwa," the applicants in court presented themselves as "one people"; in other words, they tried to consistently populate the legal identity presented in the Botswana Constitution, as interpreted to them by their lawyers. In the act of populating the concept, the applicants embodied and resignified "Bushmen" to include people – the Bakgalagadi – whom history had excluded, creating an identity that was rooted in common practices and experiences of dispossession.

The state's lawyers did not vigorously question this new, more inclusive conception of "Bushmen," probably because to do so would invoke the kind of ethnic differences that were at odds with the state's narratives of equality and cultural integration, and after all the Bakgalagadi were "people from the bush." The emphasis by the state was on national belonging as the foundation of identity, as against any kind of tribal or ethnic membership. Some of the witnesses reacted to the government lawyer's questions to delegitimize their own different cultural identity by emphasizing their ethnicity:

PILANE: And he accepts that he also is a Motswana like all others?

BOTSHELWANE: I am not a Motswana, I am Mokuaha, Mosarwa [Bushman].

PILANE:	That's okay. He accepts that he is a citizen of Botswana like all others?
BOTSHELWANE:	I say I am not a Motswana, I am a Mokuaha.
PILANE:	I said citizen of Botswana?
BOTSHELWANE:	I don't know whether I am a citizen of Botswana, but what I know is that I come from my land the land of Basarwa [Bushmen]. That is what I know. (Unofficial court transcript, July 28, 2004)

The government's lawyer was almost literally deaf to any alternative conception of belonging as he argued for the overriding significance of citizenship in the state. He followed up on this by connecting citizenship with a particular notion of property, which calls upon those with claims to property to show their certificates or purchase agreements to that land. Thus, during his examination, Pilane also asked for formal documentation showing that the applicants were in possession of their own land. To this assertion, Segootsane, the first San witness in the box, responded:

> All I know is that this land was a gift from God. I am not aware that when you are created God made some papers ... [so] that we can go around indicating that this is an evidence to show that we own this land. (Unofficial court transcript, July 27, 2004)

The applicants' witnesses also made efforts to bridge the gap between legal conceptions of property and collective belonging and their own understanding of themselves. The San witnesses under cross-examination offered narratives that – apparently unintentionally – related to the concept of "native title." Ramahoko, for example, stated: "Our forefathers were born and died in this land. Our parents died in this land so if you want to relocate us just take the whole of this soil with us and relocate us together with the soil" (unofficial court transcript, July 29, 2004).

Ultimately some of the most powerful and persuasive testimony had to do with the attachment of the applicants to permanent gravesites in the CKGR. The significance of permanent graves inside the CKGR was first brought out under Bennett's questioning of Mongwegi Thobogelo, who referred to what she called at various points "the graves of my mothers" and "the graves belonging to our forefathers, the grandparents" in Molapo.

BENNETT:	Are these graves important to you?
THOBOGELO:	They are very important to me.

BENNETT: Do you visit them?
THOBOGELO: Yes, I do visit them.
BENNETT: Do you do anything when you go to visit them?
THOBOGELO: I do something when I visited them.
BENNETT: What do you do?
THOBOGELO: When I am sick I go there to take the soil to use it for medication.
BENNETT: You take the soil from the grave itself?
THOBOGELO: I take the soil from the top of the grave [...]
BENNETT: How do you do that? (Unofficial court transcript, November 5, 2004)

In response to this last question, Thobogelo stood silently, opened her shirt and pantomimed the gesture of gathering soil, rubbing it on her bare chest, and standing in a posture of spiritual supplication. There was a long silence, broken only when Justice Dow asked Bennett whether her act could be considered purification or cleansing, to which Pilane interjected with an observation that it was simply a medicinal act involving the use of soil. "She can do all sorts of things with it, she might even just look at it" (unofficial court transcript, November 5, 2004). Despite this effort at diversion, Thobogelo's one act of wordless testimony removed all doubts about the applicants' attachments to the land – and to their ancestors – from which they had been forcibly relocated.

This did not stop the lawyer for the state from immediately taking up the issue of graves when given the opportunity to cross-examine the witness. His goal was clearly to call into question the existence or significance of permanent gravesites, a tactic that was aimed at demonstrating that the San lacked territorial belonging, first by asking about how graves were dug. In response to this line of questioning Thobogelo provided rich detail: "A deep grave [is prepared] in such a way that when it is dug we put something in it, so that the person who is inside can use that thing to climb out of the grave" (unofficial court transcript, November 22, 2004). Trying a different tactic, Pilane drew on the evidence from anthropologists, which emphasized the impermanence of the way the dead were handled among the San, consistent with a highly mobile people.

PILANE: Now, those who know the history of the Basarwa [San] say that because Basarwa were nomadic they did not bury their dead. They say that ... if a person was so ill, and it was clear to the band to his family that he was unlikely to survive they would gather fruits and berries for him, hunt an animal for him, place them next to him then collapse his hut on him, and the band would then move and go and settle somewhere and leave him to die. Do you have any comment?

THOBOGELO: What kind of person is that who says such things? Is that person around here, and can he come into court and stand up and say these things?

PILANE: I invited a comment not to ask a question.

THOBOGELO: I am answering for myself. (Unofficial court transcript, November 22, 2004)

Pilane then asked Thobogelo to remember George Silberbauer, the "white elderly gentleman" who gave testimony as the opening witness in New Xade.

PILANE: Your expert witness who studied you as a people, your culture, your ways, your beliefs goes on and says when a man dies he is buried and mourned at the grave for four days.

THOBOGELO: On that point he is correct, when someone is dead we sit there and we mourn for that person.

PILANE: He continues: "the people then leave that place and do not live there."

THOBOGELO: We have never done that at Molapo, we consider Molapo as our village, we just move out to establish cattle posts and always come back to Molapo.

PILANE: It may be that perhaps at the time that Dr. Silberbauer carried out his investigations the Basarwa people were still carrying on their nomadic way of life, and they did not live in settlements.

THOBOGELO: How would that be the case because when I grew up I was shown where he used to stay when he had come to Molapo. (Unofficial court transcript, November 22, 2004)

In a few spare words Thobogelo asserted her own narrative of place and belonging. Silberbauer had, in good faith, as the first witness for the applicants, described the way of life of the San, consistent with how it had been depicted by many other experts, himself included, as the mobile hunting and gathering way of life that captured the imaginations of those who saw the deep history of humanity represented in a living people. But what was missed in the emphasis on mobility that was being pressed by Pilane was the complexity of Silberbauer's scholarly work as well as his testimony in which he tried to explain the multifarious and changing nature of the San way of life. Complexity of this kind often went missing in court (Sapignoli 2009). What Thobogelo underscored in her testimony was the fact that, for many San, life had changed toward more permanent settlements, with graves, boreholes, and small livestock. This did not mean that the web of human relationships lost all meaning, but that the meaning changed, like everything else, toward greater permanence. This implied that the forced relocation was not imposed on a nomadic people who, it was incorrectly imagined, could easily take discontinuity in stride, but on a people that had always had a profound sense of place, whose territory was filled with symbolic and spiritual significance (Kuela 2010; Takada 2016).

In the words of the San and Bakgalagadi who gave evidence, past and future were present in the space of the court. Their testimony not only pointed to collective ecological wisdom, intergenerational transmission of a system of knowledge inherited from ages past, but also and at the same time to their historical complexity, their ability to adapt to new circumstances. They said that their land was collectively owned, that it was held by the group and not by individuals, that they had never given it up, and that many of them were not aware of the meaning of state land. They told the court that they *did* have territories (areas that they occupied and moved around in), against the government lawyer's argument that because they were mobile they did not have a sense of territorial rights and property. They testified that they moved from place to place over time, but within known areas or "traditional territories," each of which was called a *gu* (G/ui), *g!u* (G//ana), or a *nong* (Naro). The applicants described their relationship with the land and how the land was necessary for their physical and social health, charting a different path of development from that envisioned by the state.

The difficulty of conveying these essential qualities of their way of life explains in part why this trial lasted so long. A traditional territory and its use are based on abstractions that call for expert witnesses, including the applicants themselves (as witnesses of fact), to describe their relationship to that territory in detail – and to offer these descriptions in an adversarial context in which their accounts were subject to skepticism and probing in order to bring out inconsistencies that could be highlighted as sources of doubt.

The court was more directly receptive to testimony in which San and Bakgalagadi witnesses recalled their personal experiences of forced relocation, which was at the center of the case. They described the day in late January 2002 when many men in uniforms and vehicles arrived in their villages and began destroying their homes and putting people and their animals on trucks. Their narratives and stories revealed oppressive and inhumane treatment. All of the witnesses said they did not have any choice: "We were told to move, we were not asked." They used expressions such as "We gave up hope." They said that members of the same family were approached separately, at different times, to see if they would be agreeable to the relocation; this then was used as a form of pressure on the others. Some families were split because they were relocated to different resettlements. Corresponding to this experience, the word that Mongwegi Thobogelo used for "compensation" was the G//ana term *phimilo-dikeledi*, meaning "to wipe one's tears."[4]

Even though their testimonies introduced themes of suffering and spirituality, the court was oriented toward minimizing the emotional impact of testimony. As factual witnesses, they were asked to present facts related to the relocation, government consultations, their practices, their biographical data, and the origins of their families and ancestors.

This part of the witness testimony was more familiar to, and understandable by, the court. It had to do with the illegitimate use of force, with the sometimes violent control of bodies, with policies and the police that enforced them. Here the only ambiguity had to do with establishing matters of fact, in which the witnesses could present compelling narratives based on lived experience.

Arguing the case based on these legal principles thus involved a process of double translation. This occurred first in the court's language translation from Sekgalagadi, San, and Setswana into English. At the same time, a process of conceptual translation took place, from the ideas and experience of the applicants and their experts into legal reasoning, taking the terms used by witnesses and making them legally comprehensible. They did so in part by engaging in a kind of *pre-emptive translation*, preparing witnesses with the facts they were to use in their testimony so that what they had to say might be heard.

THE STATE MAKES ITS CASE

The respondents' factual witnesses and experts were called in during the year from May 2005 to May 2006. One of the experts testifying for the state, Kathleen Alexander, a veterinarian and expert on wild and domestic animal diseases, occupied the box for twenty-five days. They were experts on wildlife and natural parks, staff of the DWNP, including its minister, Ghanzi District Commissioner, land board, and central government officials, RADP officers, police and Department of Supplies Officers who took part in the removals of the San and Bakgalagadi from the reserve in 1997 and 2002. Through these testimonies, the government's lawyer pursued three central lines of argumentation: one concerned the cultural values and benefits that justifies the relocation; another underscored the incompatibility of humans and wildlife, emphasizing the values of "total preservation" of the park's resources for the benefit of all citizens; and a third focused on the voluntary nature of the relocation and the benefits that were to follow from the creation of new opportunities in the remote area communities.

The narrative of the respondents centered on the government's ideas of equality, citizenship, and development, which, as we have seen, was already present through the removal activities and which expressed the intention to integrate the San and Bakgalagadi into "the rest of the modern nation." The government's justification in court for suspending services in the reserve was their "astronomic cost." At the same time, its position was that the services were not terminated; they were just "moved" to a new location outside the reserve (author notes 2006). This narrative was based on the position that human settlements cannot exist in a game reserve – the place by definition set aside for wildlife – and relocation was presented as an act of government responsibility toward its citizens, necessary for the inhabitants' integration into the human world.

The respondents' lawyers also invoked the issue of distinct rights versus the equal rights of citizens, claiming that it was the duty of the government to protect the reserve for present and future generations and that if the right to live in the CKGR was extended to other people in the nation, the flora and fauna of the Kalahari would be completely destroyed. The lawyers for the state thus attempted to discredit the applicants' claims of their different identity from the country's other inhabitants. The applicants were represented as the "poor part" of Botswana society and not indigenous peoples with "special rights" from the rest of the nation (author notes 2006). Under these circumstances, the state was fulfilling its responsibility to all of its citizens by removing the Bushmen from the reserve and giving them the wherewithal to create new and better lives. Otherwise, they would always be a source of national shame, a people characterized by poverty and the absence of civilization.

Perhaps the clearest expression of the government's understanding of the legitimate forms of culture came from the defense witness, Pelonomi Venson, a career politician who had once rejected the pleas of the San delegation in Gaborone led by John Hardbattle and who at the time of the relocations was Minister for Wildlife. Her testimony emphasized the basic principle that "ethnicity is never pronounced or promoted above nationhood" (unofficial court transcript, May 9, 2006). She also revealed the way that the idea of culture can be restricted to settled collective life, based on values of development, private property, and material prosperity:

> Human settlements entail having a claim of ownership, having a claim to a piece of land that can be inherited by your children and grandchildren, having a place you call home. And based on the outline that I gave about our land users and their procedures, it follows that none of us can claim a piece of land and call it home in a place already designated and approved for other uses. (Unofficial court transcript, May 9, 2006)

Added to these views of property is a political agenda in which, as Venson put it, "our main focus is for an integrated society" (unofficial court transcript, May 9, 2006).

The assumption by those representing the state, to the effect that the residents of the CKGR were somehow backward and unable to adapt to the modern world, was not only expressed formally in prepared testimony, but also in spontaneous gestures of incomprehension. The verdict by Unity Dow, for example, noted how profound differences in the San and the state approaches to development were manifested in the behavior of the state's lawyer:

> When one of the Applicants gave evidence that she did not wish to relocate, because she wished to be near the graves of her ancestors, Mr. Pilane burst out laughing and when it seemed clear by the silence in the Court that he needed to explain the source of his mirth, he explained that he had not been aware that they buried their dead, but had rather thought that they collapsed a hut over their dead and moved on. (*Sesana* 2006c, Dow at para. 29: 244)

This is more than a description of a fault in manners – the government, through its lawyer, was unable to conceive of the San as a people with their own historical trajectory, their own conceptions of development and common good.

The ideas of culture as settlement and development that lay at the foundation of the state's expressions of national identity extended to the policy-oriented goal of "total preservation" of the park and its resources, completely separate from human habitation. This was most explicitly expressed by the defense witness Jan Broekhuis, Assistant Director of the Department of Wildlife and National Parks in the Ministry of Wildlife and Tourism from 1999 to the time of the trial. Through the course of his testimony, Broekhuis revealed himself to be a committed animal conservationist, indicating that he personally objected to any notion that the CKGR (or any game reserve or park for that matter) could support human habitation. This conservationism extended to mining in the game reserve, which he opposed in spite of a government policy that permitted it.

Among his responsibilities, Broekhuis was given the task of overseeing the drafting and negotiation of CKGR management plans. The Third Draft of the plan, created after extensive consultation, set out an arrangement whereby communities could remain inside the reserve and continue to hunt and gather sustainably, while engaging in some economic ventures such as tourism if they wished to. The final draft, produced after the relocations, had removed all reference to communities living inside the reserve and restricted the legal use of the reserve to two areas near the resettlement camps.

Taking this position further, Broekhuis argued that the removal of the San and Bagkalagadi from the CKGR had been, for all intents and purposes, already accomplished during the negotiations on the draft management plan:

BENNETT: It is only fair to you Mr. Broekhuis if I put to you in general terms that what you have done in the draft final plan is to remove from it anything which reflects the views of the residents and anything which might benefit those who choose to remain inside the reserve?

BROEKHUIS: [By] the time the draft was prepared there were no communities remaining within the CKGR save for a few individual families. The plan was

> brought in line with the government policy that the services should be delivered to communities elsewhere. (Unofficial court transcript, May 17, 2005)

Following from this assumed emptiness of the reserve of human habitation, Broekhuis did not feel compelled to take the (former) residents' views into consideration as he altered an extensively negotiated Third Draft of the Management Plan into the state's unilateral vision for the use of the reserve. Even the results of the assistant director's visit to Ghanzi to meet with NGOs and the District Council to seek approval of the draft plan were shelved as the government attempted to formalize the removals in a new regime, empty of human habitation. The views of those to be affected by the plan, Broekhuis told the court, were "irrelevant." "These are things that will be decided and done … when the need arises" (unofficial court transcript, May 17, 2005).

Broekhuis's top-down approach to consultation with the CKGR negotiating team derived in part from the managers' strict obedience to directives from the central government. This element of blind obedience to the highest echelons of the state stood out to the judges. The court observed in its verdict, for example, that the Director of the Department of Wildlife had refused to grant Special Game Licenses to the residents of the CKGR, despite having legally enshrined discretionary powers to do so. The sole motivation for this was "the fact that the Government took a decision to terminate services and the DWNP felt automatically bound to follow suit" (*Sesana* 2006c: 378–9).

Another motivating factor influencing the decisions taken by representatives of the Department of Wildlife and National Parks seemed to be a firmly held belief that permanent human presence was incompatible with the natural world – a view of human life, in other words, that is "domesticated" and separated from the "natural world" of the reserve. Joseph Matlhare, former Director of Wildlife and National Parks, for example (sworn in not only as a government official formerly responsible for the management of the CKGR, but also as an expert witness for the government on the basis of his training in biology) invoked the many "disturbance factors" associated with the presence of human communities in the CKGR (unofficial court transcript, May 26, 2005).

The state's third line of argumentation had to do with negating the claims made by the applicants that they were compelled to relocate, with their huts dismantled, water tanks destroyed and families divided by force. In his closing arguments Sidney Pilane asserted that consultations had taken place before the removals, and "there is undoubted evidence that the meetings started" (author notes 2006). Several defense witnesses were called to testify on the voluntary nature of the relocations and the benefits of living in the resettlement villages. Tabona Kelapaile, a social worker employed as a Principal Remote Area Development Officer (PRADO) in the Kgalagadi District Council who had been centrally involved in the 2002 relocations, testified (in contradiction to a summary he had previously prepared for the court) that he had never persuaded anybody to leave the CKGR, that his principal role in the relocations was to make arrangements for transport to go and collect those people who had made requests for relocation, and that when he arrived at a village in the CKGR he was greeted by a gentleman who had "registered some people who want to go to Kaudwane [a resettlement village]. No one complained about the removal of their belongings. No huts were dismantled without the consent of the owners." On the delicate matter of families being broken up in the relocation, Pilane persisted in emphasizing the strictly voluntary nature of the relocations: "If A and B are spouses and one wants to leave. Do we say to the other, sorry, unless your wife wants to come we will not assist you?" (*Sesana* 2006b: 10). In Pilane's hands, the forcible separation of families was nothing more than acts of benevolence toward individuals who shared the government's vision for the betterment of their lives.

THE CIRCUS

The contest for the rights of those who had been removed from the CKGR was not limited to the discourse of lawyers and testimony of witnesses in the courtroom. At the same time that the San and Bakgalagadi advanced their causes through institutional venues, they also engaged in "direct action" strategies such as rallies and media campaigns involving consumer boycotts. Beyond the procedures for entering evidence and rules of decorum presided over by the three judges, there was a chaotic series of side-contests and skirmishes, with very different rules of engagement. This was above all the struggle for supremacy in the media, the effort for control over the way the case was reported to public audiences in Botswana and abroad. The court case fed into wider contests that had more to do with control over ideas in the domestic electorate and overseas in places that were sources of the country's all-important tourism income, investment, and international political support.

As we saw in Chapters 4 and 5, this effort to shape opinion as a strategy toward social justice began well before the court case, but with the events of the 2002 removals from the CKGR there was an acceleration of media coverage and outreach by NGOs with a concern for the welfare of the San. The international media followed the case closely, including coverage by the British Broadcasting Corporation, the *New York Times*, and the *Mail and Guardian* (South Africa). In Botswana, numerous local newspapers also consistently followed the case, particularly *Mmegi Wa Dikang*, *The Voice*, *The Guardian*, and *The Daily News*.

The spate of press releases that Survival International began just prior to the court case (see Chapter 4, p. 150) continued while it was in progress, with Survival's director Stephen Corry citing himself as saying,

> The Bushmen are finally being given a public platform to refute the government's claim that the relocations were voluntary – so obviously false and believed only by the most gullible ... All the government has to offer them in the resettlement sites is alcoholism, depression and AIDS.[5]

SI also gave preference in its coverage of the court case to "Bushmen" witnesses, placing emphasis on stirring statements such as Tshokodiso Botshilwane's testimony in July, 2004, in which he stated pithily, "I prefer death to relocation."[6]

It is important not to overemphasize the influence of the SI campaign to the point of overlooking the significant impact of other players, including the independent influence of media outlets in shaping opinion surrounding the first CKGR trial. As Saugestad (2005) notes, this case had stronger national and international reverberations than similar cases of forced removal in the past. In fact, the attention from international NGOs, academics, and activists for indigenous rights, along with the involvement of the United Nations, the African Union, and the European Union (see Chapter 5), gave the situation faced by the people of the CKGR an amplified global context, which was not at all limited to the efforts of SI. A variety of prominent NGOs also threw their hats into the ring. In 2004 Roy Sesana and Jumanda Gakelebone were invited by Rupert Isaacson and Barbara Savage of the Tribal Trust Foundation to do a tour of the United States. Kalahari Peoples Fund sponsored the tour, which began with a visit to Hollywood, where they were hosted by singer-songwriter Jackson Browne to raise funds for the legal case. Significant press coverage was devoted to the visit to the US on National Public Radio, BBC, South African Radio, and Radio Botswana. *National Geographic* published an article titled "African Bushmen Tour U.S. to Fund Fight for Land" (Lovgren 2004). Various celebrities visited the reserve and the new settlements in Botswana during the first years of the legal battle, including Prince Charles, Brad Pitt, and Angelina Jolie. The cumulative effect of such campaigning was to raise the profile of the case and, at the same time, to add substantially to the awareness of the San as an icon for a disappearing indigenous way of life, whose struggle for survival followed from the harm of government policies and the ideas that inspired them.

Despite the international dimensions of the NGO-sponsored publicity campaigns, the most immediate way this struggle manifested itself in the trial was through the involvement of reporters from national and other southern African media outlets. Through this kind of media attention, San activists in Botswana had an immediate channel into national and regional popular opinion on issues surrounding the court case. Several local and national newspapers reported daily on events in the court, including regular stories on the testimony provided by each witnesses or the lines of argumentation in a cross-examination, once even publishing a story on Pilane's heated complaints to the judges about being distracted by whispering from Gordon Bennett during his cross-examination of Arthur Albertson ("Botswana: Pilane Shouts to Quell Whispers in Court" [Chwaane 2005a]). While the state newspaper *The Daily News* reported on the key events of the case in a fairly straightforward way, other outlets were more sympathetic toward the "Basarwa" applicants. *The Voice*, for example, came out with a headline that emphasized the genocidal nature of the removal: "On the Attack: Botswana Government wants to kill Basarwa and our culture" (Reporter *The Voice* 2004).

Roy Sesana in particular became a public figure through media coverage of the case, always wearing his distinctive leather hat with steenbok antlers that he had fashioned especially for the occasion. There was nothing scripted about these interviews, and the lawyers for the San and Bakgalagadi applicants occasionally had to mollify the judges when the court proceedings were commented on and their views appeared in the morning papers. The judges were particularly sensitive about articles that were critical of the court and its proceedings, as, for example, when the weekly *Botswana Guardian* printed an item titled, "Language Barrier Closes Sesana Out," which stated that Roy Sesana hardly appeared in court, preferring to stay outside smoking cigarettes because he was unable to follow the proceedings in English, and explained that the court had neglected to provide interpreters and the San lacked the means to hire their own. Sesana later claimed that he did not give an interview for this article, but merely had a casual conversation with a journalist (Chwaane 2005b). On several occasions, the day in court began with the state's lawyer objecting to just-appeared newspaper articles in which Sesana was reported to have expressed doubt about the fairness of the proceedings or to have made a connection between diamond mining and the removals. On May 9, 2005, for example, the proceedings began with a response to Pilane's complaints to the judges about recent newspaper articles that had reported on the case, with Bennett apologizing on behalf of his clients:

BENNETT: [...] If [my clients] caused offence to the Court, they offer through me their unreserved apologies. I have advised them that they should be more circumspect in any comment they need to communicate in the future and that they should confine those comments to the substance of the serious issues to which this case gives rise. They have accepted to do that and I am very much hope that there will be no further difficulty in that respect.

JUSTICE PHUMAPHI: All right. (Unofficial court transcript, May 10, 2005)

The verdict later reflected the judges' frustration with this ongoing recourse to media, pointing to the fact that Sesana did not appear as a witness, yet "outside Court, through the media and without the limitations of an oath to tell the truth, he had plenty to say" under circumstances in which he was "free to embellish and/or distort" (*Sesana* 2006c: 137–8). Clearly for the judges, Sesana's political activism was in no way a substitute for legal evidence. The verdict assigned legal costs to the applicants (eventually to be borne by Survival International), citing Sesana's statements to the media as the source of this punitive decision. It is clear from the displeasure expressed by the judges toward this journalism that the media engagement was not so much intended to directly influence the judges and their verdict, but to use the case as an opportunity, through the media interest it

Figure 9 Roy Sesana and other applicants with journalists outside the court

generated, to more broadly influence public opinion. The court was in this sense a focal point and amplifier of a wider political struggle over opinion. It is also possible that Sesana felt excluded by the proceedings, which took place in a language he did not understand, and that he used his access to the media as an outlet to express his grievances, which had no place in the courtroom.

Gordon Bennett was very much aware of the significance of the media as a dimension of the legal strategy. He once told me, for example, about his frustration in taking on the case after the order of witnesses had already been set, with George Silberbauer as the applicants' first witness (2013). This, for him, was a wasted opportunity to meet the expectations of journalists, whose attention was especially strong in the opening days of the trial and who wanted to hear about the relocation directly from the San and Bakgalagadi people who had been subjected to it. These witnesses, he felt, were a much more stirring, media-friendly source of testimony than the foreign anthropologist-as-expert.

There is a sense in which the NGO campaigns, celebrity endorsements, and media coverage of the trial in Lobatse were all interrelated, making what was happening outside the court part of a multifaceted strategy that included the court case. The key to using the media as an aspect of a legal strategy, however, was to be circumspect, not to cause offense by "sub-judicating" the case, as Pilane put it. The San and Bakgalagadi applicants were anxious for their story to be heard. Their outreach activity was not limited to what they told reporters, but on one occasion on September 6, 2006 involved applicants (including witnesses) bringing their justice lobbying into the courtroom during the closing arguments. This was the day when around a dozen applicants appeared in the gallery wearing white t-shirts with the slogan "I (heart) CKGR" provided to them by SI and FPK. Before the judges entered the courtroom, I overheard Sidney Pilane tell Gordon Bennett that he saw these t-shirts as a protest, that freedoms are good but they can go too far. That is why, he said, there is a problem in the West with terrorism. Gordon Bennett's secretary Kali Mercier, suggested that wearing tourist t-shirts might not be terrorism as we know it. Pilane's reply was, "But it begins," implying that the t-shirts were a first step down a slippery slope to violent anarchy. Bennett instructed those wearing the shirts to cover them. They duly complied, and later lined up outside the court for photographs, proudly displaying their shirts. When the issue was then discussed in closed chambers, there was no need for the judges to act, because the matter had already been resolved. The justice lobbying and media coverage may well have been a significant aspect of the trial, but, in principle at least, no part of it was ever to cross the threshold and possibly influence the proceedings.

THE RULING

The verdict in *Sesana and Others v. the Attorney General of the Republic of Botswana* was delivered in the Lobatse High Court on December 13, 2006 to a room filled to capacity. When it was apparent that the courtroom would be far too small to accommodate the many people who wanted to attend, a tent was hastily erected outside, equipped with a TV screen and loudspeakers, and with a hundred plastic chairs set up to handle the overflow, but even this was not enough and many people ended up sitting on the lawn. The press, both national and international, was there in significant numbers scattered throughout the crowd in the courtroom. At about 9:00 a.m. there was a flurry of excitement, with flash bulbs going off as Roy Sesana made his entry from a side door accompanied by around a hundred of the applicants. He was dressed in his "regalia": ostrich eggshell beads, a leather vest, a thin necktie, and his trademark cap with steenbok horns. Some of the applicants wore the "I [heart] CKGR" t-shirts, with no objection from any of the judges or respondents, in contrast to the events several months previously in which they were forced to cover the same politically-charged message. Benches in the front of the courtroom had been reserved for the applicants, and they sat there quietly and patiently. Sidney Pilane entered next, smiling broadly as he approached Gordon Bennett, who returned his smile as they embraced and took their seats. At 9:30 a.m. Justice Dibotelo began delivering the ruling, with a discourse lasting more than two hours.[7]

To properly understand the effectiveness of the lawyers' and witnesses' narratives and the consequences that going to court has had in the life of CKGR's inhabitants we need to consider the verdict, the ways that judges lent credence to or denied the validity of the evidence presented in court. This can be seen not only in the majority decisions of the ruling, which give it legal effect, but also in the individual rulings offered by each of the three judges, which point more specifically to the testimony that influenced them or that they excluded as irrelevant to the legal questions under consideration. First, let us consider the 2006 verdict as a judgment with legal effect. The three judges of the High Court unanimously ruled that the applicants were in possession of the land, which they lawfully occupied in their settlements in the CKGR. The majority decision stated that the applicants were deprived of such possession by the government forcibly or wrongfully and without their consent. The verdict stated that the government's refusal to issue Special Game Licenses and to allow the applicants to enter the reserve was unlawful and unconstitutional. The termination by the government of the provision of basic services to the applicants in the CKGR, however, *was* permissible under the law. On December 19, 2006, the Botswana government announced that it would not appeal the decision in the *Sesana* case. It now stands as a prominent reference point in the case law on indigenous rights.

Within this ruling, there are important differences expressed by the three judges. Justice Dibotelo (the Judge in Chief) was the more conservative of the three, avoiding reference to international law, tending toward a middle-of-the-road traditionalism, which inclined toward Tswana nationalism. He is a member of the Bakwena, one of the more significant "tribes" from the standpoint of population, territory, and political influence. From this starting point, he did not recognize the applicants as members of an indigenous people with a culture different from that of the dominant society, but instead argued that they are to be considered the same as any other Batswana (citizen of Botswana). He rejected the testimony offered by Silberbauer, and dismissed any discussion of the intent behind the establishment of the game reserve (Saugestad 2011: 47). He did not recognize that the applicants had been removed by force from their homes. He was also alone among the three judges in finding that the "Evidence before the Court also shows that the Applicants did not principally depend on hunting for their food because they cultivated crops such as maize, beans and melons and kept domestic animals like goats and chickens as a source for their food" (*Sesana* 2006c: 111–12). He concluded that the termination of services in the Central Kalahari was not unlawful and that people had been consulted sufficiently prior to the termination of those services (*Sesana* 2006c: 69–70). To justify his decision to deny the services to the applicants, he referred to the San and Bakgalagadi witnesses who had proudly stated their ability and their intention to live in the reserve even without government support.

Striking a note of difference with this view, Judge Unity Dow (*Sesana* 2006c: 157–8) was "the progressive" judge, having previously established a reputation as a defender of women's rights in Botswana.[8] Hers was by far the more impassioned ruling. In the courtroom she strayed somewhat from her text when pointing to the long history of prejudice and disadvantage experienced by the Bushmen:

> The CKGR residents, especially the Basarwa, are at the lowest end of the social structure ... The British used to call them "wild" and "uncivilized" ... In the pre-Independence election of 1964, the then government felt it of little value to get the "Bushmen" to vote ... They are not mentioned in Sections 77, 78, and 79 of the Constitution and have no representative in the House of Chiefs ... They are disadvantaged, marginalized, and until recently were politically silent ... The indigenous have rights ... Causing the disappearance of their culture is too big a price to pay ... They have a special relation to land as it is their spiritual base ... Until recently, perhaps it is still the case, "Mosarwa," "Lesarwa," "Lekgalagadi" and "Mokgalagadi" were common terms of insult, in the same way as "nigger" and "kaffir." Any adult Motswana who pretends otherwise is being dishonest in the extreme.[9]

Consistent with her progressive approach to equality and racism, Dow emphasized that the services the government was providing before the relocation were now "essential for the applicants livelihood, because their mobility and diet have changed over the years" (Sapignoli 2015: 13). Justice Dow (*Sesana* 2006c: 157–8) emphasized the expert evidence, which showed that the mobility of the applicants within the reserve has, during the years, been linked to availability of drinking water. She took a culturally sensitive position, stressing that the rights of the applicants and their choice not to leave the CKGR should not be judged from the "colonialist" position of the government, which sought to impose a Tswana way of life on them. She recognized the applicants as "indigenous to the Central Kgalagadi region" (*Sesana* 2006c: 160), with a different culture and different practices, traditions, and needs, emphasizing that the "Respondent view of development fails to take in consideration the knowledge, culture and ideologies of the applicants," and that this case questions the meaning of "development."

Finally, Justice Mpaphi Phumaphi, a member of the Kalanga elite that had long pressed for minority rights in Botswana (Werbner 2004), delivered his opinion. His verdict reflects his sensitivity to minority and indigenous issues by referring to common law cases such as the *Mabo* case in Australia, which recognizes "aboriginal title" to the land and refuses the "extinguishment of the native title on the land." His opinion stated "neither the declaration of the Ghanzi Crown land [in 1901] nor of CKGR [1961] extinguished the native rights of the Bushmen to the CKGR," so the applicants "were in possession of the land that they lawfully occupied" (*Sesana* 2006c). Judge Phumaphi invoked the "abundant evidence" provided by the anthropologist and the applicants' lawyer showing that "when the idea of declaring the game reserve was conceived, the intention was that it would ... provide land for the Bushmen where they could hunt freely to satisfy their nutritional needs without interference from outsiders" (*Sesana* 2006c: 344).

The three judges thus approached the verdict from different angles, producing a decision that on some points reflects divergent and contradictory readings of the evidence and philosophies of the place of minorities in the state.

The court was not impressed by the state's justifications for its policy of a settlement-free reserve. The extensive efforts that the government put into demonstrating the incompatibility of human communities and animals in the CKGR may have been important to the lawyers and their clients (not to mention the public at large), but it was ultimately irrelevant for the final verdict. Justice Phumaphi, agreeing with Dow on this specific point, found that the testimony on human/animal relations in the CKGR was a "red herring," not at all related to the issues on which the court was asked to decide: "The bulk of evidence, however highly informative as it was, could not assist the Court to determine whether force was used against the applicants during relocations, or whether the termination of services was unlawful and unconstitutional, etc." (*Sesana* 2006c: 369). The state's ideas of culture and of human relationships with the natural world may have been informative in themselves, but were not the kinds of "facts" that the judges referred to in arriving at their verdict.

The verdict reveals that the applicants and their expert witness were to a certain extent able to negotiate formalized identities and strategically navigate the structures of the court. In fact, in the process of producing evidence, the applicants introduced into the legal reasoning of the judges the troublesome concept of indigenous peoples, based in international law and embodied in their expressions of difference. They put forward an understanding of development and land use that was distant from state policies and legislation targeting them. For their part, the judges, collectively and from different angles, transformed these concepts from their own senses of diversity, fairness, and state responsibility, in ways that were to have significant consequences for the lives of the people of the Central Kalahari.

In the end, *Sesana v. the Attorney General* produced a basic paradox. The applicants' right to occupy the reserve was affirmed and the relocation was recognized by the majority as forced and illegitimate, but the same services that were cut to force the people of the reserve to leave their houses were not seen by the court as necessary for their way of life. In its conclusion, it was less about the provision of essential services to the CKGR residents (which were denied to them in the verdict) and more about recognition of the *identity* of the residents of the CKGR, as hunters and gatherers, and of the affirmation of their right to continue residing as hunters in their villages in the reserve.

Attempts to inscribe indigenous claims into national and international legal orders are frequently frustrated, as the language of law in courts tends to force fluid and ever-changing concepts into rigid, reified categories aimed at defining and fixing elusive identifications into legally recognizable forms. In the *Sesana* case, the court did this initially through the formal structures of the legal procedure, as in the requirements for registering and recognizing the applicants. There were also exceptions to the tendency toward boundaries and reification, as in Justice Dow's verdict, which emphasized the historical change and adaptability of customary practices. The overall effect of the litigation, however, was the creation and solidification of boundaries of belonging and understanding of "tradition," where only hunting rights were recognized.

In the Botswana High Court, notions of "applicant," "Bushmen," "indigenous," "property," "origins," and so on were carefully built or in some cases dismantled by the lawyers and judges. One effect of these efforts toward conceptual clarity was that the applicants were called upon to take on previously unfamiliar concepts in their own discourse and present a narrative that encapsulated their diversity. The British and Botswana lawyers could navigate the case in the courtroom and treat discourses on the "Bushman" way of life either as statements of law or as testimonial evidence of facts. A contingent Bushman identity was created, and evidence of continuity with the past was projected as a claim of land and resource rights into the future.

INDIGENOUS PEOPLES' ACCESS TO JUSTICE

In the last several decades the pursuit of justice for indigenous peoples has pushed increasing numbers of political struggles into state, regional, and international courts. This has occurred wherever a number of conditions are present: access to capable lawyers with the ability to navigate complex bodies of international and domestic law; the wherewithal to pursue costly litigation against governments and corporations with deep pockets; following from this, connections to a network of committed donors able to support litigation behind the scenes; and finally and most importantly, an independent judiciary capable of ruling against the government in a political structure that accommodates judicial review. As we have seen in the case of the San, costly trials, especially that of 2004–6, would have been impossible without international support. The Botswana government attempted to use this fact to question the legitimacy of the claims against it, emphasizing the role of "outsiders" in "putting ideas in the heads" of the San and stirring up trouble. But this support is everywhere a condition for indigenous peoples' pursuit of claims through court.

Given these daunting conditions, it is perhaps surprising that so many indigenous claimants have sought recourse in the courts, to the point that litigation has become one of the strategic anchorages of the global indigenous rights movement. There are several ways that litigation brings advantages to indigenous claimants. In some ways, if their litigation is successful it can have more "bite" in influencing states than international law. States are largely in control of global organizations and therefore are able to diminish the effects of the standards that they set. Tobias Kelly, for example, draws particular attention to the ways that states control the UN's compliance mechanisms relating to the prohibitions against torture, which contrast sharply with the immediate and far-reaching consequences of litigation in the United Kingdom. The language of the Committee against Torture (CAT), he points out, is usually "phrased in terms of diplomatic politeness, is often not hard-edged, and therefore not persuasive in a legal context," leading a decision of the British House of Lords to dismiss evidence from the CAT as "having no value" (Kelly 2012: 148). Litigation, by contrast, was more persuasive. "It was court cases that made the biggest difference in the areas on which CAT and the JCHR [the Joint Committee on Human Rights in the UK Parliament] had expressed concern," resulting in immediate reforms, including changes to the regime under which detainees suspected of terrorism were held (Kelly 2012: 148–9). In challenging a government that is responsive to its courts, litigation can be an effective way of mobilizing rights, including the human rights of indigenous peoples.

Recognizing this possibility inherent in litigation, indigenous peoples' uses of the law, sometimes involving persistent forms of "lawfare," translates their frustration, complaints, and sense of indignation into action and expresses hope for restitution, recognition, and a just future. This is occurring in a context in which the juridification of politics is intensifying. Despite the fact that state courts are often slow or reluctant to apply human rights norms to issues seen as "domestic" matters, international NGOs and indigenous peoples' organizations have sometimes turned to litigation as a way to assert collective rights, to end oppression and discrimination, to press for recognition of indigenous difference, and to secure that legal recognition in state law. State courts in many parts of the world have thus become one of the settings in which the concepts that are part of the indigenous rights movement are being elaborated, with implications for the ways that people making indigenous rights claims are seen, categorized, and defined through law.

At the same time, however, legal regimes remain in many ways inseparable from the privileged status of nation-states and from the inequalities that can result. International recognition has not always translated into state recognition, while states, as participants and responsible parties of human rights instruments, paradoxically remain the principal violators of indigenous peoples' rights.

Indigenous peoples, through their use of courts, have had some success in gaining state recognition of land and resource rights in Australia (the *Mabo* decision 1990), Japan (the Sapporo District Court decision 1997), and Nicaragua (the Awas Tingni community on the Atlantic coast 2001), among other places (Anaya 2009). Encouraged by these successes, San and other minorities of southern Africa began to employ legal means to gain land and resource access in the 1990s and early part of the new millennium. The recourse to the Botswana court system by the San and Bakgalagadi of the CKGR can therefore be seen in a global context of increasingly common litigation by indigenous rights claimants.

Where litigation fails is above all in the expense and amount of time a major case takes to argue. The slow, methodical pace of courts can result in, for example, leaving in place a ticking time bomb of environmental destruction of the kind described by Kirsch (2014b), in which litigation did not stop the dumping of mine tailings and the destruction of the Ok Tedi and Fly Rivers before it was too late. In the case of the San, the longer litigation went on, the more the facts of removal insinuated themselves in the people's everyday lives.

Not surprisingly, the increased recourse to courts has resulted in an uneven record in terms of securing recognition from states of the legitimacy of indigenous rights claims and an even more spotty record of their actual implementation of court decisions. Even liberal states can take a foot-dragging approach to court decisions that go against their interests, that compromise state or industrial access to resources and thereby derail plans for large-scale development.

The effectiveness of litigation is one issue; another is its *effects*. What is less obvious in the trend toward indigenous peoples' use of courts are its consequences for the ways that courts redefine and reshape the rights and identities of people who are the subjects of law. The Endorois case of 2009 offers an example.[10] This case brought indigenous claims to the African Commission on Human and Peoples' Rights (ACHPR) after unsuccessful litigation in the Kenyan courts, with the result being a landmark decision in which the commission ruled for the first time on the recognition of indigenous rights. The ACHPR addressed injustices that are strikingly similar to those faced by the San of the CKGR, arising from the removal of the people of the Lake Bogoria region in Rift Valley Province between 1973 and 1986 to make room for the Lake Bogoria Game Reserve and for a mining enterprise following the discovery of a deposit of rubies. In approaching its interpretation of indigeneity, the ACHPR dispensed with the controversial notion of "first comers" and emphasized instead a people's connections to territory and their subjection to systemic forms of oppression, discrimination (referring to the *Saramaka People v. Suriname* case approach to indigeneity), and forced displacement at the hands of the state. In applying this approach to African indigeneity to the claims made by the Endorois, the ACHPR found with the complainants on all counts. The Endorois, the commission found, are an indigenous people with both the rights to the benefits of development and the right to "preserve their identity through identification with ancestral lands." The most immediate consequences of this ruling, however, did not involve a reform of state policy, and did not result in improvement of the conditions of marginalization and discrimination faced by the Endorois. The commission has no compliance mechanisms built into its decisions, and the government of Kenya had little incentive to comply with the commission's decision.

The consequences for the Endorois of the litigation process itself, however, were arguably more far-reaching than the verdict. The case become part of the "travelling model" of rights that contributes to ongoing processes of defining and asserting indigenous rights. Moreover, it secured the adoption of indigeneity as a legal category at the African regional level. Gabrielle Lynch, argues that in order for the Endorois to get to the point of filing the suit, they first had to redefine themselves as "indigenous" and to, as she puts it, "market injustices in an international judicial contest" (Lynch 2011: 26). Even if states do not recognize the rights of indigenous peoples, their judiciaries can refer to case law. Landmark cases like *Mabo v. Queensland* in Australia, *Saramaka People v. Suriname* in the Inter-American Court of Human Rights, and the Endorois case in the African Commission on Human and Peoples' Rights become reference points for indigenous claims and activism, despite the rejection of the terminology and rights claims of indigenous peoples by states. Through litigation, the language of indigeneity went beyond vague notions of belonging, to involve a strategic emphasis on the Endorois's distinction from their Tugen neighbors (with whom they share many similarities), while placing ownership and control of land at the center of their communal identity (Lynch 2011: 27–9). The Endorois case makes clear that, even before rendering their verdicts, courts can be instruments for the reconceptualization and reification of identities.

In the *Sesana* case, as I have shown in this chapter, arriving at a judgment often involved a similar process of creating or refining qualities of cultural identity in ways that are both essentializing *and* requiring a kind of interpretive plasticity, with judges acting as the arbiters of the meaning and of the legitimate application of legal terms to distinct ways of life. Contrary to what happen with the Endorois case where their Tugen neighbors were excluded from indigeneity, in the case of Botswana the San and Bakgalagadi transcended their ethnic differences to unite under the banner of "peoples of the CKGR."

The consequences of this process for a reconceived sense of belonging were only the beginning. The San's and Bakgalagadi's pursuit of justice reveals other dimensions of the court's influence on their social lives and identities. Just how the verdict played out in the aftermath of the court case is one of the topics I consider in the next chapter.

7

AFTER JUDGMENT

LEGALITY FROM BELOW

Accounts of the experience of collective claimants in courts tend to emphasize the concepts and processes of litigation and focus on the claims-making process and/or the specific legal contest in which the struggles take place. This leaves little space for understanding what the recourse to adjudication produces, in particular what happens to people's understanding and activation of their rights, and leaves unanswered a simple central question: what have been the consequences for people's everyday lives of legal contests and processes? Approaching this issue from another angle, how has the activist and legal advocacy created certain types of subjectivities – such as the community of applicants, indigenous peoples, etc.?

Much of the attention in the literature on subaltern or indigenous legal struggles is focused on their ability to use sustained political/legal mobilization to exploit existing organizational frameworks or to construct alternative notions of rights (e.g. de Souza Santos and Rodríguez-Garavito 2005); there is, however, less understanding of the subjectivities and imaginaries that are generated by means of activist strategies and as outcomes of legal processes (e.g. Tate 2007: 75). Sally Merry draws attention to the significance of this shift in perspective: "Since achieving rights requires making claims, questions about how individuals come to view themselves in terms of rights and what conditions inspire them to make rights-based claims are of critical importance in promoting the transnational human rights system" (Merry

2012: 113). Consistent with this observation, the approach that I take here considers law as entrenched in the everyday, not just as a form of oppressive power but as generative, part of the way relationships are created and identities and expertise developed and experienced. I also consider how rights claimants express injustice emotionally and somatically, in ways that are externalized in bodily experience that reflects the anxieties and physical constraints that have been imposed on them.

It is clear that the multidimensional processes of activism have brought about significant changes to San social life, creating more visible engagements, alliances, strategies of representation, and political divisions, mainly between those who are experienced in the knowledge and networks of activism and those who are not. What have the strategies of creating NGOs and new networks, going to court, and dealing with donors, states, lawyers, etc., done to the San people's understanding of their rights and justice and their relationships with neighboring groups and other minorities, civil society, and the state?

Up to this point, I have shown how in multistranded justice campaigns, law becomes one (among others) of the ways to engage in politics and to challenge structural inequalities. I will begin by considering what the inseparability of law and politics does in practice, how it impacts people's lives and shapes the scope of possibility for activist engagements. I will pay particular attention here to how the views of justice and injustice felt by the people of the Central Kalahari (both within and outside the reserve) are expressed, by those who offer a clear example of new "solidaristic understandings of entitlements grounded on alternative forms of legal knowledge" (de Sousa Santos and Rodríguez-Garavito 2005: 16). Roy Sesana expressed the point straightforwardly: "I saw at that time [before the court case] a lot of people did not know their rights and were just pulled by their ear and agree [he pulls his own ear]. Not like now. I had the help of First People to teach them their rights" (author notes 2016). Sesana's words indicate that the government's powers and hypocrisies are apparent to the reserve residents, readily perceived and often deeply felt as injustice.

The literature on "legality from below" is not always shy about the tendency for local empowerment projects to "construct indigenous subjects that are professional, entrepreneurial, and increasingly distanced from their communities," while the strategies they pursue get channeled "into acceptable forms that reinforce state power through its legal regimes" (Speed 2008: 176). Anna Tsing, situating her nuanced analysis of global-scale encounters and interactions of "cultural friction" in intellectual context, expresses this notion of the hegemonic consequences of resistance in the starkest possible terms: "NGOs, human rights advocacy, and civil society spread as a transnational governmentality, a new imperial power that reaches deeply into human souls. The new subjects of liberalism are even more trapped in power because they imagine it as freedom" (Tsing 2005: 214). The contestations of social justice activism bring with them the potential for the institutional imagination to be limited by their structural imperatives and for the encroachment of neoliberal institutions into the campaigns that set out to oppose them.

This "hegemonic" side of justice campaigns adds another aspect to our assessment of what these campaigns produce, calling for us to cast a wider net and to add some descriptive substance to accounts of hegemony and its challengers. If it is important to consider the impact of justice campaigning on people's legal consciousness, it is also necessary to consider the effects of persistent injustice, made manifest in both new forms of networking and campaigning among the youth, and persistent daily forms of resistance in the communities of the Central Kalahari Game Reserve (CKGR).

A NEGOTIATION TREADMILL

The day after the ruling *in Sesana and Others v. the Attorney General of the Republic of Botswana*, on December 14, 2006, the Attorney General issued a statement that outlined the position of the Botswana government on how the court's decisions would be implemented (Molokomme 2006). The statement held that: only the 189 [*sic*] surviving applicants in the original court case along with their children could return to the Central Kalahari; in order to do so, however, they had to provide an *Omang* identity card or a passport. According to Saugestad (2011: 46), this reduced the number of beneficiaries and precluded the right for future generations to return without permits. The applicants' spouses initially seemed to have the right to go back to their villages, even if they were not included in the list, but through time the government's implementation of the case changed, leaving spaces of uncertainty and ambiguity concerning who had the right to enter the reserve without a permit.

As soon as the applicants started to go back they met other constraints in what they thought was a case that had been "resolved" in their favor: they could bring no domestic animals with them (with the exception of a few donkeys that were ear-tagged as belonging to an applicant); they could only bring in building materials for non-permanent structures; and they could bring in only as much water as the director of the DWNP felt was the amount "reasonably required." With respect to hunting rights, the High Court judgment did not automatically grant the applicants the right to Special Game Licenses. These required an application, with the DWNP considering each application individually. Furthermore, the narrow interpretation of the judgment made the case not a "collective case" where rights were recognized as belonging to a distinct class of people (the inhabitants of the CKGR). Rather, it was interpreted as a case made by individuals brought together in a list of applicants. Since the verdict, the government of Botswana has taken the list of applicants at face value, and has generally restricted access to the CKGR on the basis of the original people listed in the founding affidavit as applicants.

Gordon Bennett, not surprisingly, was of a different opinion.[1] He saw the verdict as applying to everyone who was removed in 2002 and not just those who were named as applicants in the case. It also remained possible, he felt, to press for the rights of the people who were relocated in 1997, who were not included in the *Sesana* case but who had the same constitutional right to live in the CKGR (author notes 2016).

In the political context following the 2006 verdict, some of the biggest challenges facing some of the San and Bakgalagadi in the Central Kalahari and surrounding areas included questions about the duties of the government and the rights and responsibilities it has, including provision of water, medicines, and social infrastructure. The verdict did not offer help in this regard. It did not compel the government to provide services inside the CKGR, and such services are not constitutionally guaranteed in Botswana.[2]

In its reluctance to take on the task of deciding on every possible point of detail in the conflict between the people of the reserve and the government, the court left many points of contention to be decided in negotiations. This included the services to be provided by the government, the development initiatives to be sponsored, and the place of hunting and keeping livestock as permissible activities in the reserve. The residents of the reserve thus entered into a negotiated relationship with the state, in which every aspect of their lives was subject to assessment and the possible application of law.

Negotiation was nothing new to those who identified as San activists. A "double legal strategy" that had been pursued since the 1990s consisted of "negotiations" over government services and development in the CKGR, together with the possibility of the use of courts, resumed several years after the verdict. The 2006 verdict itself explicitly referred the applicants and the government "back to the negotiation table." In accordance with this piece of guidance, a new negotiating group was convened, which had representatives from some of the NGOs that had been on the original CKGR negotiating team (notably, Ditshwanelo, FPK, and Kuru) and from some government ministries and departments, together with a representative group from the CKGR and the new settlements, later known as the "residents committee." The aim of this new phase of negotiations was to agree on what was not spelled out in the verdict and to bring the two parties to reconciliation.

Some people in the CKGR were initially quite optimistic about their dealings with then Vice-President Seretse Ian Khama, the son of the first president of the country, Seretse Khama, who in their imagination was a "friend of the Bushmen," sympathetic to the cause of the people of the CKGR and to San and Bakgalagadi generally. When President Festus Mogae opted to step down from the presidency on April 1, 2008 and named Vice-President Khama as his replacement, many people in the CKGR felt that a new space would be opened for serious negotiations about their condition.

What has occurred instead has been a shift toward what many observers of the political scene in Botswana have variously referred to "authoritarian liberalism" (Good 2009), an overreach by an "executive presidency" (Bodilenyane 2012), and a "curtailment of civil liberties such as freedom of speech/press" accompanied by "growing intolerance of opposite views by the political leadership" (Botlhomilwe, Sebudububu and Maripe 2011: 332). Appointed to the rank of Brigadier General in the Botswana military at the age of 24, Ian Khama has brought to the presidency much of the influence and personal connections of his military career, including many of the personnel appointed to the civil service. He has expressed a strong disdain for American-style democracy, particularly the influence of interest groups on political decisions. He has resorted to arresting and in some cases deporting journalists after having declared them "prohibited immigrants." His support and promotion of the *Media Practitioners Act* of 2008 in Botswana has been criticized both inside and outside of his government for placing significant and unnecessary limits on free speech. He has also been criticized for structuring judicial appointments in ways that favor the interests of the government and thereby eroding the separation between the executive and the judiciary.[3] It is with this trend toward authoritarianism and disdain for activist politics that the San's justice campaign continued its efforts in the period after the *Sesana* judgment.

On June 12, 2008, a delegation of five people, led by Roy Sesana, met with the new president, to request that the matter of the CKGR be discussed. In that meeting it was agreed that three representative bodies would be involved in the negotiation process: the government of Botswana, the residents committee of the CKGR,[4] and the CKGR NGO coalition.[5]

The residents committee's hope for a new policy line from the government did not last long, however. In fact, the narrow interpretation of the verdict was no accident, but followed from ideas and policies originating from the highest levels of government. On November 3, 2008, President Khama, in his State of the Nation report to Parliament, remarked as follows on the Central Kalahari issue:

> The notion on the part of some outsiders that any segment of our society wishes to subsist today on the basis of a *hunter-gathering lifestyle is … an archaic fantasy*. The Reserve's unique natural heritage is an important natural resource which will be preserved for the benefits of the present and future generations. (Khama 2008, emphasis added)

Khama made a similar statement two years later at Orapa, the diamond mining community east of the CKGR, in December 2010. He remarked, "The Bushmen are living a life of backwardness, a primitive life of deprivation alongside wild animals, and a primeval life of a bygone era of hardship and indignity" (IWGIA 2011: 481). Khama's statements are consistent with those made by members of his cabinet. On November 3, 2010, Kitso Mokaila, Botswana's Minister of Environment, Wildlife and Tourism, told the BBC's *Focus on Africa* program: "I don't believe you would want to see your own kind living in the dark ages in the middle of nowhere as a choice, when you know that the world has moved forward and has become so technological."[6] From these statements it is clear that, despite the verdict of *Sesana and Others v. the Attorney General*, the government still considered the consistent refusal of the San and Bakgalagadi to relocate and use what was offered in the newly established settlements to be irresponsible and undignified. The government continued to maintain the position that no permanent structures or any kind of development should be present in the CKGR because it is a national park. In spite of these restrictions, however, permanent infrastructures were present that embody state interests, such as roads, camping sites for tourists and wildlife scouts, elegant tourist lodges, new boreholes for wildlife, a working diamond mine, and camps for police and game scouts. The tension between the CKGR inhabitants and the government was once again a contrast between different understandings of development and of the significance of collective rights and responsibilities.

It is true that the 2006 judgment has shied away from directly and forcibly removing the determined residents of the CKGR, but apart from this, the Botswana government has not been dissuaded from almost punitive policies, including denials of service, oriented toward emptying the reserve of permanent inhabitants. Up to 2015 there were no government or district council officers operating inside of the reserve delivering services or assistance, with the exception of school-aged children being picked up and driven to school outside the reserve. The only state officers coming into the reserve on a regular basis were game scouts and members of a specialized military police group (the Special Support Group, the SSG). The SSG camped outside the gates of the reserve where they constantly stopped its residents in search of "illegal" meat, weapons, or ostrich eggshells. They are described by some analysts as "notorious" for their actions, particularly for their patrols in the villages of the CKGR in search of "poachers" (Mwakikagile 2010: 12).

The government was clearly torn between wanting to be seen as complying with the judgment and maintaining its reputation as a liberal state, downplaying its authoritarian impulses toward imposing its will, while moving forward with its vision of state-sponsored development. The result was a schizophrenic tension and division manifested in stark contradictions between, on the one hand, the court-sanctioned goal of dialogue with the San and Bakgalagadi as legitimate residents of the reserve and, on the other hand, policy statements denigrating their way of life and announcing another possible removal (author notes 2011).

The negotiation meetings continued, despite a climate of mistrust (by September 2011 they had met only five times) and a widespread sense that the government had already made its decision, that the negotiations were simply being done for show, to gain international approval. The idea of a new management plan for the CKGR was raised at several of the CKGR meetings, reintroducing the strategy of developing new maps and plans to get use rights over the reserve. The CKGR coalition, in conjunction with the people of the community of Molapo, along with consultants such as Arthur Albertson (whom we have already encountered as an expert witness in the *Sesana* case and who was in charge with FPK of mapping traditional territories inside the reserve in the 1990s), started to develop a new plan for their village. The idea behind the community use planning process was that a management plan for Molapo would be drawn up and submitted to the Department of Wildlife and National Parks. It was hoped that this would be the first of several CBNRM plans for each of the communities inside the reserve and that these plans would be incorporated into a new overall CKGR management plan that would spell out the rights of the communities to natural resources and services inside the reserve.

The government had yet to agree in principle, however, on the inclusion of Community Use Zones in the revised management plan. Rumors spread that the government had already taken its decision, and that only two communities would be given the rights in the CKGR: New Xade and Kaudwane, both of them resettlement villages outside the reserve. Meanwhile, people inside the reserve were worried about such practical affairs as what would happen with the possibility of a double residency, one in the reserve and one in the new settlements; could this be a first step by the government toward extinguishment of their right to live in the CKGR?

Then there was the problem of compensation for damage by elephants. They had not commonly been seen close to the villages, but in March 2011 they were suddenly and inexplicably emboldened and several herds got into the fields and destroyed the maize and sorghum crops. The residents wanted compensation for the losses, something that they could not get unless their areas were officially recognized as Community Use Zones.

Discussions of the reactions by reserve residents to this "new" CKGR negotiation process revealed that most of them had little faith in the commitment of the government to respond to the questions raised during the "consultations", which were seen not as genuine consultation but just as talks where government spokespersons bring their views/decisions. In this new negotiation phase, tension between people in the reserve and NGOs involved were common, starting with issues such as who represents whom and who should be the people involved in the process. The residents in the reserve were particularly upset with some NGOs, which in their view had abandoned them during the years of the *Sesana* trial and had now returned along with other NGOs to involve themselves in this new phase. The residents of the new settlements, who were also represented in the negotiations, were interested in knowing what would happen to their access to the reserve and the use of its resources. A common concern was that people could become divided and placed in conditions of conflict because of the government decisions on who could have access to what resources and where.

When I met with the residents of several villages in the reserve in 2011 and again in 2012, it was clear to me that many of the residents had acquired a jaded view of the negotiation processes – expressed in observations such as: "We feel that the government has forgotten us" and "We do not want to be relocated again" – and matched this view with a sense of the practical measures that needed to be followed to hold officials to account: "We want a meeting called in Gaborone. We want to talk to the president. We want CKGR representatives there." Their objective was to negotiate without the intermediation of NGOs, directly with the responsible officials, preferably the president himself. All they wanted in terms of representation was a lawyer to assist them in the meetings. The general feeling was well expressed by one participant in the "talks": "The consultations on the CKGR can only be valid when a lawyer for communities resident in the reserve presides over all [the meetings]." For them, the lawyer was their "bow and arrow," something that could protect them from the government's wrongs and create an illusion of certainty in an uncertain situation with an unpredictable state.

This "bow and arrow," however, was precisely what the government did not want them to have, as it became increasingly intolerant of anything related to the Central Kalahari and the San in general. In 2013 Gordon Bennett was placed on a list of people requiring a visa to enter the country. This occurred after his widely publicized "victories" in several cases related to the CKGR people (which I discuss below) and while he was preparing to argue in court against the government relocation of another San village (the village of Ranyane in the Ghanzi District). At the end of June 2013, Bennett was escorted by officials from the Department of Wildlife in Gaborone, where he was seeking to obtain a permit in order to visit his clients in the CKGR, to the Department of Immigration, where his new conditions of entry into the country were imposed. He was accused by immigration officials of making "political statements" in his work with the people of Ranyane (Chapter 8, p. 304). As Bennett explained to me, this occurred while he was informing his clients of their rights and, in attempting to deflect the credit that his clients were giving him for progress in the case, told them that this was *their* success, that *they* were responsible for coming together to take a stand against injustice, with words to the effect of, "this is your victory, not my victory." In making this statement, he was later accused of engaging in political advocacy. This change in his visa status in effect barred Bennett from arguing other cases in Botswana's courts, as he had done so effectively in the *Sesana* and *Mosetlhanyane* (Chapter 8) cases. Able only to work out of his London office and prevented from travelling to Botswana to plead in court, he was less effective and his clients were placed at a disadvantage in subsequent litigation. This immigration prohibition was not entirely unprecedented, but in fact was (and continues to be) a common way for governments to deal with successful, nuisance-making foreign litigators. The government of India did the same thing in response to Bennett's effectiveness in representing the Dongria Kondh, a "scheduled tribe" in northeast India whose religious practices were threatened by a bauxite mine planned by a transnational corporation, Vedanta (Temper and Martinez-Alier 2013).

At the same time, the government strictly controlled access to the sites of contestation within the reserve. Research permits for people working on issues that could be seen as politically problematic, in particular having to do with San land rights, were often withheld. The government of Botswana also sought to stem the flow of information by notifying individuals that they would be in violation of the security laws of the country if they shared information with outside agencies. A number of non-Batswana people were named as prohibited immigrants (PI), including some of those who had been involved either directly or indirectly in the *Sesana* case, several members of Survival International, some journalists, and several academics, among them Kenneth Good, then at the University of Botswana, and James Workman, who later went on to write an important book, *Heart of Dryness*, based in part on events in the CKGR (Workman 2009).

These efforts to isolate the people of the CKGR from their supporters had the effect of further stalling the negotiations. From the standpoint of the government of Botswana, these negotiations were ongoing, even though there were no formal meetings of the negotiating group after 2010. The CKGR residents committee sent several letters in an attempt to meet with President Khama to move forward on what was perceived as an "unfair and a stuck process," and to discuss issues such as development in the reserve, access of people and animals, etc. These letters went unanswered. Sesana was finally able to meet with the president and several ministers in May 2013, and again in February 2015, to have a direct dialogue on the development of services and activities in the reserve.

One of the results of the latter meeting was that in 2016, Sesana was hired with a three years' contract by the government as a "community facilitator," to act as a "liaison officer" between the residents of the reserve and the government through the Ghanzi District Council in the negotiations concerning the provision of government services in the CKGR. Given that Sesana is nonliterate, he has been assisted in this position by a secretary, an officer in the Remote Area Development Programme, who also takes the minutes of every meeting. He was also, as a government employee, prohibited from publicly criticizing the government, with an infraction likely to result in dismissal.

At the same time, a new residents consultative committee was established, composed of one representative from each community in the reserve. This has brought new tensions, concerns, and efforts at gaining recognition through a new, previously unfamiliar leadership role (which I discuss further in Chapter 8).

These are positions introduced to the negotiation process that have the people of the reserve seemingly running in place, attending meetings and having local level discussions, and then going back to the negotiations, only to find that government disregarded their positions. The High Court's affirmation of their right of occupancy of their traditional territories produced little more than an illusion of movement through "talk." The government negotiators limited the discussion to the development of mining and tourism, without allowing meaningful input or initiatives from those with rights to the land.

THE SOCIAL LIFE OF THE APPLICANT LIST

Rights can become manifested in practice in ways that are unexpected and unintended by almost everyone involved. One of the most important consequences of the *Sesana* case was simply the creation of a list of people who have the right to live in the CKGR, which distinguished them from those who did not register as an applicant. Soon after the verdict, in January 2007, some of the applicants in the case and their families started to go back to their places in the reserve. Based on fieldwork and interviews that I conducted from the 2006 verdict up to 2017, questions remain regarding people's ability to return to the reserve without difficulty.

The list of names of living applicants at the time of the judgment constituted a division of the San and Bakgalagadi into those who held certain rights and those who did not. In other words, with the list of

Figure 10 The Matswere Gate, Central Kalahari Game Reserve

applicants, "the law has replaced culture(s) as the means of inclusion or exclusion par excellence" (Karst 1989 in Hastrup 2003:16). After the verdict, in fact, the list found its way to the gate of the park, where it was checked against the identity papers of those wanting to enter.

The applicants' list in the hands of the wildlife scouts (some of whom are San) at the gate illustrates in the most tangible way possible the reification of legal concepts; but also the fact that in another sense these concepts are much less fixed than they appear to be (see Hull 2012), depending as they do on the person at the gate and how the list can be used to arbitrarily include or exclude those seeking entry. Without having one's name on the list (and even with it there, as it turned out) there was a good chance that entry would be denied, or worse, that people would be arrested (Sapignoli 2017). For non-applicants to enter the reserve, they needed to apply for a one-month certificate of permission, much like a visa, to the Ministry of Wildlife, Environment, and Tourism office, something that is difficult to obtain. All too often they were arrested or fined if they were found in the reserve with an expired permit. Families and individuals attempting to return to their village or visit relatives were surprised to have their bags searched for food and/or to find themselves turned away, even though they had been born in the reserve and then relocated, all because their names were not on a list of applicants, about which they were previously unaware. This set of issues posed huge impediments to the viability of the CKGR communities, with cases reaching the Magistrate's Court following arrests at the gate.

Another aspect of the category of applicants follows from the fact that when the list of applicants was being gathered, children under eighteen years of age were not legally permitted to sign. They were nevertheless documented as applicants without their signatures affixed to the documentation. When they "won" the case, however, their status changed. Those who went back to the CKGR with their parents as minors later lost their status as applicants – and their right to live in the reserve – when they turned eighteen. The difficulty of applying for a permit to enter the reserve sometimes resulted in the forced separation of families, with adult children unable to live in the same community as their parents in the reserve. The way the list has been interpreted and used is unclear and has been subject to change. There have been differences between what has been officially said by government representatives and the forms it takes in practice, exacerbating people's sense of insecurity, subjection to arbitrariness in the use of power, and mistrust in the state.

The prohibitions on entry to the reserve extended to their means of subsistence, particularly the small livestock that are essential to the diverse economy of the CKGR. They were not permitted to bring goats, one of their staples of subsistence, into the reserve. Whatever livestock they already had in the reserve was subject to the occasional act of confiscation, although the government made no systematic effort to empty the reserve of domestic animals.

The division between applicants and non-applicants even applied to the animals that they used for transportation. Following the government's narrow interpretation of the verdict, only the applicants were allowed to cross the gates of the CKGR with donkeys or horses. The animals they used for transport in and out of the reserve had to be registered and given ear tags with numbers, which could be readily recognized at the gates. When these animals died, they could not be replaced. This rule added to a condition among residents of the CKGR in which their rights were fluid and temporary, diminished by age and mortality.

The effects of the applicant list became profoundly arbitrary. The guards at the entrance could determine how justice was applied differentially. At times, for instance, they engaged in the exercise of power through search and seizure, and possibly arrest; at other times, they let people in unmolested, sometimes even giving them some water and a lift to their homes. The occasional kindness they were shown did not offset a sense of foreboding the reserve residents had about the checkpoint. The uncertainty about what they were to encounter there – an act of kindness or an assertion of power – was, needless to say, deeply unsettling, adding to people's mistrust in government and reinforcing their reluctance to visit relatives on the other side of a park boundary that had, for all intents and purposes, become an arbitrarily hostile border.

The origin of the distinct set of rights for applicants and non-applicants is a division that is not often known or accepted by the people of the Central Kalahari. While their knowledge of the case and its consequences varies, a clear common denominator is a sense of fairness that had been violated, a sense of injustice toward the differences imposed on them. The applicant list appeared to many people in the reserve and in the resettlement villages as a mystery from out of nowhere, a conjuring trick, something cleverly designed to divide them without leaving traces of accountability. People sometimes referred to it as "the paper that talks for us." But it was also a paper that excludes and oppresses. With no explicit policy in place, no one to whom responsibility can be attributed (apart from a distant government), it still somehow had the effect of breaking up families and leaving people more vulnerable, in ways that seem to loosen their hold on their territory and to further government interests:

> I don't know anything about the list. I don't even know who made that list. I only see it as a disturbance to our families. It is dividing us and it is destroying our unity. We are a community that lives with extended families and relatives and we support one another in raising our children and making decisions on how to manage our land. So what I see from the government is [an effort] to make all of the old people die and leaving our land with no one.[7]

It should be stressed that the relationships with family and community members who live in the relocation settlements outside the reserve, where people engage in exchanges and social networking, are crucial to maintaining social relationships and to fortifying people's "safety net" system. The residents in the reserve share and exchange meat, skins, and wild fruits, with some sugar, tea, cooking oil, and maize meal – goods that are part of the destitute food that some residents receive in the settlements of New Xade, Kaudwane, or Xere. People also move between places outside and inside the reserve to collect pensions and to go to clinics. These movements have always characterized the life of the people in the Kalahari (Chapter 2). Relationships extend into vast networks, involving mobility and cooperation across much of the country (Ikeya 2016), in a system of resource and opportunity-sharing that has now been closed at the gates.

The "magic" of the applicant list is that it produces a sense of injustice, of mystery concerning how this list, which had just some names on it and not others, was actually made. Who produced the list, and how? This was not clear to the residents of the reserve. As a woman living in Kaudwane (a resettlement village southeast of the reserve) told me: "If my child has the right, why not me, if my husband has the right, why not me ... I say that if we have the right we have the same rights" (author notes 2013). The sense of injustice produced by the list among those who were subjected to its arbitrariness has nothing to point to, no decision, no individual, just a sense of disillusionment based on something that appears as an illusion. At the same time when confronted with actions of harassment and denial of their rights to be in the reserve and to hunt, the "paper that talks for us" is part of the court's papers that they refer to as a way to concretize their claims.

This diffuse sense of injustice also applied more generally to policy decisions that seemed to originate in particular government agencies but could not be traced to a decision or attributed to anyone in particular. Discussions of the case sometimes point to the court's seeming inability to influence the government, raising questions about how useful the court can be if it results in an unequal application of the law. A man from Metseamonong expressed to me his frustrations and his sense of unfairness: "If I'm hunting and I get caught, I go to prison. But if the government doesn't comply [with the law], nothing happens" (author notes 2013). Here grievance has a focal point, the laws and decisions that produce the hunting arrests, but also a sense of impotency that the laws do not apply equally to those in power.

The ominous, spectral quality of the applicant list had to do with its capacity to bring about an unintended destruction of collective life. It separated families, denied children the heritage intended by their parents, and drained away the communities' means of survival. It did all this through the fiction of the nonpolitical, without violence, but through technicalities, the standard, routine, and bureaucratic procedures of legal process.

LAW TALK

One of the significant qualities of the *Sesana* case and its aftermath is the extent to which legal concepts continue to be used by the people of the CKGR, even those without literacy skills, to talk politics and to negotiate with the government. Many San and Bakgalagadi claim to live in a state of fear and uncertainty about the future: uncertainty whether they will be relocated again, arrested, beaten, or killed. A man in Molapo (east CKGR), speaking about the SSG, said: "Why do they see us as the enemy? … Why [does] the military [have] to be here? We are scared, we live in a state of fear. Our children and wives are very worried that something can happen. They are worried to go out for collecting food. And we are worried too. This is our land" (author notes 2012). People were arrested or harassed by game officers not only after being caught hunting but even when carrying *biltong* (dried meat) outside the reserve. A common practice of park authorities was to search those who entered or left the reserve, confiscate "contraband" food or water, and sometimes arrest those found in possession of it. Game officers also entered villages in the reserve looking for wild meat. This often led to arrests, charges, and detention, with those accused sometimes going to court or at other times discharged after a few days.

One of the things that stands out from a long view of the San's sense of justice is how much continuity can be found in their sense of grievance from the period not long after independence in 1966 to the present. When the people of the CKGR were interviewed in 1980 said things like, "they beat us and left" or "they chased us away from where we were born," or when they objected to game officials entering people's homes without permission, there is a sense that the state, through the actions of its officials, was behaving improperly. Beating someone up and leaving precludes the possibility of understanding the source of hostility and coming to terms.

The idea and practice of justice is informed in good measure by the circumstances of people's lives in the moment. The residents' attitude toward legal institutions and their perception of the use of activism as a tool for justice to bring positive social change often depended on the most recent events that affected them. It also followed from a sense of the future, the pull (but sometimes overlapping, not strictly on a continuum) between hope and disillusion. In the court hearing and their engagement with international institutions and NGOs the people of the Kalahari were putting faith in a "justice about to come" (Brunnegger 2016: 141).

Many of the reserve residents had experienced the court firsthand, either in its *in loco* visit to the CKGR in 2002, the brief period of hearings in New Xade as the trial began, or, for a few who had the means to travel, during the lengthy trial in Lobatse. The subsequent court cases in pursuit of water rights, entry rights, and hunting rights can only have had the effect of solidifying this experience and converting it into a way to recalibrate the power imbalance with the government and realize their aspirations for better lives. The "litigation chain" (which

I discuss in Chapter 8) and their fluctuating relationship with NGOs – some of which came back after years of apparent disengagement, others like FPK not having the economic capacity to continue to follow up fully on people's requests, and others being prevented from working in the reserve by the lack of a government permit – eventually transformed people's hope, their sense of justice, which they expressed in the celebration after a court victory, into a sense of disenchantment, of justice lost.

Even if it was not the first time the people involved in the CKGR cases had experience with state laws in their everyday actions (which also took place through the use of *dikgotla* and lower courts) this was the first time that they went to the highest court in the country with a collective cause. And certainly this was not the first time that people had engaged with NGOs, and "expats" on issues related to justice claims. However, a common sense of revelation, of something deeply new, was often expressed when I asked about what had changed since they had been relocated from the reserve. The revelation was expressed by one of the witnesses in the *Sesana* case, in this way:

> The court and NGOs helped me to understand my rights because the NGOs [helped us go to court] and the court made a ruling that opened my ears and showed me that what the government has done to us by relocating us was not good. They could have just let us stay in our land.[8]

The ruling was experienced almost in terms of a religious awakening, of having one's senses attuned to a new condition of truth and salvation. In other words, by actively following the case, some people arrived at a deeper sense of injustice, a clearer awareness of the harm that had been done to them.

Kirsten Hastrup, examining what she calls the "global culture of human rights," stresses that

> Legal language and rights talk may externalize implicit values and potentially bind people together in speech community, but the possibility remains that the language spoken is semantically empty, because the words refer to no actual experience. (Hastrup 2003: 21)

The language of rights is not only sometimes at odds with the lived experience of claimants; it can also be entirely detached from it and hence devoid of practical meaning.

In the case of the people of the Central Kalahari the situation is quite different. It is true that the language of the law has bound applicants and activists together in an indigenous "speech community" in situations such as in UN lobbying and during the legal process. Yet many San remain reluctant to participate in that use of language. They are disinclined to speak about anything they have not directly experienced, sensing that they do not have the authority to do so. When they do talk about their rights, the courts' judgments, and encounters with the law, what they have to say is permeated with personal experience, reflection, and insight. Even if what they say is not always framed in terms of law or rights, their perceptions are certainly not semantically empty.

People's engagement in this kind of "law talk" emerged clearly while I, accompanied by a translator, was visiting the village of Molapo in the Central Kalahari in October 2012. Sometimes we visited people in their homes, at other times in collective conversation, almost in the manner of impromptu "circle groups" in which a conversation would start and others would join in. Despite the language barrier, I often understood what people were saying before their words were translated, through a combination of English terms (they usually used English for key words without an equivalent, like "indigenous," "high court," or "constitution"), a rudimentary knowledge of some San words, and the San's and Bakgalagadi's uncanny ability to express themselves through a combination of emotion and bodily enactment. The gestural expressivity of the San takes the form almost of spontaneous, physical "speech" acts, through their bodily "way to be in the world" (see Csordas 1999), often combined with words to give presence to a metaphor, like Roy Sesana making the gesture of breast feeding while saying, "the land is like a mother," or imitating dogs fighting for a piece of meat when he was expressing his concerns about the relationships among NGOs. My lack of language skills thus had the unintended benefit of allowing me to be more attentive to the context, including the physical communication and emotions of my interlocutors, even if some of the immediate sense of what people said was sometimes "lost in translation."

One of my visits to the reserve occurred a few weeks after the residents had been visited by the ministers of Foreign Affairs and of Wildlife and the Ghanzi Council Secretary (2011). The ministers had flown to the villages of the CKGR by helicopter ostensibly to report on the talks with the government that were going on, but by the end of their tour they had not promised any kind of benefit or provided any information on the negotiations. Instead, they announced yet again to the people of the Kalahari that the land on which they were living was not theirs and that they needed to move. The timing of my visit to the CKGR was such that the resentments caused by what the government ministers said had not yet cooled down, yet people had had time to discuss it and to think deeply about its implications. Their mood was serious, with none of the joking and levity that came out in more casual gatherings. Most of those who were not speaking looked to the ground, apparently listening intently. What they said to me had an element of emotionally charged deliberation, as though they were "bearing witness" rather than talking with a visitor.

Some residents stressed the hypocrisy of policies ostensibly driven by fiscal restraint, presented in the context of what they saw as lavish spending. As one man from Metseamonong remarked, "the government has said that it is costly to bring development [to the CKGR]. But they come in helicopters!" (He gestured to the sky above the acacia trees, indicating the direction from which they had come.) A participant in a group conversation in Kikao focused on the cost of entry restrictions imposed on them:

> We see all the SSG people [mobilized there by the government for its anti-poaching campaign] people driving around in trucks, arresting people and stopping people at the gates to the reserve. It is expensive to keep them there. Why does the government not pull those people off the gates and out of the camps? This would save money if that is their story. (Author notes 2011)

By extension, disappointment with the ministerial visit prompted disillusionment with the negotiation process: "We don't see negotiations going anywhere." Another resident remarked: "The time for negotiations is over. We won the court case. This land is our land."

There were also views that reflected the accumulated knowledge acquired over years of struggle and litigation. A witness in the *Sesana* case emphasized: "We won't listen to the ministers. The government had the right to appeal the decision of the court in December 2006. They did not. Clearly they agreed with what the court said." There was also a common defensive posture, which saw legal representation as necessary in the face of an adversarial government: "The government knows that we cannot read. They bring the attorney general and lawyers. People in the CKGR do not want this. We want *our* representatives, *our* lawyers at the meetings." Evident from these views is the fact that the court system and the lawyers who represent them in it have become familiar, with grievance sometimes expressed in terms of the standards of state law: "The court decision said that the government taking us out of the reserve was illegal." A woman in New Xade drew attention to what she had learned from the case: "The constitution says we have rights, we did not know before the relocation," adding an understanding of the verdict that went well beyond its actual meaning: "the court confirmed that we are the owners of this land" (author notes 2011).

Even if the state's law and legal institutions continued to be seen as instruments of domination and colonization, it was clear to me that at least some of the residents of the reserve had an acute sense that justice called for the power of law to be applied equally to the state and its representatives, even if this was something they were not seeing in practice and from which they were not yet seeing any material benefits. One participant in a group conversation in Metseamonong, responding angrily to a possible future relocation, put such a view bluntly: "[The minister] should be put in jail for what he said. [He] is not listening to the court ruling. We should take him to court on this. We want him to be sentenced too!" (author notes 2011). The court and its power of judicial review was the way to express discontent, the juridification of the struggle in practice.

For some, legal concepts were represented materially by the "Court" and by papers that the NGOs following the case gave them, and that they kept in their homes. An example is a summary of the verdict, provided by the lawyer for the applicants, which some, despite not being able to read, have kept and used as a symbolic reference point of their rights. Despite their frustrating and unjust experiences in state courts, their difficulties following the verdict, and even though there was in what they said a strain of skepticism and fatalism with reference to the powers of government, some still had a certain amount of trust in state law, expressed almost in passing, as something taken for granted, in statements like: "This thing will be forever" or "My grandchild can quote the constitution and get his rights from there" (author notes 2015). The phrase, "We want something written on paper" was one of the constant refrains of the people of the Kalahari during the talks with the government.

The perception of what was achieved and lost through the court has changed through time in a back and forth of enchantment and disenchantment, but what remained was a common perception that, even if the ruling had not been honorably implemented by the government, "The case helped us by bringing us back to our land. Without it we could never have come back" (author notes 2013).

At other times, the people of the reserve and the resettlement villages expressed a sense of fatalism, of being subjected to forces beyond their control. A woman commenting on the situation of her family stated:

> I don't see the use of the court ruling. It was nice when the sentence was made, but now it has changed and the ruling did not materialize. I don't know what happened because we were told that we have been given back our land and now we still get harassment. It seems that the government wants to relocate us again, since now the talk is only about wildlife and [people have] forgotten that we were granted permission to stay on that land .... I do not know what to do. Now I do not even understand my life.[9]

The CKGR residents thus recognized that what they needed most was something that had the force, through the power of written words, to compel the government to keep its obligations, or at least to stabilize policy in such a way that their lives would be secured against oppression. A legal document, "something written on paper", was what was needed, something more tangible than spoken promises. The people of the CKGR, in other words, were thinking of their relationship with the government with reference to the power of a document to alter the behavior of powerful actors with a less than honorable history.

Some San activists, even those who participated in legal advocacy, were certainly aware of the limits of the law and state courts, particularly when they began to see the limited ability of the court to follow up on its verdict, to compel the government to comply with its decision. The difference of opinion toward the court belied a greater consistency that took forms depending on whether the speaker's focus was on the court's inclusion and recognition of the San's justice claims or on the government and its failure to implement the courts' verdicts.

EMBODIED INJUSTICE

One of the judges in the 2006 case, *Sesana and Others v. the Attorney General*, Justice Unity Dow, made an observation in her verdict about the apparent wellbeing of the applicants, which took place during the "inspection *in loco*" that preceded the trial: "The group that huddled for a photograph, on the suggestion of the Applicants' counsel, Mr. Bennett," Justice Dow remarked, "resembled a group one might see at a refugee camp – bare-footed, poorly clad for the weather, and the desert temperatures do, during winter nights, plummet to freezing, and obviously without sufficient water for proper hygiene"(*Sesana* 2006c: para. 17). In making this observation, Justice Dow, despite her somewhat patronizing language, cut through much of the government's argumentation about community development, resource management, and equal citizenship and brought the focus back to those who were making claims, the applicants, whose struggles to secure a livelihood on their own terms were made manifest in their suffering bodies.

Dow's remark corresponds with an observation that the San of the Central Kalahari often make about themselves, pointing to their conditions of deprivation and suffering as manifestations of injustice. From this perspective, justice and wellbeing are inseparable, and injustice is embodied in stressed bodies and sickness – often expressed as a "pain in my heart."

For those who wanted to go back to their villages in the reserve, but were forced into the resettlement villages and unable to return, there was a sense of being separated from every significant source of wellbeing, from their families, from the exchanges on which relationships were based. People often talked about not being able to visit relatives and friends often enough. The same was true for the applicants who did not want to leave the reserve because they were worried about being harassed and having their belongings confiscated by the guards at the gates. In the settlements outside the reserve people were cut off from what made them well: the graves of their ancestors, the performance of rituals to supplicate and appease them, being on the land and in the "places that healed." They were prevented from practicing the kind of ritual that Thabogelo performed with such spontaneous, dramatic effect in the courtroom, rubbing soil from the gravesite on her body in an act of supplication of the ancestors. Furthermore the loss of land implied a loss of freedom (cf. Ingstand and Fugelli 2006), as expressed by a woman who went back to her village in Molapo: "the life in the New Xade is difficult, I felt like in prison. Now here we can move. Moving gives us hope because when things are difficult we move; we do not know what we will find, but we will find food to gather" (author notes 2012). For those people who wanted to go back to the reserve, but were relegated to the life in the new settlement, injustice was often manifested through sickness (with many cases of AIDS/HIV and TB), and through being driven to drink to change the way they felt (Chapter 2).

Inside the reserve people's experience acquired another dimension. Being back helped them "to heal from the years of being forced to move," but still the return came with great personal cost in terms of their ability to live without enough food, water, or medical services. In fact, in the reserve the sense of injustice was manifested in their bodies that the "government makes unclean because it does not provide water"; that are sick because of the lack of clinics, medicine, and food and affected by illness (HIV/AIDS) contracted in the resettlements, without the medicine they need to stay alive; that are stressed – "my heart [*tcáó*] is in pain" – because of the families that are separated, the state officers that harass them, the tensions within and among communities, and the incapacity, particularly for hunters, to feed their families. In other words, justice and injustice are embodied, expressed not only in discourse but objectified in illness and emotional and somatic experience.

The lack of water was invoked as a source of injustice, not only with reference to thirst and the difficulties of irrigating and keeping small livestock, but with reference to how it compelled people to live, to the daily activities of cooking and cleaning. As a man in Metseamonong observed pointedly: "Democracy? I wear rags. I wear dirty clothes. [He pulls on his shirt.] Have you seen anyone like this in a democracy?" This was expressed similarly in a response to the way government officials had publicly depicted their lives in statements they had heard over the radio: "Dirty life is the way they are calling San life. But the government is making us dirty." Being forced into conditions of physical uncleanliness, which were then invoked by government officials as a way of denigrating their way of life, was a form of rhetorical harm that was not lost on the people of the reserve. They suffered from the illegality of hunting, from the confiscation of livestock, and from the difficulty they faced going to the settlement for food while fearing arrest; and this again manifested itself in bodily symptoms, of being starving, stressed, unwell. This source of suffering was commonly articulated in the form of an accusation: not "We are starving" but "The *government* is trying to starve us" (author notes 2013). The prohibition on transporting food across the reserve boundary (when visiting relatives and friends) had an effect on people's ability to meet expectations of sharing, particularly for men to act as providers, provoking the anxiety that followed from not being able to meet social obligations, or, more basically, of not being able to feed one's family, as expressed by an applicant visiting his relatives in New Xade: "Today I cannot bring food to my people [in this case he is referring to the people in the reserve when he goes back] and this is making me sick" (author notes 2013). Injustice for the applicants was therefore expressed in a discourse of the government causing hunger and sickness, of not having food for their children, of problems within families because of the inability to provide, with hunger combining with a particular form of isolation and loneliness as a compound outcome of the illegality of hunting and the lack of means to openly feed people and to nurture relationships.

And when sickness came, the means to deal with it were remote. Women commonly expressed the uncomfortable feeling (stress) of having sick children and not knowing what to do, with no access to medicine, transport to a hospital, and, when a ride was available, worries about the trip. Travel to the nearest clinic sometimes involved greater risk than dealing with illness in the reserve without help: "if somebody is sick, the clinics are far and it is dangerous to walk there. Our kids are sick but we cannot do anything because we do not want to walk with them so far. They can die" (author notes 2012). Again, these were not seen as accidental circumstances, not attributed to the remoteness of the villages in the reserve, but to the government policy of denying services to them. Injustice was again manifested in sick, stressed, and sometimes even dying bodies.

The notion of a bodily sense of justice and injustice follows from the observation that the body is not only a biological and material phenomenon, separated from the mind, but an unstable cultural and historical one, "defined by perceptual experience and by mode of presence and engagement in the world" (Csordas 1999: 145). The everyday sense of justice can thus be grounded in the symbols and conditions of bodiliness, but is often unspoken. It resists discourse. In a forceful and persuasive study of victim experience in post-Apartheid South Africa, Rita Kesselring finds that those who were injured by their experience of violence do not usually articulate their experience through the established forms of therapy, state law, or biomedicine, but through "a model of the body that is historical and accumulative" (2017: 108). "Social recognition," she writes, "is often lacking because victims cannot satisfyingly fulfill the social roles that have been reserved for them" (2017: 109).

Unlike the victims of Apartheid who were engaged in personal struggles to come to terms with the violence of a regime that had been overthrown, the San did not have a historical turning point to which to refer in seeking to make sense of their experience of violence. Their narratives, and their somatization of injustice, were oriented more to present conditions. The verdicts did occasionally take cognizance of their conditions of suffering, as in Dow's poignant remarks, but the legal process remained focused on questions of law, leaving little room for the conditions of victimhood. It is perhaps the disconnect between legal logic and the lived experience of injustice that stands in the way of discrimination and other forms of injustice being taken more seriously as sources of somatic expression and obstacles to wellbeing. The sense of injustice can be expressed as an emotion, articulated outside established forms of victimhood, and ultimately incommensurable with dominant pathways for the recognition of both legal and medical harm.

For the people of the CKGR, justice and injustice tended to be embodied in somewhat different ways, according to the forcible division of those who are within and outside of the reserve. Outside the reserve, it was more commonly manifest in the longing for the land, for the ancestors, for healing, for conditions of wellness; while inside the reserve it more often took the form of deprivation, of sickness resulting from want of healthy food and water, of the dirt of poverty and the bigoted labels that apply to it, the embodiment of political neglect and denigration.

And for all the people of the Central Kalahari, injustice was felt in the relationships that were ruptured, the reciprocity interrupted, the loss of people who were alive but distant, felt in terms of an almost tangible sense of loneliness and disconnection. And these things in turn were seen as a consequence of political decisions to act against their right to return to the land that, as they understood it, the High Court, in its wisdom, had given back to them.

TRUST AND REPRESENTATIVITY

Asked if he followed the court proceedings in the trial that bore his name as first applicant, Roy Sesana made reference to his regular consultations with the attorney for the applicants, Gordon Bennett:

> Each and every day after court my attorney would brief me on what happened and what we should expect, so I did follow the court proceedings. He was like a traditional healer. He told me at the end of the case [before the ruling] which two judges would support us and rule in our favor and which one would rule against us, and that was what happened. He even told me that although the other judge seemed to not like us, there were some things he would like, so all this had been giving me hope that I would go back to my land.[10]

It is worth reflecting on what Sesana's seemingly incongruous comparison between the lawyer and a traditional healer might mean. On a superficial level, the British lawyer was a male who spoke with authority and was respected in the community, all qualities regularly attributed to those San people with knowledge of healing. But the comparison goes further. For Sesana, the lawyer, with his powers of prediction, had special insight into a realm of mystery and danger, just as a healer in a trance dance enters into and comes to "know" the mysterious cause of sickness. The lawyer, like the healer, is in this sense a mediator and translator of a realm that cannot be understood by the ordinary mortal, grappling with forces that act in unpredictable ways, the sources of the fates of human lives. The healer/lawyer is able to bring knowledge from a realm of danger and use it for wellness, both of individuals and of the relationships between them. Bennett was therefore seen as someone endowed with gifts that could not be fathomed by those who did not possess them, who used them to better the conditions of the afflicted. And the court was in this sense a place of mystery, where inscrutable and potentially malevolent powers had to be brought under control. The law in practice was powerful, inscrutable, and dangerous, but at the same time a source of hope in adversity.

Trust was not always expressed through such colorful metaphors. The key to the applicants' trust in others to represent them was for some quite simply the personal relationship, the willingness to communicate in person. This emphasis on personal connection applied not just to lawyers, but broadly to activists and NGO representatives of all kinds. The importance of face-to-face meetings was also expressed in the many letters sent to the Office of the President to meet him, without intermediaries, without NGOs or ministers.

One of the refrains from those CKGR representatives involved in recent meetings with government representatives is their sense of uncertainty and lack of faith in the negotiation process in the absence of the one person they had chosen to represent them. How could they trust the government when it banned their lawyer, Gordon Bennett, from entering the country and taking care of their concerns? As a woman from Metseamonong put it, "Now that the government has put the guns down, it should also bring back our lawyer," so that he could attend all the meetings the residents hold with the government to advise them appropriately. Again they put their trust in papers, in material that could turn into evidence "an agreement with the government regarding services need to be written and signed." Residents challenged the government to provide "written evidence" to give them assurance that it was no longer "at war" with the communities, but would be providing services in good faith. Other residents continued to refuse to participate in these "talks" because "everything should be witnessed by the courts so that no one will blame the other" (author notes 2015).

If the government could not be trusted, the residents put their limited trust in their own lawyers and in documents, things that are "written and signed." To them, nothing else had moved the state to act in their interests, albeit reluctantly and with ambiguous and delayed effects. It was, from their perspective, the only way to restore, however partially and tentatively, the lives that they knew.

There was by no means a universal trust in outside advocates, and representation had to be underpinned by continuous personal consultation. Skepticism about the people's reliance on lawyers to represent them well was expressed in the words of a woman who, after talking about the difficulties of living in her village in the reserve after the relocation, underlined, "I don't know what kind of person can represent the interests of someone else. I feel better if I represent myself, because I will say what is in my heart" (author notes 2015). As I discussed above, the further one gets from the immediate source of information and emotion, the less trustworthy will be the things that people say. Knowledge is most reliable when it is proximate, a view that brings to mind the San UN delegates' reluctance to speak for others about situations on which they lacked firsthand experience (Chapter 5, p. 185). A woman from Metseamonong, referring to the work of the lawyers and NGOs who represented the people of the Central Kalahari, remarked: "They came to our village and told us that what we heard on the radio was the truth" (author notes 2012). The news reported on the radio, in other words could not be fully trusted; and only when someone she knew came in person to confirm what she had heard did she feel that the information she had was reliable.

The same trust in the person who talks with them and reports back from personal experience is what made an effective activist NGO and spokesperson. People would often complain that some of the NGOs supposedly working in their interest never sent anyone to visit them; they mainly saw the presence of NGOs in the CKGR in the form of those people sent to act as a secretariat to take notes in government meetings or in the form of consultants employed to work with them, but usually from afar. In some cases this discontent with NGOs extended into frustration with the government that did not allow people to visit and work with them. At the same time, NGOs as well as donors become the receptacle of their hopes for development on their own terms.

This approach to trust, knowledge, and representativity is strongly emphasized in San ethics. The things people say (and hence the people who say them) have to be trusted. "You only say something will help you if you have experience with it." Without that experience, you "don't know if [it] is life or death" (assistant notes 2016). The further one gets from what is seen, heard, and experienced firsthand, the less it can be relied upon for making decisions. This can explain why Sesana, who understood little that was happening during the trial while he was in the courtroom, was able to honestly say, "I did follow the court proceedings." His regular consultations with Bennett were such that he could legitimately make this claim.

This observation has important implications for activist leadership, particularly in the ability and incentives of representatives to report on international activities. The more this activity occurs in the absence of local participation, the more it will be seen by those who are being spoken for as something that "does not belong to them," and that they do not trust. The litigation process in court partially overcame this problem when the court made a visit *in loco* and the proceedings began in New Xade, at least long enough for the applicants and others to get a sense of what the court looked like, who the people involved were, and above all to see their interests as a central part of the agenda. Through this outreach as part of its inquiry, the High Court entered the claimants' realm of experience, enhancing its understanding of the reserve residents' conditions of dispossession.

THE ORIGINS OF NEW DISPOSSESSIONS

As the example of the applicant list shows, it is impossible to comprehend the San people's sense of justice, including their understanding of what the activist cause has or has not produced, without first considering the conditions in which they live and the new sources of dispossession and resistance that have arisen after several decades of struggle. The sense of justice denied is almost as poignant as an original sense of harm. The ways that the San people see their relationship with the government and with the activist networks in which they have long been engaged are colored by their conditions of deprivation and, in turn, the slow pace of efforts to overcome them.

Dispossession has taken a far-reaching form with the decision of the Botswana government to initiate a new land policy (Republic of Botswana 2015). Under this new policy, individuals with means could go anywhere in the country and take over leasehold and communal land. What had been community trust areas in Wildlife Management Areas such as those in western Ngamiland and parts of southern Ghanzi District began to be taken over by individuals and small companies. This privatization process, when combined with the TGLP changes, led to a large-scale transfer of land into the hands of the wealthy, while the poor are largely left out (Cullis and Watson 2005; Sapignoli and Hitchcock 2013b).

Dispossession has also taken the form of wide disparities of opportunity between those who chose to remain in or return to the CKGR and those who live in the resettlement villages. Once their right of return had been granted by the court, many San assumed that this right would be accompanied by all the other benefits of the state. The government's approach, however, was to minimize its obligations toward those who chose a path of defiance. This came out in the planning process of the CKGR, which might be seen as a distribution of opportunity. Once people had been removed from the CKGR, the government granted the rights to set up community trusts, to manage land inside the reserve, to those settlements that had been established on the peripheries of the reserve, New Xade, Kaudwane, and Xere, while for the communities in the reserve there is still no such agreement. Meanwhile, considerable time and resources have been spent by NGOs and the people in the reserve to come up with a management plan on how people would like to use and live in the land. One of the issues is that the CBNRM policy does not apply directly to state land, and hence cannot form the basis for land use in the reserve, at least not without an accompanying policy reform. A second problem is that since a hunting ban went into effect, community trusts in communal areas have begun to be taken over by private companies, both ones owned by Batswana and by expatriates. In fact a recent (starting in January 2014) countrywide hunting ban altered the right to hunt in the CKGR, making it into a criminal act, for which people accused of poaching are arrested and jailed; and under the current "shoot to kill policy," people can be legally killed by antipoaching units if they are suspected of engaging in illegal hunting (Konopo, Ntibinyane, and Mongudhi 2016; Vidal 2016).

The recent land policy (Republic of Botswana 2015) and other development policies that are in the process of being formulated by the Khama government could well result in the efforts of the people in the Central Kalahari and in the areas outside of the reserve going nowhere. The CBNRM policy was revised by Parliament in 2007, in a form that was more consistent with the government's centralizing, "difference blind" orientation to those for whom it was intended (Republic of Botswana 2007; Hoon 2014). With the 2007 policy on CBNRM, wildlife is redefined as a "national common," similar to minerals, where the revenues have to be divided among citizens.[11] A program that had the potential to empower marginalized communities was thus reformulated and centralized with key powers and income sources directed to the state, often leaving local participants with little to show for years of effort other than a legacy of disappointment and mistrust.

Many of the community trusts that were showing some success in terms of generating income and employment have been taken over by private companies, including those in western Ngamiland and in the Okavango Delta region, which were some of the most productive community trusts in the country (Hitchcock et al. 2015). Opposition by the San and other minorities to these state-centric land policies has been consistent and has continued to the present, even though the government claimed in a series of *kgotla* meetings in early 2016 that the CUZ would be recognized and the five existing communities in the Central Kalahari would be able to set up community trusts and control wildlife and tourism activities in their areas. The breakdown of the CBNRM program, the new land policy, and the transfer of resources from communities to private individuals have left many citizens wondering what the future will hold (Hitchcock and Frost 2017).

Tourism has become another focus of resentment, international campaigning, and potential for litigation. The CKGR is currently divided into at least three tourism zones which in the past were overseen by Bigfoot Safaris (a private operation that operated mainly in Khutse and the southern CKGR); the Department of Wildlife and National Parks; and private safari companies (e.g. Wilderness Safaris and Kwandu Safaris which have rights over areas in the north of the CKGR). There are also some mobile tourism operators that enter the CKGR periodically. Besides these operations, there are plans for at least half a dozen more high-end residential tourism camps in the CKGR. In the eyes of some of the residents, the Botswana government has made major moves toward privatizing tourism in the Central Kalahari, leaving relatively little space for CBNRM activities, community campsites, or mobile safaris run by local communities.

When in December 2009 a tourist lodge was opened in Deception Valley, north of Molapo, the home of Roy Sesana, the people in the village pointed out the irony of large numbers of wealthy tourists and mining company personnel spending time in the Central Kalahari, seeing animals and magnificent vistas, driving around on delicate pan surfaces and fossil river beds and drinking ice water when the residents themselves were not allowed to access water sources, or to utilize the resources in the reserve in the name of conservation (author notes 2013). Wilderness Safaris, the owner of Kalahari Plains Camp, defended its actions, saying that it had been operating in the twenty-three established camps for tourists in the CKGR since 1990, and the construction of the tourist lodge was done with the full consent of the Ghanzi District Council and the government of Botswana (Wilderness Safaris 2010). Wilderness Safaris also maintained that the majority of their employees at Kalahari Plains Camp had their origins in the CKGR region. On occasion, tourists would engage San as guides or would purchase crafts from them. By and large, however, tourism activities were organized by safari companies, and the San played little, if any, role other than working on occasion as camp assistants (Hitchcock and Babchuk 2017). With Ian Khama as president and his brother Tshekedi Khama as Minister of Environment, Wildlife and Tourism, nature conservation has been touted as a priority in the country's interests, and large investments have been made in this sector, including setting up a Tourism Intelligence Security to fight poaching activities and to develop antipoaching camps (*Patriot Reporter* 2016).

Meanwhile, the government pursued a second pathway to large-scale development in the reserve through mineral extraction. For the many people in the CKGR and resettlement villages who experienced the worst effects of the mining projects but who were excluded from employment opportunities, it was this fact above all that added poignancy to their dispossession and lack of resources and services.

As I discussed in Chapter 2, the mine in Gope, as a focal point of the anti-relocation campaign, was a major presence among the extractive enterprises in the CKGR. In June 2007 Gem Diamonds purchased the mining licenses for sites around Gope in the CKGR, an area of 745 km^2 where De Beers and Falconbridge, Ltd (Xstrata) had found kimberlite deposits indicating the presence of diamonds. The company paid a reported US $34 million for the license. By 2011 Gem Diamonds and the government of Botswana were ready to jointly announce that a 53 billion Pula (US $7.3 billion) diamond mine, which was to be established at Gope in the relatively near future. In response to those critics who were concerned about the impact of the mine on the residents of the CKGR, Gem Diamonds maintained that it had policies in place that govern its relationship with local communities and that these would ensure environmentally sustainable exploitation of mineral resources and engage with the people inside and outside the reserve. New assessments were done relating to the mine's corporate responsibility and its promise to provide services, training, and jobs to the people in the reserve. At the same time, however, the few San miners working in the reserve were transported in from the resettlement villages. As it happened, the mine suspended operations in February 2017 before many of its anticipated benefits could be seen by the residents of the CKGR and the surrounding villages, but narratives of prosperity, hope, and, for many, exclusion still reverberated widely and continue to do so.

While I focus on the diamond mine here, the very same issues were raised with reference to copper mining in the reserve. Fracking (or, more precisely, hydraulic fracturing) has also taken place in the reserve, as well as several mineral explorations that the residents are witnessing, with mining equipment and trucks close to their villages, but without efforts being made to consult them and keep them informed. People often lamented that the mines (diamonds and copper) were already established when interviews were conducted for the projects' social impact studies, and no one had consulted them earlier. The only information they had about the projects came from seeing prospecting and excavation activity on their territories and in some cases from NGOs such as First People of the Kalahari which were visiting the reserve. There was a sense of being left behind by events and of not being listened to. Fracking was initially denied and then, faced with clear evidence, admitted by the government.[12]

In the case of the copper mine that extended from the northern part of the Ghanzi ridge to the Toteng area of Ngamiland, and cut through the north-west corner of the reserve, for some people with whom I spoke (mainly San people) in the villages of Kuke, Qabo and in the farms (Ghanzi District) the mine was seen as another source of dispossession and they were worried that they would lose their jobs in the farms, and at the same time lose their animals and access to graves and houses.[13] (As Guenther [1986: 282] notes, "It is the location of their relatives' graves, rather than where they work or live that defines *//ai* [home] for the Naro.") Others instead saw the mine as a possibility for jobs, and maybe better-paid jobs (clearly many were not informed of the fact that the mine would probably employ people from other parts of the country or from neighboring countries with more specialized skills). One even joked about the fact that the mine was about to accomplish something the Naro had never been able to do, "take the land from the farmers" (author notes 2012).

Similar views (absent those of the farmers) were expressed about the possible diamond mine in Gope. Often when I spoke with people in the reserve about the mine opinions were divided. A major concern was that the mineral development in the reserve could lead to their relocation, because "whenever there are good things ... we are always moved." Following from their past experience, any discussion of development in the CKGR translated into concerns about forced relocation. This included a shrewd observation from one resident, to the effect that mining in other parts of the country did not necessarily involve moving people away, but the opposite: bringing them in to the area of the project to share in its benefits (author notes 2011).

Some were concerned that it would have negative impacts on their land and the wildlife, especially on wildlife and flora in the immediate vicinity of the mine. Others, particularly thinking short term, were hopeful that the mining company would employ them in some of the early work in the Gope area, then later as mine workers, and possibly provide them with compensation for using what they saw as their land. Still others anticipated that they would be able to get water from boreholes drilled as part of the mining activities, something that in fact happened with De Beers first and Gem later, allowing people to use their borehole and in the case of Gem providing some support for drilling boreholes once people won the right in court to build them in the reserve (Chapter 8, p. 292). Hope for benefits from the project extended to some advocates of the San such as Kiema (2010: 122–3) who argued that the Gope mine would bring the benefits of "development" to the people of the reserve. Meanwhile, Haile Mphusu, Managing Director of the Gope Exploration Company, pointed out some of the limits to these hopes, including the fact that the conditions of the company's contract with the government prohibit allowing the "Basarwa" to use the boreholes that are drilled for the Gope project (SIAPAC 2011: 3).

Despite the fact that many of those interviewed in an environmental and social impact studies (2008) felt that they had been forcibly moved out of the area to make way for mining, they almost uniformly expected benefits from the mine now that they had returned to their territory. Even though jobs were by far seen as the main potential benefit of the project, the discussion sometimes turned to "concern about the employability of people in directly-affected communities" (cited in SIAPAC 2008: 31). Few households (14.6 percent) had any members with skilled employment experience. This was compounded by the experience of racism, or discrimination by other ethnic groups, which came up frequently in the interviews: "Even when our children go out to look for jobs they mostly come back empty-handed due to discrimination against our tribe" (cited in SIAPAC 2008: 36).

The residents of the CKGR, in the years immediately following the *Sesana* case, were thus both hopeful about the possibility of benefits from a diamond mine at Gope and highly skeptical of the possibility that these benefits would ever reach them. As it happened, many of their concerns were borne out. The people I spoke with more recently (2014), before there was any indication that the operations would soon close down, reported that the mine was very noisy, that they did not see any benefit in terms of jobs and that the few people from the CKGR working in the mine came from the settlements. People were often disturbed by the comings and goings of equipment involved in exploration of the area around their village in search of "not sure what, probably diamonds" without being consulted or informed, adding to the sense of insecurity over the threat of relocation. Their experience throughout was marked by discrimination against them as "Basarwa," exclusion from the processes of information-sharing and decision-making, and a looming threat of yet another forced removal from the territory that was the repository of their knowledge, social lives, and security.

The exclusion of the people of the CKGR from the benefits of mining and tourism is informative when viewed in the context of their social justice campaign. From this perspective, it becomes apparent that none of the international NGOs that acted in support of the CKGR inhabitants' right to live in the reserve were prepared to advocate for their right to benefit from the mines and tourist lodges that were imposed on them and their territories. The contours of injustice were fairly clear to them, consisting mainly of the hypocrisy of insisting that people relocate outside the reserve for the purposes of wildlife conservation, while actively promoting conservation-compromising mining and tourism activities inside the reserve as sources of revenue for the state.

For the people of the reserve, including those who had been forcibly relocated from it, injustice was experienced in the everyday, encountered in struggles to subsist and survive, manifested in such things as guards, gates, licenses, lists of names, identity papers, ear tags on animals, and, perhaps above all, in the arbitrariness of their use. For them, hypocrisy and the sense of justice/injustice were etched into their bodies and their sense of sickness and wellbeing. As we will see in the next chapter, the sense of injustice was also tied in with the shifting alignments of activist strategies in law and politics, the sense of the possibilities that remained for change, on their own terms.

8

LITIGATING A WAY OF LIFE

LAW AND POLITICS IN THE JUSTICE CAUSE

What happens to activism when it goes to court? What does legal confrontation with powerful adversaries do to the wider struggle against their abuses? In principle at least, a nonauthoritarian state will accede to the decisions of all courts (state and international) with which it is honor-bound to comply, and this is why litigation has proven to be a common strategy of indigenous rights claimants. It is generally understood that any political regime characterized by the "rule of law" will require all parties involved in a dispute – but with a particular onus on the government – to submit to the decisions of the court as originating from a higher authority, which, in principle at least, serves as a politically unbiased source of justice anchored in the law. If that higher authority forms part of an authoritarian regime or a colonial project, then it is fairly clear that prospects for using the courts as a source of leverage to influence public policy are minimal. Under these circumstances, the prospects of pursuing rights claims in court will be conditioned by the reality of working with a system marked by disrespect of the law and suppression of litigants who dare to challenge the will of the powerful. This opposition to judicial review and the rule of law is not always explicit. The question then arises whether governments, like that of Botswana, that have the appearance of promoting liberal democracy, are also able to use their courts as tools of repression. And, if so, how do they do it?

One of the ways that this can occur happens when governments defy the decisions of courts in ways that attract little notice, such as violating the terms of the verdict, or implementing them in bad faith, in small, cumulative actions, which are intended to undermine the effects of a judicial decision while discursively accepting it. This forces rights claimants into a position where they have to pursue one or more of several options: to accept without question the accumulation of injustices, sometimes in the form of blatant human rights violations, to intensify international pressure through media outreach and activism at the UN; or to reduce their expectations and engage in a process of negotiation in which they are expected to dilute and compromise their claims. As a last resort (if they have the means), they can also return to litigation, producing a situation in which major verdicts become broken up into particular claims, producing a litigation chain requiring ever-increasing engagement with lawyers and courts, with ever more recourse to judgments that may or may not conclude by bringing the powerful to account.

The big issue with which litigation began – the cause that attracted notice, that got people to pause as they scrolled through their Facebook posts, that attracted commitments and provoked responses – all this becomes dissipated into secondary contests. There may still be media coverage, as would be expected when the powerful are summoned to court as defendants/respondents, but the newness and urgency of the story fade into a *normalization of litigation*. The routinization of struggle is not only something that the litigants themselves experience; it pervades the dynamics of activism.

Under these circumstances, do we find an increasing imbrication or a separation (purification) of law and politics as an outcome of legally oriented activism? Does increased recourse to courts end up emptying justice causes of politics as it captures them in litigation? What ultimately happens to politics when activist campaigns reframe their causes as "cases" and take them to court? Can politics be really differentiated from law? As I will show in this chapter and discuss further in the Conclusion (Chapter 9), there is no straightforward answer to these interrelated questions, with the domains that are commonly understood as "law" and as "politics" interpenetrating and inseparable.

The imbrication of law and politics in justice campaigns goes well beyond the courts and their reach of influence. It can be seen more clearly when the multiple points of leverage used in activist campaigns are taken into consideration, without restricting law to courts and politics to government offices. As I will show in this chapter, law and politics find expression in the aftermath of judgments, in the ways that verdicts are implemented or ignored. The legal/political field also extends to the international domain, where prominent verdicts can be the focal points of contests framed as human rights issues between indigenous activists and states.

I will also consider whether, with litigation (with consequences relating to judicialization) as part of a justice campaign, political struggle goes silent and dissent becomes emptied of politics. This question should be understood with reference to the process by which activists supplement or substitute their legal strategies by engaging directly in electoral politics, joining political parties, and taking positions as civil servants in efforts to change laws and policies affecting them. Under these circumstances, does recourse to courts, combined with UN lobbying and other sources of leverage, continue to have a place in political activism? Although the strategies of activism have multiplied, while being subjected to increased pressures of co-optation, it remains clear that the courts have not been abandoned in the face of the government's narrow interpretations of their verdicts. It is also clear that the consequences of these prominent cases tend to be greater than their immediate verdicts (Kirsch 2014b: 123). As one outcome of the San's multistranded activist engagements, litigating a way of life has become a permanent feature of the political process.

THE LITIGATION CHAIN

As more and more indigenous peoples and organizations take governments and corporations to court as a way to defend their rights, an important phenomenon begins to appear: legal contests, even supposedly victorious ones, do not always produce stable conditions for justice or even meet the basic obligations assigned to them by the courts. Instead, governments and industries often approach verdicts by digging in their heels, obstructing compensation, delaying or derailing the action they are called upon to take, provoking the need for more intervention by the supposedly victorious applicants, producing more litigation, repeating legal contests over and over. This can take the momentum out of a justice campaign. The initial euphoria of court victory is replaced by a kind of dull apathy in which litigation becomes almost a form of bureaucratic routine, a tedious, drawn-out process necessary for securing the practicalities of life and livelihood. This strategy of delayed or minimized remedy resembles the initial gambit taken by some defendants with deep pockets of strategic delay of proceedings, forcing plaintiffs with more limited resources to drop their suits or accept derisory settlements, except that delays often also occur once judgments have been rendered or settlement agreements concluded.

This can be seen, for example, among the James Bay Crees of northern Quebec, who took the provincial utility Hydro Québec to court in 1972 in an effort to secure an injunction to stop unwanted hydro-electric megaproject development on their territories.[1] After an epic trial, they won a resounding initial victory, only to have it overturned on appeal. Ultimately, the Crees lost their case. Yet their initial success brought the province and the utility to the negotiating table, eventually producing the *James Bay and Northern Québec Agreement* of 1975. This agreement, in large part through provisions for land use and regimes of resource extraction, created a legal framework that ostensibly defined the Crees' rights with some precision, but was in practice repeatedly violated by logging and mining companies, forcing the band councils of the Cree communities to hire lawyers and go to court, again and again. By the time a second phase of hydro-electric development was negotiated leading up to the 2002 *New Relationship Agreement* (popularly known as the "Paix des Braves"), the Crees faced a situation of entrenched legal struggle, culminating in an unsuccessful effort to secure an injunction in Quebec Superior Court against twenty-six forest companies acting in violation of aboriginal title and the provisions of the *James Bay and Northern Québec Agreement* (Niezen 2009: 104).

Much the same situation is described by Stuart Kirsch in his account of the litigation on behalf of indigenous plaintiffs from Papua New Guinea against the mining conglomerate Broken Hill Proprietary Ltd (BHP) in the late 1990s. When an initial settlement, which included cash compensation and construction of a processing system for mine tailings, was stalled, the plaintiffs were compelled to return to court. In this follow-up litigation, instead of charging ahead against the mining corporation with bravado, the law firm "reluctantly returned to court out of responsibility to their clients" (Kirsch 2014b: 114).

A very similar form of what might be called "litigation chains" or "litigation entrenchment" followed by "litigation fatigue" descended on the San. While securing a verdict in 2006 that many saw as a "victory" and vindication of their rights claims, the contempt with which the government of Botswana approached the verdict and their need to secure further legal protection brought the Central Kalahari Game Reserve (CKGR) inhabitants back to court again and again. By making activities oriented to meeting basic needs "illegal," such as hunting (even with a license) or the transport of water into the reserve, the government created conditions of deprivation and legal ambiguity that had to be repeatedly resolved through recourse to courts. The narrow approach to the applicant list and the bad faith toward the implementation of the *Sesana* verdict can be seen as the sources of a series of secondary claims, which increased the San and Bakgalagadi's involvement with lawyers and legal processes, producing judgments that may or may not lead to the reform of government they are looking for, but that certainly involved them more intimately in the ideas and outcomes of legal action. Some of the cases were significant and precedent-setting, such as their effort to secure access to water in the Central Kalahari. Others were related to more specific complaints, as in arrests for illegal hunting or the effort to seek compensation for goats that were killed or confiscated in raids by park rangers. To get a sense of the way that litigation became almost an aspect of daily life for the San in the Central Kalahari, let me now briefly outline some of the specific cases or kinds of cases that followed directly from the conditions created by the 2006 *Sesana* verdict and the government's approach to the obligations it imposed.

The "Water" Case

Since the suspension of services in 2002, the availability of water has been a constant problem for the CKGR inhabitants. After several failed attempts to convince the government to restore the services or allow people in the CKGR to have their own borehole and/or to carry water in the reserve, in February 2010 two people from the communities of Kikao and Mothomelo in the CKGR, with the help of First People of the Kalahari, decided to file a new case in the High Court in Lobatse to affirm their right to drill or use boreholes in the CKGR. Gordon Bennett was happy to be able to lead this case from the beginning, in contrast to the *Sesana* case when much had already been done and decided by the time he was hired. The founding affidavit of the case, *Matsipane Mosetlhanyane and Gakenyatsiwe Matsipane v. the Attorney General*, eloquently expresses the motivation behind the decision to take the government to court for a second time:

> [We] have returned to the CKGR because it is our home and it is where we want to live and die. It is where our ancestors are buried, and it is the only place we know. This is why we travelled for many days to get here. It is why when our huts were burnt down we slept in the open until we had replaced them, without a thought of returning to New Xade. It is why we have put up with many difficulties, and will continue

> to do all we can to survive in the CKGR, with or without the Borehole. (*Mosetlhanyane* 2010 Conclusion, para. 75)

Some of the applicants in the case were original applicants (those of the 2006 *Sesana* case) and others new applicants who had been relocated in 2002 but were not among the applicants in the 2006 case and who were nevertheless able to get past the gates and return to the reserve. Matsipane Mosetlhanyene, the first applicant, was one of the original applicants and a witness in the 2006 case. The second applicant was his wife. He identifies as Mokgalagadi. He described to me the difficulties of living in the villages without water, and how "the lack of water frequently makes us weak and vulnerable to sickness." The applicants stressed their concern that, without an alternative source of water in the dry season, the elderly in particular will suffer, as will young children, whose mothers sometimes do not have enough milk to feed them. He described the new conditions after the *Sesana* case, in which people were left without any government service or borehole and had to travel long distances to get water, thus risking their lives. And the people in Mothomelo depended in particular on the pan in Kikao, where they collected water, and on their use of vehicles to transport it (even if this then depends on the availability of cash to buy petrol). People also got water in Kaudwane, the new settlement outside the reserve, and brought it back into the CKGR, sometimes being stopped at the gate in doing so. They also relied on plants and roots, but lacked sufficient water for their small livestock, resulting in the loss of many of their animals.

The answering affidavit, deposed by Trevor Mmopelwa, the Director of DWNP, stressed simply that, "The Basarwa have chosen to settle in areas far from those facilities. They have become *victims of their own decision* to settle an inconveniently long distance from the services and facilities provided by the government" (*Mosetlhanyane* 2010).

The applicants initially lost the case in 2010, partly on the grounds of the "uncertainty" of the number of applicants, with High Court Judge Walia pointing to the fact that eight of the applicants were not part of the "original" *Sesana* case and were therefore not "properly before" the court (*Mosetlhanyane* 2010: 3). In agreement with the government position, the judge stated that the applicants "were victims of their own choice," having the possibility, which they did not act on, to relocate to places in closer proximity to water sources such as those provided in the new settlements (*Mosetlhanyane* 2010: 28, para. 24).

A final decision on the CKGR water case was made by the Court of Appeal on January 27, 2011. The five judges of the Court of Appeal unanimously agreed that since the applicants have the right of "continuing occupation of the reserve" as was established in the 2006 verdict, they had the right to water. The judgment states that in accordance with the *Botswana Water Act* the applicants have the right to use existing boreholes and/or drill their borehole for "domestic purposes only" because they are in lawful possession of the CKGR land (*Mosetlhanyane* 2011).

Parts of the verdict went further than a mere vindication of the inhabitants' rights to water. Judge Ramodibedi described the case as a "harrowing story of human suffering and despair caused by a shortage of water in the harsh climatic conditions of the Kalahari Desert where the appellants and their 'Basarwa' community live" (*Mosetlhanyane* 2011: at para. 4). In grounding the verdict in the law, the judgment referred to the International Covenant on Economic, Social and Cultural Rights (even if Botswana is not signatory) and in particular the African Commission's report on the implementation of the covenant, particularly paragraph 16 (d), which says: "States should provide resources for indigenous peoples to design, deliver and control their access to water." The July 2010 UN General Assembly's recognition of access to water as a fundamental human right was quoted as well (*Mosetlhanyane* 2011: 21). The Court of Appeal, summarizing its position, delivered a devastating appraisal: "Government seems to be saying to the appellants: you can live in your settlement in the [reserve] as long as you don't abstract water other than from plants" (*Mosetlhanyane* 2011: 23).

This judgment showed that Botswana's Court of Appeal was willing to take into consideration nonbinding but profoundly important statements emanating from the emerging international consensus on the fundamental importance of socioeconomic rights in fulfilling human dignity. With this legal reference point influencing the verdict, the government's refusal to allow the applicants to have a borehole was seen as a "degrading treatment of the appellants" (*Mosetlhanyane* 2011: 24). Even if in winning the case the applicants acquired the right to drill boreholes at their own expense, this judgment does not recognize water as a human right and the government was not made responsible for the delivery of water services.

On April 22, 2011, the government of Botswana stipulated that the Department of Wildlife and National Parks could go ahead and allow water drilling for people in the CKGR. In June, Gem Diamonds agreed to pay for the drilling of four boreholes, one of which was found to have potable water (Mothomelo). On September 4, 2011, a celebration was held that marked the establishment of the new borehole. Residents of the reserve were able to drink their own water for the first time in nearly a decade. A commemorative plaque (see Chapter 1, p. 7) was mounted near the borehole, and Survival International posted a video on their website to mark the victory.

The feeling of celebration, however, was short lived. When I went back to the reserve one year later the borehole in Mothomelo was malfunctioning and not pumping enough water for everyone (and their animals) in the community. Some of their livestock had died in the days just before my arrival. For the other communities in the reserve like Metseamonong, Gugamma, and Molapo the situation was worse. With their water supply scarce, people were walking to the closest resettlement villages or using trucks when available and risking "smuggling" water back into the reserve. At Molapo, a borehole was also drilled and there was a plan for desalinization of the water, but the equipment provided was never fully operational and some pieces of equipment were lost or stolen. Even with a verdict in their favor, their lives were precarious, with conditions of survival shaped by the vagaries of engine parts and policy.

The "Entrance" Case

In October 2012 I went to the reserve again, this time as a consultant/facilitator for First Peoples Worldwide (FPW), a US-based organization that had collaborated with FPK in the 1990s and that since then had followed the situation of the people in the CKGR. I was travelling with a young American working for FPW, an Australian Aboriginal human right activist, and Jumanda Gakelebone, who was our facilitator/translator. We spent several days in the villages in the reserve after – highly unusually – getting a permit from the DWNP. In the permit several points were stressed, including that the permit "does not grant you permission to bring food and water to the CKGR residents," and "No weapons of whatever form, whether spears, bows, traps ... capable of injuring or killing wildlife may be brought into the reserve." Before we were ready to go back to Gaborone, we spent a few days in Molapo.

On our way back Roy Sesana asked us if we could give him a lift to Rakops because he was not feeling well and wanted to see a doctor. We left the village with Sesana in the car and Gakelebone driving.

When we arrived at the Matswere gate in the northeast of the reserve, a Special Support Group (SSG) member came to our vehicle and took over from the game scouts who normally perform the routine questions and identity check. He spent a lot of time alleging that Sesana was not among the people listed in the permit, so we were all "in trouble" for that. We tried to calm things down and explain that Sesana was sick, that we were bringing him to a doctor, and that he did not need a permit because he was on the list of applicants.

The officer persisted with his accusations. Then he started to look in our bags, and soon found a small bow and arrow in my bag that had been given to me by a resident in the reserve. He accused me of being in possession of an undeclared weapon, which I could have used to kill wildlife in the park. I explained that it was a harmless craft product, the kind that you can buy in a tourist shop in Gaborone. He repeated that he would bring me to jail. Sesana and Gakelebone shouted almost in unison, "is a craft, not a weapon!" and "There is no poison, you cannot kill an animal!" The officer decided to "confiscate the weapon" and to let us go on condition that "you go straight to Gaborone, you do not talk with anyone on the way and do not stop anywhere. You go to Gaborone and leave tomorrow [those of us who were not Botswana residents all had flights to go back to where we came from] and if you do not do as I say we will arrest you. I will instruct the police to monitor you" (author notes 2012).

Clearly this was an empty threat, and no one followed us back to the capital. This was a situation familiar to many people in the reserve, but in their case the threats were not empty. Compared with the life-threatening situations faced by other human rights activists, journalists, and anthropologists in more volatile conditions, this was of course a minor case of police intimidation, but it gave me personal insight into the kinds of encounter with authority that are part of the everyday experience of the San and their supporters.

The uncertainty over entrance permits has been an ongoing issue with the people of the Central Kalahari, many of whom felt that they were not free to leave the reserve if they so chose, for fear of not being allowed to return, and who were concerned that their horses, goats, and donkeys could be confiscated once they were at the gates. Many people who were not applicants in the *Sesana* case took for granted that they could go back with their families and animals and return to the lives they led before the relocation. In practice, however, this was not possible because of government opposition. Without having their names on the applicant list, they were refused entry.

These issues also became the basis for a third CKGR legal case filed in 2013, *Keotlhabetsi Ithutseng and Mosimane Malefo et al. v. the Attorney General*, with the applicants represented by the office of the lawyer Duma Boko (one of the lawyers of the *Sesana* case, and currently leader of the main opposition party, the Botswana National Front) with High Court justice Walia presiding, the same judge who dismissed the water case. Gordon Bennett was at this time – July 2013 – prevented from entering the country and could not argue the case.

The principles of the third CKGR court case revolved around two main issues: (1) who has right to enter and live in the CKGR – (a) the original applicants in the 2004–6 case or (b) all of the people who were relocated from the CKGR in 2002. And (2) the right to bring domestic animals such as donkeys into and out of the CKGR.[2] The case was therefore about who had rights to go in and out of and live in the CKGR and what animals they could have inside the boundaries of the Central Kalahari in order to sustain their livelihoods.

Judge Walia dismissed the case in August 2013 on technical grounds, particularly because the applicants lacked the necessary "*locus standi* to bring this application" and lacked proof that they were residents of the CKGR, a lack of evidence that could not be evaluated by the judge through the founding and answering affidavits. The inclusion and exclusion from the applicant list was thus not just a criterion for crossing the gate of the reserve, but was applied to a decision concerning whether a case could be accepted by a court. Some of the applicants in this case had been forcibly relocated but were not part of the 2002 list of applicants, and were not accepted as new applicants as an extension of the *Sesana* case. Instead, the judge asked for further proof of the legitimacy of their claim to residency in the CKGR.

What further complicated matters was the fact that the dates in the papers signed were contradictory: the power of attorney from the applicants to the first applicant was dated later than the power of attorney that the first applicants gave to the lawyers. Boko asked the judge to "interpret the rules of court liberally to avoid injustice to a party" (*Ithutseng* 2013: 11), but for the judge this was unacceptable. These are the kinds of difficulties that emerge when a collective claim (or a claim that includes many individuals) gets put forward in conditions in which travel and communication make it difficult for the case to be organized according to the rules of the court. The government-imposed conditions of isolation and impoverishment also make it impossible for a case to be properly filed in order to address some of those very conditions.

In his decision, Walia referred (as he did in the 2010 water case judgment) to the *Sesana* case, particularly to the High Court judge's comment concerning the "laxity and carefree manner in which the applicants' papers in a case of such immense public interest have been prepared" as a reason for the dismissal (*Ithutseng* 2013: 17–18). He stated that the applicants' claim of being relocated in 2002 as the people of the *Sesana* case have to be sustained with evidence, but contrary to the Court of Appeal (2003) he did not refer the matter to oral evidence or to trial because of "the cumulative effect of disregard of the rules" (*Ithutseng* 2013: 18 para. 52).

The structure of litigation thus made its appearance once again, this time well beyond the original process that led to the creation of the applicant list. The chaotic nature of producing this list – particularly in the context of a people who required translation to understand their role in the litigation process and who lacked the financial means to find, and maintain regular contact with, a lawyer who would have their cause as a priority – was later used against them in their efforts to secure their rights. There could be no better illustration of the circular logic and hegemonic effects of the structures of state law.

The "Livestock" Cases

Litigation chains do not only result directly from the government's response to a particular verdict; they can also stem from the cases produced by a wider condition of legal uncertainty or schizophrenia, in which policy and criminality are applied apparently arbitrarily and unpredictably. Government arrests, fines, and confiscation of property in the CKGR did not always follow a predictable pattern, and when they did occur, the residents of the reserve had become familiar enough with the use of law as a remedy that, in the rare circumstances that they had the resources to defend their rights, they did not hesitate to do so.

At the same time that people and livestock were prevented from entering the reserve, there were operations mounted by government authorities to go into the reserve and confiscate goats and other domestic stock belonging to residents and former residents, something that occurred on many occasions, including in raids and "roundups" that took place in 2005, 2006, and 2009. Ostensibly, the reason for these confiscations was that the goats were harming the environment and were potential carriers of disease, as had been argued by one of the government witnesses in the *Sesana* case, an American veterinarian.

This prohibition had consequences that went well beyond the mere denial of ownership rights. In response to the prohibition, families would often "decide" to separate with one of them staying in the villages outside the reserve to take care of the animals left behind out of concern that they would be confiscated. At other times the entire family would move to the settlement villages, where there was less risk of losing their animals. People in the reserve saw this as one of the main concerns that prevented them from engaging in government projects, such as the development of tourism camps close to their villages or participating in the Community-Based Natural Resource Management Plan to be submitted to the DWNP. Their concern was that these activities could imply a new relocation, particularly given that "if land is for tourism, we will be limited again on the livestock." A woman shared a concern that was often reported to me in the villages inside and outside the reserve: "we want to be involved with tourism. We were used to dance for them, to sell them jewelry," she said, but "if we agree to tourism another round of relocation is in earnest. In an area where there is tourism, people are not allowed to rear livestock" (author notes 2012). (As I discussed in Chapter 7, the development of mining in the reserve inspired similar concerns about forced relocation.)

As with the hunting arrests, the government seemed to be purposefully acting in defiance of its own laws in furtherance of a strategic goal: the removal of the San and Bakgalagadi from the CKGR. One of these cases gained somewhat greater prominence and resulted in some press coverage. It emerged in a High Court ruling in 2016 that some years before the government had confiscated and auctioned livestock belonging to the San leader, Roy Sesana and some of his "tribesmen." The six applicants – Roy Sesana, Xamme Gaotlhobogwe, Dube Ngwanaosele, Kanyo Kaingotla, Sister Gaotlhobogwe and Kealotswe Motsoketso – all residents of Molapo, applied to the court claiming that the government had confiscated over ninety-five goats and a horse from them on the grounds that these animals had been brought into the reserve unlawfully. Sesana told the court that he had owned these goats prior to the removal of all residents to New Xade by the government. Other applicants also said that their goats had always been in the game reserve, even before the High Court ruled that residents of Molapo could keep their livestock within the park. They said the incident occurred in their absence in 2009.

The government's lawyer denied that the livestock had been removed without the "Basarwa's consent," arguing that numerous meetings and consultations were held between them and Ghanzi District authorities prior to the removal of the livestock from the CKGR. Only following the refusal of the "Basarwa" to comply with government instructions was the livestock forcefully removed. Asked about the location of the inventory that was prepared when the goats were removed from Molapo and the photos that were taken of the goats, the wildlife official testified that the inventory was at the office. As for the photos, he had no idea what had happened to them.

In his 2016 decision, Justice Abednego Tafa overruled the government's actions and ordered the state to reimburse the complainants. In the judgment, he mentioned that officials of the Department of Wildlife and National Parks had auctioned all the goats in March or June 2010, but said that dogs had killed the horse. The judge found that the lack of documentation by the state was problematic. He said that he was satisfied that the Basarwa had proven their claim, and that all the goats had been illegally removed by the DWNP and later auctioned, with the proceeds deposited in the national treasury, adding that, "There was no order from a competent authority for such proceeds to be forfeited to the state." He ordered the government to compensate the applicants, valuing a goat at P800 (US$ 75) and a donkey at P1,500 (US$ 141). The state was further ordered to pay the legal costs of the suit.[3]

The "Hunting" Cases

With the restrictions on resource use and mobility, food security for many people in the reserve became a near-constant problem. A central aspect of this situation stemmed in part from restrictions on hunting, with arrests occurring despite the verdict of the *Sesana* case, which recognizes the rights of applicants to hunt. On May 5, 2012, for example, the government sent Special Support Group (SSG) (Botswana Police Service) officers to the community at Metseamonong to control what was seen as illegal hunting in the reserve. The SSG expended considerable energy in searching people and arresting them. By the end of the year, over twenty people, some of them minors, had been arrested in the CKGR and in the resettlement sites of New Xade and Kaudwane (Hitchcock, personal communication, 2017). According to the International Work Group for Indigenous Affairs, there were allegations of "mistreatment, torture and brutalization of people who were suspected of having illegal wildlife products. Some of these individuals were later brought for trial and had to pay substantial fines" (Gakelebone and Hitchcock 2013). In October 2012, I met some of the people who had been arrested. One of them, the headman or *ayaco*,[4] stressed that the way they were treated by the government was painful, that they were criminalized, arrested like thieves because they wanted to eat. He was particularly upset and claimed that the president himself sent the SSG to the area after flying over the reserve and, by chance, seeing them hunting.

If anything, the situation became worse after hunting was banned across the country in 2014. The inhabitants of the CKGR were again in a situation of legal liminality, not knowing what their "illegal" subsistence activities would lead to. Questions were raised at the Ghanzi District level, in parliament, and in international meetings regarding what the universal hunting ban implied for the people for whom hunting was a main source of subsistence and a source of their identity. A few contradictory explanations eventually emerged in statements by government officials. When I spoke with a high government official in the DWNP in Gaborone in 2012, a year or so before the hunting ban was promulgated, his position was that "everything that Khama says is law," meaning that the hunting ban was about to take place (essentially by decree), but that the "people of the CKGR are an exception. They do not need a permit, we have the applicant list and we know who can hunt and who cannot." This was an interesting explanation concerning why Special Game Licenses were not given out, but this was not in fact the way things turned out: people were arrested for hunting, even if they were among the applicants in the *Sesana* case. Again, the San were faced with a sense of living in uncertainty, with government officials saying one thing, while enforcement agents like game officials and police acted on what appeared to be quite different directives. The state continued to be something inscrutable, unpredictable, and dangerous.

Despite the announcement of the hunting ban, the CKGR inhabitants (as well as the people in the resettlement villages) persisted in their practice of hunting, with the state using the justice system to enforce the ban under its poaching laws and the reserve residents having recourse to the court to defend their right to legally hunt. Some of these cases resulted from hunting arrests, while the case-in-progress that I will now introduce was a positive assertion of hunting rights.

In August 2014, five residents who were applicants in the *Sesana* case and the *Mosetlhanyane* case filed a motion of intention to sue – officially

Nare Gaoberekwe, Mosetlhanyane Matsipane, Amogelang Segootsane, and Mogoba Tshiamiso v. the Attorney General and Minister of Environment and Tourism – over their hunting rights, particularly requesting "that the director of the Department of Wildlife and National Parks be instructed to make all arrangements necessary to enable the claimants to apply for Special Game Licenses or hunting permits and to determine those applications on their merits."[5] The first applicant, Nare Gaoberekwe, an eighty-two-year-old man from Metseamonong, was accused of poaching in the reserve some years earlier, even though he was an applicant in the *Sesana* case and one of the few people who never left the reserve during the relocations. The application challenged the 2014 hunting ban and its lawfulness (*Gaoberekwe* 2014: 3), adding, "We have always depended on hunting [and] gathering [... as] an important part our culture" (*Gaoberekwe* 2014: 5, 6). With the San litigants lacking the funds to follow up on this claim, the case has languished as a motion of intent to sue, without actually being heard. Their claim was essentially that the hunting ban conferred arbitrary powers on the Minister of Environment, Wildlife and Tourism. They also claimed that "the ban violated the Constitution of Botswana by excluding those who hunt on private game farms from the ban" (Babchuk and Hitchcock 2014). The logic of this lawsuit followed directly from the earlier case that (in a limited way) secured water rights: "in order to exercise our right to reside in the CKGR under the Sesana ruling ... we need not only access to water but the ability to feed ourselves" (*Gaoberekwe* 2014: 4).

An incident in May 2016 brought the repression of subsistence hunting in the CKGR further into the spotlight: a poorly trained antipoaching police unit crashed their helicopter in the CKGR, thereby bringing media attention to the extent of their activities, which, at least according to initial reports, ostensibly involved shooting at San hunters from the air. I first heard about the event immediately after it occurred from phone conversations with people in the Ghanzi District. The following day the crash was reported in Botswana's newspapers, emphasizing the routine nature of the antipoaching mission and the fact that six game officers had been injured, but making no mention of any San hunters. This was quickly followed by a story released by Survival International, which emphasized accusations by the reserve residents that the antipoaching unit had been firing on San hunters at the time of the crash, and that nine Bushmen had then been arrested and stripped naked and beaten while they were in custody. The SI article condemned the militarization of conservation efforts, which had resulted in "a situation in which Bushmen are accused of 'poaching' because they hunt to feed their families and face arrest and beatings, torture and death while big game trophy hunters are encouraged" (Survival International 2016).

This story was quickly picked up by the Botswana press, with the addition of denials from government officials. Police Senior Superintendent Dipheko Motube was quoted in the *Sunday Standard* as saying that the antipoaching activity was routine and that the arrest of the poachers in the area of the crash was "just a coincidence" (Ontebetse 2016b). Again, Survival International and the Botswana government were pitted against one another in a media flare-up, with SI highlighting the rights to hunt and the violent oppression of the San, and the government engaged in denial. The controversy gained intensity as the press contacted Gakelebone, who confirmed the story put out by SI, reporting that as councilor of New Xade, he had met with the men in custody and confirmed their story of mistreatment and being shot at from the helicopter. Despite the claims and counter-claims of SI and the government, this incident has been relegated to an uncertain status, with neither the government's story nor that of the San (and certainly not both together) producing a coherent narrative based on recognized or unequivocal facts.

In a separate, more "factual" incident that occurred around the same time, Roy Sesana's son, Tshoganetso, was arrested along with two others on charges of hunting in a protected area. This incident added impetus to the lawsuit filed in the Botswana courts to confirm the hunting rights of the San and the illegality of the antipoaching policy, which had been applied indiscriminately to them. Media coverage added energy and commitment to the lawsuit, which had been lagging for want of support, though at the time of writing no court action following from the original motion has yet materialized. The series of lawsuits following upon the 2006 *Sesana* case thus continued with this newest lawsuit looming on the horizon, further demonstrating the tendency toward litigation chains as an aftereffect of prominent cases.

TAKING INSPIRATION

The 2006 *Sesana* verdict had effects far beyond its instigation of a chain of litigation that centered on its unfulfilled obligations and unresolved conflicts. It also acted as a source of inspiration for other cases based on injustices occurring outside the CKGR, and in some cases outside

Botswana. It encouraged other cases, not only out of necessity but also out of inspiration.

The influence of court decisions is often considered in terms of the legal standards they establish. The *Mabo v. Queensland* case in Australia, for example, stands as a prominent point of reference for indigenous rights in many parts of the world through its repudiation of the concept of *terra nullius* (the idea that the law of colonial powers could be used to take possession of territories where there were already people present) and its affirmation of those people's native title to the territories they occupied. By providing guidance to other courts on difficult questions of law, some pivotal decisions carry influence far beyond the immediate issues that they are called upon to address.

There is another sense in which some cases are influential, which has more to do with their capacity to serve as reference points of inspiration to networks of activists. They sometimes give people the sense that they can challenge a condition of oppression that has been naturalized. In the Ranyane case (officially *Ditlhame Mmakgomo and 12 others v. the Ghanzi Land Board, the Ghanzi District Council, and the Ghanzi District Commissioner*), to which I now turn, many people in the Ghanzi District with whom I spoke felt that their case was similar to that of the people of the Central Kalahari. The Central Kalahari cases gave them hope – and the model – that they could use to stop their displacement, the awareness that they were in possession of rights that could be recognized in court. In a way, this insight activated their rights. Claimants who may be reluctant to file suit against the state may see inspiration in actions successfully taken elsewhere. Advocacy organizations can use "successful" cases to explain to their clients what can be achieved by taking the risky step of going to court against their government or a powerful corporation. It is this dimension of a court's influence that I want to briefly explore here with reference to two cases, the 2011 Ranyane case in Botswana and the ongoing Etosha case in Namibia, both of which, in different ways, took direct inspiration from the litigation undertaken by the people of the CKGR.

The Ranyane Case, Ghanzi, Botswana, 2010–16

Ranyane is a small village west of Kule-Ncojane in the southern part of Ghanzi District in western Botswana, the residents of which were mostly Naro San along with a few Ngologa Bakgalagadi and Herero (see Figure 3, p. xix). Ranyane is also located in a Wildlife Management Area (WMA) and in a corridor between two of Botswana's major protected areas: the Kgalagadi Transfrontier Park and the CKGR. Since 2010 the Ghanzi District Council had repeatedly told the people of Ranyane that they must move because the area is in a wildlife corridor and is not a government-recognized settlement. NGOs such as First People of the Kalahari, the Botswana Khwedom Council, and Ditshwanelo monitored what was happening. Several people in the Ghanzi area noted independently of one another that at least one aim of this removal was to enable the Ghanzi Land Board to grant rights over the area to a rancher (author notes 2012–5).

Eventually, at the end of 2011, the Ghanzi District Council sent in a team, which proceeded to dismantle the borehole equipment, leaving the people and livestock of the area without water. (The borehole engine was eventually brought back by the residents themselves, who then had to provide diesel and maintenance at their own expense.) Several families moved to other areas due to the lack of water. A letter was sent by the residents of Ranyane to the Ghanzi Land Board and the Department of Wildlife and National Parks, protesting the stoppage of the water. They did not receive a formal reply.

As a result of the government pressure to relocate, thirteen residents of Ranyane sought legal assistance and filed a motion against the Ghanzi District Council, the Ghanzi Land Board, and the Ghanzi District Commissioner to stop the relocation. As a result of this motion, the relocation of the people remaining in the village was stopped with a temporary injunction by Justice Moroka in the High Court, in May 2013 (*Mmakgomo* 2013a). In filing these cases, the people of Ranyane, and the NGOs working with them, were clearly inspired by the *Sesana* case. Some of those who participated in researching the background to the Ranyane removals also had experience in *Sesana v. the Attorney General*, including Robert Hitchcock (who provided a deposition) and Gordon Bennett, who was initially among the lawyers who took charge of preparing the Ranyane case.

In the days following the verdict, government officials held a *kgotla* meeting over several days trying to convince the residents to relocate and stopping them from accessing the village's water pipe. Then the District Council sent more than twenty vehicles to Ranyane to forcibly relocate everyone who was not among the thirteen applicants named in the order. Again, the government used a list of applicants to deny the same rights granted in court to the relatives and other Ranyane inhabitants who were not part of the case. But according to Ditshwanelo's fact-finding mission, the Ranyane residents had taken courage from the verdict and "refused to be relocated because they know about the interdict prohibiting their relocation."[6]

Like *Sesana v. the Attorney General*, the Ranyane case became the subject of debate in the United Nations. In the 2013 session of the Permanent Forum on Indigenous Issues, a state delegate from the Ministry of Local Government and Rural Development, Halakanfwa Mbulai, read a statement to the UNPFII that emphasized the government's new Botswana Land Policy and the RAD settlements scheme, singling out Ranyane as a village that "has already benefited from the rationalization exercise" of land use with the aim of balancing between "conservation and human requirements." Mbulai stressed the "intensive consultations" with the residents, in which the latter "indicated a desire to relocate elsewhere," and that "there are other families at Ranyane who have indicated the desire to remain. The government of Botswana has no plans to remove those who wish to remain and continue to stay in Ranyane." The San in the room answered the government's statement by underscoring the fact that "numerous San have been dispossessed" as a result of the new land policy and that some people of Ranyane had been relocated and others threatened with relocation (author notes 2013).

Back in Botswana, the Ranyane residents' lawyers sent a letter to the Ghanzi District Council to stop a series of new relocations that were taking place in spite of the High Court ruling. On June 18, 2013, the High Court ruled with another order in favor of the Ranyane people, stating that government personnel could not enter people's compounds without their consent, could not remove the borehole's engine (which had been reinstalled by the residents after the local government dismantled it) and could not remove the applicants from their homes without previously informing their lawyer (*Mmakgomo* 2013c). This is the point at which Gordon Bennett, in talking with his clients, was accused of inciting political mobilization and was expelled from the country (see Chapter 7, p. 259). This ruling, however, did not stop the Ghanzi District Council in its plans to follow through on the removal. The delivery of destitute food was suspended, as were the payments for labor-based drought relief projects, *ipelepeng*, which had employed as many as 40 people in the village who at one point were each making approximately US $47 (P400.00) per month. A report titled *Ranyane Relocation Phase 2* was written behind the scenes by the Ghanzi District Council (Ghanzi District Council 2012).[7] When this was discovered, the people of Ranyane along with their lawyers filed suit in the High

Court in Gaborone, with their case, *Heebe Karakubis and 114 Other Applicants v. Ghanzi District Council*, intended to stop the relocation and restore services (water, pensions, mobile clinics, etc.).

The final decision of the High Court on the Ranyane cases was a dismissal of the applicants' claims, issued by a High Court Judge on November 21, 2015 (*Karakubis* 2015), by which time most of the people of the village had already been relocated. This dismissal was announced in a judgment that called Ranyane an "unrecognized settlement" in a Wildlife Management Area and maintained that the services that had been provided there were "only temporary," overlooking the fact that the borehole had existed on a trek route between Nojane and the main Ghanzi–Lobatse road for decades and that the Ghanzi District Council had provided food, water, and diesel for the borehole to Ranyane at least since the 1970s. The judgment essentially reaffirmed the position of the Ghanzi District Council and the central government that the people had no right to stay at Ranyane. It questioned their depositions, raised issues about their birthplaces and backgrounds, and said that they did not have rights to services such as water.

The government and the Ghanzi District Council moved the people of Ranyane in spite of legal cases brought against them by the villagers. Some residents of Ranyane decided to appeal the decision in February 2016 (Baaitse 2016), but as of the beginning of 2017 no response had been forthcoming from the Court of Appeal.

This judgment is an illustration of what happens when litigation fails in the courts. It signaled an abrupt end to the legal battle against removal and dispossession. Losing the case after all possibilities of appeal had been exhausted meant subjection to the authority of the state, unless of course the financial means could be found to file another claim that addresses the same cause under different circumstances. Again, capture in a cycle of court cases is a consequence of victory, and litigation chains are a luxury of the few.

The Ranyane case also illustrates the importance of time, and the oppressive effects of delay, in court processes. The case was filed to prevent a relocation that had already been set in motion. As in the *Sesana* case, judgment was delayed, much to the disappointment of the applicants and their support community. Without an effective emergency injunction, the "politics of time" (see Kirsch 2014b) played in the government's favor. The government was able to legally continue the removals and delay the case until they were more or less accomplished, a fait accompli. The hegemony of the court process, its congruence with the goals of the state, can sometimes be found as much in what it does not do as in the verdicts that rule on issues more conclusively.

The Etosha Case (Namibia)

The influence of the San's justice campaign in the CKGR can also be seen outside the country, in a case with somewhat similar contours, involving evictions from a game reserve, and oriented toward a group of San applicants, breaking new ground with the submission of a class action lawsuit. The Hai//om people were evicted from the Etosha National Park roughly sixty years ago, in 1954. The claim asks the Namibian High Court to find the government of Namibia and a variety of other parties with interests in the Etosha National Park in breach of their obligations to compensate the Hai//om for the dispossession of their traditional territories (*Tsumib* 2015, 2016).

The arguments made in the founding affidavits of the Etosha case (*Jan Tsumib and 8 Others v. the Government of the Republic of Namibia and 19 Others*) would be immediately familiar to anyone who worked on the rights of the San in Botswana. The Hai//om argued for their rights to traditional territory and their rights to share in the activities and benefits of the park from which they had been removed, while the government denied the claims of communal ownership while asserting a state-centric view of the need for undifferentiated rights and the need to widely share the national benefits of the park.

One of the key supporters of the Etosha case was James Anaya, the Special Rapporteur on the Rights of Indigenous Peoples, who had visited Botswana and Namibia in 2012. In an expert affidavit in favor of the Hai//om filed in 2016, he presented an argument outlining their distinct rights, including the facts that they share basic features with other indigenous peoples worldwide, such as cultural distinctiveness, non-dominance relative to the majority, and attachment to ancestral land.

Another supporter of the Hai//om, who can be seen as a direct carrier of the "travelling model" of the CKGR case, was Robert Hitchcock, who had been directly involved in the *Sesana* case as well as in the Ranyane case as one of the applicants' advisors and witnesses. Other anthropologists have also been involved, including Thomas Widlok and Ute Dieckmann, both working at the University of Cologne, and each with long experience in Namibia and with the Legal Assistance Centre of Namibia based in Windhoek. Preparing a "class action" based on the Hai//om as a collective identity was difficult for the anthropologists engaged in the case, in that it entailed risking a personal association with and responsibility for the processes of "invented traditions" and "identity classifications" that they often study and deconstruct. Coming up with a collective legal case meant engaging in the legal construction or creation of the people who had to be represented as claimants. Dieckmann set about this challenging task by presenting a point-by-point refutation of the Namibian Prime Minister's misuse of her work, responding with an ethnographically rich description of Hai//om approaches to the interconnections between property and the networks of social relations that the Hai//om value as essential to their way of life, and have in common with other indigenous groups.

It is significant to note that the suit was filed some twenty-five years after Namibia's independence from South Africa in 1990, and that in the interim, the Hai//om developed the very sorts of connections to NGOs and UN institutions that we saw developing among the San of the CKGR. Members of the team that prepared the case at the Legal Assistance Centre told me that the *Sesana* case, known widely in the circles of southern African indigenous activists, was a significant point of reference for them and the Hai//om in the decision-making and preparations involved in filing their case.

It was more than the idea of legal activism and a lawsuit that travelled from the CKGR to the Etosha case, but also the complexities of representing a group of people like the San in a state structure of adversarial litigation. In preparing the Etosha case, one of the difficulties encountered was that of including the Hai//om claimants in a class action suit in a way that would avoid the vexations and exclusions of the applicant list as was used in the CKGR case. The difficulties follow, in part from the tendencies toward what Kesselring (2016: 76) refers to as "individuation" in class action lawsuits, the tendency for the law to use individual cases of guilt or victimhood to single out actions and identify the collective harm that had been suffered. While it may yet be possible to avoid the kind of arbitrary exclusions that followed from the applicant list in the *Sesana* case, it is all but a foregone conclusion, following Kesselring's analysis, that the litigation process will define the collective experience behind claims of injustice with reference to the templates provided by single instances.

A decision in this case is still pending. The trial and the outcomes of this class action litigation have yet to occur.

A PARALLEL STRATEGY: BRINGING THE VERDICT TO THE UN

In the 12th session of the Permanent Forum on Indigenous Issues (PFII) in 2013 held at the UN Headquarters in New York, Job Morris, founder of SYN, took the floor, under the "Agenda Item 7: human rights" in a conference room filled with some 500 indigenous representatives, state and NGOs delegates, and UN officials. Reading from a carefully prepared statement, he outlined the main human rights-related grievances of the peoples of the Central Kalahari:

> Botswana has not implemented the recommendations of the Special Rapporteur on the rights of indigenous peoples of 2010, nor has it honored the Botswana High Court decisions on the Central Kalahari case of 2006 … We would like to have access to clinics and drugs in the places where our communities live such as the Central Kalahari Game Reserve, D'Kar, Qabo and others. The government should work to ensure the effective and direct participation in the negotiations regarding the Central Kalahari peoples. (Author notes 2013)

This "intervention" in the Permanent Forum was one of the several follow-ups to the verdicts in the CKGR cases, intended to pressure the Botswana government to change its policies and practices.

Morris was building on a legacy of indigenous activism in the UN, in which San delegates had already been active for several decades. From the 1990s up to 2015, the San of southern Africa brought the CKGR case to the attention of the international public more than any other cause or claim that they brought to the UN (Chapter 5). The meetings in which they participated constituted a distinct space for activism, with its own language of protest and cultural romance, its own rules of diplomacy and etiquette, its own structures of inclusion and exclusion. Here judgment did not take the form of a binding verdict in a court ruling, but was more diffuse and indirect, reaching out to the people present in the room, inserting information into discursive spaces of diplomacy, appealing to the general public, and in doing all these things, engaging in the "politics of shame" as a way to influence the policies and actions of the state. The verdict was used as a technology of truth-making.

The 2006 *Sesana* case had a tangible influence on the strategy in the UN, with the verdict becoming a consistent point of reference in San interventions. The case offered a "handle" with which to focus discussion of state injustices toward indigenous peoples. It became popular, like a meme or a sound bite, almost commodity-like, in the way it was picked up by indigenous representatives, particularly among the southern African delegations. In 2007 a statement made by WIMSA referred to the CKGR court case verdict as "a hollow victory." In the same meeting FPK submitted a collective statement addressing the Permanent Forum by calling on the government of Botswana to "allow the San people to return to their homeland free from harassment and with full access to water and health care." The CKGR case was also mentioned almost every year in the Permanent Forum as well as other meetings in the UN system.

This social justice lobbying in international institutions went outside the UN system as well. In November 2010, a San delegate from Metseamonong (CKGR), Smith Moeti (a relative of some of the people arrested and accused of poaching), spoke at the African Commission on Human and Peoples' Rights 48th Ordinary Session (November 10–24, 2010). He described the complex situations facing the people in the Central Kalahari, their lack of access to water and the fact that they had not been given hunting licenses to legally sustain themselves. He reported that some of his relatives living in the reserve had told him, "We have been abandoned. Thirst and hunger are hunting us, and even our health is under threat." Moeti's grandmother, Xoroxloo [Qoroxloo] Duxee, had died of thirst in the CKGR in 2005.[8]

Lobbying also took place online. Facebook networking was a significant part of the San's participation in the 2015 Climate Change Conference, COP 21, in Paris, where the Central Kalahari was a theme in the efforts by the San delegates to again bring the San's issues to the attention of the general public. This effort was given additional impetus from an article that had just appeared in the British newspaper *The Guardian* (Barbee 2015), which revealed that Botswana had sold fracking rights in the CKGR to a private company. This connection between resource extraction and removal was reflected in a statement made by a young San activist and Botswana-based NGO delegate on Facebook:

> Currently the world has gathered in Paris for COP21 to talk about bio-diversity, sustainable development and clean energy ... Meanwhile, Botswana is busy selling fracking rights to companies that will damage the entire park. Diamonds and fracking in a national park ... and here I thought that the San were relocated from the park to preserve and maintain the natural resources. (Author notes 2015)

This is one example among many of the way that the priorities of San delegates to UN meetings have an independent presence online, with various sources of information and opinion feeding inspiration to one another as the meetings unfold.

In the course of these more recent lobby efforts, a different tone seemed to have emerged, inspired largely by the CKGR case and its aftermath. The indigenous delegations appeared to have found a weak spot in the government's self-representation in international forums: in response to the San's claims of indigenous rights focused on distinct rights, the government had always been able to deflect the argumentation into its sustained efforts to promote equality; but after the 2006 *Sesana* decision, with reference to the CKGR and the desperate conditions of the residents there, Botswana was being accused of human rights violations *based on a refusal to abide by the decisions of its own courts*. This was different. The impact of the argument put out by the San delegates was more difficult to escape. After hearing the San present their case to the UNPFII, a UN official remarked to me that he had always thought of Botswana as "a tolerant and democratic country. The situation of its indigenous peoples is a surprise indeed" (author notes 2009). As an indictment of Botswana's human rights record, the story was persuasive.

The recommendations made by San delegates in the Permanent Forum meetings had never reached the final report of the session, at least not until 2013. In that year Morris's statement was picked up in the final report under the item "human rights," where the report addressed the need for African states to implement court decisions regarding indigenous peoples' rights, particularly recalling the Endorois case in the African Commission of Human and Peoples' Rights, the Ogiek case in the African Court, and the "decision of the High Court of Botswana in the case concerning the Kalahari Game Reserve."[9] These few words in a list of ignored court decisions were, in terms of international law and global governance, the formal culmination of the San's years of efforts to bring their human rights grievances to the attention of the world community.

The Permanent Forum on Indigenous Issues' 15th annual session in 2016 brought the situation of the San to the fore in a way that indicates some of the cumulative effects of the San's campaign as an indigenous people. One prominent indication of the effects of the campaign was the fact that the government of Botswana came to the meeting with more state delegates than ever before, with the Minister of Local Government, Slumber Tsogwane, leading a delegation of six other members. It was the first time in Forum history that a minister from Botswana took the floor and also the first time that the government directly and voluntarily addressed the situation of the people in the CKGR. In Tsogwane's statement, which emphasized the government's steps toward implementing the *UN Declaration on the Rights of Indigenous Peoples*, there was a familiar reiteration of the position against the concept of indigenous peoples, to the effect that "all tribes and ethnic groups in Botswana are indigenous to the country, but being mindful of the fact that there are other sections of our population, especially Remote Area Communities, that are generally socially and economically marginalized and still deserve special attention" (author notes 2016). He did add, however, that the government had considered and approved the use of mother tongue language and early childhood development through the Presidential Commission of Education, an apparent breakthrough in the recognition of cultural rights, against the policies and practices of assimilation. Regarding the Central Kalahari situation, he stressed that,

> In consultation with communities living in the Central Kalahari Game Reserve, the government has established a consultative structure, for remote area communities to preserve their interest. This process has proved to be fruitful and government has acceded to the needs of the communities by providing water to the Central Kgalagadi Game Reserve (CKGR) human settlements. (Slumber Tsogwane, statement at the UNPFII 2016)

There was nothing new in this government statement. The one difference was that this time around a "consultative structure" was in place, with Roy Sesana as chair; and one seemingly small but significant truth had been spoken: water had in fact been delivered to the villages in the reserve, though without any policy in place to make it anything more than a gesture.

The minister also seemed to indirectly respond to the criticism of the country's now-challenged CBNRM policy and its threats to community economic wellbeing. He stated that, "Remote Area Communities living in the periphery of wildlife management areas and natural monuments are given the opportunity to form community trusts to benefit from the natural and cultural resources through the Community Based Natural Resource Management Programme" (Tsogwane 2016). Progressive as the minister's intervention may have sounded, the education and CBNRM policies he touted simply did not exist, at least not in the forms or with the effects that were key to the persuasive qualities of his speech.

The minister's intervention, despite the untruths apparent to anyone knowledgeable on the issues, was greeted with scattered applause. It was the first time that I could remember seeing indigenous delegates clapping for a Botswana government statement. This was one of those moments when it was crucial for a delegate from civil society to immediately take the floor and call attention to a state's falsehoods.

Speaking on behalf of the "Khwedom Council and the Indigenous San people of Botswana," Keikabile Mogodu was called by the chair to take the floor few minutes after the Botswana statement. He stated that, "in all the reports that Botswana has made and will continue to present, she [Botswana] talks about Remote Area Communities. She fails to recognize the San people of Botswana as indigenous, but chooses to refer to us as Remote Area Dwellers or Basarwa." He went on to rebut the government's claims regarding education, reporting that the government "continues to teach the language of the dominant tribe," a practice that is leading to the "extinction of San languages" (author notes 2016).

In making its statement, the government of Botswana seemed to be motivated by a sense that it had prepared the ground for exposing its treatment of the San to public view. In international diplomacy, this is what progress looks like, how it is measured.

INDIGENOUS RIGHTS UNDER REVIEW

One way that Botswana responded to the negative publicity on the CKGR was to reverse an earlier decision and invite James Anaya, the Special Rapporteur on indigenous peoples' rights, to visit the country. This was in response to the mounting pressure put on the government by indigenous NGOs, regional coalitions of NGOs, and transnational organizations and lobby groups.[10] To maintain its reputation as a responsible member of the global community, Botswana had to be seen to respond fairly and openly to its critics. Between March 19 and 27, 2009, Anaya visited Botswana, where he met with government officials in Gaborone and undertook a field visit to several villages in the reserve, the relocation settlements, and RAD villages.[11] He consulted with local authorities, indigenous leaders, and community members.

In his report on this visit, Anaya noted the challenges facing the indigenous peoples of Botswana, including poverty, lack of secure access to land tenure, and lack of a voice in decision-making regarding policy.

Referring specifically to the people living in the CKGR, Anaya stated, "Those people currently in the reserve are struggling due to lack of water and social services and have asked to receive services at their communities within the reserve; even just the provision of water would significantly improve their current living conditions" (Anaya 2010: 30). In the typical understated language of UN reporting, he observed that the denial of services to the San and Bakgalagadi in the CKGR "does not appear to be in keeping with the spirit and underlying logic of the (High Court) decision, nor with the relevant international human rights standards" (Anaya 2010: 30).[12]

Botswana's reply to the Anaya report reiterated its standard position in response to negative publicity on the CKGR, to the effect that "all Batswana are indigenous to Botswana." The government maintained that it was addressing all of the concerns raised by Anaya, including providing assistance to Botswana citizens who were disadvantaged and marginalized. Finally, the government claimed that a wide-ranging negotiation process had been established on the CKGR issue and that all stakeholders were involved in the discussions. Since then, San delegates to UN meetings have periodically met with the special rapporteurs in private meetings, in which the rapporteurs would ask questions on the status of the San in the country and particularly on the people of the CKGR.

Not only indigenous delegates but also other state representatives, UN independent experts, the African Commission on Human and Peoples' Rights, and global opinion leaders like Bishop Desmond Tutu have at various times criticized Botswana's behavior toward the San and the people of the CKGR in particular. In the UN's human rights system, Botswana was questioned by a variety of committees about what was happening regarding minorities and indigenous peoples, particularly in the CKGR.

In the latter part of 2008, for example, the situation in Botswana was reviewed by the Human Rights Committee in Geneva as part of the 3rd session of the UN Working Group on the Universal Periodic Review (UPR) (December 1–15, 2008). The UPR, introduced to the UN in a reform of human rights processes in 2008, is a periodically held supervisory review of a state's human rights situation, based largely upon "peer reviews" by other states, in which participants are encouraged to be constructively critical and to share best practices. It is based on three distinct reports: a national report written by the State under Review (SuR); a compilation of extracts from reports of UN agencies, treaty bodies and special procedures; and a stakeholders summary, based on submissions from NGOs. Since the NGOs involved in this process must to have a considerable degree of knowledge of the UN system and of human rights, it usually falls on the most experienced organizations to take on this role, leaving out the kind of civil society organizations that are lacking in resources and expertise. To participate in the UPR process, therefore, indigenous peoples from Botswana have to count on the intervention of international NGOs such as Minority Rights Group, or some established national human rights NGOs such as Ditshwanelo and Reteng.

Here too, reference to the court ruling was a significant part of the pressure brought to bear on the government of Botswana to reform its policies and practices toward the San. Legal decision-making in one forum (the court) was a source of leverage in a very different legal venue (the UPR). The key to the justice campaign, in other words, was the imbrication of its various strategies, such that they reinforced one another. Without the *Sesana* verdict, the government's policies in the CKGR would have been more easily framed as "development" and attracted little notice in the UN.

In the compilation of UN information prepared by the Office of the High Commissioner for Human Rights (OHCHR) as part of the review in 2008,[13] the Committee on the Elimination of Racial Discrimination (CERD) noted in particular Botswana's "reluctance to recognize the existence of indigenous peoples on its territory" and urged "the State to respect and protect the existence and cultural identity of all ethnic groups within its territory and to review its policy regarding indigenous peoples."[14] The document specifically refers to the issue of the CKGR under the item "minorities and indigenous peoples":

> The State [of Botswana] should pay particular attention to the close cultural ties that bind the San/Basarwa to their ancestral land; protect the economic activities of the San/Basarwa that are an essential element of their culture, such as hunting and gathering practices, whether conducted by traditional or modern means; study all possible alternatives to relocation; and seek the prior free and informed consent of the persons and groups concerned ... The Special Rapporteurs informed the government that despite this court ruling, they continued to receive numerous communications indicating that the court's decision was not being fully implemented by the authorities.[15]

Botswana's reply,[16] included in the Report of the Working Group[17] at the 10th session of the HRC, stated simply that it was complying fully with the 2006 court judgment and that it was engaged in a negotiation with the people of the CKGR and the NGOs working with them.[18]

NGOs also had their say. In the summary of stakeholders' information[19] prepared by the OHCHR as part of this review, a report by the Botswana-based NGO Reteng: The Multicultural Coalition of Botswana finds that "the Basarwa of the Central Kalahari Game Reserve are struggling for the implementation of the December 2006 ruling to return to their ancestral land. They need water, food, school medical facilities and roads in the CKGR."[20] It is noteworthy that Reteng places emphasis on the incompleteness of the services provided, in other words, questioning the state's human rights record on its own terms by demonstrating the neglect of services that followed its refusal to implement the CKGR ruling (even though services are not strictly an obligation arising from the verdict), thereby avoiding any engagement with claims of distinct rights.

Botswana did not accept the recommendations made by several states and NGOs to ensure that indigenous peoples' rights were recognized and in particular to guarantee the rights of the people in the reserve. Instead, the government argued that it "already has a clear and effective policy and land tenure system that addresses issues related to access to land for all Batswana, including residents of the reserve."[21] In its national report presented by the Minister for Defence, Justice, and Security, Dikgakgamatso Seretse, and submitted in 2008 to the UPR, Botswana mentions nothing about the CKGR case, the San, or even indigenous issues in general.[22] Noting this absence, several states, including Japan, Spain, Canada, Denmark, and the Vatican, raised questions about the CKGR situation and what was going to happen with its people.

The second cycle of the UPR of Botswana in 2013 (January 21–February 1) produced much the same result: the UPR process accomplished little in the way of directly shifting the government toward greater acceptance of indigenous rights. In its report,[23] Botswana presented the implementation of the first cycle recommendations, including the issues relating to indigenous peoples, by pointing out that the Special Rapporteur had visited the country in April 2009,[24] as though this fact alone constituted a form of human rights compliance that obviated the need to address the human rights violations that the Special Rapporteur encountered. The government engaged in the *violence of repetition*. As one of the key national priorities for Botswana's human rights implementation, the San were mentioned along the following lines: the government of Botswana has "adopted affirmative action strategies for the benefit of the marginalised groups i.e. Basarwa and remote area dwellers, affording them preference in schools, vocational institutions and employment."[25]

No mention was made of the CKGR. What had seemed to be progress toward justice turned out once more to have been like movement on a treadmill.

In the stakeholders' information,[26] provided to raise questions and monitor Botswana's position, only the Society for Threatened Peoples (STP), an international NGO based in Germany, mentioned the CKGR issues, particularly its observation that, "though the San were allowed to hunt inside the CKGR, they were regularly refused a hunting permit by the Government."[27] The resulting report of the Working Group on the Universal Periodic Review[28] to the HRC referred several times to the CKGR cases and to the unmet promises of the government, including its failure in reporting (i.e., the case of CERD). The recommendations of the Special Rapporteur were also included in several parts of the document, particularly with respect to indigenous rights to justice, political representation, culture and education, and recognition of indigenous land tenure. In the same report, the USA "expressed concern at a narrow interpretation by the High Court, which prevented hundreds of San people from living and hunting on their ancestral lands,"[29] and recommended that Botswana "fully implement the 2006 High Court ruling and allow all San individuals who want to live on the Central Kalahari Game Reserve to do so."[30] Spain, the United Kingdom, Finland, Norway, Italy, and Mexico included similar recommendations.

Botswana was largely impervious to the recommendations made through the UPR process, in part because they are just that – remarks intended to guide the state under review toward more consistent compliance with its human rights obligations. More than this, however, Botswana was able to deflect much of the criticism of its human rights record regarding the San by repeatedly invoking its efforts to implement *equal* rights. In these terms, removal was represented as opportunity, assimilation as education, and prohibition of subsistence activities as protection of a valuable resource for the benefit of all citizens.

This is not to say that activism in international forums has no effect. Most states are, in fact, very protective of their reputations in the international scene. This is reflected in the diplomatic language and courtesies that are insisted upon in the day-to-day interactions that permeate global organizations. Confrontation is avoided by the structure and organization of discourse. In the UPR, states are the vehicles by which the human rights records of other states are assessed, but usually in diplomatic language, avoiding a confrontational approach to human rights violations that might cause offense.

When we track a document like the 2006 *Sesana* verdict, however, it becomes apparent that, through the international legitimacy of the rule of law, it actually sharpened the contours of politics, no matter how diplomatically it might have been presented. The Botswana government's challenge to the rule of law through its ongoing repression of the residents of the reserve set off alarm bells for the UPR reviewers, which drew further attention to the discredited policy of forced removal and assimilation of the residents of the reserve. The campaign of exposure and embarrassment in the UN ratcheted up the political stakes of the removal policy internationally and at home. While the political stakes of the contest intensified, the life of the people of the reserve, with its daily struggles, continued unchanged, permeated by a sense of everyday injustice.

POLITICS BY POLITICAL MEANS

In a meeting organized at Columbia University, New York, during the yearly UNPFII session in 2016, several indigenous representatives spoke about issues of conflicts and how to bring peace to indigenous lands. A common concern expressed by several indigenous activists from the South concerned what to do when going to court, an "expensive, uncertain and lengthy process" that does not resolve their problems, because even when the court rules in their favor, there is commonly a lack of implementation. A Forum member from Bangladesh, reporting on his people's experience, suggested that the importance of pursuing a multifaceted strategy of resistance was key to political advocacy, engaging not just in litigation but also in government politics with the aim of achieving parliamentary representation. Jumanda Gakelebone, still an outspoken figure in the San movement, was present in the room. He had recently entered national politics, having been elected councilor in one of the resettlement villages, New Xade, representing the opposition party, the Umbrella for Democratic Change (the union, established in 2013, of the Botswana Movement for Democracy, Botswana National Front, and Botswana People's Party). Gakelebone later commented on the remark by his colleague from Bangladesh with reference to his position as councilor: "When I saw that the law was not enough to help my people, and the government did not respect the verdict, the next thing that I thought I could do was enter politics, hoping to change the government" (author notes 2016). This insight became for him almost a mantra, a reference point for his new strategic convictions.

Writing in the mid-1990s, Holm, Molutsi, and Somolekae (1996) noted that Botswana's civil society was only beginning to become partisan. This was in part a result of political disincentives. When leaders of civil society organizations began to associate with political parties, civil servants representing the interests of the government had a tendency to reject their "mandate" to represent their members (Holm et al. 1996: 59). The ability of politicians and civil servants to dampen the political leverage of organizations, in turn, was related to the structure of the one-party dominant system. Group leaders at that time were fully aware that the Botswana Democratic Party (BDP) would win the next election. "In this context, to back the opposition angers the ruling party; to support the ruling party brings little gratitude since it is already insured of victory" (1996: 60).

Several scholars have analyzed the Botswana political system and the role that the BDP has had since independence in what is effectively a one-party system (see de Jager and Taylor 2015). The dominant party system that characterizes Botswana's procedural democracy brings the state into the service of the government. This produces significant "incumbency advantages" that in Botswana have given the BDP preferred access to media and state institutions. The dominant party system raises questions concerning the competiveness of the electoral system, and the absence of possibilities that other parties have to influence policy and challenge the dominant party in national politics (de Jager and Taylor 2015: 26).

This calculus might change, however, if the BDP, despite its advantages, significantly loses its share of the total vote. Since independence in 1966, the BDP has won the large majority of seats in parliament in ten general elections, with as much as 90 percent of the vote compared to 10 percent for opposition parties (Molomo and Molefe 2005; Good 2009: 44–65). In the 2014 general election, however, this support was for the first time reduced to a minority of the popular vote, a little more than 46 percent, corresponding with a movement toward the contraction of the BDP electoral base and support of the main opposition parties

(Poteete 2015: 3). The Botswana National Front (BNF) as well as other opposition parties such as the Botswana Congress Party (BCP), riding the wave of minority activism, have long argued that the resettlement of the San was a violation of human rights. For instance, in September 2006 the BCP presented a report titled "Position Paper on the Relocation of Communities: The Case of the Gana and the Gwi of the Central Kalahari Game Reserve (CKGR)," in which it encouraged the government to recognize the "Basarwa" as "indigenous peoples." As the BCP position paper noted: "The Basarwa should neither be treated as fauna and flora nor forcefully assimilated or integrated into mainstream Botswana" (BCP 2006: 16). Coming at the conclusion of the *Sesana* trial, this position paper reinforced the strategic appeal of party politics by strongly opposing the government's resettlement schemes and formally accepted the idea of the San being an indigenous people in Botswana. Under these circumstances, given viable multiparty conditions, the payoffs for partisan engagement increase. With its lock on power (even with a reduced majority), the government can still afford to ignore appeals for political reform. But the more the opposition parties gain influence, the more the government is incentivized to take critical groups seriously and be attentive to grievances that have a chance of gaining political traction. This situation, according to some San activists, leaves open a possibility for them to engage directly in electoral politics as a way to redress their people's grievances.

Indigenous activism among the residents of the CKGR and their supporters thus involves multiple strategies, subjecting them to constant assessment and switching between them as the occasion (and opportunity) demands. The courts, for all their value as a check on the abuse of government power, are never sufficient in themselves, and seemingly never completely autonomous, never quite able to bring enough pressure to bear on the government to make it comply in good faith with their verdicts. The trust of the people is one thing, but for those who think and act strategically, there is always room to shift tactics, to try something else.

The engagement of African indigenous representatives with political parties is not new, going back at least to the Tanzanian activist and parliamentarian Lazaro Moringe Parkipuny whose path-breaking work in the UN created space for indigenous peoples from Africa in the 1980s (Hodgson 2011). Indigenous peoples' activists historically engaged first in state politics through joining political parties, so the resistance was national wherever possible, particularly before the globalization of NGO advocacy and the global currency of human rights. It also has a long history in Botswana, both in the main government party, ruling since independence, and in the opposition parties. For instance, Roy Sesana's activism goes as far back as the 1970s, when he returned from working in the mines in South Africa and joined the opposition party BNF, under the tutelage of the late BNF leader Kenneth Koma, accompanying him on countrywide tours as he campaigned (Keoreng 2011). Sesana had an almost rock star status at BNF rallies that gave him the podium in 2011, when he was still basking in the glow of publicity that followed his namesake court case and the political contentions that followed (Keoreng, 2011). (Recall that the BNF leader Duma Boko has legally represented Sesana and the cause of the people of the CKGR in the 2006 case as well as in several subsequent cases.) In 2015, when I asked Sesana about his engagement in political parties he told me about his disillusionment with politics and expressed his sense that political parties take advantage of the San cause, trying to co-opt and manipulate their leaders to gain their constituencies' support. He added that "when lion cubs start to fight, they have no teeth but when they are adults, then they have teeth," by which I suppose he meant that when politicians come to power they are basically the same, only more dangerous than when they began their careers – they "have teeth," and he does not trust them (author notes 2015).

Gakelebone's election as councilor in October 2014 was united symbolically with his activist agenda when he attempted to wear "Kua [San] traditional dress" to his swearing-in at the Ghanzi District Council. He wanted to make a political statement regarding "indigenous peoples culture and dignity" (as he reported the event to me). He has found that his closer connection with state politics through his position as an elected member of the district council opens doors to more direct dialogue with higher officials: "Now as councillor I can speak and people listen, I can call for a meeting, I have legitimacy because I have been elected, [which] is not like when I was only an NGOs representative" (author notes 2015).

National politics are very powerful among the youth, with some of them engaging directly in political campaigning. There is prestige in being elected, and this can produce social and political leverage in one's own community – but also divisions, facilitating space for cooptation, corruption, and development of political elites that are distant from their constituencies. This is particularly the case when indigenous peoples are structurally disadvantaged and marginalized in an unsupportive and unfamiliar institutional context.[31]

"Ethnopolitics" has also become an organizational strategy, and this has come with the risk of producing factionalism. For the 2014 general election, the Khwedom Council invited the San as part of the organization's agenda to prepare for the 2014 and 2019 elections, to have more representatives involved in political and decision-making positions and to reach districts and parliament. This created heated discussions among the participants, who were supporters of different parties, including that of the ruling party in government. This raised concerns about how the Khwedom Council would select candidates to support, and in particular from which parties, without causing divisions or losing its representativity as an organization working for the all the San.[32]

This shift in the San leadership's political consciousness highlights one of the ways in which the government's intransigent implementation of policies of removal and assimilation is self-defeating. The more these policies are insisted upon, the more the San will feel a poignant sense of injustice, a sense of exclusion, a feeling of being treated as *balata* (recall, for example, the minister who said to a San delegation, "we will always own you"). And out of these passions of injustice, the more they will seek an answer in terms of identity attachments, which seek to overcome the impositions of the state and its projects of unwanted development and assimilation. Ethnogenesis was built into the ambitions of a government that insisted on its opposite in ethnocentric terms, through the absorption of the San, Bakgalagadi, and other indigenous and minority groups into a Tswana-centric state.

All the while that San activists were forming political strategies as part of the activist support of the CKGR residents and indigenous rights most broadly, the government was engaging in a countervailing strategy of co-optation, transforming activists into civil servants. The most prominent example of this has been Roy Sesana's employment on the residents committee, the committee that is meeting with government officials to negotiate the provision of services and development initiatives (mainly tourism) inside the reserve.

The move to hire Sesana harkens back to the political strategy of the expansionist proto-state, in which leaders of the Tswana *merafe* systematically brought their political opponents into ties of delegated leadership, rather than excluding, offending, and provoking them in the direction of greater antagonism. The flip side of inclusion in governance is a modicum of obedience. Several young educated activists have become civil servants working for a variety of ministries and local governments. A young activist from New Xade (whose family was relocated in the 1990s), with an MA degree and training in indigenous peoples' rights, landed a job with the Ministry of Foreign Affairs as soon as he finished his studies. After serving for some years in its office in Gaborone, he was reassigned to the Botswana embassy in London. He probably joined the government because of the good position, which was particularly attractive after many years of study and the difficulty of finding any other job. He also had the good intention of influencing politics from the "inside," a space that he thought the job could offer. However, other activists continue to see this as a government strategy "to shut his mouth" (which, in effect, it did in terms of his public statements). As Hale points out with reference to other such situations, "it would be a mistake to equate the increasing indigenous presence in the corridors of power with indigenous empowerment" (Hale 2004: 17). This can be seen in the regimes of discipline imposed on government employees. For instance, the Ghanzi Council sometimes sanctions employees who "misbehave" by engaging in politics. Recently (in January 2017), an employee originally from Metseamonong was called to a disciplinary hearing in response to his pointed inquiries into the provision of government services in the reserve.

Personal motives for Sesana's decision to become a civil servant are not difficult to find. When I spoke to him in the summer of 2015, he made it clear that he was experiencing economic difficulties, which were at this point particularly acute with the addition of a newborn to his family. But he stressed his unique position to contribute favorably to the negotiation process. He later on explained (in the FPK record files 2016) that, "I thought it was a way to resolve our problems … I wanted to show everybody that is not that we are difficult and we are refusing development, but because we want things to be done the way we want [them] to be done," and "I do not want to betray my people." He underlined to me how he was "hurt" by the feelings of his people who accused him of betraying them. He compared his decision to accept the job with his decision to go to court: "I want to bring evidence," he said, "I wanted to prove to all people that the government was wrong." And now with his new position he can "see things from the perspective of an insider;" he can talk with them and see what they are doing, and "bring evidence of that." If the government lies in the process he would return to protesting, "to say what is going on again," and if things do not change, "I do not give up, only death will stop me." His opinion has swung back and forth between feelings of hope and reconciliation with government officials and distrust of them, the latter particularly following his son's arrest for "poaching." When his son was arrested Sesana immediately broke the civil service prohibition on public criticism of the government by denouncing the arrest of his son to the press, resulting in the headline "Now Sesana fights government" in *The Monitor*, despite the risk that he would be dismissed from his position as a community facilitator (Pheage 2016c). Again on September, 10, 2017, a *Sunday Standard* article titled "Khama's CKGR Plan Unravels as Sesana Refuses to Play Ball," reported that Sesana had "stuck out his middle finger at an offer by government to be transported from the CKGR to Gantsi village to receive his salary" (Ontebeste 2017). Sesana had travelled from the CKGR to Gaborone to press officials in the Office of the President about the *Sesana* verdict, in particular the right of siblings and offspring of the applicants to return and live in the reserve and the need for the government to issue Special Game Licenses and revoke the hunting ban. When he was advised that, as a civil servant, he needed to tone down his voice and stop disparaging the government, Sesana is said to have told the officials in the Office of the President that he would say what he wanted and "that he did not approach the government seeking employment" (Ontebeste 2017). Despite his outburst, he remained in his position as a government employee.

From the perspective of the government, it is much less difficult to find reasons for bringing Sesana on board as an employee. His position in the government divided those who were opposing government policies and in particular reduced the leverage of Survival International, for whom Sesana had been the most active and effective spokesperson. With Sesana as an employee, the government had less concern about him and the damage he could do in his role as the media-friendly representative of the San engaging in activist politics. Through his employment, the government has tried to buy his silence, and perhaps even permanently destroy his popular standing as an outspoken activist. Seen from the perspective of the Tswana's long history of capture and co-optation, the government's recruitment of activists is an indication of the success of their efforts, or at least of the fact that they have made a strong impact. Co-optation in these circumstances is an outcome of having acquired a certain degree of influence, of being a political threat, more than a reflection of an activist's modernist or assimilationist ideals.

As might be expected, the move caused controversy and consternation in the close-knit circle of San activists, together with accusations of collusion and co-optation by some who were deeply skeptical of the government's motives in hiring Sesana. One of these critics surmised that the only rationale for the government's move was to cause confusion and factionalism among the communities in order to weaken them and advance its political goals. One of the two main national newspapers headlined these moves "Basarwa Reject Roy Sesana; Govt deal in the CKGR" (Ontebetse 2016a).

Others saw the negotiations, particularly with Sesana as a government employee, as a way to break a deadlock that had left the residents of the reserve without services for nearly a decade. Many people in the CKGR continued to respect and trust him. His acceptance of an employment contract with the government was part of a flexible strategy of resistance, which did not prevent him from being a spokesperson for his people and to denounce the government if things went wrong. With his deep knowledge of the territory and its people, Sesana was quite possibly exactly the right person for the job, able to bridge the divide between the government's goals for development in the CKGR and the interests of its residents. With Sesana's involvement (whether or not he can claim credit), the newest phase of negotiations with the government concerning services and development in the reserve began to bear fruit, with new regimes of water delivery and visits from mobile clinics. In February and March 2016, several government ministers visited the communities inside the Central Kalahari with a new message: they promised the people that the government would not only restore services, but also that the communities would henceforth be allowed to benefit directly from tourism.

At the time of writing, it is still not fully clear whether the government decision to start the provision of basic services like water, "destitute rations," and mobile clinics was a permanent commitment or a short-term effort to deflect criticism. Certainly, the provision of basic services was not accompanied by any form of acknowledgement of past harm or symbolic gesture of reconciliation. The absence of formal acknowledgement of a change in policy, in turn, brought out concerns that the promised development of tourist facilities would entail yet another relocation to a central village, together with the removal and prohibition of livestock. Just as the occasional kindness shown by guards at the gate did not change the basic sense of uncertainty caused by the general practice of "search and seizure," there was little celebration associated with these benefits, and little trust in the work of the committee. The services were accepted with a cautious wait-and-see attitude.

PRODUCING EFFECTS

In circumstances in which the government was reluctant to abide by the court's decisions, interpreting them narrowly and engaging in fruitless "negotiations," it became clear to the original litigants in the CKGR case that it would be impossible for them to maintain a viable way of life in the reserve without a simultaneous and contradictory subjection to criminal procedure and recourse to the courts in defense of their rights. In essence, the legal system became both a source of repression and a necessary instrument of subsistence, without which survival on one's own terms would be unfeasible.

The San's engagement in social justice activism can thus be seen as caught in a "litigation chain," a succession of court cases that follow from a particular verdict or negotiated agreement, based on conflicts arising from violations, bad faith, or narrow interpretations of the legal obligations of those who are bound by the verdict or agreement. Even nonauthoritarian states can act with impunity in ignoring the decisions of their own courts. One of the ways this occurred was through numerous arrests and "petty" cases brought to the Magistrate's Court, resulting in acquittals, fines, or short jail terms for hunting or possession of "contraband" meat. Small, cumulative violations of a verdict do little to attract notice or mobilize public opinion. This means that states can engage in provocations – like some of those we have just seen: unlawfully enforcing hunting bans or impounding livestock, and so on – with little cost to their honor. And if their policies are to be opposed by litigation, states can count on their own resources, and their ability to out-litigate and deny their opponents the possibility of access to justice. This is part of the process referred to by Jean and John Comaroff (2006: 30) as "lawfare."

In these circumstances, why does there continue to be trust and hope in the law on the part of the San and Bakgalagadi? Why this litigation chain? Why not to give up these efforts? One possible partial answer might be that litigation has the potential to produce results more quickly than other forms of activism, or at least to have the appearance of producing results, even if court cases can take years for a verdict to be reached.

Another reason might be that in asserting their disagreements in court, indigenous litigants are resisting through a language that is heard in the resonance of the law and the legitimacy of courts. Through this legitimacy, they act on the hope that a "true story" will emerge and that the government cannot simply avoid responding to their claims. The *Sesana* case and its aftermath showed that the government may indeed be found in breach of the law by the High Court, even if it is able to interpret the law narrowly to continue its agenda and frustrate the course of justice. Despite this limitation, Pnina Werbner sees promise in the Botswana courts' powers of judicial review, and sees the courts being "utilized as a tool to control the arbitrary power of the postcolonial state" (2014: 504). This trust in the power of the judiciary to correct the wrongs of the state similarly seems to have motivated the San and other African indigenous peoples in their struggle for rights.

Not surprisingly, however, this possibility of the courts as an expeditious source of justice was not consistently realized in practice, including most prominently in the aftermath of the *Sesana* case. The lack of implementation of some of the items in the ruling and lack of movement on a negotiated solution left communities in the CKGR with chronic conditions of deprivation and a sense that the government cared about them only to the extent that it was determined to remove them from their territories in the reserve. On the other hand, the fact that there were discussions at the international, national, and local levels about how to address the concerns of the people of the CKGR gave them some hope that there may be a way for them to stay on their land and to conduct their lives according to their own vision of its value and possibilities for the future. For some of these people in their particular circumstances, the strategy of litigation clearly had benefits, above all in terms of the "visibility" and exposure of their claims, which outweighed its costs, compromises, and disappointments.

Litigating a way of life seems to be a widely recognized global phenomenon, with a long history (see Shattuck and Norgren 1979). In the UN, cases such as that of the CKGR in national courts or of the African Court and African Commission on Human and Peoples' Rights are mentioned by indigenous delegates, states and UN reports in a positive light, as a way to influence global policy and politics, and as one of the "best practices" to bring justice when a fair settlement out of court cannot be reached. These verdicts are used as a tool, or weapon, to lobby governments at the international level, to give legitimacy – a sense of truth – to their claims and have some kind of leverage (clearly, if the verdict is in their favor). However, indigenous delegates to the UN, brought together to discuss their experiences, end up sharing their concerns and frustrations, noting that a proliferation of the use of courts is not enough to bring governments to respect their rights. Even if the verdicts are in their favor, they are often not implemented and do not make a significant difference to their everyday experience of injustice.

Litigation chains only occur in circumstances in which those who are engaged in legal contests with the state have the resources and the support network to hire effective lawyers and repeatedly hold the state to account in its own courts. The James Bay Crees were able to do this because they had a fairly secure financial base through the *James Bay and Northern Québec Agreement* of 1975, which made it possible for them to return to court again and again in response to encroachments on their territories and resources in violation of the agreement. And the people of the CKGR had donors, the IWGIA and Survival International in particular, that were committed to litigation as a strategy of furthering the rights and survival of indigenous or tribal peoples. Where claimants have the resources to return to court, their leadership almost inevitably experiences a kind of "court fatigue," in which litigation undergoes a transformation from a strategy driven by enthusiasm and hope to a grinding routine, an obligation of leadership, with few expected benefits and no end of legal struggle in sight.

In most cases, however, it does not come to this. Ironically, litigation chains are a privilege of the fortunate few, those with the financial resources and connections needed to engage repeatedly in litigation. Even liberal states are able to violate their own laws with impunity, while those who have legitimate justice claims are usually prevented from acting on them through the courts by the very conditions of marginalization and destitution they would struggle against in litigation, if only they could.

This brings us to the question concerning the effectiveness of justice campaigns like those of the San. What are the consequences for indigenous peoples of the changes and contests that take place in the period after legal verdicts or negotiated agreements? Are they consistently captured or co-opted by states, their grievances rendered inert in the chemical conversion of UN reports? Do they inevitably get caught up litigation chains in contests with governments that refuse the legitimacy of major verdicts and disperse them into smaller, lower-profile, more manageable claims? Or do they have the "counter-hegemonic" effects that derive from the mere fact of being heard, from engaging in "legality from below"?

By focusing on the period after judgment to address these questions, I am in a better position to provide some (at least tentative) answers than if I had restricted my attention to the courtroom and the verdict itself. From this longer-term perspective, we can see the emergence of a widened net of criminalization and, partly in response, litigation chains. Recourse to court in the landmark *Sesana* case, therefore, did not result in an attenuation of politics, but, on the contrary, a *hyperpoliticization*, in which the verdicts and "law talk" were used as political weapons in a justice campaign that returned to court and extended beyond.

Legal activism and the litigation chains do not appear to have fundamentally reformed or corrected the deep structures of the state. For the state, the residents of the CKGR remain a marginalized community along the lines of other remote area communities in the country. The many years of political engagement and advocacy in international meetings by San advocates and their supporters contributed more to the wider efforts of the indigenous peoples' movement than to addressing their own conditions of displacement. Alliances were created and fortified between San representatives and other indigenous delegates, NGOs, donors, and UN delegates. The fact remains, however, that those people of the Central Kalahari who were able to participate in the judicial process and who chose to return to their homes in the reserve are still there, without much in the way of government services, it is true, but fighting against the will of the state to remove them.

The *Sesana* verdict and its aftermath, considered together with the activism that the San undertook at the UN and elsewhere, reflect an unremitting tension and opposition between the law as an empowering influence and as an oppressive, marginalizing force. The struggle to be San today fits into a wider narrative of justice causes and collaborations that signal fundamental transformations in the way that systemic grievances can be acted on by those who are oppressed by their own states.

The one constant in this process has been greater reliance on legal remedies and professional expertise, sometimes resulting in an apparent advancement of the cause, at other times resulting in co-optation and defeat, but always producing greater influence of and dependency on formal organizations and systems of law. Under circumstances in which the government was insistent on eliminating permanent human settlement from the CKGR and refusing to recognize the distinct rights of the people who lived there, new relationships and networking among various categories of people became necessary for social support: NGO representatives, activists, journalists, experts, anthropologists, and lawyers became indispensable for defense of their rights to subsist and persist in their territories. The litigation and lobbying in defense of a specific way of life has reached a point at which these professionals have in at least one respect become like digging sticks – an ordinary tool of subsistence necessary for survival on the land.

9

CONCLUSION

OBJECTS AND SUBJECTS OF LAW

One approach that might be taken in trying to represent the history of San engagement with state and international law might tell a story of a long period of isolation and marginalization, of a people living in simplicity as hunters and gatherers, without their own laws or even concepts of ownership. According to this narrative, their simple lives would be followed by a sudden discovery of themselves as rights holders and might depict their use of this discovery, their alliances with the people who brought it to them, and their use of justice activism as a new tool of survival. It might narrate something like the "Coke Bottle in the Kalahari Syndrome" (Solway and Lee 1990), where modernity falls from the sky, but in this case with activism-and-law as single entity falling from the sky as a tool of liberation and a sign of progress. This story, despite its appeal, however, would overlook the San's own history of organizing themselves as a society, their norms and rules, not to mention their diversified subsistence and economy, which have been unrecognized by dominant legal systems. The simple story would overlook the fact that the several San peoples who today call themselves "Kua," "San," "First Peoples," "Bushmen," or "Indigenous" were effectively excluded from decisions concerning their lives, while being classified and clientalized as *malata* in the Tswana proto-states. It would also overlook their space for maneuvering and resistance within (and around) these dominant systems.

The San's inclusion in the nation-state was initiated on the assumption that they had rights, but understood by the government as limited to rights to equal citizenship. At the same time, there was a civic dimension to the policies designed to address poverty or the "Bushmen problem" that set the stage for the later emergence of activist organizations and networks. The term is not entirely dissimilar to the "Indian problem," expressed in various forms and at different times throughout the Americas, one of them being Carl Schurz's 1881 essay on US Indian policy, "Present Aspects of the Indian Problem," in which he bemoans the "greedy encroachments of white men upon Indian lands [with] hostilities being brought about in this manner" (Schurz 1881: 2).

The "Bushmen problem," like the "Indian problem" of the Americas, was in part shorthand for the difficulties posed to ambitious, control-seeking states by those people with subsistence-based economies who were unwilling to let go of their territories and ways of life to make way for ambitious projects of resource exploitation and nation-building. The "Bushmen problem," however, also took on elements of rights and development intended to address their conditions of landlessness and dependency. The context of displacement was the backdrop of the San's activism, oriented toward assertions of rights and identity from multiple leverage points. In effect, through the San's assertion of rights claims, the "Bushmen problem" became no longer merely a matter of assimilationist policy implementation, but a concerted challenge to the state's logic of national homogeneity.

The San challenge to assimilation and national homogeneity also took place on the international stage as an indigenous people. Russel Barsh, writing in the mid-1990s, observed that indigenous peoples were "gaining recognition of their legal personality as distinct societies with special collective rights and a distinct role in national and international decision-making" (1994: 34). This trend continued with the more complete influence of African and Asian indigenous peoples in international law and organizations, producing what has become a global indigenous movement. Yet in the case of Botswana, such recognition was obstructed by a persistent reluctance to extend an indigenous legal personality to peoples such as the San.

The high-profile justice campaign that was pursued by the San and their allies is part of a much wider phenomenon that is occurring in many parts of the world: the pursuit of justice by marginalized peoples acting in opposition to much more powerful agents, states, and corporations.

The North Dakota Access pipeline protest of 2016, for example, brought together representatives of some 280 native American nations to block pipeline construction at an important river crossing, after the Standing Rock tribe sued for an injunction and brought a petition to the U.S. Army Corps of Engineers in Washington, DC, supported by their NGO ReZpect Our Water (Healy 2016). It was not only the unprecedented intertribal support of the protest but also (and perhaps above all) social networks and media exposure that brought the Standing Rock protest to international attention, putting remarkable pressure on the Army Corps of Engineers to draw up plans to reroute the pipeline around the disputed territory. An executive order on February 7, 2017 by a newly inaugurated President Trump authorized the Army Corps of Engineers to proceed with the construction of the pipeline, putting to an abrupt end the environmental impact assessments of the project. The protesters were soon evicted and the protest camp dismantled, with courts remaining the next available avenue of recourse.[1] One of the basic lessons to take away from this example, which could well also apply to the San's justice campaign, is that a protest movement can do everything "right," have a broad base of support and global media exposure, and can still be obstructed by a powerful government or corporation that refuses to be deterred in pursuit of its perceived interests. When the San and their allies crossed the line, when they used their leverage with international publics to go after the country's diamonds and tourism, the gloves came off and the government took punitive measures – notable among them the strict control of the movement of people and goods in and out of the CKGR – apparently meant to dampen the enthusiasm of dissent. As with the Standing Rock process, the position of a government can change almost from one day to the next, for good or ill, and can sometimes incorporate inherent contradictions, with some officials saying one thing and others doing quite another in practice.

States (and some large corporations) that promote rights-oriented civil society organizations, independent judiciaries, free presses, and other conditions favorable to popular protest and the correction of state policy do not usually act quite so visibly and precipitously to suppress dissent. They will sometimes seek to accomplish two contradictory goals in meeting their legal obligations: first, to publicly maintain their reputations as honorable, human rights-observant members of the international community; but, second, at the same time to less visibly shut down a justice campaign that is interrupting other key economic and political objectives. They occasionally do this by waiting out campaigns of dissent, absorbing and then ignoring censure, letting memories fade, and meanwhile saying one thing publicly while privately continuing with their original agendas. Botswana made use of this deny-and-persist strategy by emphasizing its furtherance of the equal rights of citizens (e.g. through programs of poverty reduction in the RAD villages) to draw attention from its violations of the distinct rights of the San.

The Botswana government has invoked neoliberal good governance and goals of equality alongside a more implicit obstacle to justice: an element of perverse and perduring racism that gives the San's struggle for justice some of its distinct qualities. The state's goals of economic development and equal citizenship ran up against the aspirations of the San for recognition as a distinct people, with access to and control over their territories, that much is clear. But the San could not participate as equal citizens in the project of the nation even if they wanted to, not only because the state's plans for development had the effect of displacing them from their land, but also because they were prevented from doing so by their consistent categorization as poor and inferior, needing to be improved and uplifted by their exposure to Tswana language and values.

As this book has illustrated, the way that powerful actors counteract the justice claims that stand in the way of their objectives is less often to be found in dramatic action like mass arrests; but more often, it takes the form of cumulative, small-scale uses of law and discourse to hamper and discredit rights claimants over the long term. States' interventions in the UN are repeated again and again, with words changed only slightly, like hammer blows that have little effect at first but increasingly take hold as the nail sinks deeper. This is the *violence of repetition*, the form of discursive power that takes effect through reiteration, with simple messages conveyed the same way in multiple venues year after year (Chapter 5). The powers of the state, applied against rights claimants who threaten its interests, are able to produce formidable accumulations of refutation, baseless assertions, and crude falsehoods that, to be counteracted, call for the kind of institutional and ideological resources that few marginalized peoples are able to muster.

The only way for activists to counter this strategy is to maintain a sufficient level of noise – on an international scale and over a long period of time – and not allow the state to repress them or wait them out.

And this is easier said than done. The difficulties that stand in the way, particularly among groups that are struggling against social and economic marginalization as a source of their oppression, are formidable. Again, only those claimants with the widest networks and the greatest resources can overcome the violence of repetition with counter-narratives that expose the weaknesses in and move beyond the persuasive powers of the state. The justice campaign that I have described in the pages of this book is therefore a remarkable exception, in which an unusual degree of support from donors and celebrities added energy to a campaign that in other circumstances would have floundered and disappeared from public view.

One of the themes that has emerged clearly from this book is that the San and their supporters have engaged in an impressive, multifaceted set of efforts to achieve the elusive promise of justice – on their own terms. Among the San's multiple strategies of activism, litigation was one of the most consequential, especially in terms of shaping the lives of the claimants. The *Sesana* case, as one of the landmarks of indigenous litigation in Africa, informs us particularly clearly about the social consequences of indigenous activism through state courts. As the case became more complex, it opened a window into the ways activism was turned toward producing legal evidence, the law converted experience into evidence, and evidence into facts, and the way that, like facts, the applicants themselves first had to be transformed into a cognizable entity before the court was able to consider their rights and whether or not they were violated. Following its grounding in facts and categories, procedural law and the law of precedent structured the evidence in a way that depicted a particular (and limited) understanding of who the applicants were as a people (Chapter 6).

Even at its completion, with judgment rendered, the case left many questions unanswered, leading to more failures of negotiation, more lawsuits, more loose ends – in sum, a situation, lasting to the present, in which the San of the CKGR are called upon to litigate their way of life (Chapter 8). The litigation process itself, much like the process of accreditation to the UN, involved a technology of identity. Through this technology, the court was able to produce one category, the "Bushmen" of the CKGR, out of the different but interconnected identities of the San and Bakgalagadi. It also, perhaps more consequentially, created a category of "applicants" as a source of social membership, who, as an outcome of the verdict, acquired a number of distinct rights (and grounds for further claims) that set them apart from those who were not included on the applicant list.

Although the court was concerned with arriving at a reliable number and description of the "applicants," the reality of life in the Kalahari region does not easily lend itself to certainty. People occasionally move, and with them their identity attachments change, sometimes between the categories of San and Bakgalagadi. They shift between hunting and agro-pastoralism, find seasonal labor in ranches or mines, live between remote area settlements and the reserve, and migrate to and return from cities. And through this flux of life among those who declared basic attachments to their territories in the Central Kalahari, the capacity to participate in the resistance against their removal came down to a thumbprint on a document, and having that document accepted by their lawyers and the court through the process of creating a cohort of applicants. The applicant list that resulted clearly did not correspond to all those whose experience of removal was the same and who similarly wanted justice through the courts. Above all, it created a group of people from among the San and Bakgalagadi of the CKGR who had the right to return to their ancestral territory. With the imposition of restrictive rules of entry, the simple act of inclusion in the case took on a life of its own. It divided the people of the CKGR between those who had the right of return and those who did not. In simple and stark terms, it created different regimes of suffering, with those in the reserve lacking such basic services as delivery of water, food, and medicine, and those outside the reserve lacking access to their traditional territories, their connection to the land, and the graves of their ancestors. The applicant list constituted a technology of legal and social identity with important implications for the struggles and rights claims of daily life. It is a clear example of the fact that, even if recognition succeeds in a shallow way, it can produce forms of exclusion that limit the potential of restitution and redistribution.

In the process of these struggles, law became part of the everyday, with experiences of distress and restrictions on freedom commonly understood as manifestations of injustice. Law entered into subjectivity as a way for the claimants to think about the world, in particular about affliction and remedy. Injustice was embodied, made manifest in the physical experience of illegitimate suffering.

In the period "after judgment" (Chapter 7), the litigation process added another element of insecurity – the need for complex negotiations, with uncertain outcomes following from the litigants' weak bargaining position. This is a phenomenon that others have noted as result of negotiation between indigenous peoples and governments and industries elsewhere, including the native title holders of Western Australia, who were dismayed to find that even with the recognition of their rights, they actually had little power other than the right to "negotiate." With conditions for the receipt of benefits unfulfilled, and with the complexity of the agreements requiring high levels of expertise in commercial law and finance, the indigenous Australians were not in a position to secure the benefits that they had expected would follow from the recognition of their rights of native title (Wahlquist 2017). In this way, collective justice claimants commonly face a broken connection between recognition and redistribution. In Nancy Fraser's terms (2005), this broken condition can be understood as an outcome of misrepresentation, a lack of parity in the social arrangements that define the relevant subjects who are entitled to justice (Chapter 1).

Many of the legal battles engaged in by the San leadership and their advocates came down to not just a struggle for recognition in the law as a distinct people, but above all an effort to secure just conditions in the representation of those who are arguably the most marginalized in Botswana. Taking this point further, what we see clearly behind the multistranded justice lobbying on behalf of the San was an equally varied set of economic motives, efforts to secure a livelihood, create income-generating opportunities, or sponsor careers. Claims to recognition as a distinct people were inextricably connected to those that were, in Nancy Fraser's terms (2005, 2010), representative and redistributive, that had important implications for the terms of their access to justice and, in turn, their access to land and resources, development on their own terms, food security, and equal access to government benefits.

I have followed San representatives in their efforts toward changes of policy and representation in government, efforts that might be seen as encountering, and perhaps being captured by, the structures of state and international law through which they are compelled to seek justice. In many parts of this book, we have encountered a basic tension between social justice activism as a check on the abuses of states (including liberal democratic ones), and the actual results of justice-seeking: the limits on redistribution, the negotiations in bad faith, and the further imposition of "fortress conservation," including criminalization of subsistence practices. Taking this longer perspective raises a basic question: Under what circumstances do campaigns succeed or fail, and in what conditions are their agreements with states honored or obstructed?

Jo Becker, in a wide-ranging comparative study of human rights advocacy, finds that successful results are more likely when advocacy is "based on broad-based alliances, organizing by those most affected by human rights abuses, strategic timing and 'opportunistic advocacy', credible research and documentation, and multiple points of leverage" (Becker 2013: 259). The San's justice campaign did all of these things. They built broad alliances with international NGOs and participated actively in the international movement of indigenous peoples (Chapter 5). The people who were most affected by the removals of the residents of the CKGR were prominently among those who represented the cause, with Roy Sesana taking up this role with his own distinct, charismatic style. The justice campaign did not let opportunities go by for getting their message out to a wide, international public. It drew attention to key issues like mining and tourism in the reserve that highlighted the hypocrisy of the removals and the illegitimate suffering that resulted from the government's conservation policy. The campaign made use of credible and reputable experts, whose research and testimonies were at the highest level of professional standards. And they employed multiple points of leverage in various strategies of social justice campaigning, including litigation in state courts, participation in international forums, and pursuit of elected office.

Yet, their justice cause stagnated. On the surface at least, the campaign ultimately fared no better than many other justice campaigns. Its results were negligible, and slow in coming. The "victory" achieved by the San and Bakgalagadi and their legal team eventually ensnared them in a litigation chain, ultimately resulting from the government's narrow, almost punitive approach to implementing the judgment. The San were compelled to return to court again and again, to litigate their way of life. There are recent indications that this battle has at least been partially won and that there are improvements in the process of service delivery, but not through any form of policy pronouncement or statement of reconciliation that would give its beneficiaries a secure sense that change, a long time coming, has finally come.

THE REFUSAL OF RECOGNITION

One of the distinctive features of the indigenous peoples' movement in Africa is that it has involved exporting and translating an emerging regime of human rights – the rights of indigenous peoples – to national contexts that refuse it. This persistent denial of recognition raises the question concerning whether it makes sense to pursue claims of collective rights based on the legal category of indigenous peoples in the African context. While the San have asserted their distinct collective rights as an indigenous people, the government of Botswana has contested these rights claims by invoking the individual rights of the poor as citizens. What are the effects of this disjuncture nationally and internationally? And how has it influenced the justice campaign pursued by the San and their allies?

The San's positioning as an indigenous people has allowed them to take part in the international indigenous movement and to learn about the ways that other groups promote their rights and cope with the political abuses of states. Their connections with other delegates in the UN have given them a sense that their struggles are part of a common justice movement.

Youth activists in particular are not always (or often) recognized leaders or spokespersons of the people for whom they speak. Yet at the UN they take the floor with authority in an effort to present the virtues and struggles of their people. They are pursuing avenues for the vernacularization of human rights to their localities and, together with other indigenous delegates, are contributing to the participatory energy necessary for the legitimacy of UN initiatives concerning indigenous peoples. The creation of a youth elite, with the requisite skills to navigate the UN's demands for effective contributions to international meetings, followed almost directly from the rules of accreditation and participation. Like the court system, the UN was active in its creation of categories and structures, forms of knowledge to which activists were expected to conform. This included the accountability structures of NGOs. It also included knowledge about the essence of human rights claimants, about who *they* were in relation to the global phenomenon of indigenous peoples. The international organizations that deal with issues related to these groups have exponentially multiplied. The resulting competition over indigeneity has occasionally led to the reification of cultures and group divisions that produce new forms of exclusion. At the same time that reification occurs, specific claims become subsumed into wider and longer-term issues that are the result of regional and international alliances. Ultimately, the concept of indigenous peoples as a source of human rights remains an abstraction in practice for many of those whom the concept is meant to represent (Chapters 4 and 5).

The government resistance to the indigenous category in the African context can have the effect of pushing indigenous activists toward alternative discourses and legal identities in efforts to avoid the pitfalls of misrecognition. In the case of the Maasai in Tanzania presented by Hodgson (2011), for instance, after many years of international and national struggle with indigeneity as a core advocacy tool, they shifted away from indigenous rights and toward those associated with pastoral livelihoods as a precondition of being able to effectively engage in policy reform. This did not happen in the same way with the San, for whom the language of indigeneity as a legal and economic instrument in multiple strategies has remained more constant, despite the government's adamant position of nonrecognition of their rights as indigenous peoples and any benefits that might result. Under these circumstances of government refusal, San advocates for indigenous rights at the national level are called upon to engage in multiple acts of translation in an effort to insert such rights into national policies and institutions.

Even in conditions of state refusal of recognition, right claimants still gain certain advantages from adopting the concept of indigenous peoples. Being indigenous today means access to global spaces of interaction, such as the United Nations, and to a long-term vision of their possibilities for political, legal, and economic resources. State and regional courts have occasionally recognized the standards of international law, building indigenous rights into several landmark decisions, including the Sesana, Ogiek, and Endorois cases. Under the impetus of these developments, being indigenous means making claims to justice, rights, and restitution. It also means acting on opportunities for redistribution, making use of international legal standards such as that of FPIC, and of whatever economic opportunities there may be from the international community of donors and activists for the improvement of their material conditions. In the eyes of many marginalized people in Africa, being indigenous today means to be political and legal subjects at the international level, and to take part in global discourses on economic, environmental, and political crises.

HYPER-POLITICIZATION

I have presented two aspects of the common qualities among many indigenous peoples' justice campaigns, which relate closely to the question of the state law's hegemonic effects through "depoliticization." In one direction, law has a marked tendency to facilitate displacement in furthering the interests of the state (Ramanathan 1996). It underpins utilitarian justifications such as the "public purpose" or "balance of convenience" that make necessary the relocation of communities or whole populations to make way for large-scale projects such as transportation infrastructure, pipelines, hydro-electric facilities, and the like. In the case of removals of indigenous peoples from territories designated as parks or nature reserves, law tends to serve the (at times contradictory) commercial and conservation interests of the state. In the case of Botswana, arguments in favor of land privatization initiatives, such as that of the Tribal Grazing Land Policy (TGLP) and the 2015 *Botswana Land Act* (Republic of Botswana 2015), were supplemented with quasi-evolutionist arguments concerning the benefits of civilization and assimilation into the project of the unified, civilized state.

For all of these reasons, people have to move, and the law is there to assist in doing it. Even though the San were the intended beneficiaries of laws like those that gave them distinct access to parks and/or subsistence practices, they were also subjected to law as a mechanism of dispossession. Policies like the TGLP and various regimes of hunting regulation dispossessed the San without recognition that their dispossession had even occurred. The Botswana government also relied on policy provisions intended to put pressure on the people of the reserve to relocate (Chapter 2 and 3). The power of law to dispossess was rendered invisible in the forms of legislation and policy; it was naturalized, built into the order of things through the pursuit of development goals oriented toward an abstract conception of the public good (see Ferguson 1994: 255). Even in circumstances in which law was applied in the San's favor through successful litigation, there was always a trade off in which legal technologies had the effect of facilitating conditions of "lawfare" and legal dependency.

One of the simplest and most direct ways that the concept of juridification is used in the literature is to focus on just this kind of encroachment of state law as a tool of the powerful into the lives of the oppressed. In this sense, juridification serves as shorthand to represent the use of law by those with power to outflank and essentially victimize those who have the potential to make claims against state and corporate interests. The rule of law and the primacy of rights, as Jean and John Comaroff (2006: 23) argue, are emphasized, "even when both the spirit and the letter of that law are violated, offended, distended, purloined." This recourse to law as an instrument of political leverage or coercion "becomes most readily visible when those who act in the name of the state conjure with legalities to act against some or all of its citizens" (Comaroff and Comaroff 2006: 30). Peter Zoettl (2016) provides an illustration of this in his description of the way that, in the process of demarcating indigenous territory, the Tupinamba of Brazil have been subjected to a variety of forms of legal domination: they are increasingly bureaucratized by public administration; their land rights and indigenous status are constantly subject to formal scrutiny and requirements of often unattainable forms of proof by public and private agents; and their leaders are regularly prosecuted and criminalized by the police and the judiciary (Zoettl 2016: 3). As we have already seen at many points in this book, there has been a similar use of state law as a political tool of the state to dispossess indigenous peoples, sometimes involving carefully calibrated mechanisms of regulation and control over their movements and sources of subsistence. It is in this sense that the increased recourse to law involved a process of depoliticization. The "lawfare" that is oriented to the furtherance of state interests against the interests of those on the margins converts political decisions that might provoke resistance into legal decisions that are more readily naturalized and accepted. In this conception of juridification, the legitimacy attached to legal processes is seen as rendering state actions apolitical and beyond the realm of public debate and contestation.

A second approach to juridification considers law as entrenched in the everyday, not just as part of a structure of oppression, but as facilitating resistance to it, and in the process creating new relationships, identities, and forms of expertise. In the case of the San's pursuit of justice, NGOs in particular were sites and sources of legal activism in which they had to navigate new standards of audit and accountability and, at the same time, were able to acquire new structures and vocabularies of rights and development. Seen from the perspective of the San in the CKGR, the NGO that most completely represented their interests continue to have an almost spectral existence beyond its formal financing and accreditation had came to an end, built on memory and personal relationships that produced a certain institutional immortality that lived beyond the official demise of the organization (Chapter 4).

Considered more broadly, building their justice claims around NGOs resulted in new forms of dependency on donors and power inequalities between donors and recipient agencies and between formally educated leaders and their constituents; yet the development of formal organizations with their legal mandates and bureaucratic structures enabled San activists to bring their grievance to the UN, to act on their rights in the judicial system, and to raise the profile of their cause nationally and internationally. Some members of the San leadership acquired greater knowledge of nation-state and international law, and the various strategies of activism that could be employed in conjunction with it. The increased reach of legal processes can also include its use as a publicly visible tool of activism and legal resistance in opposition to oppression. This is one of the central themes of the volume by Julia Eckert and her colleagues, *Law Against the State*, in which the increased recourse to law is discussed in the context of organized opposition to the designs of the state. Juridification in this sense occurs through a growing capacity for law to be employed as a tool of activism.

Sesana and Others v. the Attorney General introduced litigation against the state, together with the "advocacy circus" that surrounded the case, as vehicles for the expression of intractable political differences. This reflects a *hyper-politicization* of the courts, in which recourse to legal remedies both embodied and intensified the political struggles taking place between the San/Bakgalagadi and the state, both within and outside the courtroom. The people of the CKGR continued to pursue rights and act on ideals of justice, even after many years of legal struggle, with implications that went beyond the courtroom, to struggles between indigenous peoples and states occurring elsewhere (see Chapter 8, p. 301).

In the various uses of state and international law in the San's justice campaign, politics were deeply – and openly – implicated in legal processes. Two of the actors in the *Sesana* case were themselves political figures, each representing political interests, one in the party in power (Pilane), the other in the opposition (Boko). Each of these attorneys clearly imagined that they might further their personal political ambitions through their involvement in the case. Beyond the key people involved, the legal process was inherently political. It offered an adversarial process in a closely watched public forum by which policy could be shaped.

Politicization can occur when the court amplifies the impact of political action that takes place in other forums. In the legal struggles of the people of the CKGR, there was never a clear, all-encompassing shift of energy from a political realm to the courts. Law and politics were in some ways inseparable, part of one and the same phenomenon. Even as they pursued their claims in the country's highest court and in UN meetings, their spokespeople sought (and in a few instances achieved) political office, and were appointed or elected to negotiating committees involving very political struggles centered on campaigning, lobbying, and, in other instances, succumbing to or resisting co-optation by the government. Besides this immediately recognizable form of engagement in local and national politics, their representatives also maintained a presence in international forums, in particular by lobbying and making statements at the annual sessions of the United Nations Permanent Forum on Indigenous Issues. More than this, their connections to a global network of advocacy groups and NGOs included high-profile sponsors and donors, one of which, Survival International, raised the political stakes of their struggle by initiating an international campaign intended to impugn the Botswana government's assertions of goodwill in its accounts of the removals. The courts were never the exclusive domain of justice-seeking by the San, and the politics of their cause was never limited to influence-seeking through political offices. Law and politics intersected in a dizzying array of stratagems and struggles as the judges of the High Court tried in vain to keep politics from crossing over into the proceedings of the court and to keep the case over which they were presiding from spilling out into wider contests. The fiction of the non-political was in this case impossible to maintain. Judicialization in this sense was part of a multistranded intensification of political struggle, not a process by which politics were captured or shifted on to the judiciary at the expense of civil engagement.

It is therefore in the realm of the uses of law outside the courtroom that we see the political imbrications with legal process most clearly. The court and its drama became a lightning rod for public attention. Politics were played out in the media attention given to the trials in which the San and their supporters gave voice to their grievances. This was clearest in *Sesana and Others v. the Attorney General*, in which the media brought attention not only to the daily events of the case, including Roy Sesana's antics in the courtroom, but to some of the underlying issues, with a focus on the "newsworthy" qualities of the litigants: the precariousness of the "Basarwa's" picturesque hunting way of life (this theme preferred by the foreign media), the deprivation they experienced in the absence of services, their removal, the violence perpetrated against them, the guns fired, the families torn apart. This was the essential stuff of politics, for which the narratives of the court served as an anchorage for public attention and debate.

The process and outcomes of litigation were inseparable from the San acquiring and cultivating their status as an indigenous people in international law. This was in part facilitated by the circumstances of their relationship with the state and with NGOs. First, more than most marginalized peoples in Africa, the San could lay indisputable claim to being the "first inhabitants" and therefore "indigenous to" the southern Africa region, over and against the state's insistence on nonrecognition of any form of ethnic or tribal difference. More than this, however, there was a strong political dimension to their indigenous status. Botswana shared with settler states elsewhere and at other times in history the justifications for the elimination of original inhabitants whose lives were based on subsistence economies. It practiced forms of racism and assimilation that connected the San to those indigenous peoples in other places with similar experiences who formed the global indigenous movement (Chapter 3). This historical background thus further opened the door to the San's pursuit of the politics of identity – and to the hyper-politicization of their struggle.

HEGEMONY AND COUNTER-HEGEMONY

The San's justice campaign has produced more than a complex example of the tensions and trade-offs between legal "hegemony" and "counter-hegemonic anti-globalization." I have been attentive to the ways that the campaign and the opposition to it have produced new forms of group membership and categorization, which, in turn, also had implications for the campaign's success. The "victories" that the San and Bakgalagadi and their supporters achieved in court belie the ways that the litigation process and the implementation of the verdicts compounded and multiplied the injustices they faced.

The hegemonic qualities of the litigation process were felt before the trial even began, in the preparation of the case and, above all, in the creation of the "applicant list." But establishing the identity of claimants is only the beginning. As we have seen, courts also seek a similar kind of clarity about the history and customs of those who are making claims to a territory and distinct way of life. The court's recourse to fact tends to create remoteness from the conceptions and priorities of those whom they attempt to hear as rights claimants. Ambiguity cannot be readily tolerated by courts, but in some way has to be reconciled with the need for certainty, a demand that requires images, artifacts, practices, and life histories to be chosen with a view to their legibility, translatability, and reliability. To some degree, the High Court was receptive to ideas of mobility and change, but, as we shall see, its verdict still left the CKGR's inhabitants with a judgment based on a reified identity as hunters, which was exploited by the government in a narrow interpretation of its obligations (Sapignoli 2017).

The legal structures and processes of the state and of international law, however, should not be exclusively treated as sources of domination and hegemony, but also, in some circumstances, as resources that are malleable, offering possibilities for resistance or negotiation. The emphasis on legal victimization does not present the complete story of how state and international law become part of the lives of those on the margins of a dominant society; above all, it does not tell the story of their uses of law, how it can be a rallying point for claims-making, for using the state's courts to call the state to account. The verdicts that were the result of the San and Bakgalagadi's "litigation chain" became a reference point and a presence in people's discourse and action, and in their relationships with the state and global institutions (Chapter 7).

In this regard, Boaventura de Sousa Santos and César Rodríguez-Garavito (2005: 2) call for more attention to be given to an "unprecedented effervescence of debate and experimentation in bottom-up legal reform and new international legal regimes." In their view a "subaltern cosmopolitan legality" is upending the common assumption that those on the margins lack political and legal agency. These once-excluded actors are now the beneficiaries of "new forms of global politics and legality" (de Sousa Santos and Rodríguez-Garavito 2005: 9). Similarly, De Gaay Fortman (2011) emphasizes the significance of "human rights upstreaming" in an approach that leaves more room to consider the impact of claimants on the legal structures and discourses through which they pursue their rights.

Change undoubtedly occurs through activist campaigning, even if not uniformly in ways that meets the immediate expectations of activists. The behavior of states and corporations can be modified by litigation and international activism, largely through the reputational costs of prominent public causes that put policies and their consequences under scrutiny (Kirsch 2014b: 229). While many of the efforts of indigenous rights claimants may seem to go nowhere, there are benefits from them that go beyond mere words on paper, that at the very least have influence as a check on the worst abuses against those on the margins. Stuart Kirsch, drawing from his experience with litigation by the Yonggom people of Papua New Guinea in Australia's courts against the mining conglomerate BHP and the disastrous environmental and social impacts of the Ok Tedi mine, takes pains to argue that critiques of litigation are often incomplete and unrepresentative of the consequences and possibilities of legal activism. Kirsch shows how a particular justice cause can widely transform the interpretation of legal principles and, in the process, alter the power relationship between a once-marginalized people and powerful governments and industrial agents. His account calls into question the fatalism of the critiques of legal activism and their failure to consider how law can be used to bring about positive change, which makes it difficult to see the actual complex consequences of "mobilizing law from below." Ultimately, law is "a resource for promoting political and economic transformation" (Kirsch 2014b: 87).

Taking a "bottom-up" perspective does not, of course, consistently reveal the success of counter-hegemonic projects or legal alternatives to hegemonic regimes. De Sousa Santos and Rodríguez-Garavito do mention the "constant danger of cooptation and obliteration" (2005: 17), though in the context of a celebration of the overlooked possibilities for resistance that persist and alternatives that continue to be put forward, despite opposition from the powerful (2005: 12).

This brings us back to the question concerning what indigenous peoples' engagement in legal activism actually accomplishes. Despite the odds that seem stacked against them, indigenous spokespeople continue to engage in justice campaigns with no sign that these efforts are abating. In fact, for many people, cases like that of the Central Kalahari represent a source of motivation to remain politically engaged and a source of hope for other possible futures. Sesana expressed this point when he said,

> The cases gave hope to the Kua. Now we have more support from the people in Botswana and from the people in the government too. People now are more aware that what the government does is wrong because the law showed that; they know what our problems are. (Author notes 2011).

There is no doubt that San activism has raised their profile as a people who have been wronged by a misguided, even callously profit-seeking government. But even if we remain skeptical that the San of the Central Kalahari have achieved any of their goals in the face of the state's powerful opposition, or any greater security in their subsistence and sense of place, they have at least accomplished this much: they have brought their hopes for the future to wide attention, challenged the stereotypes that limited their possibilities as a people, and forced the government to recognize them as rights claimants with unusual obstacles to prosperity and a powerful sense of place. They made clear to a government that was set upon policies of removal and assimilation that it could no longer afford to ignore its critics, leaving open possibilities for policy change that would otherwise not have existed. They have also provided examples for others to follow the multiple ways that activism exerts influence, with the potential for those involved in justice campaigns to carve out spaces of opposition, compromise, negotiation, and possibly, just possibly, creating more favorable conditions for the lives toward which they aspire.

NOTES

CHAPTER 1

1. In this book I make frequent reference to a "San" struggle, which actually includes an important element of diversity. It was defined as a "Bushmen" case by the Botswana High Court because this is how it was framed by the CKGR inhabitants, the court, and their supporters. In fact, the San's struggle included the Bakgalagadi residents (with individuals referred to as *Mokgalagadi*) of the CKGR, who thus became integral to the "San" claims and causes.
2. The current San population is estimated at 130,000 in seven southern African countries: Angola (10,000), Botswana (62,500), Lesotho (400), Namibia (38,000), South Africa (7,800), Zambia (1,300), and Zimbabwe (2,600). There are some sixty self-identified groups who fall into three language categories Ju/'hoan (northern Kalahari), Khoe-Kwadi (central Kalahari), and Tuu (southern Kalahari) (Guldemann 2014). There are several ways in which the San people are referred to by outsiders and refer to themselves. In this book I choose to use mostly the word San as a collectivity, and the name of the specific groups, because that is the way they refer to themselves when they talk as a people to wider audiences such as those of United Nations meetings.
3. See, for example, Marshall (2003), Lee (1979), Lee and DeVore (1976), Tanaka (1980), Silberbauer (1981), Solway and Lee (1990), Barnard (2007: 98).
4. See Wilmsen (1989, 2002), Wilmsen and Denbow (1990), Gordon and Douglas (2000).
5. The history of indigenous involvement in the UN and the place of indigenous peoples and organizations in the formation of a new legal category and identity has been discussed extensively by a variety of authors (see, e.g., Engle 2010, Xanthaki 2010, Minde 2008, Morgan 2007, Niezen 2003).
6. See Sanders (1989), Muehlebach (2001), Lindroth (2006).
7. United Nations adopts *Declaration on Rights of Indigenous Peoples*. www.un.org/apps/news/story.asp?NewsID=23794&Cr=indigenous&Cr1=#.WL1xK2XUDzI. Accessed March 6, 2017.
8. Starting in 2014, discussions and consultations took place in the UN on new criteria for increasing the participation of "indigenous representative institutions" in UN initiatives, including the General Assembly. The opposition of several key states, including China, Egypt, Morocco, and

India, which sought to define indigenous peoples and have a final say on their recognition, resulted in an intractable divide and failure to reach an agreement.

CHAPTER 2

1. *Sesana* 2006c Bundle 1A 104 (ExP32), Letter from Minister Margaret Nasha to Ditshwanelo, dated January 7, 2002; emphasis added.
2. Kiema (2010: 80–1) calls the CKGR invalid and says that the stated aims of declaring the area a game reserve were not entirely for the benefit of the area's inhabitants. A report that the NGO Ditshwanelo produced in 1996 after its fact-finding visit in the reserve states, "they were not part of the consultation process when the CKGR became a game reserve. They acknowledged that perhaps they were not enlightened at that time, but argue that this has changed and that they ought to be consulted properly in relation to their lives now that they are citizens of an independent Botswana" (Ditshwanelo 1996: 7).
3. For more on hunting in the Central Kalahari, see Silberbauer (1965) and Hitchcock (1988, 2002).
4. See Silberbauer and Kuper (1966); Ikeya (1999); Osaki (2001); Sugawara (2002); Kuela (2010: 67–72).
5. In the 1970s and 1980s, G/ui and G//ana San people represented between 48 and 63 percent of the overall CKGR population, while Bakgalagadi made up between 25 and 43 percent (Murray 1976; Sheller 1977; English et al. 1980; Hitchcock 1988). The figures are complicated in part because of the issue of self-identification and also because the census approaches varied; in some cases the interviews were extensive, and in other cases they were relatively cursory. In addition, other people were in the CKGR at the time of the various studies, including Tsila and visitors from outside the reserve, and they may have been counted as residents.
6. See Cashdan (1984: 447–9), Barnard (1992: 223–6), Valiente-Noailles (1993: 55–7), and Kuela (2010: 30–2).
7. Veterinary cordon fences were long fences erected in rural parts of the country in order to prevent the spread of livestock or other animals that might have foot-and-mouth disease (FMD). The Protectorate Administration and later the Botswana government erected these fences as part of the Veterinary Department's programs aimed at maintaining livestock health through preventing cattle movement which could result in the transmission of disease such as FMD and lung sickness.
8. See also www.owensfoundation.org. Accessed 17 September 2016.
9. Data from the DWNP; see Hitchcock and Masilo (1995) and the CKGR and Khutse Management Plan, DWNP (2001).
10. Of the different kinds of boreholes in the CKGR, only a few had direct effects on San and Bakgalagadi mobility. The boreholes drilled for wildlife attracted animals that could be hunted, but people were generally afraid to hunt in those places because of fear of arrest by DWNP game scouts. The

boreholes drilled for mineral prospecting by De Beers and other mining companies were usually saline, and people did not drink from them. Only one borehole was accessible to people living in the CKGR in the period between 1997 and 2002 – that of Mothomelo. After the government destroyed the borehole in Mothomelo in 2002, there were no boreholes where residents or visitors (other than tourists, government officials, and mining company personnel) could get water.

11. For further discussion on RADP, see Wily (1979); Hitchcock (1980) and Saugestad (2001).
12. The Mothomelo borehole had a Lister engine and was powered by diesel, supplied periodically by the Ghanzi or the Kweneng district councils. There were two large 10,000-gallon water tanks at Mothomelo, which stored the water from the borehole.
13. For a discussion of some of the craft production and purchasing issues, see Hitchcock and Masilo (1995) and Ikeya (1996).
14. See, for example, Owens and Owens (1981) and Spinage (1991), and some of the discussions in the *Kalahari Conservation Society Newsletter*.
15. I am grateful to Robert Hitchcock for providing much of the information on which this section is based, drawing from his expertise on the San people and many years of experience as a consultant specializing in issues of resource extraction, resettlement, and relocation in southern Africa.
16. The timing of the discovery of diamonds was likely important in this debate. Some officials said that diamonds were discovered in the early 1980s, but the decision to develop the diamond mine at Gope was not made until late in the first decade of the new millennium, several years after people had been relocated.
17. Those who have questioned the connection between mining and the removals include some national and regional NGOs and researchers as I discuss further in pp. 152 and 192.
18. For a summary of some of the reasons given by the government for the relocation, see Hitchcock (1988, 2002); Ikeya (2001); Saugestad (2001, 2011) and Sapignoli (2009). The Botswana government website in the 1990s and early part of the new millennium also contained information on the CKGR, but this was removed in around 2007 or 2008.
19. See Harden (1988); Saugestad (2001); Hitchcock (2002); Nthomang (2004) and Kiema (2010).
20. This information was drawn from a webpage (www.gov.bw/index.php/) that has since been removed.
21. For further details on the 1997 removal, see Ikeya (2001); Hitchcock (2002) and Maruyama (2003).

CHAPTER 3

1. For a discussion of the conditions of the San in the *morafe*, see Livingstone (1857: 56); MacKenzie (1871: 128–33); Mohr (1876: 156) and Bryden (1893: 142–3).

2. On the *botlhanka*, see Tlou (1977: 367). The system of serfdom is discussed by Gadibolae 1985 as *bolata*. See also Schapera (1952: 198); Datta and Murray (1989: 58–9), and Morton (1994).
3. The categories of those excluded from access to land, and hence from the "rights to speak and be heard", included impoverished households (including cattle post employees), recently established male-headed households, female-headed households, and rural employees (Gulbrandsen 1987: 60).
4. See Schapera (1938: 30–2, 66–8, 120–3, 250–2; 1943: 26–31, 260–2; 1970: 80–91).
5. See Schapera (1952) and Gulbrandsen (2012). On the meaning of *kagiso* and *kutlisiswano*, see Pöntinen (2013: 278, n. 330).
6. Some tribal capitals are: Shoshong, Old Palapye, and Serowe in the Ngwato territory (now Central District); Molepolole in Kweneng District; Tsau and later Maun in the Tawana tribal territory (later, North West District); and Kanye in Southern District (Ngwaketse).
7. Under Rey's administration, the British introduced the *Native Administration Proclamation* of 1934, aimed at reducing the chiefs' powers, and the *Native Tribunals Proclamation* of 1934, which made the *kgotla* (in the administration's terms) a legal entity. In enacting these measures, Rey and the British administration were opposed by Tshekedi Khama, chief of the powerful Bamangwato, who argued that these proclamations had no force because they did not recognize native law and custom, which was the basis of the original foundation of the *Protectorate and the Order in Council* of 1891 (see Ifezue 2015: 278–9).
8. See Botswana National Archives [BNA] files DCS 5/2 and DCS 8/6 and Parsons (1973).
9. The influence of British parliamentarians on Protectorate policy toward Bushmen can be found in Brantlinger (2003: 73–93) and Penn (2006: 147–9, 222–4, 230–6).
10. For further details on mistreatment of San in cattle posts, see Parsons (1973); Hermans (1977); Hitchcock (1978) and Miers and Crowder (1988).
11. For a discussion of the Bamangwato, see Parsons (1973).
12. For a thorough assessment of Seretse Khama, see Parsons, Henderson, and Tlou (1995) and Williams (2007).
13. Also called Boers, people of Dutch ancestry who have lived in South Africa from 1652 to the present. Afrikaners first came to Botswana beginning in the 1850s, and sizable numbers settled in Ghanzi in 1898–99 and in the twentieth century.
14. See above, and Sillery (1965: 188–91), Wily (1979b: 12–17), and Russell and Russell (1979: 10–15).
15. There were also San who had moved out of the Central Kalahari Game Reserve during drought periods, especially in the early 1960s (Sheller 1977; Alec Campbell, personal communication, 2010), and itinerant San in the region who moved from one farm to another, seeking employment.
16. For discussions of the RAD settlements, see Gulbrandsen et al. (1986).

17. This strategy worked until 2014 when the Botswana government essentially turned most of the community trusts over to private operators.
18. For further discussions of the TGLP and its impacts in Western Central District, one of the areas just to the east of the Central Kalahari Game Reserve, see Hitchcock (1978, 1980, 1990), Campbell and Main (1991), Campbell et al. (2006), and Sapignoli and Hitchcock (2013b).
19. Such perceptions have a long history, as reported by Sylvain (1999) in her study of farms workers and farmers in the Omaheke region of Namibia.
20. Schools were created trough the Bushmen Development Office (BDO) and RAD programs, and by 1979 over 400 Bushmen children attended the ten schools of the district (Wily 1979a: 38).
21. The Dutch Reformed Church later opened schools in Xangas in 1970 and Kuke in 1977, though the impact of these schools in promoting San identity was negated when they were taken over by the government in 1977–78 as part of a new national education policy (Lawy 2016: 111).
22. For further analysis of discriminatory legislation in Botswana, see Ng'ong'ola (1997); Mazonde (2002); and Nyati-Ramahobo (2009).

CHAPTER 4

1. For more on the proliferation of NGOs, see Kamat (2003), Ahmed and Potter (2006), Alvaré (2010), and Lewis (2014).
2. See, for example, Thomas (1958) and Van der Post (1958).
3. The key scholarly works on the San as hunter-gatherers include Lee and DeVore (1976), Marshall (1976), Lee (1979), Tanaka (1980, 2014), and Silberbauer (1981).
4. See, for example, Guenther (1986), Mogwe (1992), Gordon and Douglas (2000), and Gordon (2009).
5. I obtained information on First People of the Kalahari from the following sources: FPK members themselves; the files of FPK; reports of organizations that funded FPK, such as the International Work Group for Indigenous Affairs and the Saami Council; media sources; documents on file in the University of Botswana library; and the private collections of individuals who worked with and reviewed FPK over the years.
6. These events have been discussed in detail in a number of publications, including those of Saugestad (2001) and Hitchcock (2002). The year 1992 was also the quincentenary of the arrival of Europeans in the New World and an important year for indigenous peoples who were pressuring governments and the international community for better treatment.
7. Later on, other groups were incorporated such as //Au//eisi in the Groot Laagte and Qabo areas in northern Ghanzi District and the !Xoo of southern Ghanzi.
8. The official founding members of FPK were Komtsha Komtsha (Naro), Roy Sesana (G//ana), Saikuta (G/ui), Tsao (Ju/'hoansi), Gomme Kgao (Ju/'hoansi), Aron Johannes (Naro), and John Hardbattle (Naro).

9. The First Regional Conference on San Peoples was held in June 1992 in Windhoek, Namibia. For discussions of these meetings and their significance, see Saugestad (2001); see also scenes from John Marshall's film *A Kalahari Family* (Marshall 2003).
10. Komtsha was a member of the NGO Kuru.
11. "The Khwe Speak Out," *Mmegi/The Reporter*, 13 (20), May 23–30, 1996.
12. See The Right Livelihood Award, http://www.rightlivelihoodaward.org/laureates/roy-sesana-first-people-of-the-kalahari-fr/ Accessed December 2016.
13. The trickster is a key figure in San religion and mythology, an ambiguous, multifaceted individual, one that confounds binary categories such as natural/supernatural, human/divine, and human/animal. Known as *//Gawama* to the G/ui and *Piisi/koagu* to the G//ana, the trickster is seen variously as a prankster, a divine creator, a goblin, and a god (Guenther 2000: 4, 95–125). Roy Sesana, in the various roles he played during the trial, shifted from one persona to another and thus can definitely be characterized as a trickster. His various personae contributed to his leadership abilities, meaning that he could appeal to different audiences.
14. In 1895, three Tswana chiefs went to England to try to stop the British government from giving Bechuanaland to Cecil Rhodes's British South Africa Company (Parsons 1973; Tlou and Campbell 1984: 218–20).
15. Tragically, Mama Rampadi passed away as a result of an automobile accident a month after representing her people at the Molopo workshop on hoodia benefit-sharing, held in Molopo, South Africa, on September 20–21, 2006. Her fate in October 2006 was reminiscent of the death of Khamana Phetso of Kuru, who had been with her at the Geneva WGIP meeting in 1999, who also died as a result of a car accident.
16. Minutes of the Botswana Khwedom Council meeting on San leadership, July 25–26, 2015.
17. The negotiating team included Kuru Development Trust (now the Kuru Family of Organizations [KFO]), the Working Group of Indigenous Minorities in Southern Africa (WIMSA), and several other Botswana-based NGOs: Ditshwanelo, the Botswana Council of Non-Government Organizations (BOCONGO), and the Botswana Christian Council.
18. San Youth Network webpage, https://sanyouthnetwork.wordpress.com. Accessed January 2017.
19. Ditshwanelo website. http://www.ditshwanelo.org.bw/press.html. Accessed 3 February 2007.
20. See, https://www.survivalinternational.org/news/24 Accessed 10 November 2016.
21. The intervention of SI in the CKGR case and its relationship with FPK have also been discussed by several scholars (see, for example, Taylor and Mokhawa 2003; Good 2009; Solway 2009, 2011; Saugestad 2011; Zips-Mairitsch 2013).
22. See www.ditshwanelo.org.bw/july018pres.html. Accessed October 4, 2016.
23. Williams and Albertson, December 3, 2001, "Report NT meeting with Vice-President 30 Nov 2001," p. 4.

24. See Qobe Xhukuri in Ditshwanelo (2002: 44–5).
26. The Khwedom Council has more recently suffered a similar fate, with the Executive Director Keikabile Mogodu reporting to a meeting of the organization in D'Kar in 2015 that the staff had not been paid since 2014 and had even pooled 200 pula per month to pay for rent, which, it turned out, was insufficient. The report of this meeting noted further that "the organisation is in debt, and it has failed to submit its Annual Returns which may lead to cancellation at [the] Registry of Societies" (Botswana Khwedom Council 2015: 2). BKC did, however, have an annual general meeting on August 7–8, 2017 at which it was announced that the organization had received some additional funding.
26. See https://en.wikipedia.org/wiki/First_People_of_the_Kalahari. Accessed March 10, 2017.
27. See, www.africanprosperity.com. Accessed 20 October 2017.

CHAPTER 5

1. See Engle (2010: 17–18) and Niezen (2003) for background on the early indigenous peoples movement in the UN.
2. On the historical relationship between Khoi and San people, see Barnard (1992); Elphick (1977); Boonzaier et al. (1996).
3. UN WGIP Final Report, E/CN.4/Sub.2/1994/30, p. 20.
4. While it is certainly easier to identify the original inhabitants in the Americas, some complexities surrounding indigenous identity remain, particularly in Latin America, as discussed by Canessa (2007).
5. The few states that attended intermittently were Nigeria, Morocco, Senegal, and, since the 1995 session, South Africa. Only at the beginning of the twenty-first century did Botswana start to send delegates to the PFII sessions in New York, not surprisingly beginning in 2004, a key year in the struggle in the CKGR, corresponding to the beginning of a major court battle (see Chapter 6).
6. UN WGIP Final Report, E/CN.4/Sub.2/1998/16, p. 29.
7. Kxao Moses=Oma took part in various conferences and meetings involving San, including the First Regional San Conference held in Windhoek in June 1992, the Second Regional San Conference held in Gaborone, Botswana, in October 1993, and the 1997 Khoisan Conference in Cape Town. He is the brother of the Ju/'hoan traditional authority Txamkxao=Oma. For the statement see http://cendoc.docip.org/collect/cendocdo/index/assoc/HASH0112/9bba985c.dir/210233.pdf. Accessed December 10, 2016.
8. Indigenous Peoples' Centre for Documentation, Research and Information (DOCIP) has archived the statements from San and other indigenous peoples' organizations, UN agencies and governments attending UN meetings on indigenous peoples' rights. Most of the statements quoted in this chapter can be found at www.docip.org.
9. UN WGIP Final Report, E/CN.4/Sub.2/1998/16, p. 21.
10. See, http://cendoc.docip.org/collect/cendocdo/index/assoc/HASH014f/aea602a9.dir/210232.pdf Accessed 1 October 2016.

11. Although Macklem makes this point with reference to the *Declaration of the Rights of Indigenous Peoples*, the same argument applies to indigenous identity in the absence of a definition in the Working Group on Indigenous Populations, together with the elaboration of new indigenous rights.
12. ECOSOC Resolution E/2000/22 art. 1.
13. For discussions of the WGIP, see Muehlebach (2001) and (Niezen 2003).
14. These include the Kuru Family of Organizations (KFO), based in Botswana; the South African San Institute (SASI), based in South Africa; the Indigenous Peoples of Africa Co-ordination Committee (IPAAC), a network of African-based indigenous organizations; the Open Society Foundation for Southern Africa (OSISA); and IWGIA.
15. The following section draws from my chapter "A Kaleidoscopic Institutional Form." In *Palaces of Hope: The Anthropology of Global Organizations*. Ronald Niezen and Maria Sapignoli (eds.) Cambridge: Cambridge University Press, 2017.
16. Perhaps the most prominent example of an alternative to the Permanent Forum is the Expert Mechanism on the Rights of Indigenous Peoples in Geneva.
17. Indigenous participants submit four kinds of statements: (1) indigenous caucus statements, (2) joint NGO statements, (3) individual statements, and (4) "cooperative statements" made collaboratively by NGOs, UN agencies and states. These statements are usually prepared a few days before or during the PFII sessions.
18. For the strategic importance and implications of indigenous use of language, see Graham (2002).
19. The significance of the distinction for the San once reached the point where they presented a statement to the Permanent Forum decrying the fact that anthropologists and others had failed to make a proper distinction between them: "The Khoi are traditionally herders with a hierarchical society and the San are traditionally hunter-gatherers who had an egalitarian social order. Self-determination is largely accepted by both the Khoi and the San and both groups prefer to be recognized as either San or Khoi." Then the spokespersons, after reporting that the San have been vulnerable to imposed leadership not only by Bantu groups but also by Khoi, concluded: "We appeal to the governments and the academic world to honor our wish to be called San and not Khoisan, which we expressed in the Penduka Declaration of 2001" (Baba Festus, as !Khawa ttu and WIMSA, 9th UNPFII 2010). See, http://cendoc.docip.org/collect/cendocdo/index/assoc/HASH2387/d2f873da.dir/PF10delaria045.PDF Accessed 1 October 2016.
20. This is a view shared by other indigenous peoples as well as scholars. See Taylor (2007), Ng'ong'ola (2007), Good (2009), Solway (2009), and Saugestad (2011).
21. Fairly current information on connectivity can be found on the Central Intelligence Agency's World Factbook: www.cia.gov/library/publications/the-world-factbook/geos/bc.html.

22. See the *Daily News*, Botswana's official newspaper, in October and November 2004; contrast with *The Voice* and *Mmegi wa Dikang* in October to December 2004.
23. Part of this concern was addressed by the introduction, in 2016 PFII session, of closed-door dialogues between indigenous delegates and Forum members without the presence of state representatives.
24. See, http://cendoc.docip.org/collect/cendocdo/index/assoc/HASH013e.dir/199_as.pdf. Accessed 20 October 2016.
25. See, http://cendoc.docip.org/collect/cendocdo/index/assoc/HASH01c5/9c8c45ed.dir/275_as.pdf. Accessed 20 October 2016.
26. See, http://cendoc.docip.org/collect/cendocdo/index/assoc/HASH4924/5a052ff2.dir/272_as.pdf. Accessed 4 September 2016.
27. The report of the Special Rapporteur on the Situation of Human Rights and Fundamental Freedoms of Indigenous People, James Anaya, Addendum: Preliminary Note on the Situation of Indigenous Peoples in Botswana. Geneva: Human Rights Council. A/12/34/Add. 4, 23 September 2009.
28. Ludick, Steven, Director, Department of Community Development, Ministry of Local Government and Rural Development of the Republic of Botswana (2014) On Agenda item 4: Human Rights, during the 13th session of the Permanent Forum on Indigenous Issues, May 12–13, May 2014. p. 9. Emphasis in original.
29. Author notes, UNPFII 2013 Botswana, Agenda Item 4: "Half-day discussion on African region."
30. See Wily (1979a); Saugestad (2011); Republic of Botswana (2009, 2014); Chapter 3, p. 92–97.
31. Author notes, UNPFII 2015, Agenda Item: 7 "Human Rights: Ngamiland Council of NGOs." This statement was submitted and is on the UN website, but he was not actually called from the speaker list to deliver his statement in person.
32. My summary of the controversy is based on information provided by Wynberg (2010), and from the more detailed analyses in Chennels (2016).
33. The controversy eventually also found its way to the Expert Mechanism on the Rights of Indigenous Peoples in Geneva in 2014, where Festus stated, "The Intellectual Property Rights with regards to Free and Prior Informed Consent must be reviewed and effective monitoring models should be established in addressing the matter of further exploitation, with special emphasizing on the situation of the San communities within southern Africa" (7th meeting, EMRIP, Geneva).

CHAPTER 6

1. The following discussion of the applicants in the *Sesana* case draws from an article that appears in the *Political and Legal Anthropology Review, PoLAR* (Sapignoli 2017).

2. In common law systems (Botswana's Roman-Dutch procedural law draws heavily on common law), witness testimony plays a crucial role in presenting evidence. Even documents, which stand authoritatively alone in other judicial systems, tend to be introduced through witnesses who are asked not only to comment on documents and their origin, but also to read important passages into the record of the trial transcripts to give them more weight.
3. See Silberbauer (1981) and Kiema (2010) for a discussion of San's connections to the land.
4. This was reported by *The Voice*, in an article titled, "We were told to move, we were not asked," November 26, 2004: 4.
5. www.survivalinternational.org/news/168. Accessed November 2016.
6. www.survivalinternational.fr/news/2. Accessed November 2016.
7. I am grateful to the late Janet Hermans for her generosity in allowing me to use this information from her unpublished notes, which were originally provided to the Kalahari Peoples Fund.
8. This reputation was based on the case that she brought against the Attorney General. This was the landmark case, *Unity Dow v. the Attorney General of Botswana* (1992), which challenged the *Citizenship Act* of 1984 and the Botswana Constitution (Lockwood 1990).
9. This verbatim report of Justice Dow's ruling comes from unpublished field notes by Janet Hermans, provided to the Kalahari Peoples Fund.
10. 276/03 Centre for Minority Rights Development (Kenya) and Minority Rights Group (on behalf of Endorois Welfare Council) Kenya. African Commission on Human and Peoples' Rights, November 25, 2009. http://caselaw.ihrda.org/doc/276.03/. Accessed March 18, 2017.

CHAPTER 7

1. This observation comes from his personal correspondence with the applicants and representatives of FPK in 2011.
2. Botswana does not have a constitutional provision relating to economic and social rights, it has not ratified the International Covenant on Economic and Social Rights, and the *Sesana* verdict did not call for the provision of services. Thus, it was not strictly speaking unlawful when the government, in accordance with the letter of the 2006 judgment, decided not to restore the services that were provided before the relocation (water, mobile clinics, village schools, pensions, destitute food rations, training, etc.).
3. The *Sunday Standard* published several articles on the issue: "Secret documents raise questions about Botswana's independence of the judiciary," September 20, 2015; "Khama replaces suspended judges amid international outcry," October 11, 2015; "Khama in fighting for judicial control – fresh evidence," November 1, 2015.
4. The residents committee of the CKGR originally comprised representatives from the villages of Xere, Molapo, Mothomelo, Kikao, Gope, Gugamma, New Xade, and Kaudwane. The village of Metseamonong, as I will discuss later, had decided not to participate in the process.

The committee was chosen through consultative processes facilitated by a team that included the CKGR coalition NGOs (Kuru, FPK, and Ditshwanelo).

5. The function of the coalition was to facilitate the process of engagement between the current and former residents of the CKGR and the government of Botswana.
6. www.bbc.com/news/world-africa-11685932. Accessed May 2011.
7. Recorded interview, conducted by an assistant, 2016.
8. Recorded interview, conducted by an assistant, 2016.
9. Recorded interview, conducted by an assistant, 2016.
10. Recorded interview, conducted by an assistant, 2016.
11. The 2007 policy opted to split wildlife revenues in two, where the CBOs will continue to receive 35 percent of the revenues and a newly created National Environment Fund will receive 65 percent, with the task of redistributing the money being done at the national level (Poteete 2009: 292). This has meant recentralization of CBRNM and nationalization of revenues and more power to the central government and district councils, with the government intending "to stop malfeasance in current projects" (Hoon 2014: 58).
12. Botswana has allocated a large number of licenses for companies to engage in hydraulic fracturing in various parts of the country. According to the Open Society Initiative for Southern Africa (OSISA), this has included protected areas, notably the Okavango Delta, the Tsodilo Hills, the Central Kalahari Game Reserve, and the Kgalagadi Transfrontier Park (Barbee [2015]; African News Agency [2016]; OSISA [2016]).
13. I was part of a team doing the environmental and social impact assessment in which we interviewed mining personnel, farmers, and San laborers to get their views about the potential impacts of the mine.

CHAPTER 8

1. On the James Bay Crees and their litigation, see Richardson (1991); Niezen (2009); Desbiens (2013).
2. The donkeys, which were surveyed by the government in 2005–6, are crucial to the wellbeing of people in the CKGR, in that they provide the means for bringing people and water into reserve, and are used for getting water from water points and pans inside the CKGR to the villages. They are also used to carry melons, which people depend on for moisture.
3. Without access to court documents or hearings, I have based my account of this case on phone interviews and in-depth local reporting of the verdict. See also, *Mmegi Online*, "Govt ordered to compensate Sesana, fellow tribesmen," October 28, 2016. www.mmegi.bw/index.php?aid=64195&dir=2016/october/28. Accessed November 29, 2016.
4. The term *ayako* has been adopted by the G/ui and G//ana for "headman," but normally the word that they both use in their language is *x'aiga* (see Maruyama 2007: 373).

5. Without access to court documents or hearings, I have based my account of this case on phone interviews and in-depth local reporting of the verdict and on some documents provided to me by FPK. See also "Basarwa sue Khama," August 19, 2014, *Mmegi Online*, www.mmegi.bw/index.php?aid=45294. Accessed December 2014.
6. Ditshwanelo Press Statement 2 on the relocation of residents of Ranyane settlement, June 13, 2013. www.osisa.org/sites/default/files/ditshwanelo_press_statement_ranyane_update_2.pdf. Accessed December 24, 2016.
7. Part of the liking of the information appeared on the Survival International website in August 2013 (www.survivalinternational.org/news/9469).
8. For a discussion of this event and its significance, see Workman (2009: 15–19, 24–6, 203–21, 241–2).
9. UNPFII 2013, 12th session, Report E/2013/43-E/C.19/2013/25, p. 8, para. 30.
10. In the past, the former Special Rapporteur on the human rights and fundamental freedoms of indigenous peoples, Rodolfo Stavenhagen, had wanted to visit Botswana (notably in 2004, around the time the *Sesana* case began), but Botswana refused to allow him into the country. Instead, the Special Rapporteur went to South Africa, where he reported on the situations of indigenous peoples, including Khoekhoe and San, there (Stavenhagen 2005).
11. These were: Kaudwane in Kweneng District; Gugamma and Metseamonong in the CKGR; New Xade, West Hanahai, and D'Kar in Ghanzi District; and Tsodilo Hills, Shaikarawe, and Mababe in North West District.
12. A draft report of this visit was presented to the government in September 2009, and a final version was produced by the HRC on February 22, 2010. Anaya referred to the CKGR issue as "an emblematic case" (Anaya 2010: 16), and he devoted significant attention to the CKGR issue in his report (Anaya 2010: 16–18). He reported on the Botswana visit at the 2010 PFII meeting in New York.
13. Human Rights Council, Working Group on the Universal Periodic Review, 3rd Session, Geneva, December 1–15, 2008. Compilation prepared by the Office of the High Commissioner of Human Rights, in accordance with paragraph 15(B) of the annex to Human Rights Council Resolution 5/1. Botswana, A/HRC/WG.6/3/BWA/2, October 2, 2008.
14. Human Rights Council. 2008a. A/HRC/WG.6/3/BWA/2, para. 11, p. 5.
15. Human Rights Council. 2008a. A/HRC/WG.6/3/BWA/2, pp. 9–10.
16. Human Rights Council, 10th Session, Agenda Item 6: Universal Periodic Review, Report of the Working Group on the Universal Periodic Review. Botswana, Addendum Views on conclusions and/or recommendations, voluntary commitments and replies presented by the State under review, A/HRC/10/69/Add. 1, March 17, 2009.
17. Human Rights Council, 10th Session, Agenda Item 6: Universal Periodic Review, Report of the Working Group on the Universal Periodic Review. Botswana. A/HRC/10/69, January 13, 2009.

18. Human Rights Council. 2009. A/HRC/10/69/Add. 1, p. 5, 16.
19. Human Rights Council, Working Group on the Universal Periodic Review, 3rd Session, Geneva, December 1–15, 2008, Summary prepared by the Office of the High Commissioner of Human Rights, in accordance with paragraph 15(C) of the annex to Human Rights Council Resolution 5/1. Botswana. A/HRC/WG.6/3/BWA/3, September 15, 2008b.
20. Human Rights Council. 2008b. A/HCR/WG.6/3/BWA/3, p. 6
21. Human Rights Council. 2009b. A/HRC/10/69/Add. 1, p. 5.
22. Human Rights Council, Working Group on the Universal Periodic Review, 3th Session, Geneva, 1–15 December, 2008, National Report Submitted in Accordance with paragraph 15(a) of the Annex to Human Rights Council Resolution 5/1, Botswana, A/HRC/WG.6/3/BWA/1.
23. Human Rights Council, Working Group on the Universal Periodic Review, 15th Session, Geneva, January 21–February 1, 2013, National report submitted in accordance with para. 5 of the annex to Human Rights Council Resolution 16/21. Botswana, A/HRC/WG.6/15/BWA/1, December 4, 2012a.
24. Human Rights Council 2012a. A /HRC/WG.6/15/BWA/1, p. 6.
25. Human Rights Council 2012a. A /HRC/WG.6/15/BWA/1, p. 17.
26. Human Rights Council, Working Group on the Universal Periodic Review, 15th Session, Geneva, January 21–February 1, 2013. Summary prepared by the Office of the High Commissioner for Human Rights in accordance with paragraph 5 of the annex to Human Rights Council Resolution 16/21. Botswana, A/HRC/WG.6/15/BWA/3, October 29, 2012b.
27. Human Rights Council, 2012b. A/HRC/WG.6/15/BWA/3, p. 6.
28. Human Rights Council, 23rd Session, Agenda Item 6: Universal Periodic Review, Report of the Working Group on the Universal Periodic Review. Botswana, A/HRC/23/7, March 22, 2013.
29. Human Rights Council, 2013. A/HRC/23/7, p. 7.
30. Human Rights Council, 2013. A/HRC/23/7, p. 24.
31. Excerpt from the IWGIA publication *Challenging Politics: Indigenous Peoples' Experiences with Political Parties and Elections*, ed. Kathrin Wessendorf (IWGIA 2001).
32. This was also reported in the national media in an article headlined "Politics Divides Basarwa Community" (Letsididi, 2011), which discussed "notorious activists" who were engaged in the discussion to support or criticize the organization.

CHAPTER 9

1. An initial Federal Court ruling in July 2017, which the Standing Rock Sioux Tribe and their allies hail as a victory, suspended of the pipeline's permits and called for impacts of the project to be more thoroughly assessed before it can proceed.

BIBLIOGRAPHY

ACHPR. 2005. *Report of the African Commission's Working Group of Experts on Indigenous Populations/Communities*. Banjul, The Gambia: ACHPR, and Copenhagen: International Work Group for Indigenous Affairs.

2006. *Indigenous Peoples in Africa: The Forgotten Peoples? The African Commission's Work on Indigenous Peoples in Africa*. Banjul, The Gambia: ACHPR, and Copenhagen: International Work Group for Indigenous Affairs.

2007. *Advisory Opinion of the African Commission on Human and Peoples' Rights on the United Nations Declaration on the Rights of Indigenous Peoples*. Banjul, The Gambia: ACHPR, African Union, and Copenhagen: International Work Group for Indigenous Affairs.

2008. *Working Group on Indigenous Populations/Communities*. *Africa Report of the Working Group on Indigenous Populations/Communities in Africa Mission to the Republic of Botswana, June, 2005*. Banjul, The Gambia: ACHPR, African Union, and Copenhagen: International Work Group for Indigenous Affairs.

African Group of States. 2006. *Draft Aide Memoire: United Nations Declaration on the Rights of Indigenous People, 9 November, 2006*. New York and Geneva: United Nations.

African News Agency. 2016. "Botswana Dismisses Reports of Fracking Rights in Pristine Kgalagadi Transfrontier Park." *Mining Weekly*. 16 February.

Ahmed, Shamina, and David Potter. 2006. *NGOs and International Politics*. West Hartford: Kumarian Press.

Albertson, Arthur. 2000a. *Traditional Areas (N!oresi) of the !Goshe Community*. Botswana: Trust for Okavango Cultural and Development Initiatives.

2000b. *Traditional Land-Use Systems of Selected Traditional Territories in the Central Kalahari Game Reserve*. Botswana: Report to First People of the Kalahari, Ghanzi, Botswana.

Alvaré, Bretton. T. 2010. "'Babylon Makes the Rules': Compliance, Fear, and Self-Discipline in the Quest for Official NGO Status." *Political and Legal Anthropology Review. (PoLAR)*, 33(2): 178–200.

Anaya, James. 2009. *International Human Rights and Indigenous Peoples*. Aspen Publishers.

2010. *Promotion and Protection of Human Rights, Civil, Political, Economic, Social and Cultural Rights, Including the Right to Development. Report of the Special Rapporteur on the Situation of Human Rights and Fundamental Freedoms of Indigenous People, James Anaya, Addendum: The Situation of Indigenous Peoples in Botswana*, Geneva: Human Rights Council, Tenth Session, Agenda Item 3, A/HRC/13, 22 February 2010.

Baaitse, Francihah. 2016. "Basarwa clash with Gov't over human/Wildlife co-existence." *Weekend Post*. 11 February.

Babchuk, Wayne and Hitchcock, Robert. 2014. "Botswana." *Indigenous World*. Copenahgen: IWGIA. pp. 468–74.

Barbee, Jeff. 2015. "Botswana Sells Fracking Rights in National Parks." *The Guardian*. 2 December.

Barelli, Mauro. 2012. "Free, Prior, and Informed Consent in the Aftermath of the Declaration on the Rights of Indigenous Peoples: Developments and Challenges Ahead." *International Journal of Human Rights*. 16(1): 1–24.

Barnard, Alan. 1992. *The Hunters and Herders of Southern Africa: A Comparative Ethnography of Khoisan Peoples*. Cambridge: Cambridge University Press.

2006. "Kalahari Revisionism, Vienna and the Indigenous Peoples Debate." *Social Anthropology*. 14(1): 1–16.

2007. *Anthropology and the Bushmen*. Oxford and New York: Berg.

Barsh, Russel L. 1994. "Indigenous Peoples in the 1990s: From Object to Subject of International Law." *Harvard Human Rights Journal*. 7: 33–86.

Barume, Albert. 2010. *The Land Rights of Indigenous Peoples in Africa*. Copenhagen: International Work Group for Indigenous Affairs.

Bechuanaland Protectorate. 1961. *Fauna Conservation Proclamation 1961*. Gaberones: Bechuanaland Government.

Bechuanaland Protectorate Administration. 1963. *The Central Kalahari Game Reserve Regulations*. Mafeking: Bechuanaland Protectorate Administration.

Becker, Jo. 2013. *Campaigning for Justice: Human Rights Advocacy in Practice*. Stanford, CA: Stanford University Press.

Bennett, Bruce. 2008. "Mogotse's Goats and Other Cases before the Gaberones Magistrate in 1908." *Botswana Notes and Records*. 40: 21–34.

Biesele, Megan. 2006. "The Kalahari Peoples Fund: The Activist Legacy of the Harvard Kalahari Research Group." In *The Politics of Egalitarianism: Theory and Practice*. Jacqueline Solway (ed.). London and New York: Berghahn Books. pp. 131–48.

Biesele, Megan and Robert Hitchcock K. 2013. *The Ju/'hoan San of Nyae Nyae and Namibian Independence: Development, Democracy, and Indigenous Voices in Southern Africa*. New York and Oxford: Berghahn Books.

Bishop, Kristyna. 1998. "Squatters on Their Own Land: Khwe Territoriality in Western Botswana." *Comparative and International Law Journal of Southern Africa*. 31: 92–121.

Blichner, Lars and Anders Molander. 2008. "Mapping Juridification." *European Law Journal*. 14(1): 36–54.

Bodilenyane, Keratilwe. 2012. "Botswana's Executive Presidency: Implications for Democracy." *Journal of Public Administration and Governance*. 2(4): 188–201.

Bodley, John H. 2015. *Victims of Progress*. Sixth Edition. Lanham, MD: AltaMira Press.

Bolaane, Maitseo. 2013. *Chiefs, Hunters, and San in the Creation of the Moremi Game Reserve, Okavango Delta: Multiracial Interactions and Initiatives, 1956–1979*. *Senri Ethnological Studies 83*. Osaka: National Museum of Ethnology.

Bollig, Micheal, Robert Hitchcock, Cordelia Nduku, and Jan Reynders. 2000. *At the Crossroads: The Future of a Development Initiative: Evaluation of KDT (Kuru Development Trust), Ghanzi and Ngamiland Districts of Botswana*. Harare, Zimbabwe: Hivos Foundation.

Boonzaier, Emile, Candy Malherbe, Penny Berens, and Andy Smith. 1996. *The Cape Herders: A History of the Khoikhoi of Southern Africa*. Cape Town: David Phillip.

Borchgrevink, Axel. 2004. "Indigenous to Indigenous Development Cooperation: Review Blichner of the Saami Council Projects in Africa." *The Norwegian Institute of International Affairs (NUPI)*.

Botlhomilwe, Mokganedi Zara and David Sebudubudu. 2011. "Limited freedom and intolerance in Botswana." *Journal of Contemporary African Studies*. 29(3): 331–48.

Botswana Khwedom Council. 2012. *San Youth Network: Proposal for [a] San Youth Summit to [be] held on October2013*. Unpublished document.

2015. *Conference Proceedings Report*. D'Kar, 27-28 July. Unpublished report.

Boustany, Nora. 1995. "The Bushmen's Advocate: Straddling Two Worlds, John Hardbattle Speaks to the Plight of the No'akwe of Botswana." *Washington Post*, 18 December. pp. 1–4. www.washingtonpost.com/archive/lifestyle/1995/12/18/the-bushmens-advocate/927fed08-26eb-4494-b889-898c63829fc6/.

Brantlinger, Patrick. 2003. *Dark Vanishings: Discourse on the Extinction of Primitive Races, 1800–1930*. Ithaca, NY: Cornell University Press.

Brockington, Daniel and Jim Igoe. 2006. "Eviction for Conservation: A Global Overview." *Conservation and Society*. 2(2): 411–432.

Brockington, Daniel, Rosaleen Duffy, and Jim Igoe. 2008. *Nature Unbound: Conservation Capitalism, and the Future of Protected Areas*. London: Earthsca.

Brunnegger, Sandra. 2016. "The Craft of Justice-Making through the Permament Peoples' Tribunal in Colombia." In *A Sense of Justice: Legal Knowledge and Lived Experience in Latin America*. Sandra Brunnegger and Karen Falk (eds.) Stanford, CA: Stanford University Press, pp. 123–46.

Bryden, H.A. 1893. *Gun and Camera in Southern Africa: A Year of Wanderings in Bechuanaland, the Kalahari Desert, and the Lake Country, Ngamiland with Notes on Colonization, Natives, Natural History, and Sport*. Edward Stanford, London.

Brysk, Alison. 2000. *From Tribal Village to Global village. Indian Rights and International Relations in Latin America.* Palo Alto, CA: Stanford University Press.

Campbell, Alec. C. 1973. "The National Park and Reserve System in Botswana." *Biological Conservation*. 5(1): 7–14.

Campbell, Alec and Michael Main. 1991. *North West District Remote Area Dwellers: Socio-Economic Survey, Remote Area Development Region South of Lake Ngami*. Report to the North West District Administration, Maun and the Remote Area Development Programme, Ministry of Local Government and Lands, Gaborone, Botswana.

Campbell, Alec, Michael Main, and Robert K. Hitchcock. 2006. "Land, Livestock, and Labor in Rural Botswana: The Western Sandveld Region of Central District as a Case Study." In *Updating the San: Image and Reality of an African People in the 21st Century*. Robert K. Hitchcock, Kazunobu Ikeya, Megan Biesele, and Richard B. Lee (eds.) Senri Ethnological Studies 70. Osaka, Japan: National Museum of Ethnology. pp. 183–228.

Canessa, Andrew. 2007. "Who Is Indigenous? Self-Identification, Indigeneity, and Claims to Justice in Contemporary Bolivia." *Urban Anthropology & Studies of Cultural Systems and World Economic Development*. 36(3): 195–237.

Carroll, Terrance and Barbara Wake Carroll. 2004. "The Rapid Emergence of Civil Society in Botswana." *Commonwealth & Comparative Politics*. 42(3): 333–55.

Cashdan, Elizabeth. 1984. "G//ana Territorial Organization." *Human Ecology*. 12(4): 443–63.

Chanock, Martin. 1998. *Law, Custom, and Social Order: The Colonial Experience in Malawi and Zambia*. Portsmouth, N.H. Heinemann. Original edition, New York: Cambridge University Press 1985.

Charters, Claire and Rodolfo, Stavenhagen. 2009. *Making the Declaration Work: The United Nations Declaration on the Rights of Indigenous Peoples*. Copenhagen: International Work Group for Indigenous Affairs.

Chennells, Roger. 2016. *Equitable Access to Human Biological Resources in Developing Countries: Benefit Sharing Without Undue Inducement*. New York: Springer.

Childers, G. W. 1976. *Report on the Survey/Investigation of the Ghanzi Farm Basarwa Situation*. Gaborone, Botswana: Government Printer.

Chr. Michelsen Institute. 1996. *NORAD's Support of the Remote Area Development Programme in Botswana (RADP) in Botswana*. Bergen,

Norway: Chr. Michelsen Institute, University of Bergen, Oslo, Norway: Royal Norwegian Ministry of Foreign Affairs and Gaborone, Botswana: Ministry of Local Government, Lands, and Housing.

Chwaane, Thato. 2005a. "Botswana: Pilane shouts to Quell Whispers in court." *Mmegi* (Botswana). 10 February. http://allafrica.com/stories/200502100696.html. Accessed 5 March 2016.

2005b. "Botswana: Sesana Denies granting Botswana guardian interview." *Mmegi* (Botswana). http://allafrica.com/stories/200505180127.html. Accessed 7 March 2016.

Comaroff, Jean and John Comaroff. 1991. *Of Revelation and Revolution. Christianity, Colonialism, and Consciousness in South Africa.* Volume One. Chicago, IL: University of Chicago Press.

(eds.) 2006. *Law and Disorder in the Postcolony*. Chicago, IL: University of Chicago Press.

2009. *Ethnicity, Inc*. Chicago, IL: University of Chicago Press.

Cook, Amelia and Jeremy Sarkin. 2009. "Who Is Indigenous? Indigenous Rights Globally, in Africa, and among the San in Botswana." *Tulane Journal of International and Comparative Law*. 18, 93–130.

Corntassel, Jeff. 2007. "Partnership in Action? Indigenous Political Mobilization and Co-option during the First UN Indigenous Decade (1995–2004)." *Human Rights Quarterly*. 29: 137–66.

Corry, Stephen. 2011. *Tribal Peoples for Tomorrow's World*. London: Survival International.

Couso, Javier, Huneeus Alexandra and Rachel Sieder. (eds.) 2013. *Cultures of Legality: Judicialization and Political Activism in Latin America*. Cambridge University Press.

Crawhall, Nigel. 2011. "Africa and the UN Declaration on the Rights of Indigenous Peoples." *The International Journal of Human Rights*. 15(1): 11–36.

Crosette, Barbara. 1990. "Rising variety of groups vie for attention at U.N. rights forum." *New York Times*. 31 March.

Crowder, Michael. 1985. "Tshekedi Khama and Opposition to the British Administration of the Bechuanaland Protectorate, 1926–1936." *Journal of African History*. 26(2–3): 193–214.

Csordas, Thomas. 1999. "Embodiment and Cultural Phenomenology." In *Perspectives on Embodiment: The Intersections of Nature and Culture*. Gail Weiss and Honi Fern Haber (eds.) New York and London: Routledge. pp. 143–64.

Cullis, Adrian and Cathy Watson. 2005. *Winners and Losers: Privatizing the Commons in Botswana*. London: International Institute of Environment and Development.

Cumming, R. G. 1870. *Five Years Adventure in the Far Interior of South Africa*. London: Murray.

Daes, Erica. 2008. *Indigenous Peoples: Keepers of Our Past-Custodian of Our Future*, Copenhagen: International Work Group for Indigenous Affairs.

Dahl, Jens. 2009. *IWGIA: A History*. Copenhagen: International Work Group for Indigenous Affairs (IWGIA).

2012. *The Indigenous Space and Marginalized Peoples in the United Nations*. New York: Palgrave Macmillan.

Datta, Kusum and Andrew Murray. 1989. "The Rights of Minorities and Subject Peoples in Botswana: A Historical Evaluation." In *Democracy in Botswana*. John Holm and Patrick Molutsi (eds.) Gaborone: Macmillan Botswana. pp. 58–74.

de Gaay Fortman, Bastian. 2011. *Political Economy of Human Rights: The Quest for Relevance and Realization*. New York: Routledge.

de Jager, Nicola and Ian Taylor. 2015. "Democratic Contestetion in Botswana." In *Democratic Contestation on the Margins: Regimes in Small African Countries*. Claire Metelits and Stephanie Matti (eds.) Lextington Books. pp. 25–48

Dekker, Reinder Albertus. 2002. *The Design of a Microfinance Programme in San Communities in Western Botswana*. PhD Dissertation, Pretoria: Development Administration, University of South Africa.

Department of Wildlife and National Parks. 1996. *Botswana's Community Based Natural Resource Management Program*. Gaborone, Botswana: Department of Wildlife and National Parks.

1998a. *Second Draft Management Plan for the Central Kalahari Game Reserve and Khutse Game Reserve*. Gaborone, Botswana: Department of Wildlife and National Parks.

1998b. *Botswana Wildlife Aerial Census Data*. Gaborone, Botswana: Department of Wildlife and National Parks.

2001. *Third Draft Management Plan for the Central Kalahari Game Reserve and Khutse Game Reserve*. Gaborone, Botswana: Department of Wildlife and National Parks.

Desbiens, Caroline. 2013. *Power from the North: Territory, Identity, and the Culture of Hydroelectricity in Quebec*. Vancouver: University of British Columbia Press.

Descola, Philippe. 1994. *In the Society of Nature*. Cambridge: Cambridge University Press.

de Sousa Santos, Boaventura and César Rodríguez-Garavito. 2005. "Law Politics, and the Subaltern in Counter-Hegemonic Globalization." In *Law and Globalization from Below: Towards a Cosmopolitan Legality*. Boaventura de Sousa Santos and César Rodríguez-Garavito (eds.) Cambridge, UK: Cambridge University Press, pp. 1–26.

Dibeela, Lebogang. 2014. "The Gope Gem Diamonds Mine: A Jewel or Blight in the History of Basarwa Resistance?" *Sunday Standard. Commentary Monday*, 8 September, 2014.

Dieckmann, Ute. 2007. *Hai//om in the Etosha Region: A History of Colonial Settlement, Ethnicity, and Nature Conservation*. Basel: Basler Afrika Bibliographien.

Dinokopila, Bonolo Ramadi. 2011. "The Right to Water in Botswana: The Review of the Matsipane Mosetlhanyane Case." *African Human Rights Law Journal*. 11(1): 282–95.

Ditshwanelo. 1996. *When Will This Moving Stop? Report on a Fact-Finding Mission of the Central Kgalagadi Game Reserve, April 10–14, 1996*. Gaborone, Botswana: Ditshwanelo, the Botswana Center for Human Rights.

1998. *Steps toward Your Land Rights: A Booklet about the Land Allocation Process in Botswana*. Gaborone, Botswana: Ditshwanelo, the Botswana Center for Human Rights.

2002. *The Central Kalahari Game Reserve. Seminar*. Gaborone: Pyramid Publishing.

Durham, Deborah. 1999. "Civil Lives: Leadership and Accomplishment in Botswana." In *Civil Society and the Political Imagination in Africa*. John Comaroff and Jean Comaroff (eds.) Chicago, IL: University of Chicago Press, pp. 192–218.

Eckert, Julia, Brian Donahoe, Christian Strümpell, and Zerrim Özlem Biner, (eds.) 2014. *Law Against the State: Ethnographic Forays into Law's Transformations*. Cambridge, UK: Cambridge University Press.

Egner, Brian. 1987. *The District Councils and Decentralization: 1978–1986. Report to SIDA (Swedish International Development Authority)*. Gaborone: Economic Consultancies.

Egner, E. Brian and Anna-Lise Klausen 1980. *Poverty in Botswana*. Working Paper No. 29. Gaborone: National Institute of Development and Cultural Research.

Elphick, Richard. 1977. *Kraal and Castle: Khoikhoi and the Founding of White South Africa*. New Haven, CT: Yale University Press.

Engle, Karen. 2010. *The Elusive Promise of Indigenous Development: Rights, Culture, Strategy*. Durham and London: Duke University Press.

English, Mark, Bernhard Clauss, Wynand Swartz, and Jan Xhari. 1980. *We, the People of the Short Blanket: Development Proposals Based on the Needs and Aspirations of the Central Kalahari Game Reserve Population*. Unpublished report, Ghanzi District Council Remote Area Development Office.

Erueti, Andrew. 2011. "The International Labour Organization and the Internationalization of the Concept of Indigenous Peoples." In *Reflections on the UN Declaration on the Rights of Indigenous Peoples*. Allen Stephen and Xanthaki Alexandra (eds.) Oxford and Portland: Hart. pp. 93–120.

Escarcega, Sylvia. 2003. *Internationalization of the Politics of Indigenousness: A Case Study of Mexican Indigenous Intellectuals and Activists at the United Nations*, PhD Dissertation, University of Davis, California.

Escobar, Arturo. 2008. *Territories of Difference: Place, Movements, Life, Redes*. Durham, NC: Duke University Press.

Falk, Karen and Sandra Brunnegger. 2016. "Introduction: Making Sense of Justice." In *A Sense of Justice: Legal Knowledge and Lived Experience in*

Latin America. Sandra Brunnegger and Karen Falk (eds.) Stanford, CA: Stanford University Press. pp. 1–21.

Fawcus, Peter and Alan Tilbury. 2000. *Botswana: The Road to Independence*. Gaborone: Pula Press and the Botswana Society.

Ferguson, James. 1994. *The Anti-Politics Machine: Development, Depoliticization, and Bureaucratic Power in Lesotho*. University of Minnesota Press.

Festus, Baba. 2004a. "The patenting of the Hoodia Gordonia and the San People of Southern Africa." Indigenous Peoples of Africa Coordinating Committee. Statement to the 22nd Session of the Working Group on Indigenous Populations; Agenda Item 5(a) Prior Informed Consent. Geneva. http://cendoc.docip.org/collect/cendocdo/index/assoc/HASH0199/41a8d137.dir/163_as.pdf. Accessed 12 October 2016.

2004b. WGIP 22th Session. *Conflict Resolutions*.

First People of the Kalahari. 1993. *Constitution*. Ghanzi: Botswana.

Fisher, F. William. 1997. "Doing Good? The Politics and Antipolitics of NGO Practices." *Annual Review of Anthropology*. 26: 439–64.

Fraser, Nancy. 2003. "Social Justice in the Age of Identity Politics: Redistribution, Recognition, and Participation." In *Redistribution or Recognition: A Political-Philosophical Exchange*. Nancy Fraser and Axel Honneth (eds.) London: Verso, pp. 7–109.

2005. "Reframing Justice in a Globalizing World." *New Left Review*. 36: 69–88.

2010. *Scales of Justice. Reimagining Political Space in a Globalized World*. Polity Press.

Gadibolae, M.N. 1985. "Serfdom (Bolata) in the Nata Area, 1926–1960." *Botswana Notes and Records*. 17: 25–32.

Gakelebone, Jumanda and Robert Hitchcock. 2013. "Botswana." *Indigenous World*. Copenhagen: IWGIA. pp. 25–32.

Gall, Sandy. 2001. *The Bushmen of Southern Africa: Slaughter of the Innocent*. London: Chatto and Windus.

Gellner, David, Sondra Hausner, and Chiara Letizia. (eds.) 2016. *Religion, Secularism, and Ethnicity in Contemporary Nepal*. Oxford, UK: Oxford University Press.

Ghanzi District Council. 2012. *Ranyane Relocation Phase 2*. Ghanzi: Ghanzi District Council.

Gilbert, Jeremie. 2007. "Historical Indigenous Peoples' Land Claims: A Comparative and International Approach to the Common Law Doctrine on Indigenous Title." *International and Comparative Law Quarterly*. 56: 583–612.

Giraudo, Rachael. 2011. *Intangible Heritage and Tourism Development at the Tsodilo Hills World Heritage Site*. Ph.D. dissertation, Berkeley, CA: University of California.

Good, Kenneth. 2009. *Diamonds, Dispossession and Democracy in Botswana*. Johannesburg: James Currey and Jacana Media.

1999. "The State and Extreme Poverty in Botswana: The San and Destitutes." *Journal of Modern African Studies*. 37(2), 185–205.

Goodale, Mark. 2009. *Surrendering to Utopia: An Anthropology of Human Rights*. Stanford, CA: Stanford University Press.

2016. "Dark matter: Toward a Political Economy of Indigenous Rights and Aspirational Politics." *Critique of Anthropology*. 36(4): 439–57.

Gordon, Robert J. 2009. "Hiding in Full View: The 'Forgotten' Bushman Genocides in Namibia." *Genocide Studies and Prevention*. 4(1): 29–57.

Gordon, Robert J. and Stuart Sholto Douglas. 2000. *The Bushman Myth: The Making of a Namibian Underclass*. Second Edition. Boulder, CO: Westview Press.

Graham, Laura. 2002. "How Should an Indian Speak? Amazonian Indians and the Symbolic Politics of Language in Global Public Sphere." In *Indigenous Movements, Self-Representation and the State in Latin America*. Kay B. Warren and Jean E. Jackson (eds.). Austin: University of Texas Press. pp. 181–228.

Guenther, Mathias. 1975. "The Trance Dancer as an Agent of Social Change among the Farm Bushmen of the Ghanzi District." *Botswana Notes and Records*. 7: 161–6.

1977. "Bushmen Hunters as Farm Laborers." *Canadian Journal of African Studies*. 11(2): 195–203.

1986 *The Nharo Bushmen of Botswana: Tradition and Change*. Hamburg: Helmut Buske Verlag.

1997. "Lords of the Desert Land: Politics and Resistance of the Ghanzi Basarwa in the Nineteenth Century." *Botswana Notes and Records*. 29: 121–40.

1998. *Kuru Household Survey*. D'Kar, Botswana: Kuru Development Trust.

2000. *Tricksters and Trancers: Bushman Religion and Society*. Bloomington, IN: Indiana University Press.

2014. "War and Peace among Kalahari San." *Journal of Aggression, Conflict and Peace Research*. 6(4): 229–39.

2015. "Why Racial Paternalism and not Genocide? The Case of the Ghanzi Bushmen of Bechuanaland." In *Genocide on Settler Frontiers: When Hunter-Gatherers and Commercial Stock Farmers Clash*. Mohamed Adhikari (ed.) New York and Oxford: Berghahn books. pp. 134–58.

Gulbrandsen, Ørnulf. 1987. *Privilege and Responsibility: On Transformations of Hierarchical Relations in a Tswana Society*. Bergen, Norway: Department of Anthropology, University of Bergen.

2012. *The State and the Social: State Formation in Botswana and Its Pre-colonial and Colonial Genealogies*. New York and Oxford: Berghahn Books.

Gulbrandsen, Ørnulf, Marit Karlsen, and Janne Lexow. 1986. *Remote Area Development Programme*. Gaborone, Botswana: Government Printer.
Güldemann, Tom. 2014. "'Khoisan' linguistic classification today." In *Beyond "Khoisan": Historical Relations in the Kalahari Basin*. Tom Güldemann and Anne-Maria Fehn. (eds.) pp. 1–44. Amsterdam: John Benjamins.
Hale, Charles. 2004. "Rethinking Indigenous Politics in the Era of the 'Indio Permitido'." *NACLA Report on the Americas*. 38(2): 16–21.
2006. "Activist Research v. Cultural Critique: Indigenous Land Rights and the Contradictions of Politically Engaged Anthropology." *Cultural Anthropology*. 21(1): 96–120.
Hardbattle, John. 1992. *First People of the Kalahari: A Report*. Ghanzi: First People of the Kalahari.
1993a. "Statement on Behalf of the First People of the Kalahari." In *Never Drink from the Same Cup: Proceedings of the Conference on Indigenous Peoples in Africa, Tune, Denmark, 1993*. Hanne Veber, Jens Dahl, Fiona Wilson, and Espen Waehle (eds.) CDR/IWGIA Document No. 74, Copenhagen: Center for Development Research and the International Working Group for Indigenous Affairs. pp. 141–7.
1993b. "Echoes of the Ancestors." *First People of the Kalahari*. pp. 1–13.
1994. "First People of the Kalahari." *Contact. Plenty Canada*. 3(4): 1–6.
1996. *UN Trip Report*. Ghanzi: First People of the Kalahari.
Hastrup, Kirsten. 2003. "Representing the Common Good: The Limit of Legal Language." In *Human Rights in Global Perspective. Anthropological studies of rights, claims and entitlements*. Wilson A. Richard and Mitchell John (eds.) London and New York: Routledge Press. pp 16–32.
Healy, Jack. 2016. "From 280 Tribes, a Protest on the Plains." *New York Times*. www.nytimes.com/interactive/2016/09/12/us/12tribes.html?_r=0. Accessed 3 January 2017.
Hermans, Janet. 1977. "Official Policy towards the Bushmen of Botswana: A Review, Part I." *Botswana Notes and Records*. 9: 55–67.
Hirschl, Ran. 2008. "The Judicialization of Mega Politics and the Rise of Political Courts." *Annual Review of Political Science*, 11: 93–118.
Hitchcock, Robert. K. 1978. *Kalahari Cattle Posts: A Regional Study of Hunter-Gatherers, Pastoralists and Agriculturalists in the Western Sandveld Region, Central District, Botswana*. Two Volumes. Gaborone, Botswana: Government Printer.
1980. "Tradition, Social Justice, and Land Reform in Central Botswana." *Journal of African Law*. 24(1): 1–34.
1988. *Monitoring, Research, and Development in the Remote Areas of Botswana*. Gaborone, Botswana: Ministry of Local Government, Lands, and Housing, and Oslo: Norwegian Agency for Development Cooperation.
1996. "Subsistence Hunting and Special Game Licenses in Botswana." *Botswana Notes and Records*. 28: 55–64.

2001. "'Hunting Is Our Heritage': The Struggle for Hunting and Gathering Rights among the San of Southern Africa." In *Parks, Property, and Power: Managing Hunting Practice and Identity within State Policy Regimes*. David G. Anderson and Kazunobu Ikeya (eds.) Senri Ethnological Studies 59. Osaka, Japan: National Museum of Ethnology, pp. 139–56.

2002. "'We Are the First People': Land, Natural Resources and Identity in the Central Kalahari, Botswana." *Journal of Southern Africa Studies* 28(4): 797–824.

2015. "Authenticity, Identity, and Humanity: The Hai||om San and the State of Namibia." *Anthropological Forum: A Journal of Social Anthropology and Comparative Sociology*. 25(3): 262–84.

Hitchcock, Robert K. and Wayne A. Babchuk. 2017. "Challenges of Ecotourism among the San of Botswana and Namibia." Paper presented at 77th annual meetings of the Society for Applied Anthropology (SfAA), Santa Fe, New Mexico. Friday, 31 March, 2017.

Hitchcock, Robert K., Benjamin Begbie-Clench, and Ashton Murwira 2016. *The San in Zimbabwe: Livelihoods, Land, and Human Rights*. Report No. 22. Copenhagen: International Work Group for Indigenous Affairs (IWGIA); Johannesburg: Open Society Initiative for Southern Africa (OSISA); and Harare: University of Zimbabwe.

Hitchcock, Robert K. and Martin Enghoff. 2004. *Capacity-Building of First People of the Kalahari, Botswana: An Evaluation*. Copenhagen, Denmark: International Work Group for Indigenous Affairs.

Hitchcock, Robert K. and John Holm. 1993. "Bureaucratic Domination of Hunter and Gatherer Societies: A Study of the San in Botswana." *Development and Change* 24(3): 305–38.

Hitchcock, Robert K., Ikeya Kazanobu, Megan Biesele and Richard. B Lee. (eds.) 2006. *Updating the San: Image and Reality of an African People in the 21st Century*, Osaka, Japan: National Museum of Ethnology. Senri Ethnological Studies 70.

Hitchcock, Robert K. and Rosinah Rose B. Masilo. 1995. *Subsistence Hunting and Resource Rights in Botswana*. Gaborone, Botswana: Department of Wildlife and National Parks.

Hitchcock, Robert K., Maria Sapignoli, Mike Main, and Wayne A. Babchuk. 2015. "The Politics and Economics of Community-Based Natural Resource Management in /Xai/Xai, Ngamiland, Botswana." *African Study Monographs*. 36(4): 211–60.

Hitchcock, Robert K., Diana Vinding, and Karen Bungaard Andersen. 2000. *Recognition of the Bushmen's Land Rights, Human Rights, and Cultural Rights in Botswana*. Gaborone, Botswana and Copenhagen, Denmark: International Work Group for Indigenous Affairs.

Hiveluah, Ulitala. 1993. "Statement by the Permanent Secretary Ministry of Land, Resettlement, Rehabilitation Namibia." In *Never Drink from the*

Same Cup: Proceedings of the Conference on Indigenous Peoples in Africa, Tune, Denmark, 1993. Hanne Veber, Jens Dahl, Fiona Wilson, and Espen Waehle (eds.) CDR/IWGIA Document No. 74, Copenhagen: Center for Development Research and the International Working Group for Indigenous Affairs. pp. 139–40.

Hoag, Colin. 2011. "Assembling Partial Perspectives: Thoughts on the Anthropology of Bureaucracy." *Political and Legal Anthropology Review (PoLAR)*. 34(1): 81–94.

Hodgson, Dorhoty. 2011. *Being Maasai, Becoming Indigenous: Postcolonial Politics in a Neoliberal World.* Bloomington, IN: University of Indiana Press.

Holm, John, Patrick Molutsi, and Gloria Somolekae. 1996. "The Development of Civil Society in a Democratic State: The Botswana Model." *African Studies Review*. 39(2): 43–69.

Hoon, Parakh. 2014. "Elephants Are Like Our Diamonds: Recentralizing Community Based Natural Resource Management in Botswana 1996–2012." *African Studies Quarterly*. 15(1): 55–70.

Hull, Matthew S. 2012. *Government of Paper: The Materiality of Bureaucracy in Urban Pakistan.* Berkley, CA: University of California Press.

Human Rights Council. 2008a. *Compilation prepared by the Office of the High Commissioner of Human Rights, in accordance with paragraph 15(B) of the annex to Human Rights Council Resolution 5/1. Botswana.* Working Group on the Universal Periodic Review, 3rd Session, Geneva, December 1–15, 2008. A/HRC/WG.6/3/BWA/2, October 2, 2008.

2008b. *Summary prepared by the Office of the High Commissioner of Human Rights, in accordance with paragraph 15(C) of the annex to Human Rights Council Resolution 5/1. Botswana.* Working Group on the Universal Periodic Review, 3rd Session, Geneva, December 1–15, 2008. A/HRC/WG.6/3/BWA/3, September 15, 2008.

2008c. *National Report Submitted in Accordance with paragraph 15(a) of the Annex to Human Rights Council Resolution 5/1 ,Botswana.* Working Group on the Universal Periodic Review, 3th Session, Geneva, 1-15 December, 2008, A/HRC/WG.6/3/BWA/1.

2009a. *Report of the Working Group on the Universal Periodic Review. Botswana.* 10th Session, Agenda Item 6: Universal Periodic Review. A/HRC/10/69, January 13, 2009.

2009b. *Botswana, Addendum Views on conclusions and/or recommendations, voluntary commitments and replies presented by the State under review.* 10th Session, Agenda Item 6: Universal Periodic Review, Report of the Working Group on the Universal Periodic Review. A/HRC/10/69/Add. 1, March 17, 2009.

2012a. *National report submitted in accordance with para. 5 of the annex to Human Rights Council Resolution 16/21. Botswana.* Working Group on the

Universal Periodic Review, 15th Session, Geneva, January 21–February 1, 2013. A/HRC/WG.6/15/BWA/1, December 4, 2012.

2012b. *Summary prepared by the Office of the High Commissioner for Human Rights in accordance with paragraph 5 of the annex to Human Rights Council Resolution 16/21. Botswana.* Working Group on the Universal Periodic Review, 15th Session, Geneva, January 21–February 1, 2013. A/HRC/WG.6/15/BWA/3, October 29, 2012.

2013. *23rd Session, Agenda Item 6: Universal Periodic Review, Report of the Working Group on the Universal Periodic Review. Botswana.* A/HRC/23/7, March 22, 2013.

Ifezue, Godsglory. 2015. "Understanding Chieftainship in Botswana: The Status and Powers of Chiefs in Present Day Botswana." *Journal of African Law*. 59(2): 271–93.

Ikeya, Kazonubu. 1996. "Road Construction and Handicraft Production in the Xade Area, Botswana." *African Study Monographs*. Supplement 22: 67–84.

1999. "The Historical Dynamics of the Socioeconomic Relationships between the Nomadic San and the Rural Kgalagadi." *Botswana Notes and Records*. 31: 19–32.

2001. "Some Changes among the San under the Influence of Relocation Plan in Botswana." In *Parks, Property, and Power: Managing Hunting Practice and Identity Within State Policy Regimes*. David G. Anderson and Kazunobu Ikeya (eds.) Senri Ethnological Studies No. 59. Osaka, Japan: National Museum of Ethnology, pp. 183–98.

2016. "Interaction of the San, NGOs, and the State." In *Hunter-Gatherers and Their Neighbours in Asia, Africa, and South America*. Kazunobu Ikeya and Robert K. Hitchcock (eds.) Senri Ethnological Studies No. 94. Osaka, Japan: National Museum of Ethnology, pp. 255–67.

Ingstand Benedicte, Fugelli Per. 2006. "'Our Health, was Better in the Time of Queen Elisabeth': The Importance of Land to the Health Perception of the Botswana San." In *Updating the San: Image and Reality of an African People in the 21st Century*. Robert K. Hitchcock, Kazunobu Ikeya, Megan Biesele, and Richard B. Lee (eds.) Senri Ethnological Studies 70. Osaka, Japan: National Museum of Ethnology, pp. 61–81.

International Work Group for Indigenous Affairs (IWGIA). 1997. *Annual Report*. Copenhagen: Denmark.

1998. *Annual Report*. Copenhagen: Denmark.

1999. *Annual Report*. Copenhagen: Denmark.

2000. *Annual Report*. Copenhagen: Denmark.

2011. *The Indigenous World*. Copenhagen: IWGIA.

IPACC. 2004. WGIP 22th Session. *This intervention refers to the San people of the Central Kalahari Game Reserve, Botswana*. Agenda Item 4(a).

Isaacs, S.M. and B.T. Manatsha 2016. "Will the Dreaded 'Yellow Monster' Stop Roaring Again?: An Appraisal of Botswana's 2015 Land Policy." *Botswana Notes and Records*. 48: 383–95.

Isaacson, Rupert. 2002. *Last Exit from the Kalahari. The Slow Genocide of the Bushmen/San*. www.opendemocracy.net/content/articles/pdf/267.pdf.

Jefferis, Keith. 2009. "The Role of TNCs in the Extractive Industry of Botswana." *Transnational Corporations*. 18(1): 61–92.

Johannes, Aaron and Komtsa Komtsa. 1993. "Statement by Representatives of the First People of the Kalahari." In *Never Drink from the Same Cup: Proceedings of the Conference on Indigenous Peoples in Africa, Tune, Denmark, 1993*. Hanne Veber, Jens Dahl, Fiona Wilson, and Espen Waehle (eds.) CDR/IWGIA Document No. 74, Copenhagen: Center for Development Research and the International Working Group for Indigenous Affairs, pp. 149–52.

Joyce, J.W. 1937. "Report on the Masarwa in the Bamangwato Reserve, Bechuanaland Protectorate." League of Nations Publications VI. B.: Slavery. *Annex*. 6: 57–76.

Kalahari Conservation Society. 1988. *Management Plan for Central Kalahari and Khutse Game Reserves*. Gaborone, Botswana: Kalahari Conservation Society (KCS).

Kamat, Sangeeta. 2003. "NGOs and the new democracy." *Harvard International Review* 25(1): 65.

Karlsson, Bengt. 2003. "Anthropology and the 'Indigenous Slot': Debates about Indigenous Peoples' Status in India." *Critique of Anthropology*. 23(4): 403–23.

Kelly, Tobias. 2012. *This Side of Silence: Human Rights, Torture and the Recognition of Cruelty*. Philadelphia: University of Pennsylvania Press.

Kelso, Casey. 1993. "The Landless Bushmen." *Africa Report*. 38(2): 51+.

Kenrick, Justin and Lewis Jerome. 2004. "Indigenous Peoples' Rights and the Politics of the Term 'Indigenous'." *Anthropology Today*. 20(2): 4–9.

Kent, Susan. 1992. "The Current Forager Controversy: Real Versus Ideal Views of Hunter-Gatherers." *Man* 27(1): 45–70.

(ed.) 2002. *Ethnicity, Hunter-Gatherers and the Other. Association or Assimilation in Africa?* Washington, DC: Smithsonian Institution Press.

Kenyon, Paul. 2005. "Row over Bushmen 'genocide'." *BBC News, Crossing Continents Programs*. London: BBC. 11 June.

Keoreng, Ephraim. 2011. "Sesana the Rock Star at BNF." *Mmegi* 29 July, 2011.

Kesselring, Rita. 2016. "An Injury to One is an Injury to All? Class Actions in South African Courts and their Effects on Plaintiffs." *Political and Legal Anthropology Review (PoLAR)*. 39(S1): 74–88.

2017. *Bodies of Truth: Law, Memory, and Emancipation in Post-Apartheid South Africa*. Stanford, CA: Stanford University Press.

Khama, Seretse Ian. 2008. *State of the Nation Address*. Gaborone: Government Printer.

2010. *State of the Nation Address*. Gaborone: Government Printer.

2012. *State of the Nation Address*. Gaborone: Government Printer.

Kiema, Kuela. 2010. *Tears for My Land: A Social History of the Kua of the Central Kalahari Game Reserve, Tc'amnqo*. Gaborone: Mmegi Publishing House.

Kings, Sipho. 2015. "Mining Tests the Spirit of the Kalahari." *Mail and Guardian*, 30 October, 2015.

Kirsch, Stuart. 2014a. "Juridification of Indigenous Politics." In *Law against the State: Ethnographic Forays into Law's Transformations*. Julia Eckert, Brian Donahoe, Christian Strümpell, and Zerrim Özlem Biner (eds.) Cambridge, UK: Cambridge University Press, pp. 23–43.

2014b. *Mining Capitalism: The Relationship between Corporations and their Critics*. Oakland, CA: University of California Press.

Konopo, J., N. Ntibinyane, and T. Mongudhi, 2016. "Botswana's 'shoot-to-kill policy' against suspected poachers." *Mail and Guardian*, 18 March.

Kuper, Adam. 1970. *Kalahari Village Politics: An African Democracy*. Cambridge: Cambridge University Press.

2003. "The Return of the Native." *Current Anthropology*. 44(3): 389–95.

Landzelius, Kyra. 2006. "Introduction: Native on the Net." In *Native on the Net: Indigenous and Diasporic Peoples in the Virtual Age*. Kyra Landzelius (ed.) New York: Routledge, pp. 1–42.

Lawy, Jenny. 2016. *An Ethnography of San: Minority Recognition and Voice in Botswana*. Doctoral dissertation, Social Anthropology, University of Edinburgh.

Lebotse, Tshepang Denise. 2009. *Victims or Actors of Development: The Case of the San People at D'Kar, Botswana*. MA thesis. Norway: University of Tromso, Tromso.

Lee, Richard B. 1969. "Eating Christmas in the Kalahari." *Natural History*. 78(10): 14–22, 60–63.

1976. "Introduction." In *Kalahari Hunter-Gatherers: Studies of the !Kung San and Their Neighbors*. Richard B. Lee and Irven DeVore (eds.) Cambridge: Harvard University Press, pp. 3–24.

1979. *The !Kung San: Men, Women, and Work in a Foraging Society*. Cambridge: Cambridge University Press.

2006. "Twenty-First Century Indigenism." *Anthropological Theory*. 6(4): 455–79.

Lee, R. B. and I. DeVore (eds.) 1976. *Kalahari Hunter-Gatherers: Studies of the !Kung San and Their Neighbours*. Cambridge, MA: Harvard University Press.

LeRoux, Braam. 1996. Community-Owned Development amongst the Marginalized San Communities of the Kalahari, as Adopted by a San

Community Development Organization, the Kuru Development Trust. Working Papers in Early Childhood Development 22. The Hague, The Netherlands: Bernard van Leer Foundation.

Letshwiti, Monty. 1981. "Basarwa Demand Social Justice." *Daily News* (Botswana) 1 September.

Letsididi, Bashi. 2011. "Politics Divides Basarwa Community." *Sunday Standard* (Botswana) 28 November. www.sundaystandard.info/politics-divides-basarwa-community. Accessed 11 March 2017.

Lewis, David. 2014. *Non-Governmental Organizations, Management and Development*. Third Edition. London: Routledge.

Li, Tania Murray. 2000. "Articulating Indigenous Identity in Indonesia: Resource Politics and the Tribal Slot." *Comparative Studies in Society and History* 42(1): 149–79.

Lindroth, Marjo 2006. "Indigenous-State Relations in the UN: Establishing the Indigenous Forum." *Political and Anthropological Review (PoLAR)*. 42: 239–48.

Livingston, Julie. 2008. "Disgust, Bodily Aesthetics, and the Ethic of Being Human in Botswana." *Africa*. 78(2): 288–307.

Livingstone, David. 1857. *Missionary Travels and Researches in South Africa*. London: John Murray.

Lock, Margaret. 2002. *Twice Dead: Organ Transplants and the Reinvention of Death*. Berkeley and Los Angeles: University of California Press.

Lockwood, Bert B. 1990. *In the High Court of the Republic of Botswana. In the Matter Between Unity Dow and the Attorney General of Botswana*. Cincinnati, OH: Urban Morgan Institute for Human Rights, University of Cincinnati College of Law.

Lovgren, Stefan. 2004. "African Bushmen Tour U.S. to Fund Fight for Land." *National Geographic*. 14 September. http://news.nationalgeographic.com/news/2004/09/0914_040914_labushmen.html. Accessed 3 March 2016.

Lynch, Gabrielle. 2011. "Becoming Indigenous in the Pursuit of Justice: The African Commission on Human and Peoples' Rights and the Endorois." *African Affairs*. 111/442: 24–45.

MacKenzie, J. 1871. *Ten Years North of the Orange River: A Story of Everyday Life and Work among the South African Tribes from 1859 to1869*. Edinburgh: Edmonston and Douglas.

Macklem, Patrick. 2015. *The Sovereignty of Human Rights*. Oxford: Oxford University Press.

Magnussen, Anne-Mette and Anna Banasiak. 2013. "Juridification: Disrupting the Relationship between Law and Politics?" *European Law Journal*. 19(3): 325–39.

Mamdani, Mahmood. 2012. *Define and Rule. Native as Political Identity*. Harvard University Press.

Maphangela, Peter. 1988. "P30m is Set for Remote Projects." *Daily News* (Botswana) 22 February.

Marcus, George. 1995. "Ethnography in the World System: The Emergence of Multi-Sited Ethnography." *Annual Review of Anthropology*. 24: 95–117.

Marshall, John. 2003. A *Kalahari Family*. (videos). Watertown, MA: Documentary Educational Resources.

Marshall, Lorna. 1976. *The !Kung of Nyae Nyae*. Cambridge: Harvard University Press.

Martínez, Miguel Alfonso. 1992. "First Progress Report: Study on Treaties, Agreements and Other Constructive Arrangements between States and Indigenous Populations." United Nations E/CN.4/Sub.2/1992/32.

1995. "Second Progress Report: Study on Treaties, Agreements and Other Constructive Arrangements between States and Indigenous Populations." United Nations E/CN.4/Sub.2/1995/27.

1999. "Final Report: Human Rights of Indigenous Peoples, Study on Treaties, Agreements and other Constructive Arrangements between States and Indigenous Populations." United Nations E/CN.4/Sub.2/1999/20.

Maruyama, Junko. 2003. "The Impact of Resettlement on Livelihood and Social Relationships among the Central Kalahari San." *African Study Monographs*. 14(4), 223–45.

2007. "Between 'Nation' and 'Indigenous People': Micropolitics over the Legitimacy of a Newly Established Headmanship among the /Gui and //Gana San in Botswana." *Departmental Bulletin Paper*. Kyoto University.

Masarwa Commission. 1931. Report by E.S.B. Tagart, CBE on Masarwa and Corporatl Punishment in the Bamangwato Reserve, 1931, Testimony. BNA S.204/8, 15 July 1931.

Maxwell, Elizabeth and Alice Mogwe. 2006. *In the Shadow of the Noose*. Gaborone: Ditshwanelo: The Botswana Centre for Human Rights.

Mazonde, Isac N. 2002. "The San in Botswana and the Issue of Subjectivities: National Disintegration or Cultural Diversity?" In Isac. N. Mazonde (ed.) *Minorities of the Millennium: Perspectives from Botswana*. Gabarone: Lentswe la Lesedi. Pp. 57–71.

Meldrum, Andrew. 1988. "A Better Life for the Bushmen?" *Africa Report*. 33(4): 58–61.

2004. "Man cuts De Beers links in ethics row." *The Guardian*. 9 May. www.theguardian.com/world/2004/may/09/humanrights.andrewmeldrum. Accessed October 27, 2016.

Merlan, Francesca. 2009. "Indigeneity: Global and Local." *Current Anthropology*. 50(3): 303–53.

Merry, Sally Engle. 2003. "From Law and Colonialism to Law and Globalization." *Law & Social Inquiry*. 28(2): 569–90.

2005. "Anthropology and Activism: Researching Human Rights across Porous Boundaries." *Political and Legal Anthropology Review (PoLAR)* 28(2): 240–57.

2006. "Transnational Human Rights and Local Activism: Mapping the Middle." *American Anthropologist*. 108(1): 38–51.

2012. "Anthropology and Law." In *The Sage Handbook of Anthropology*. Richard Fardon, Olivia Harris, Trevor H.J. Marchand, Mark Nuttall, Cris Shore, Veronica Strand, and Richard Wilson (eds.) London and Los Angeles: Sage, pp. 105–120.

Merry, Sally and Susan Coutin. 2014. "Technologies of Truth in the Anthropology of Conflict." *American Ethnologist*. 41(1): 1–16.

Miers, Suzanne and Michael Crowder. 1988. "The Politics of Slavery in Bechuanaland: Power Struggles and the Plight of the Basarwa in the Bamangwato Reserve, 1926-1940." In *The End of Slavery in Africa*. Suzanne Miers and Richard Roberts (eds.) Madison, WI: University of Wisconsin Press, pp. 172–200.

Minde, Herry. 2008. "The Destination and the Journey: Indigenous Peoples and the United Nations from the 1960s through 1985." In *Indigenous Peoples: Self-Determination, Knowledge and Indigeneity*. Delft, The Netherlands: Eburon Delf, pp. 49–86.

Ministry of Commerce and Industry. 1986. *Report of the Central Kalahari Game Reserve Fact Finding Mission*. MCI Circular No. 1 of 1986. Gaborone, Botswana: Ministry of Commerce and Industry.

Mmegi/the Reporter. 1992. *Editorial: Basarwa*. Volume 9, no 20 - 29 May - 4 June, 1992.

Mogalakwe, Monageng. 1986. *Inside Ghanzi Freehold Farms: A Look at the Conditions of Basarwa Farm Workers*. Gaborone, Botswana: Applied Research Unit: Ministry of Local Government and Lands.

Mogwe, Alice. 1992. *Who Was (T)here First? An Assessment of the Human Rights Situation of Basarwa in Selected Communities in the Gantsi District, Botswana*. Gaborone: Botswana Christian Council.

2011. "Human Rights Struggles: Where Social Conflicts and Confrontations are Negotiated – The Case of the Displacement of 'Basarwa' from the Central Kalahari Game Reserve." In *The Governance of Legal Pluralism*. Werner Zips and Markus Weilenmann (eds.) Münster and Hamburg: LIT Verlag, pp. 163–79.

Mohr, Edward. 1876. *To the Victoria Falls of the Zambezi*. London: Sampson Low, Marston, Searle, and Rivington.

Molokomme, Athalia. 2006. *Attorney General's Statement on the Outcome of the Case of Roy Seasana and Others v. the Attorney General*. 14th December 2006. Gaborone, Botswana: Attorney General's Chambers, Government of Botswana.

Molomo, Mpho and Wilford Molefe. 2005. "Voters and electoral performance of political parties in Botswana." In *40 Years of Democracy in Botswana 1965–2005*. Zibani Maundeni (ed.)Gaborone: Mmegi Publishing House, pp. 94–121.

Mooketsi, Lekopanye. 1989. "Farm workers ill-treated in Ghanzi." *The Guardian* (Botswana) 10 November.

Morgan, Rhiannon. 2007. "On Political Institutions and Social Movement Dynamics: The Case of the United Nations and the Global Indigenous Movement." *International Political Science Review*. 28(3): 273–92.

Morocco. 1985. "Statement before the United Nations Working Group on Indigenous Populations." U.N. doc. no. E/CN.4/Sub.2/AC.4/1985/WP.1/Add.1.

Morris, Job. 2011. Political Participation: Autonomy without Marginalization. Paper presented to The Challenge of Respecting Indigenous Peoples' Rights: Comparative Experiences from Africa, Latin America, and North America, Institute for the Study of International Development, McGill University, 2011. https://sanyouthnetwork.wordpress.com/2017/03/13/411/. Accessed 2 April 2017.

Morton, Barry. 1994. "Servitude, Slave Trading, and Slavery in the Kalahari." In *Slavery in South Africa: Captive Labor on the Dutch Frontier*. Elizabeth A. Eldredge and Fred Morton (eds.) Boulder, CO: Westview Press and Pietermaritzburg: University of Natal Press, pp. 215–50.

Morton, Fred and Robert Hitchcock. 2014. "Tswana Hunting: Continuities and Changes in the Transvaal and Kalahari after 1600." *South African Historical Journal*. 66(3): 418–39.

Mosse, David. 2001. "'People's Knowledge,' Participation and Patronage: Operations and Representations in Rural Development." In *Participation: The New Tyranny?* B. Cook and U. Kothari (eds.) London: Zed Books, pp. 16–35.

Motzafi-Haller, Pnina. 1994. "When Bushmen are Known as Basarwa: Gender, Ethnicity and Differentiation in Rural Botswana." *American Ethnologist*. 21(3): 539–63.

1995. "Liberal Discourses of Cultural Diversity and Hegemonic Construction of Difference. Basarwa in Contemporary Botswana." *Political and Legal Anthropology Review (PoLAR)*. 18(2): 99–104.

2002. *Fragmented Worlds, Coherent Lives: The Politics of Difference in Botswana*. Westport, CT and London: Bergin and Garvey.

Moyn, Samuel. 2010. *The Last Utopia: Human Rights in History*. Cambridge, MA: Harvard University Press.

Muehlebach, Andrea. 2001. "Making Place at the United Nations: Indigenous Cultural Politics at the U.N. Working Group on Indigenous Populations." *Cultural Anthropology*. 16(3): 415–48.

Murray, Mark. 1976. *Present Wildlife Utilization in the Central Kalahari Game Reserve, Botswana: A Report on the C.K.G.R. Reconnaissance Survey*. Gaborone, Botswana: Report to the Department of Wildlife, National Parks, and Tourism.

1979. *Botswana's Unified Hunting Regulations: An Analysis*. Gaborone, Botswana: Department of Wildlife, National Parks, and Tourism.
Mwakikagile, Godfrey. 2010. *Botswana: Profile of a Nation*. Elizabethtown, PA: Continental Press.
Myburgh, Paul John. 2013. *The Bushman Winter Has Come: The True Story of the Last Band of G/wikwe Bushmen on the Great Sand Face*. Johannesburg: Penguin Books (South Africa).
Ndahinda, Felix Mukwiza. 2011. *Indigenousness in Africa: A Contested Legal Framework for Empowerment of "Marginalized" Communities*. The Hague, The Netherlands: T.M.C. Asser Press and New York: Springer.
Ng'ong'ola, Clement. 1997. "Land Rights for Marginalized Ethnic Groups in Botswana, with special reference to the Basarwa." *Journal of African Law*. 41(1): 1–26.
2007. "Sneaking Aboriginal Title into Botswana's Legal System through a Side Door: Review of Sesana and Others v. The Attorney General." *University of Botswana Law Journal*. December: 103–23.
Niezen, Ronald. 2003. *The Origins of Indigenism: Human Rights and the Politics of Identity*. Berkeley, CA and London: University of California Press.
2005. "Digital Identity: The Construction of Virtual Selfhood in the Indigenous Peoples' Movement." *Comparative Studies in Society and History*. 45(2): 532–51.
2009. *Defending the Land: Sovereignty and Forest Life in James Bay Cree Society*. Second Edition. Upper Saddle River, NJ: Pearson/Prentice Hall.
2010. *Public Justice and the Anthropology of Law*. Cambridge, UK: Cambridge University Press.
Norwegian Church Aid. 2007. *First People of the Kalahari Evaluation Report*. Oslo: Norwegian Church Aid.
Nthomang, K. 2004. "Relentless Colonialism: The Case of the Remote Area Development Programme (RADP) and the Botswana." *Journal of Modern African Studies* 42(3): 415–35.
Nyati-Ramahobo, Lydia. 2009. *Minority Tribes in Botswana: The Politics of Recognition*. London: Minority Rights Group International.
Oliver-Smith, Anthony. 2009. "Introduction: Development-Forced Displacement and Resettlement: A Global Human Rights Crisis." In *Development and Dispossession: The Crisis of Forced Displacement and Resettlement*. Anthony Oliver-Smith (ed.) Santa Fe, NM: School for Advanced Research Press, pp. 3–24.
Ontebetse, Khonani. 2016a. "Basarwa Reject Roy Sesana; Govt Deal in the CKGR." *Sunday Standard* (Botswana) 4 February.
2016b. "Crashed Police Chopper was 'In Pursuit of Basarwa Hunters'." *Sunday Standard* (Botswana) 18 August, www.sundaystandard.info/crashed-police-chopper-was-'-pursuit-basarwa-hunters'. Accessed 18 August 2016.

2017. "Khama's CKGR Plan Unravels as Sesana Refuses to Play Ball." *Sunday Standard* (Botswana) 10 September.

Osaki, Masakazu. 1984. "The Social Influence of Change in Hunting Technique among the Central Kalahari San." *African Study Monographs*. 5: 49–62.

2001. "Reconstructing the Recent History of the G/ui and G//ana Bushmen." *African Study Monographs*, Supplement. 26: 27–39.

OSISA. 2016. *Botswana's Diamond Deception*. Johannesburg: OSISA.

Owens, Mark and Delia Owens. 1981. *Preliminary Final Report on the Central Kalahari Predator Research Project*. Gaborone, Botswana: Report to the Department of Wildlife and National Parks.

Paine, Robert. 1977. *The White Arctic: Anthropological Essays on Tutelage and Ethnicity. St. Johns: Institute of Economic and Social Research*. Memorial University of Newfoundland.

Pariser, Eli. 2011. *The Filter Bubble: What the Internet Is Hiding from You*. London. Penguin Books.

Parmar, Pooja. 2015. *Indigeneity and Legal Pluralism in India*. Cambridge University Press.

Parsons, Quentin Neil. 1973. *Khama III, the Bamangwato, and the British, with Special Reference to 1895-1923*. Ph.D. Dissertation. Edinburgh, Scotland: University of Edinburgh.

Patriot Reporter. 2016. "Botswana: Tshekedi – The Almighty." *The Patriot*. 24 October.

Penn, Nigel. 2006. *The Forgotten Frontier: Colonist and Khoisan on the Cape's Northern Frontier in the 18th Century*. Athens: Ohio University Press.

Peters, Paulina. 1994. *Dividing the Commons: Politics, Policy, and Culture in Botswana*. Charlottesville and London: University Press of Virginia.

Pheage, Tefo. 2016a. "Khama - Sesana Deal." *Mmegi-on-line, Friday*, 22 January 2016.

2016b. "Basarwa Confused over Sesana's Employment." *Mmegi On-Line* (Botswana) 22 January.

2016c. "Now Sesana fights government." *The Monitor* (Botswana) 15 August. www.mmegi.bw/index.php?aid=62293&dir=2016%2Faugust%2F15. Accessed 18 August.

2016d. "Basarwa Report Govt to the UN." *Mmegi* (Botswana) 20 May.

Picard, Louis A. 1987. *The Politics of Development in Botswana: A Model for Success?* Boulder, Colorado: Lynne Rienner Publishers.

Pöntinen, Mari-Anna. 2013. *African Theology as Liberating Wisdom: Celebrating Life and Harmony in the Evangelical Lutheran Church in Botswana*. Leiden and Boston: Brill.

Poteete, Amy. 2009. "Defining Political Community and Rights to Natural Resources in Botswana." *Development and Change*. 40(2): 281–305.

2015. "Election Note: Botswana's 2014 Parliamentary Elections." *Electoral Studies*. http://dx.doi.org/10.1016/j.electstud.2015.05.001.

Povinelli, Elizabeth. 2002. *The Cunning of Recognition: Indigenous Alterities and the Making of Australian Multiculturalism*. Durham and London: Duke University Press.

Quansah, E.K. 2007. "The Present State of the Hearsay Rule in Botswana." *University of Botswana Law Journal*. December: 61–80.

Ramanathan, Usha. 1996. "Displacement in the Law." Special Issue Development, Displacement and Rehabilitation. *Economic and Political Weekly*. 31(24): 1486–91.

Ramos, Alcida. 2003. Comment on "The Return of the Native." by A. Kuper, *Current Anthropology*. 44(3): 397–8.

Ramsay, Jeff, Barry Morton, and Part Themba Mgadla. 1996. *Building a Nation: A History of Botswana from 1800 to 1910*. Gaborone: Longman Botswana.

Randeria, Shalini. 2007. "De-Politicization of Democracy and Judicialization of Politics." *Theory, Culture and Society*. 24(4): 38–44.

Ratshosa, Simon. 1926. *How the Masarwa Became Slaves. Report to the Bamangwato Tribal Administration, 1926*. Swerowe: Bamangwato Tribal Administration.

Reporter Daily News. 1992. "Basarwa Demand Self-Rule." *Daily News* (Botswana) 21 May.

Reporter Mmegi. 1996. "The Khwe Speak Out." *Mmegi/The Reporter*. (Botswana) 13 (20), May 23–30 1996

Reporter The Gazette. 1992. "We Were Insulted – Basarwa." *The Gazette* (Botswana) 3 June.

Reporter The Voice. 2004. "On the Attack: Botswana Government wants to kill Basarwa and our culture." *The Voice* (Botswana) October 8.

Republic of Botswana. 1966. *Constitution of Botswana*. Gaborone, Botswana: Government Printer.

1968. *Tribal Land Act (1968)*, *No. 54*, Gaborone: Government Printer.

1975. *National Policy on Tribal Grazing Land*. Government Paper No. 2. Gaborone: Government Printer.

1979. *Unified Hunting Regulations, under the Revision of the Fauna Conservation* Act (Laws of Botswana, Chap. 38:01). Gaborone: Government Printer.

1980. *National Settlement Policy*. Gaborone, Botswana: Government Printer.

1985. *Central Kalahari Game Reserve Fact Finding Mission*. Unpublished report.

1986. *Wildlife Conservation Policy*, Government Paper l. Gaborone: Government Printer.

1990. *Community based Natural Resource Management Policy*. Gaborone: Government Printer.

1992. *Wildlife Conservation and National Parks Act, 1992*. Act No. 28 of 1992. Gaborone, Botswana: Government Printer.

1994. *Ostrich Management Plan Policy*. Government Paper 1. Gaborone: Government Printer.
1998. *National Settlement Policy*. Government Paper No. 2 of 1998. August 1998. Gaborone, Botswana: Government Printer.
2000a. *National Parks and Game Reserves Regulations*. Gaborone, Botswana: Government Printer.
2000b. *Report of the Presidential Commission of Inquiry into Sections 77,78, and 79 of the Constitution of Botswana*. Gaborone, Botswana: Government Printer.
2001. *Wildlife Conservation (Hunting and Licensing) Regulations, 2001*. Gaborone, Botswana: Government Printer.
2002. *Revised National Policy on Destitute Persons*. Gaborone: Government Printer.
2007a. *Community Based Natural Resources Management Policy*. Gaborone, Botswana: Government of Botswana.
2007b. *Constitution of Botswana (1961)*. Gaborone, Botswana: Government Printer.
2009. *Revised Remote Area Development Programme Policy*. Gaborone: Republic of Botswana.
2012. *Botswana National Water Policy, October 2012*. Gaborone: Ministry of Minerals, Energy and Water Resources.
2014a. *Supplement C. Wildlife Conservation and National Parks (Prohibition of Hunting, Capturing, or Removal of Animals Order, 2014). Statutory Instrument No. 2 of 2014. Botswana Government Gazette, Volume LII, No. 2, 10 January, 2014*. Gaborone: Botswana Government Gazette.
2014b. *Affirmative Action Framework (2014)*. Gaborone: Ministry of Local Government and Rural Development.
2015. *National Land Policy*. Gaborone, Botswana: Government Printer.
Richardson, Boyce. 1991. *Strangers Devour the Land*. Vancouver: Douglas & McIntyre.
Robins, Steven. 2001. "NGOs, 'Bushmen' and Double Vision: The /Khomani San Land Claim and the Cultural Politics of 'Community' and 'Development' in the Kalahari." *Journal of Southern African Studies*. 27(4): 833–53.
2003. Comment on "The Return of the Native." by A. Kuper, *Cultural Anthropology*. 44(3): 398–9.
Robinson, James A, Daron Acemoglu, and Simon Johnson. 2003. "An African Success Story: Botswana." In *In Search of Prosperity: Analytic Narratives on Economic Growth*. Dani Rodrik (ed.) Princeton: Princeton University Press, pp. 80–119.
Russell, Margo. 1976. "Slaves or Workers? Relations between Bushmen, Tswana and Boers in the Kalahari." *Journal of Southern African Studies*. 2(2): 178–97.

Russell, Margo and Martin Russell. 1979. *Afrikaners of the Kalahari: White Minorities in a Black State*. Cambridge: Cambridge University Press.

Samatar, A.I. 1999. *An African Miracle: State and Class Leadership and Colonial Legacy in Botswana Development*. Portsmouth: Heinemann.

Samson, Colin. 2003. "Rights as the Reward for Simulated Cultural Sameness: The Innue in the Canadian Colonial Context." In *Culture and Rights: Anthropological Perspectives*, Jane K. Cowan, Marie Bénédicte Dembour, and Richard A. Wilson (eds.) Cambridge and New York: Cambridge University Press, pp. 226–48.

Sanders, Douglas. 1989. "The UN Working Group on Indigenous Populations." *Human Rights Quarterly*. 11(3): 406–33.

Sapignoli, Maria. 2009. "Indigeneity and the Expert: Negotiating Identity in the Case of the Central Kalahari Game Reserve." In *Law and Anthropology*. Michael Freeman and David Napier (eds.) Oxford: Oxford University Press, , pp. 247–68.

2012. *Local Power through Globalised Indigenous Identities: The San, the State, and the International Community*. Ph.D. Dissertation. Colchester, United Kingdom: University of Essex.

2015. "Dispossession in the Age of Humanity: Human Rights, Citizenship, and Indigeneity in the Central Kalahari." *Anthropological Forum: A Journal of Social Anthropology and Comparative Sociology*. 25(3): 285–305.

2017. "A Kaleidoscopic Institutional Form: Expertise and Transformation in the UN Permanent Forum on Indigenous Issues." In *Palaces of Hope: The Anthropology of Global Organizations*. Ronald Niezen and Maria Sapignoli (eds.) Cambridge, UK: Cambridge University Press, pp. 78–105.

2017. "'Bushmen' in the Law: Evidence and Identity in Botswana's High Court." *Political and Legal Anthropology Review (PoLAR)*.40(2): 210–225.

Sapignoli, Maria and Robert Hitchcock. 2013a. "Indigenous Peoples in Southern Africa." *The Round Table: The Commonwealth Journal of International Affairs*. 102(4): 355–65.

2013b. "Development and Dispossession: Land Reform in Botswana." In *Africa for Sale? Positioning the State, Land and Society in Foreign Large-Scale Land Acquisitions in Africa*. Sandra J. T. M. Evers, Caroline Seagle, and Froukje Krijtenburg (eds.) Leiden, Boston, and Tokyo: Brill Academic Publishers, pp. 131–57.

Sapignoli, Maria. and Robert K. Hitchcock. 2014. *Social Impact Assessment Anthropological Analysis of the Ghanzi Copper Project Area, Western Botswana*. Gaborone: Social Impact Assessment and Policy Analysis Corporation (SIAPAC) and Loci Environmental.

Sarkin, Jeremie and Amelia Cook. 2010–2011. "The Human Rights of the San (Bushmen) of Botswana – the Clash of the Rights of Indigenous Communities and Their Access to Water with the Rights of the State

to Environmental Conservation and Mineral Resource Exploitation." *Journal of Transnational Law and Policy*. 20, 1–40.
Saugestad, Sidsel. 2001. *The Inconvenient Indigenous: Remote Area Development in Botswana, Donor Assistance and the First People of the Kalahari*. Uppsala: Nordic Africa Institute.
2005. "'Improving their Lives': State Policies and San Resistance in Botswana." *Before Farming*. 4: 1–11.
2011. "Impact of International Mechanisms on Indigenous Rights in Botswana." *International Journal of Human Rights*. 15(1): 37–61.
Schapera, Isaac. 1930. *Khoisan Peoples of South Africa: Bushmen and Hottentots*. London: Routledge and Kegan Paul.
1938. *A Handbook of Tswana Law and Custom*. London: Frank Cass.
1939. 'A Survey of the Bushman Question'. *Race Relations*. 6(2): 68–83.
1943. *Native Land Tenure in the Bechuanaland Protectorate*. Alice, South Africa: Lovedale Press.
1952. *The Ethnic Composition of Tswana Tribes*. London: London School of Economics and Political Science.
1970. *Tribal Innovators: Tswana Chiefs and Social Change l795-1940*. London School of Economics Monographs on Social Anthropology No. 43. London: Athlone Press.
Scheper-Hughes, Nancy and Philippe Bourgois. 2004. *Violence in War and Peace*. Oxford: Blackwell.
Schurz, Carl. 1881. "Present Aspects of the Indian Problem." *The North American Review*. 133(296): 1–24.
Scott, James C. 1985. *Weapons of the Weak: Everyday forms of Peasant Resistance*. New Haven and London: Yale University Press.
Sekere, Biela. 2011. "Secondary Education for San Students in Botswana: A New Xade Case Study." *Diaspora, Indigenous and Minority Education*. 5(2): 76–87.
Seleka, T., H. Siphambe, D. Ntseana, N. Mbere, C. Kerapeletswe and C. Sharp. 2007. *Social Safety Nets in Botswana: Administration, Targeting, and Sustainability*. Gaborone: Lightbooks.
Shattuck, Petra and Jill Norgren. 1979. "Political Use of the Legal Process by Black and American Indian Minorities." *Howard Law Journal*. 22: 1–26.
Sheller, Paul. 1977. "The People of the Central Kalahari Game Reserve: A Report on the Reconnaissance of the Reserve, July-September, 1976." Report to the Ministry of Local Government and Lands, Gaborone, Botswana.
SIAPAC (Social Impact Assessment and Policy Analysis Corporation). 2008. Specialist Social Impact Assessment Sub-Report: Gope Diamond Mining Project, Botswana Social and Environmental Impact Assessment and Statement (SEIS). Unpublished report, prepared for MARSH Environmental Services (Pty) Ltd.

2011. Social Assessment Hana Mining (Ltd) Ghanzi Copper/Silver Project. National, District and Local Key Informant Interview Guide. Unpublished interview, 26 November 2011.

Silberbauer, George B. 1965. *Report to the Government of Bechuanaland on the Bushman Survey*. Gaborone: Bechuanaland Government.

1981. *Hunter and Habitat in the Central Kalahari Desert*. New York: Cambridge University Press.

1982. "Political Process in G/wi Bands." In *Politics and History in Band Societies*. E. Leacock and R. Lee (eds.) Cambridge: Cambridge University Press.

1994. "A Sense of Place." In *Key Issues in Hunter-Gatherer Research*. Ernest Burch, Jr. and Linda Ellanna (eds.) Oxford and Providence: Berg Publishers.

2012. "Why the Central Kalahari Game Reserve?" *Botswana Notes and Records*. 44: 201–3.

Silberbauer, George and Adam J. Kuper. 1966. "Kgalagari Masters and Bushman Serfs: Some Observations." *African Studies* 25(4) 171–9.

Sillery, Anthony. 1965. *Founding a Protectorate*. The Hague: Mouton.

Solway, Jacqueline. 1994. "From Shame to Pride: Politicized Ethnicity in the Kalahari, Botswana." *Canadian Journal of African Studies*. 28(2): 254–74.

2002. "Navigating the 'Neutral' State: 'Minority' Rights in Botswana." *Journal of Southern African Studies*. 28(4): 711–29.

2009. "Human Rights and NGO 'Wrongs': Conflict Diamonds, Culture Wars, and the 'Bushman Question'." *Africa*. 79(3): 329–43.

2011. "'Culture Fatigue': The State and Minority Rights in Botswana." *Indian Journal of Global Legal Studies*. 18(1): 211–40.

Solway, Jaquiline and Richard B. Lee. 1990. "Foragers, Genuine or Spurious? Situating the Kalahari San in History." *Current Anthropology*. 31(2): 109–46.

Speed, Shannon. 2008. *Rights in Rebellion: Indigenous Struggle and Human Rights in Chiapas*. Stanford, CA: Stanford University Press.

SPFII. 2015. Questionnaire to Government. Botswana. http://www.un.org/esa/socdev/unpfii/documents/2015/states-info/Botswana.pdf. Accessed 10 August 2016.

Spinage, Clive. 1991. *History and Evolution of the Fauna Conservation Laws of Botswana*. Gaborone, Botswana: The Botswana Society.

Stavenhagen, Rodolfo. 2005. *Human Rights and Indigenous Issues: Report of the Special Rapporteur on the Situation of Human Rights and Fundamental Freedoms of Indigenous People, Rodolfo Stavenhagen*. Addendum: Mission to South Africa, Economic and Social Council, Human Rights Council, Sixty-second Session, Item 15, E/CN.4/2006/78/Add.2, 15 December 2005.

Sugawara, Kazuyoshi. 1988. "Visiting Relations and Social Interactions between Residential Groups of the Central Kalahari San: Hunter-Gatherer Camp as a Micro-territory." *African Study Monographs*. 8(4): 173–211.

2002. "Optimistic Realism or Opportunistic Subordination? The Interaction of G/wi and G//ana and with Outsider." In *Ethnicity, Hunter-gatherers and the Other: Association or Assimilation in Africa*, Susan Kent (ed.) Washington, DC: Smithsonian Institution Press, pp. 93–126.

Survival International. 1989. "Botswana: Kalahari Peoples Threatened with Expulsion from Game Reserve." *Urgent Action Bulletin UAB/BOT/1/APR/1989*. London: Survival International.

2003a. *Bushmen. Botswana: Bushman Land Carved Up for Diamond Exploration*. Urgent Action Bulletin. London: Survival International. April.

2003b. *Bushmen. Botswana: Diamonds Bring Despair for the Bushmen. Urgent Action Bulletin*. London: Survival International.

2016. *Botswana: Helicopter Crashes after Shooting at Bushmen*. 11 August. www.survivalinternational.org/news/11385. Accessed 18 August 2016.

Sylvain, Renee. 1999. *"We Work to Have Life": Ju/'hoan Women, Work and Survival in the Omaheke Region, Namibia*. Ph. D. Dissertation, Toronto, Ontario, Canada: University of Toronto.

2003. "Class, Culture, and Recognition: San Farm Workers and Indigenous Identities." *Anthropologica*. 45(1), 105–13.

2014. "Essentialism and the Indigenous Politics of Recognition in Southern Africa." *American Anthropologist*. 16(2): 1–14.

2015. "Foragers and Fictions in the Kalahari: Indigenous Identities and the Politics of Deconstruction." *Anthropological Theory*. 15(2): 158–78.

Tagart, E.S.B. 1933. *Report on the Conditions Existing among the Masarwa in the Bamangwato Reserve of the Bechuanaland Protectorate and Certain Other Matters Appertaining to the Natives Living Therein*. Pretoria, South Africa: Government Printer.

Tanaka, Jiro. 1980. *The San, Hunter-Gatherers of the Kalahari. A Study in Ecological Anthropology*. David W. Hughes, Translator. Tokyo: Tokyo University Press.

1987. "The Recent Changes in the Life and Society of the Central Kalahari San." *African Study Monographs*. 7: 37–51.

2014. *The Bushmen: A Half-Century Chronicle of Transformation in Hunter-Gatherer Life and Ecology*. Translated by Minako Sato. Kyoto: Kyoto University Press and Melbourne: Trans Pacific Press.

Tate, Winnifred. 2007. *Counting the Dead: The Culture and Politics of Human Rights Activism in Colombia*. Berkeley and Los Angeles: University of California Press.

Tauli-Corpuz, Victoria. 2016. "Conservation and Indigenous Peoples' Rights." Report to the General Assembly, 2016. UN doc. no. A/71/50. July 29, 2016. http://unsr.vtaulicorpuz.org/site/index.php/documents/annual-reports/149-report-ga-2016. Accessed 16 December 2016.

Taylor, Ian. 2006. "The Limits of the 'African Miracle': Academic Freedom in Botswana and the Deportation of Kenneth Good." *Journal of Contemporary African Studies* 24(1): 101–122.

Taylor, Ian and Gladys Mokhawa. 2003. "Not Forever: Botswana, Conflict Diamonds and the Bushmen." *African Affairs*. 102: 261–83.

Taylor, Julie. J. 2007. "Celebrating San Victory Too Soon? Reflections on the Outcome of the Central Kalahari Game Reserve Case." *Anthropology Today*. 23(5): 3–5.

Taylor, Michael. 1996. "John Hardbattle. The Khwe's Champion." *The Guardian*, 18 December.

1997. "The Politics of Being Basarwa: Identity, Entitlement and Development among Bugakhwe, Tsega and //Anakhwe in Eastern Ngamiland. Thoughts after Preliminary Fieldwork." In *Indigenous Peoples in Modern Nation-States. Proceedings from an International Workshop, Tromso, Norway, 13-16 October 1997*. Sidsel Saugestad (ed.) Tromso: Occasional Papers Series A, No. 90, Faculty of Social Science, University of Tromso.

2003. "Wilderness, Development, and San Ethnicity in Contemporary Botswana." In *San and the State. Contesting Land, Development, Identity and Representation*, Thekla Hohmann (ed.) Koln: Rudiger Koppe Verlag, pp. 255–80.

Temper, Leah and Joan Martinez-Alier. 2013. "The God of the Mountain and Godavarman: Net Present Value, Indigenous Territorial Rights and Sacredness in a Bauxite Mining Conflict in India." *Ecological Economics*. 96(1): 79–87.

The Lawyer. 2010. "Gordon Bennett, the Go-To Tribal Rights Guy." www.thelawyer.com/gordon-bennett-the-go-to-tribal-rights-guy/?mm_56838e903ee92=56838e903ef34. Accessed 30 December 2015.

Thomas, Elizabeth Marshall. 1958. *The Harmless People*. New York: Vintage Books.

Thornberry, Patrick. 2002. *Indigenous Peoples and Human Rights*, Manchester, UK: Juris Publishing, Manchester University Press.

Tlou, Thomas. 1977. "Servility and Political Control: Botlhanka among the BaTawana of Northwestern Botswana, ca. 1750–1906." In *Slavery in Africa: Historical and Anthropological Perspectives*. Suzanne Miers and Igor Koptytoff (eds.) Madison, WI: University of Wisconsin Press, pp. 367–90.

1985. *A History of Ngamiland, 1750–1906: The History of an African State*. Madison, WI: University of Wisconsin Press.

Tlou, Thomas and Alec Campell. 1984. *History of Botswana*. Second Edition. Gaborone: Macmillan Botswana Publishing.

Tlou, Thomas, Neil Parsons, and Willie Henderson. 1995. *Seretse Khama, 1921–1980*. Gaborone: Botswana Society.
Tsing, Anna. L. 2005. *Friction: An Ethnography of Global Connection*, Princeton, NJ: Princeton University Press.
Tsogwane Slumber. 2016. *Statement by Honourable Slumber Tsogwane, Minister of Local Government and Rural Development on Agenda Item 4: Implementation of the Six Mandated Areas of the Permanent Forum with Reference to the Declaration on the Rights of Indigenous Peoples*. 15th Session of the United Nations Permanent Forum on Indigenous Issues (UNPFII), May 19, 2016.
Tutwane, Letshwiti. 2004. "Basarwa Lawyer Seeks To Repair Damage." *Mmegi* (Botswana). 20 July.
UNPFII. 2013. 12th Session. Report E/2013/43-E/C.19/2013/25.
Useb, Joram. 2004. UNPFII Third Session. *Indigenous Women*. Item 4 (d) Human Rights.
Valiente-Noailles, Carlos. 1993. *The Kua: Life and Soul of the Central Kalahari Bushmen*. Amsterdam: A.A. Balkema.
Vallinder, Torbjörn. 1994. "The Judicialization of Politics—A World-wide Phenomenon: Introduction." *International Political Science Review*. 15(2): 91–9.
Van Der Post, Laurens. 1958. *The Lost World of the Kalahari*. London: British Broadcasting Corporation.
1984. *Testament to the Bushmen*. London: British Broadcasting Corporation.
Veber, Hanne, Jens Dahl, Fiona Wilson, and Espen Waehle. 1993. *Never Drink from the Same Cup: Proceedings of the Conference on Indigenous Peoples in Africa*. Tune, Denmark, Copenhagen: IWGIA Document 74.
Vidal, John. 2016. "The Tribes Paying the Brutal Price of Conservation." *The Guardian*. 24 August 2016.
Wahlquist, Calla. 2017. "Native Title System Restricting Benefits for Indigenous Australians, Research Finds." *The Guardian*. 21 March. www.theguardian.com/australia-news/2017/mar/22/native-title-system-restricting-benefits-for-indigenous-australians-research-finds?CMP=share_btn_fb. Accessed 4 April 2017.
Warren Kay, B., and Jean E. Jackson (eds.) 2002. *Indigenous Movements, Self-Representation, and the State in Latin America*. University of Texas Press.
Werbner, Pnina. 2014. "'The Duty to Act Fairly': Ethics, Legal Anthropology, and Labor Justice in the Manual Workers Union of Botswana." *Comparative Studies in Society and History*. 56(2): 479–507.
Werbner, Richard. 2002. "Introduction: Challenging Minorities, Difference and Tribal Citizenship in Botswana." *Journal of Southern African Studies*. 28(4): 670–84.
2004. *Reasonable Radicals and Citizenship in Botswana: The Public Anthropology of Kalanga Elites*. Bloomington and Indianapolis: Indiana University Press.

Wessendorf, Kathrin. (ed.). 2001. *Challenging Politics: Indigenous Peoples' Experiences with Political Parties and Elections*. Copenahgen: IWGIA.

WGIP. 1994. *Final Report*. E/CN.4/Sub.2/1994/30.

1998. *Final Report*. E/CN.4/Sub.2/1998/16.

Wicksteed, Richard. 2008. *My Land is My Dignity (Film on the Central Kalahari Game Reserve Resettlement Issue)*. Cape Town: Onetime Films.

Wilderness Safaris. 2010. *Statement on Kalahari Plains Camp*. Johannesburg: Wilderness Safaris.

Williams, Susan. 2007. *Colour Bar: The Triumph of Seretse Khama and his Nation*. Harmondsworth, United Kingdom: Penguin Books.

Wilmsen, Edwin N. 1989. *Land Filled with Flies: A Political Economy of the Kalahari*. Chicago: University of Chicago Press.

1990. "The Real Bushman is the Male One: Labour and Power in the Creation of Basarwa Ethnicicy." *Botswana Notes & Records*. 22: 21–35.

2002. "Mutable Identities: Moving beyond Ethnicity in Botswana." *Journal of Southern African Studies*. 28(4): 825–41.

2009. "The Structure of San Property Relations: Constitutional Issues and Interventionist Politics." *Anthropologica*. 51(1): 153–63.

Wilmsen, Edwin N. and James R. Denbow. 1990. "Paradigmatic History of San-Speaking Peoples and Current Attempts at Revision." *Current Anthropology*. 31(5): 489–524.

Wilson, Richard A. (ed.). 1997. *Human Rights, Culture & Context: Anthropological Perspectives*. London and Ann Arbor, MI: Pluto.

2007. "Tyrannosaurus Lex: The Anthropology of Human Rights and Transnational Law." In *The Practice of Human Rights: Tracking Law between the Global and the Local*. Mark Goodale and Sally Engle Merry (eds.) Cambridge, UK: Cambridge University Press. pp. 342–68.

Wilson, Richard A. and John P. Mitchell. 2003. "Introduction: The Social Life of Rights." In *Human Rights in Global Perspective. Anthropological Studies of Rights, Claims and Entitlements*. Wilson A. Richard and Mitchell John (eds.) London and New York: Routledge Press, pp. 1–16.

Wily, Elizabeth A. 1975. *Bushmen and Tourism*. Gaborone, Botswana: Ministry of Local Government and Lands, Government of Botswana.

1979a. *Official Policy Towards San (Bushmen) Hunter Gatherers in Modern Botswana: 1966–1978*. Gaborone, Botswana: National Institute of Development and Cultural Research.

1979b. *Settlement as a Strategy for Securing Land for Nomads: An Examination of the Botswana Government's Current Programme for Settling the Kalahari San*. London: Agricultural Administration Unit, Overseas Development Institute.

1980. *Land Allocation and Hunter Gatherer Land Rights in Botswana: The Impact of the Tribal Grazing Land Policy*. Human Rights and Development Working Papers No. 4. London: Anti Slavery Society.

1981. *The TGLP and Hunter Gatherers: A Case Study in Land Politics*. Gaborone, Botswana: National Institute of Development and Cultural Research.

1982. "A Strategy of Self Determination for the Kalahari San (The Botswana Government's Programme of Action in the Ghanzi Farms)." *Development and Change*. 13(2): 291–308.

Workman, James. L. 2009. *Heart of Dryness: How the Last Bushmen Can Help Us Endure the Coming Age of Permanent Drought*. New York: Walker.

Wylie, Diana. 1990. *A Little God: The Twilight of Patriarchy in a Southern African Chiefdom*. New Haven: Yale University Press.

Wynberg, Rachel. 2004. "Rhetoric, Realism, and Benefit Sharing." *The Journal of World Intellectual Property*. 7(6): 851–76.

2010. "Hot Air over Hoodia." *Seedling*. October, pp. 22–4.

Xanthaki, Alexandra. 2010. *Indigenous Rights and the United Nations Standards: Selfdetennination, Culture and Land*. Cambridge: Cambridge University Press.

Zenker, Olaf. 2012. "The Juridification of Political Protest and the Politicization of Legalism in South African land Restitution." In *Law against the State: Ethnographic Forays into Law's Transformations*. Julia Eckert, Brian Donahoe, Christian Strümpell, and Zerrim Özlem Biner (eds.) Cambridge, UK: Cambridge University Press, pp. 118–46.

Zips-Mairitsch, Manuela. 2013. *Lost Land? (Land) Rights of the San in Botswana and the Legal Concept of Indigeneity in Africa*. Berlin and Zurich: Lit Verlag and Copenhagen: International Work Group for Indigenous Affairs.

Zoettl, Peter Anton. 2016. "The (Il)legal Indian: The Tupinambà and the Juridification of Indigenous Rights and Lives in North-Eastern Brazil." *Social and Legal Studies*. 25(1): 3–21.

INTERNATIONAL INSTRUMENTS

African Charter on Human and Peoples' Rights, 27 June 1981. CAB/LEG/67/3 rev. 5, 21 I.L.M. 58 (1982).

Convention on Biological Diversity, 5 June 1992. 1760 UNTS 79; 31 ILM 818.

Declaration on the Rights of Indigenous Peoples, 2 October 2007. A/RES/61/295.

International Labour Organization Convention (No. 107) Concerning the Protection and Integration of Indigenous and Other Tribal and Semi-Tribal Populations in Independent Countries. 26 June 1957, 328 U.N.T.S. 247.

International Labour Organization Convention (No. 169) Concerning Indigenous and Tribal Peoples in Independent Countries. 27 June 1989.

United Nations Declaration on the Rights of Indigenous Peoples, 2007.

LEGAL CASES

African Commission on Human and Peoples' Rights v. Republic of Kenya App. No. 006/2012. (Ogiek case). African Court on Human and Peoples' Rights. Judgment May 26, 2017.

Centre for Minority Rights Development (Kenya) and Minority Rights Group International on behalf of Endorois Welfare Council v. Kenya. 276/2003. African Commission on Human and People's Rights. Judgment. 2010.

Dongria Kondh case Survival International v. Vedanta Resources plc. Supreme Court of India. Judgment September 25, 2009.

Gaoberekwe, Nare, Mosetlhanyane Matsipane, Amogelang Segootsane, Gaorapelwe Kgwathiwa v. Attorney General and Minister of Environment, Wildlife, and Tourism. 2014.

Ithutseng, Keotlhabetsi, First Applicant and Mosimane Malefo 2nd & Further Applicants v. Attorney General, Respondent. 2013. No. MAHGB-000140-13. Gaborone, Botswana: High Court (29 August, Judge L.S. Walia).

Kamanakao Association and Other v. Attorney General. Misca No 377 of 1999. Lobatse High Court. 2002 *(1) BLR 110 (HC)*

Kanatewat et al. v. James Bay Development Corp. et al. Supreme Court Judgements. 1973.

Karakubis, Heebe and 114 others, applicants v. Ghanzi District Council, Respondent, 2015. MAHGB-0043-*14, Judge T.T. Ratowanne. Lobatse: High Court of Botswana. 21st November.*

Kayano v. Hokkaido Expropriation Committee. The Nibutani Dam Decision. Judgment of the Sapporo District Court. 1997.

Mabo v. Queensland case in Australia Eddie Mabo, David Passi, and James Rice v. State of Queensland. High Court of Australia. 1992. *166 CLR 186.*

Mmakgomo, Ditlhame, First Applicant, and 11 others v. Ghanzi Land Board, First Respondent, Ghanzi District Council, Second Respondent, and Ghanzi District Commissioner, Third Respondent, 2013a. MAHGB-000295-139. Lobatse: High Court of Botswana. 24 May.

2013b. Founding Affidavit. MAHGB-000295-13. Lobatse: Botswana High Court. 18 June.

2013c. High Court Order Justice Lot Moroke MAHGB-000295-139. Lobatse: High Court of Botswana. 18 June.

Mosetlhanyane, Matsipane, First Applicant, and Gakenyatsiwe Matsipane, Second Applicant, and Further Applicants, v. Attorney General of Botswana Respondent. 2009. Founding Affidavit. MAHLB-0393-09. Lobatse: High Court of Botswana.

2010. Judgment. MAHLB-0393-09. Lobatse: High Court of Botswana.

2011. Court of Appeal Judgement. No. CACLB-074-10 [High Court Civil Case No. MAHLB 000 393-09] Lobatse, Botswana: Court of Appeal. Heard 17 January, and delivered 27 January.

Saramaka People v. Suriname. Inter-American Court of Human Rights. Judgement November 28, 2007.

Sesana, Roy, First Applicant, Keiwa Setlhobogwa and 241 others, Second and Further Applicants, v. the Attorney General (in his capacity as the recognized agent of the Government of the Republic of Botswana). 2002. MISCA 52/2002 Founding Affidavit. Gaborone. Botswana.

2006a. Applicants' Submission. No. MISCA 52/2002. Lobatse: High Court of Botswana.

2006b. Respondent's Submission. No. MISCA 52/2002. Lobatse: High Court of Botswana.

2006c. Judgement. No. MISCA 52/2002. Lobatse: High Court of Botswana.

The Mayagna (Sumo) Awas Tingni Community v. Nicaragua Inter-Am. Ct. H.R., (Ser. C) No. 79 (2001). Judgment of August 31, 2001.

Tsumib, Jan, and 8 Others v. the Government of the Republic of Namibia and 19 Others on the matter of the Hai//om People and their land. 2015. *Case No A 201/2015*. Windhoek: High Court of Namibia.

2016. Case No A 201/2015. First Respondent's Answering Affidavit Windhoek: High Court of Namibia.

2017. Case No A 201/15. Replying Affidavit. Windhoek: High Court of Namibia.

Unity Dow v. The Attorney General of Botswana. High Court of Botswana. 1992.

INDEX

CAMBRIDGE STUDIES IN LAW AND SOCIETY

Books in the Series

Diseases of the Will,
Mariana Valverde

The Politics of Truth and Reconciliation in South Africa: Legitimizing the Post-Apartheid State,
Richard A. Wilson

Modernism and the Grounds of Law,
Peter Fitzpatrick

Unemployment and Government: Genealogies of the Social,
William Walters

Autonomy and Ethnicity: Negotiating Competing Claims in Multi-Ethnic States,
Yash Ghai

Constituting Democracy: Law, Globalism and South Africa's Political Reconstruction,
Heinz Klug

The Ritual of Rights in Japan: Law, Society, and Health Policy,
Eric A. Feldman

The Invention of the Passport: Surveillance, Citizenship and the State,
John Torpey

Governing Morals: A Social History of Moral Regulation,
Alan Hunt

The Colonies of Law: Colonialism, Zionism and Law in Early Mandate Palestine,
Ronen Shamir

Law and Nature,
David Delaney

Social Citizenship and Workfare in the United States and Western Europe: The Paradox of Inclusion,
Joel F. Handler

Law, Anthropology and the Constitution of the Social: Making Persons and Things,
Edited by Alain Pottage and Martha Mundy

Judicial Review and Bureaucratic Impact: International and Interdisciplinary Perspectives,
Edited by Marc Hertogh and Simon Halliday

Immigrants at the Margins: Law, Race, and Exclusion in Southern Europe,
Kitty Calavita

Lawyers and Regulation: The Politics of the Administrative Process,
Patrick Schmidt

Law and Globalization from Below: Toward a Cosmopolitan Legality,
Edited by Boaventura de Sousa Santos and Cesar A. Rodríguez-Garavito

Public Accountability: Designs, Dilemmas and Experiences,
Edited by Michael W. Dowdle

Law, Violence and Sovereignty among West Bank Palestinians,
Tobias Kelly

Legal Reform and Administrative Detention Powers in China,
Sarah Biddulph

The Practice of Human Rights: Tracking Law Between the Global and the Local,
Edited by Mark Goodale and Sally Engle Merry

Judges Beyond Politics in Democracy and Dictatorship: Lessons from Chile,
Lisa Hilbink

Paths to International Justice: Social and Legal Perspectives,
Edited by Marie-Bénédicte Dembour and Tobias Kelly

Law and Society in Vietnam: The Transition from Socialism in Comparative Perspective,
Mark Sidel

Constitutionalizing Economic Globalization: Investment Rules and Democracy's Promise,
David Schneiderman

The New World Trade Organization Knowledge Agreements: 2nd Edition,
Christopher Arup

Justice and Reconciliation in Post-Apartheid South Africa,
Edited by François du Bois and Antje du Bois-Pedain

Militarization and Violence against Women in Conflict Zones in the Middle East: A Palestinian Case-Study,
Nadera Shalhoub-Kevorkian

Child Pornography and Sexual Grooming: Legal and Societal Responses,
Suzanne Ost

Darfur and the Crime of Genocide,
John Hagan and Wenona Rymond-Richmond

Fictions of Justice: The International Criminal Court and the Challenge of Legal Pluralism in Sub-Saharan Africa,
Kamari Maxine Clarke

Conducting Law and Society Research: Reflections on Methods and Practices,
Simon Halliday and Patrick Schmidt

Planted Flags: Trees, Land, and Law in Israel/Palestine,
Irus Braverman

Culture under Cross-Examination: International Justice and the Special Court for Sierra Leone,
Tim Kelsall

Cultures of Legality: Judicialization and Political Activism in Latin America,
Javier Couso, Alexandra Huneeus, and Rachel Sieder

Courting Democracy in Bosnia and Herzegovina: The Hague Tribunal's Impact in a Postwar State,
Lara J. Nettelfield

The Gacaca Courts and Post-Genocide Justice and Reconciliation in Rwanda: Justice without Lawyers,
Phil Clark

Law, Society, and History: Themes in the Legal Sociology and Legal History of Lawrence M. Friedman,
Robert W. Gordon and Morton J. Horwitz

After Abu Ghraib: Exploring Human Rights in America and the Middle East,
Shadi Mokhtari

Adjudication in Religious Family Laws: Cultural Accommodation: Legal Pluralism, and Gender Equality in India,
Gopika Solanki

Water On Tap: Rights and Regulation in the Transnational Governance of Urban Water Services,
Bronwen Morgan

Elements of Moral Cognition: Rawls' Linguistic Analogy and the Cognitive Science of Moral and Legal Judgment,
John Mikhail

A Sociology of Transnational Constitutions: Social Foundations of the Post-National Legal Structure,
Chris Thornhill

Mitigation and Aggravation at Sentencing,
Edited by Julian Roberts

Institutional Inequality and the Mobilization of the Family and Medical Leave Act: Rights on Leave,
Catherine R. Albiston

Authoritarian Rule of Law: Legislation, Discourse and Legitimacy in Singapore,
Jothie Rajah

Law and Development and the Global Discourses of Legal Transfers,
Edited by John Gillespie and Pip Nicholson

Law against the State: Ethnographic Forays into Law's Transformations,
Edited by Julia Eckert, Brian Donahoe, Christian Strümpell, and Zerrin Özlem Biner

Transnational Legal Process and State Change,
Edited by Gregory C. Shaffer

Legal Mobilization under Authoritarianism: The Case of Post-Colonial Hong Kong,
Edited by Waikeung Tam

Complementarity in the Line of Fire: The Catalysing Effect of the International Criminal Court in Uganda and Sudan,
Sarah M. H. Nouwen

Political and Legal Transformations of an Indonesian Polity: The Nagari from Colonisation to Decentralisation,
Franz von Benda-Beckmann and Keebet von Benda-Beckmann

Pakistan's Experience with Formal Law: An Alien Justice,
Osama Siddique

Human Rights under State-Enforced Religious Family Laws in Israel, Egypt, and India,
Yüksel Sezgin

Why Prison?,
Edited by David Scott

Law's Fragile State: Colonial, Authoritarian, and Humanitarian Legacies in Sudan,
Mark Fathi Massoud

Rights for Others: The Slow Home-Coming of Human Rights in the Netherlands,
Barbara Oomen

European States and their Muslim Citizens: The Impact of Institutions on Perceptions and Boundaries,
Edited by John R. Bowen, Christophe Bertossi,
Jan Willem Duyvendak, and Mona Lena Krook

Environmental Litigation in China,
Rachel E. Stern

Indigeneity and Legal Pluralism in India: Claims, Histories, Meanings,
Pooja Parmar

Paper Tiger: Law, Bureaucracy and the Developmental State in Himalayan India,
Nayanika Mathur

Religion, Law and Society,
Russell Sandberg

The Experiences of Face Veil Wearers in Europe and the Law,
Edited by Eva Brems

The Contentious History of the International Bill of Human Rights,
Christopher N. J. Roberts

Transnational Legal Orders,
Edited by Terence C. Halliday and Gregory Shaffer

Lost in China? Law, Culture and Society in Post-1997 Hong Kong,
Carol A. G. Jones

Security Theology, Surveillance and the Politics of Fear,
Nadera Shalhoub-Kevorkian

Opposing the Rule of Law: How Myanmar's Courts Make Law and Order,
Nick Cheesman

The Ironies of Colonial Governance: Law, Custom and Justice in Colonial India,
James Jaffe

The Clinic and the Court: Law, Medicine and Anthropology,
Edited by Tobias Kelly, Ian Harper, and Akshay Khanna

A World of Indicators: The Making of Government Knowledge Through Quantification,
Edited by Richard Rottenburg, Sally E. Merry, Sung-Joon Park, and Johanna Mugler

Contesting Immigration Policy in Court: Legal Activism and its Radiating Effects in the United States and France,
Leila Kawar

The Quiet Power of Indicators: Measuring Governance, Corruption, and Rule of Law,
Edited by Sally Engle Merry, Kevin Davis, and Benedict Kingsbury

Investing in Authoritarian Rule: Punishment and Patronage in Rwanda's Gacaca Courts for Genocide Crimes,
Anuradha Chakravarty

Contractual Knowledge: One Hundred Years of Legal Experimentation in Global Markets,
Edited by Grégoire Mallard and Jérôme Sgard

Iraq and the Crimes of Aggressive War: The Legal Cynicism of Criminal Militarism,
John Hagan, Joshua Kaiser, and Anna Hanson

Culture in the Domains of Law,
Edited by René Provost

China and Islam: The Prophet, the Party, and Law,
Matthew S. Erie

Diversity in Practice: Race, Gender, and Class in Legal and Professional Careers,
Edited by Spencer Headworth and Robert Nelson

A Sociology of Transnational Constitutions: Social Foundations of the Post-National Legal Structure,
Chris Thornhill

Shifting Legal Visions: Judicial Change and Human Rights Trials in Latin America,
Ezequiel A. González Ocantos

The Demographic Transformations of Citizenship,
Heli Askola

Criminal Defense in China: The Politics of Lawyers at Work,
Sida Liu and Terence C. Halliday

Contesting Economic and Social Rights in Ireland: Constitution, State and Society, 1848–2016,
Thomas Murray

Buried in the Heart: Women, Complex Victimhood and the War in Northern Uganda,
Erin Baines

Palaces of Hope: The Anthropology of Global Organizations,
Edited by Ronald Niezen and Maria Sapignoli

The Politics of Bureaucratic Corruption in Post-Transitional Eastern Europe,
Marina Zaloznaya

Revisiting the Law and Governance of Trafficking, Forced Labor and Modern Slavery,
Prabha Kotiswaran

Incitement on Trial: Prosecuting International Speech Crimes,
Richard Ashby Wilson

Criminalizing Children: A History of Welfare and the State in Australia,
David McCallum

Global Legislators: How International Organizations Make Trade Law for the World,
Terrence C. Halliday and Susan Block-Lieb

Duties to Care: Dementia, Relationality and Law,
Rosie Harding

Hunting Justice: Displacement, Law, and Activism in the Kalahari,
Maria Sapignoli